GW01375274

HITLER'S FORTRESSES

OSPREY
PUBLISHING

HITLER'S FORTRESSES

GERMAN FORTIFICATIONS AND DEFENCES 1939–45

EDITED BY
CHRIS McNAB

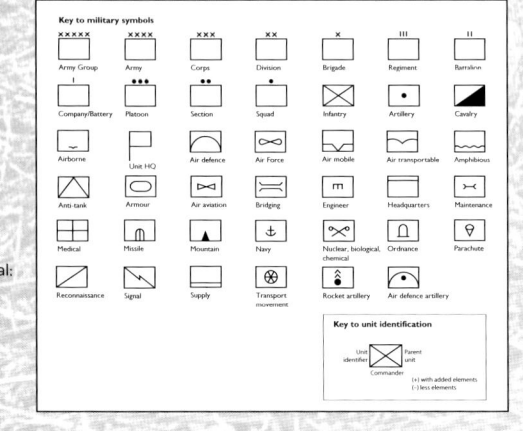

First published in Great Britain in 2014 by Osprey Publishing,
PO Box 883, Oxford, OX1 9PL, UK
PO Box 3985, New York, NY 10185-3985, USA

E-mail: info@ospreypublishing.com

Osprey Publishing is part of the Osprey Group

© 2014 Osprey Publishing

All rights reserved. Apart from any fair dealing for the purpose of private study, research, criticism or review, as permitted under the Copyright, Designs and Patents Act, 1988, no part of this publication may be reproduced, stored in a retrieval system, or transmitted in any form or by any means, electronic, electrical, chemical, mechanical, optical, photocopying, recording or otherwise, without the prior written permission of the copyright owner. Enquiries should be addressed to the Publishers.

Every attempt has been made by the Publisher to secure the appropriate permissions for material reproduced in this book. If there has been any oversight we will be happy to rectify the situation and written submission should be made to the Publishers.

A CIP catalogue record for this book is available from the British Library

ISBN: 978 1 78200 828 6

Page design by Ken Vail Graphic Design, Cambridge, UK
Index by Sharon Redmayne
Cartography by Boundford and The Map Studio
Typeset in Bembo and Conduit ITC
Originated by PDQ Media, Bungay, UK
Printed in China through Worldprint Ltd.

13 14 15 16 17 18   10 9 8 7 6 5 4 3 2 1

Osprey Publishing is supporting the Woodland Trust, the UK's leading woodland conservation charity, by funding the dedication of trees.

www.ospreypublishing.com

IMAGE RIGHTS:
Front cover: (left) 15cm naval gun (Imperial War Museum, NA18992);
(right) tank turret (courtesy of A. Chazette, via Steven J. Zaloga);
(bottom) dragon's teeth defence (NARA).
Back cover: A camouflaged bunker in France. (NARA)
Previous page: Hitler welcomes a number of officers to his fortified headquarters. (Topfoto)
This page: A Panther turret and shelter ready for installation. (Imperial War Museum, NA18343)

EDITOR'S NOTE:
This work is a compilation of several Osprey books. All books used are listed below:
FOR 3 *U-Boat Bases and Bunkers 1941–45*, Gordon Williamson
FOR 15 *Germany's West Wall*, Neil Short
FOR 23 *German Field Fortifications 1939–45*, Gordon Rottman
FOR 37 *D-Day Fortifications in Normandy*, Steven J. Zaloga
FOR 41 *The Channel Islands 1941–45*, Charles Stephenson
FOR 45 *German Defences in Italy in World War II*, Neil Short
FOR 63 *The Atlantic Wall (1)*, Steven J. Zaloga
FOR 72 *German V-Weapon Sites 1943–45*, Steven J. Zaloga
FOR 89 *The Atlantic Wall (2)*, Steven J. Zaloga
FOR 100 *The Führer's Headquarters*, Neil Short
FOR 102 *Defence of the Rhine 1944–45*, Steven J. Zaloga

The following will help in converting other measurements between metric and imperial:
1 mile = 1.6km
1lb = 0.45kg
1 yard = 0.9m
1ft = 0.3m
1in = 25.4mm
1°C = 33.8°F

CONTENTS

Introduction	6
Hitler's Headquarters – The Führer's Command Bunkers	12
Protecting the Homeland – Germany's Border Defences	68
Defence of the Periphery – The Atlantic Wall	136
Mountain Barriers – German Defensive Lines in Italy	218
Etched in the Earth – Field Fortifications	270
Specialist Fortifications – Protecting the U-Boats and V-Weapons	318
Conclusion	376
Glossary	381
Further Reading	384
Index	387

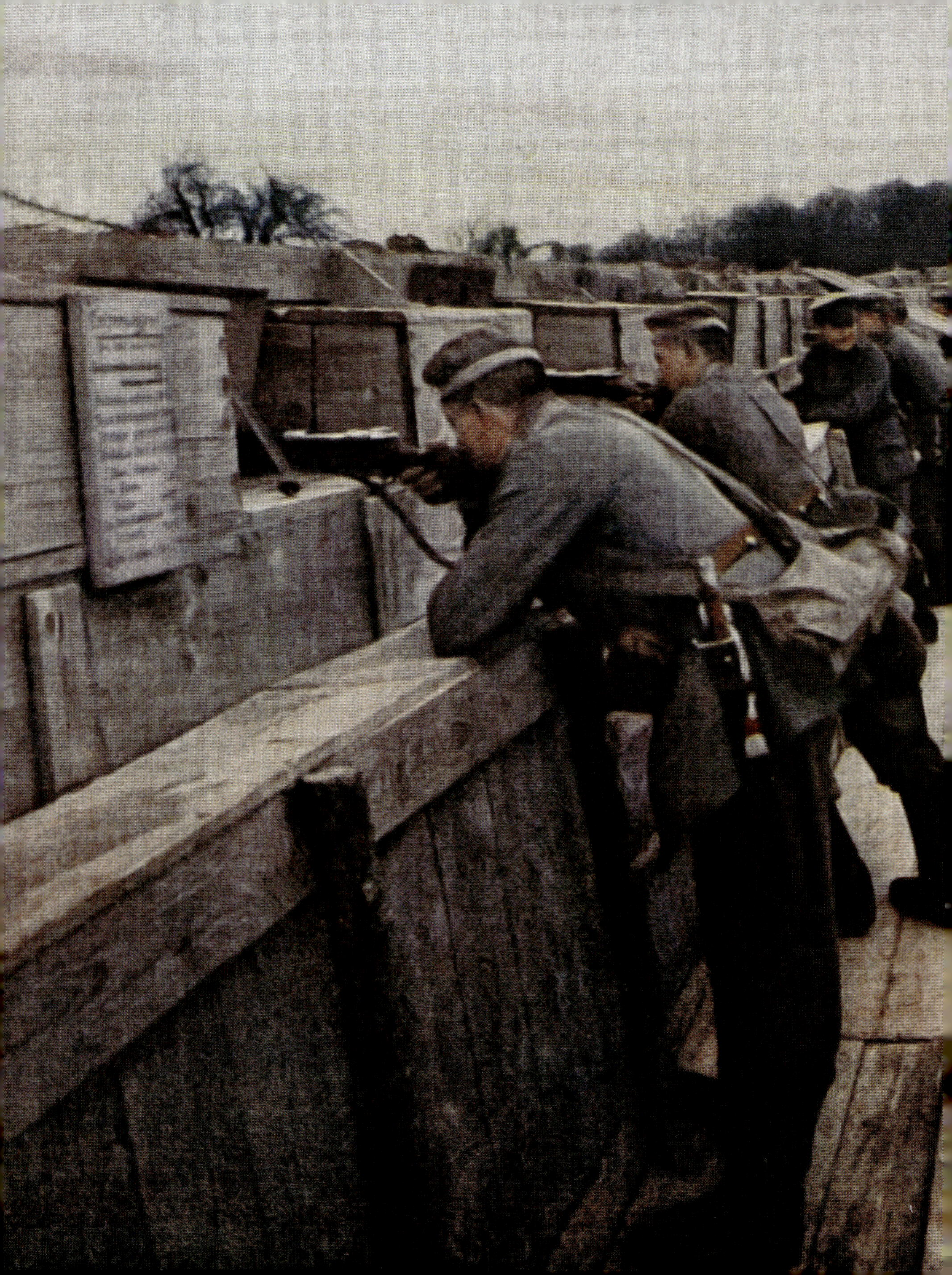

INTRODUCTION

LEFT: At the beginning of World War II, defensive systems such as these – seen in the Vosges Mountains in 1915 – were critically out of date. (Topfoto)

Inevitably, the experiences on the Western Front during World War I had a strong influence, both negative and positive, on Germany's post-war defence doctrine. The positive aspect of World War I to the German military, from the doctrinal standpoint, was the development of what is informally known as the *elastische Kampfverfahren* (elastic defence, lit. 'elastic battle procedures'). By 1916 it had been realized that solid multi-layered trench systems and an unyielding defence, aimed at holding on to every metre of ground, were impractical. Massive six-day artillery barrages would shatter both defences and the defenders. General der Infanterie Erich Ludendorff endorsed a more in-depth defence. While still relying on continuous interconnected trench lines, the defences were subdivided into three zones: (1) combat outpost zone with minimal lookouts to warn of attacks and keep patrols from penetrating deeper; (2) 1,500–3,000m-deep main battle zone with complex trench systems concentrated on key terrain (rather than rigid lines covering all areas) intended to halt the attack; and (3) rear zone with artillery and reserves. While the battle zone still relied on trench lines, to establish the new defences the German troops actually withdrew (previously unheard of) in some sectors to more easily defended terrain, placed many of the trenches on reverse slopes to mask them from enemy observation and fire, and established strongpoints on key terrain. The establishment of the combat zone, supported by long-range artillery, disrupted Allied attacks. After fighting its way through the outpost zone the attack would often exhaust itself in the battle zone. Rather than attempting to halt the attack outright, penetration of the battle zone was accepted. The attack would become bogged down among the defences, battered by artillery fire and counter-attacks. This was first implemented in April 1917, and by war's end in November 1918 the defences were completely rearranged under this concept. It had proved itself, and was adopted by the post-war Reichsheer in 1921.

There were negative influences too of the experiences on the Western Front. The horror, misery and prolonged stalemate of trench or positional warfare (Stellungskrieg) encouraged many, like Hans von Seeckt, to find another way to wage war. Some form of mobile offensive was preferred and defence was regarded as necessary only for local holding actions or a temporary situation until the initiative was regained and the offensive resumed.

The elastic defence was codified in the two-volume manual called *Führung und Gefecht der verbundenen Waffen* (Leadership and Combat of the Combined Arms), published in 1921/23. This codification managed a compromise between those who still favoured the elastic defence (the old 'trench school') and those espousing a more mobile form of warfare. The manual stated that either form of warfare could be employed depending on the situation, but it clearly preferred the elastic defence, with improvements. These entailed more depth (both within each zone and in the distances between zones), and in fluid situations it called for a fourth zone forward of the three traditional ones. This was an 'advanced position' of light mobile units, infantry and artillery, which would disrupt the attack and force the enemy to deploy early into battle formation. The advance units would then withdraw and constitute part of the reserve. Anti-armour defence was addressed, but there were few effective anti-armour weapons at the time, being prohibited for the Reichsheer by international treaties. What anti-armour defence there was took the form of artillery concentrations and obstacles. The combat outpost zone would consist only of individual and infantry weapon positions not connected by trenches.

Such was the theory. In practice, Generaloberst Hans von Seeckt, acting chief of staff, strongly discouraged any officer (with some being relieved of duty) from practising the elastic defence. Seeckt desired a mobile war of manoeuvre and shunned defence. Though Seeckt resigned in 1926, his successors continued to abide by his views, which remained in effect until the early 1930s. The practice of the elastic defence was permitted in exercises though. The rearmament of Germany in 1933 gradually saw the means become available to utilize a highly evolved form of mobile warfare. This was by no means army-wide, as the new Deutsches Heer (German Army) was still largely an infantry force relying on horse artillery and horse-drawn supply columns (4,000–6,000 horses per division). The infantry division's 27 rifle companies may have walked, but the division did possess a degree of mechanization via truck transport for headquarters, signal, anti-armour and pioneer elements. Divisional reconnaissance battalions too were increasingly mechanized, receiving motorcycles and scout cars, though horses and bicycles were still relied on.

The new defence doctrine, laid out in *Truppenführung* (Troop Command) in 1933, allowed the four previous zones a greater use of anti-armour obstacles, minefields, anti-armour guns behind the main battle position, and tanks assembled in the rear zone to support counter-attacks. The use of armour as a mobile counter-attack and manoeuvre force was not fully appreciated at this time, however, as German tanks had played no role in defeating Allied tank breakthroughs in World War I. They would be held in the rear to engage enemy tanks that had broken through and to destroy them piecemeal as they wandered through the rear zone. There was disagreement on the employment of anti-armour guns. While some might be attached to the advanced-position forces, most were to be positioned behind the main battle position to block tank breakthroughs. Others urged that they be positioned forward to pick off approaching enemy armour and break up the attack early. Individual infantrymen were to attack roaming tanks with anti-armour rifles and hand mines, which proved to be inadequate. As the Blitzkrieg (lit. 'lightning war') concept developed, the German Army became so offensively orientated that anything appearing too defensive in nature was at risk of being minimized.

HITLER'S FORTRESSES

This being said, Germany did invest, and invest heavily, in defensive structures, although the value and tactical purpose of these often sat awkwardly with Hitler's perspective on warfare. As this volume will show, the Third Reich sank millions of Reichsmarks, huge amounts of manpower and awesome volumes of concrete and steel into major defensive outworks. During the 1930s, the focus was on building up the Westwall (West Wall) on Germany's western border, and (to a lesser extent) the defences along the border with Poland. In many ways, however, the commitment made to these defences was less than total, and during the first two years of World War II they were largely irrelevant anyway. Poland was conquered in a rapid Blitzkrieg campaign in 1939, and Western Europe fell to an ascendant Wehrmacht (German Armed Forces) in 1940. Offence seemed to be the motive power of German success, so the defensive mindset took second rank in the thinking of the High Command.

Nevertheless, as Hitler turned his attention to the Soviet Union in 1941, and spurred on by British coastal raids, Hitler authorized the construction of his Atlantikwall (Atlantic Wall), a massive system of defensive works along the western European coastline, stretching from Norway to Spain. Then, as the tide of the war turned against Germany from 1942, the defensive impetus became more urgent. The West Wall was revitalized, and further defences built along the Rhine; the Atlantic Wall received fresh investment and a reinvigorated leadership; the so-called Panther–Wotan Line was partially built as an (inadequate) buttress against the Soviets from the east; various cities and enclaves were declared to be *Festungen* (fortresses), to be held at all costs.

The rear end of the Valentin U-boat bunker, containing the various workshop areas, under construction. One of the roof-supporting arches (top left) has been partially encased in its concrete shell. Just below this can be seen the floor of the topmost workshop level. (Gordon Williamson)

INTRODUCTION

Yet ultimately, although the Allies paid a heavy price to take some of Hitler's fortresses, the defences were never able to control the outcome of the war. This book explores why this is so. It ranges across a broad spectrum of what we might designate 'Hitler's fortresses', from his personal headquarters through Atlantic Wall casemates to field positions carved into the sodden or frozen earth of the Eastern Front. In these positions, tens of thousands of German soldiers often spent their time in structured boredom, watching quiescent landscapes, but also fought to the death, the roofs above their heads pounded by artillery and aerial ordnance. Whatever the technicalities of the study to follow, we should always remind ourselves that Hitler's fortresses were both homes and graves to many men.

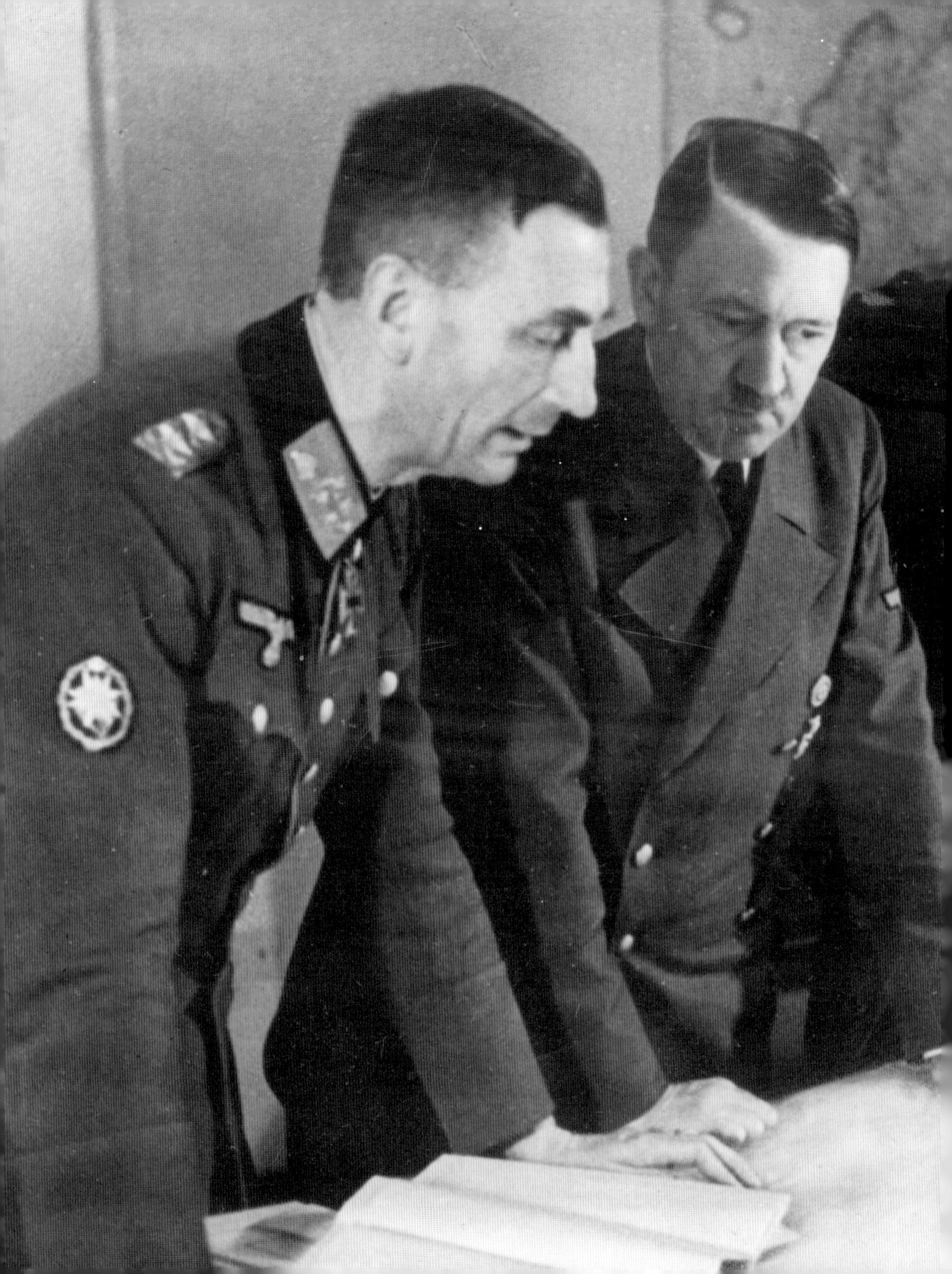

HITLER'S HEADQUARTERS – THE FÜHRER'S COMMAND BUNKERS

LEFT: Hitler in conference with Keitel (right) and Dietl at his headquarters near Rastenburg, known as Wolfsschanze, in 1941. (Scherl/SZ Photo)

As early as 1924, Hitler laid down his ambitions for territorial gains in his book *Mein Kampf* (My Struggle). At this time these were little more than pipe dreams, since he was languishing in Landsberg Prison. In the next decade, however, his fortunes improved. In 1933 he was made Chancellor of Germany and following the death of President Hindenburg he became supreme leader, or Führer. Being all-powerful, his ambitions could now begin to be realized. At first his aims were relatively modest: the remilitarization of the Rhineland, Anschluss (union) with Austria and the absorption into the Reich of the Sudeten Germans. Unchecked, he grew in confidence and now annexed the rump of Czechoslovakia, and on 1 September 1939 he took an even greater gamble by invading Poland.

Up until this point the German Army had been greeted as liberators, or at least had not met any resistance. Poland was different. A sovereign state, Poland had always been fearful of its powerful neighbours and had taken steps to defend itself. This, understandably,

Führerhauptquartier locations.

14

The concrete rail tunnel at Stepina was almost 500m long. Along its length entrances secured with steel doors were built into the wall to allow access. These could be secured from the inside with a simple locking mechanism. (Neil Short)

made Hitler nervous, and although he was not at this time intimately involved in the planning and direction of the campaign, he nevertheless wanted to be near the frontline to oversee the operation as it unfolded. Consequently, Hitler's personal train – codenamed 'Amerika' – was adapted as an improvised headquarters. This expedient was considered acceptable because the planners anticipated that the fighting in Poland would be over relatively quickly. Moreover, Führersonderzug (lit. 'Führer Special Train') 'Amerika' had the advantage of flexibility; in the unlikely event that the western democracies came to the aid of their ally, the train would enable Hitler to shuttle between fronts.

Somewhat surprisingly, for Hitler at least, Britain and France honoured their pledge to protect Poland, but their attacks in the west were so ineffectual that they were little more than a minor irritation for the Wehrmacht, which was able to concentrate all of its might against Poland, and on 27 September the government in Warsaw capitulated. This favourable turn of events enabled Hitler and the Oberkommando der Wehrmacht (OKW; Armed Forces High Command) to monitor the campaign from their mobile headquarters without any major alarms. However, the shortcomings of this 'wandering camp', as Walter Warlimont (Deputy Chief of the OKW Operations Staff) dubbed it, were recognized and it was concluded that a permanent solution would be needed for

Hitler oversaw the invasion of Poland not from a permanent Führerhauptquartier, but from his personal train 'Amerika'. Here the Führer is flanked by adjutants Schmundt (right) and Engel (left). In the left foreground Generalfeldmarschall Brauchitsch (left) and Generalfeldmarschall Keitel are in discussion. (Topfoto)

any attack in the west, which Hitler hoped to launch late in 1939. Thus, in September, key German figures Erwin Rommel, Dr Fritz Todt and Albert Speer were sent to the western border to identify possible sites.

Three sites were shortlisted and, because there was no time to build a bespoke headquarters, all of them were based on pre-existing, but very different, structures. One was near Bad Münstereifel in the Eifel mountains, one near Bad Nauheim in the Taunus mountains and one near Freudenstadt in the Black Forest. The headquarters favoured by Speer was in the Taunus mountains, an area he had explored as a young man. It was based around Schloß Ziegenberg and was codenamed Führerhauptquartier (FHQ; Führer Headquarters) Adlerhorst (Eagle's Eyrie). However, in spite of all the work to renovate the castle there, it was clear that it would not be ready for the invasion, and more significantly Hitler was not enamoured with it. Speer later recollected how Hitler, following a visit to the castle, concluded that 'It was too luxurious … not his

Entrance to the concrete rail tunnel at Stepina where Hitler met Mussolini in August 1941. Today the tunnel is used as a museum to house military memorabilia and is open to the public. (Neil Short)

style, too grand, "something for a horse-loving aristocrat". In wartime, he said, he as Führer must inspire the soldiers at the front with the Spartan simplicity of his daily life.'

Having served as a Gefreiter with the List Regiment in World War I, Hitler was familiar with the privations of the humble soldier. He was also well aware of the value of concrete bunkers to protect against heavy artillery and, on the modern battlefield, air attack. With this in mind, Hitler chose FHQ Felsennest (Mountain Nest), part of a Flak position in the West Wall. Located in the Eifel it was in an ideal position for Hitler to oversee the campaign in the west and on 9 May 1940 Hitler and his staff moved in.

The rapid advance of the German forces in the spring of 1940 soon left Hitler somewhat detached in his hilltop bunker and he insisted that a new site be identified from where he could oversee the second phase of the attack. Once again there was no time to build a bespoke headquarters, so various other alternatives were considered. Dr Todt, together with members of the Führer Begleit Bataillon (Führer Escort Battalion), inspected a series of Maginot Line bunkers in the vicinity of Maubeuge, but this idea was quickly dismissed and a second reconnaissance mission was instigated, which identified a number of small villages that were considered suitable for adaptation. Of these Brûly-de-Pesche in Belgium was selected. A series of temporary and permanent buildings were erected in the village and existing buildings were modified to create what became known as FHQ Wolfsschlucht (Wolf's Gorge). Yet no sooner had Hitler moved in than approval was given to identify a site for a further Führerhauptquartier from where he could oversee operations deep inside France. North of Margival, between Reims and Soissons, was a railway tunnel that was considered suitable to house the Führersonderzug. Dr Todt and Oberstleutnant Thomas (the new head of security) surveyed the site and orders were given for the construction of a bunker ready for Hitler's use. Work on FHQ Wolfsschlucht II began on 15 June 1940, but two days later France sought an armistice and the plans were shelved.

With the threat in the west all but extinguished, Hitler's gaze once again turned east. Hitler's view of the Soviet Union was contemptuous, but his outward disdain masked a genuine fear that the Red Army, in spite of its shortcomings, was capable of delivering a powerful counter-strike. Thus, in late 1940 Hitler ordered Dr Todt and two of his adjutants, Schmundt and Engel, to identify three locations from where it would be possible to oversee operations against the Soviet Union. One of the sites was to be in East Prussia and would be the principal Führerhauptquartier, with two further smaller, less elaborate, sites in German-occupied Poland. The logic was that should the Red Army launch a counter-attack – particularly from the Bialystok salient – and threaten the main Führerhauptquartier, then Hitler could move to an alternative and oversee operations from there. These three headquarters – FHQ Wolfsschanze (Wolf's Lair) at Rastenburg in East Prussia, Askania Mitte (Askania Centre) near Tomaszów and Askania

Süd (Askania South) near Strzyzów (better known as Anlage Mitte/Camp Centre and Anlage Süd) – were unique at the time because they were specially constructed to act as Führerhauptquartiere.

As it transpired, Hitler's concerns about a Soviet counter-attack proved groundless and although the Russian troops fought tenaciously, they were poorly led and were unable to stem the German advance. Consequently, Anlage Mitte was not used and Anlage Süd served only as a venue for talks with Mussolini in August 1941.

In that same summer German forces forged east and, as in France, the swift advance left Hitler far to the rear and unable to direct operations personally. Therefore, in September 1941, Thomas, Schmundt and Oberstleutnant Below (another of Hitler's adjutants) were ordered to identify three further sites for Führerhauptquartiere broadly corresponding to the axis of advance of the three German army groups: one in the

Most of Hitler's headquarters were constructed by German workers of the OT. However, FHQ Wehrwolf, which was located deep inside the Soviet Union, was built with forced labour, including prisoners of war. Many of these died in the process and a memorial was erected to their memory after the war. (Topfoto)

HITLER'S FORTRESSES

During the war Hitler stayed in a number of purpose-built headquarters. The chart shows which Führerhauptquartiere Hitler occupied, when and for how long. (Neil Short)

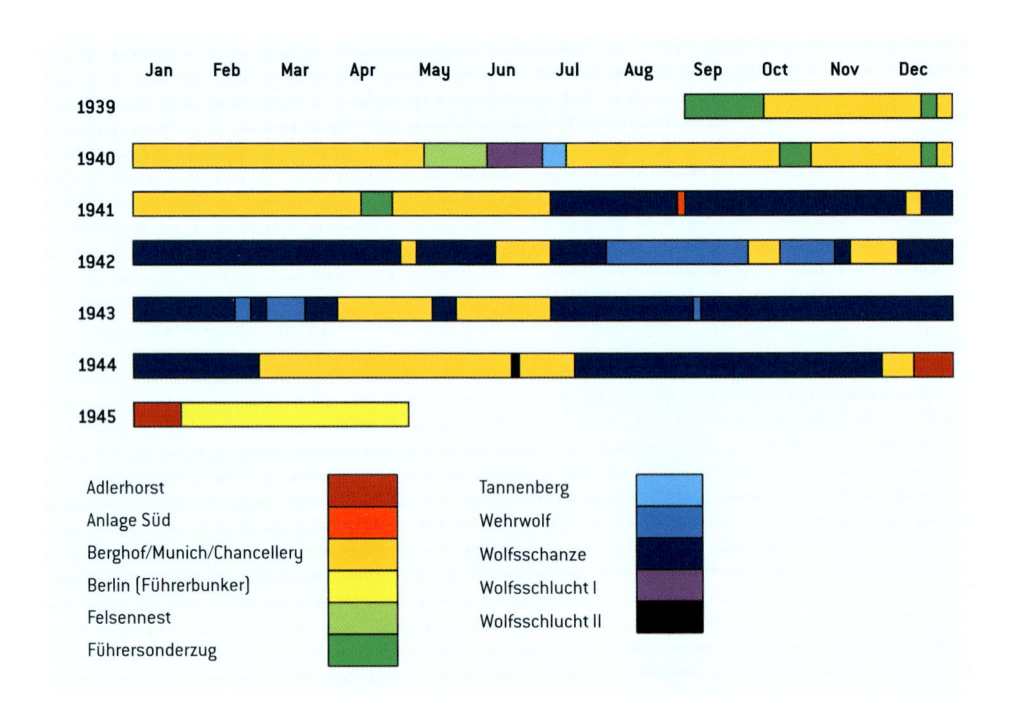

Adlerhorst	▇
Anlage Süd	▇
Berghof/Munich/Chancellery	▇
Berlin (Führerbunker)	▇
Felsennest	▇
Führersonderzug	▇
Tannenberg	▇
Wehrwolf	▇
Wolfsschanze	▇
Wolfsschlucht I	▇
Wolfsschlucht II	▇

north near Leningrad, one in the centre for the attack on Moscow and one in the Ukraine so that Hitler could direct operations in the Caucasus.

In October 1941 the Organisation Todt (OT; Todt Organization) was ordered to begin work at a former Red Army base near Gniesdovo, west of Smolensk, which lay on the main road to Moscow. Work on FHQ Bärenhöhle (Bear Cave), as it was called, involved converting existing structures and building a number of new blockhouses. However, although he was keen to capture the Soviet capital, Hitler's focus was increasingly fixed on the south and the vast natural resources located there. To enable him to oversee operations better in this theatre, orders were given for a second Führerhauptquartier to be built on Soviet territory. In November 1941 work began on Anlage Eichenhain (Camp Oak Grove) later renamed FHQ Wehrwolf. The new Führerhauptquartier was located in a wood some 8km north of Vinnitsa in the Ukraine.

By the summer of 1942 work on these two Führerhauptquartiere was nearing completion ready for Hitler to take up residence and oversee the new offensive. The main effort was to be made in the south, with holding operations around Moscow and Leningrad. The latter had been blockaded by Axis forces since July 1941, but although symbolically important its capture was not a priority and troops were gradually redeployed to more important sections of the front. Consequently, it was not until November 1942 that work began on FHQ Wasserburg some 300km south-west of Leningrad. From here Hitler would oversee the capture of Russia's second city, but as it transpired he never visited the headquarters and in the summer of 1943 Axis forces around the city went on the defensive. Elsewhere offensive operations continued, as did the building of a new Führerhauptquartier. In July 1943 work began on FHQ Olga, to the north of Minsk. Some 400m³ of concrete were poured, but it was never completed.

Meanwhile, in the west, British and Commonwealth forces launched a series of raids against German-occupied Europe and forced Hitler to start fortifying the coast against further attacks. More significantly, following Hitler's decision to declare war on the United States there was an increasing threat of a full-scale invasion. To prepare for such an eventuality, work began on FHQ Wolfsschlucht III near Vendôme in May 1942, and soon after (September 1942) work resumed on the Führerhauptquartier at Margival.

By the spring of 1944 the threat of invasion was acute and would, it was believed, be delivered in the region around Calais. If successful, such a landing would endanger the Führerhauptquartiere in France, and so work began in April 1944 near Diedenhofen

After the war Hitler's bunker in Berlin was partially demolished, but in 1988 a decision was taken to remove the last vestiges. The concrete structure was reduced to a tangle of reinforcing rods and lumps of concrete. The I-beams that supported the roof are clearly visible. (W. Fleischer)

The largest bunker at Wolfsschlucht II was some 90m in length. It was captured by the Allies and after the war it was used by the Americans. The building was originally christened 'Constance' but when this photograph was taken in 2009 the name appears to have changed to 'Patricia'. (Neil Short)

(Thionville) in Lorraine on FHQ Brunhilde and in the autumn at the Ohrdruf training ground in Thuringia.

By the spring of 1944, FHQ Wolfsschanze was threatened not only from the air, but also by Red Army ground forces. To mitigate this risk, work started in October 1943 on a further site near Bad Charlottenbrunn (Jedlina-Zdrój) in Silesia. This was in a more central position and was therefore easier to defend and less vulnerable to attack from the air. FHQ Riese (Giant) was incredibly resource intensive with manpower from the OT, forced labour from the nearby Groß-Rosen concentration camp and later Poles captured in the Warsaw uprising working on the project. In October 1944, 23,000 workers were employed on the building work. The Führerhauptquartier was also a logistical nightmare, requiring the transportation of tons of raw materials into this mountainous region and the removal of similar amounts of spoil. Unsurprisingly, FHQ Riese was never finished and in the closing stages of the war Hitler was instead forced to use Führerhauptquartiere from an earlier era or to improvise.

For the ill-fated Ardennes offensive Hitler stayed at FHQ Adlerhorst, though not in the palatial Schloß Ziegenberg – that was given over to Oberbefehlshaber West

(OB West; Commander-in-Chief West) Generalfeldmarschall Gerd von Rundstedt and his staff. Hitler stayed in a series of bunkers at the rear of the castle. When Operation *Wacht am Rhein* (Watch on the Rhine) failed, Hitler was forced to return to Berlin where he retreated to a series of bunkers located under key government buildings in the heart of the city. Work on the first of these shelters began soon after Hitler became chancellor in 1933. Later, in 1936, he insisted that an air-raid shelter be included in the design for the banqueting hall in the garden behind the Reich Chancellery. Then, in 1942, perhaps anticipating the devastating air raids to come, Hitler asked Speer to develop plans for a much deeper and stronger bunker under the Reich Chancellery, but only in 1943 did work begin. The new shelter, known as the Führerbunker, became Hitler's last Führerhauptquartier, but even by the time of his suicide in April 1945 the work was incomplete.

A TOUR OF THE SITES

ADLERHORST

FHQ Adlerhorst was based around the imposing Schloß Ziegenberg, which had been compulsorily purchased at the outbreak of the war. No expense was spared in renovating the interior of the castle so that it was fit for a head of state; it was finished with walnut doors and window frames, had panelled walls and was furnished with paintings and sculptures. From the castle, steps led down to a series of subterranean concrete bunkers. The first of these, Bunker 1, was arranged like an old-style railway carriage with the various rooms (which included a map room, recreation room and toilets) accessed from a single corridor. A passageway led from here to four further bunkers. The first of these was Bunker 5, which housed the fuel tanks, ventilation system, machine room and generator, coal store and the heating and water boiler. From here the corridor continued to Bunkers 6 and 7. The former housed the telephone exchange (Amt 600) and the latter an accommodation block. The last bunker, Bunker 3, was adjacent to Bunker 1 and was an accommodation block consisting of some 16 rooms.

Some 2km north of the castle seven 'houses' were built, each with a reinforced concrete cellar. Where the cellar stood proud of the ground the walls were clad with natural stone and then on top a Swiss-style chalet was constructed, which provided the day-to-day accommodation for the residents. Haus I was designated as Hitler's quarters and included a map room, rooms for his aides-de-camp and servants and his own private quarters, which consisted of a bedroom, bathroom, dressing room and study. The cellar was reached by a flight of stairs and provided a pared-down version of the upstairs accommodation.

A roofed walkway led from Hitler's accommodation to Haus II – the officers' mess. This consisted of a large dining hall, two lounges and a kitchen. Next to the mess or Kasino was Haus IV – the Generalshaus – which could accommodate 12 people in a mixture of single and double rooms and also had a lounge and two offices. Next to this was Haus III, the Pressehaus where Otto Dietrich, the Third Reich's Chief Press Officer, and his staff worked, and finally there was Haus V, which was allotted to Martin Bormann, Hitler's private secretary. To the north of Hitler's house was Haus VI, which was home to the OKW staff and a telephone exchange. At the bottom of the rise on which the other six 'houses' sat, and separated by a small road, was Haus VII – the guardhouse. This was much larger than the others and was of a slightly different design, with a porch at one end and a garage at the other.

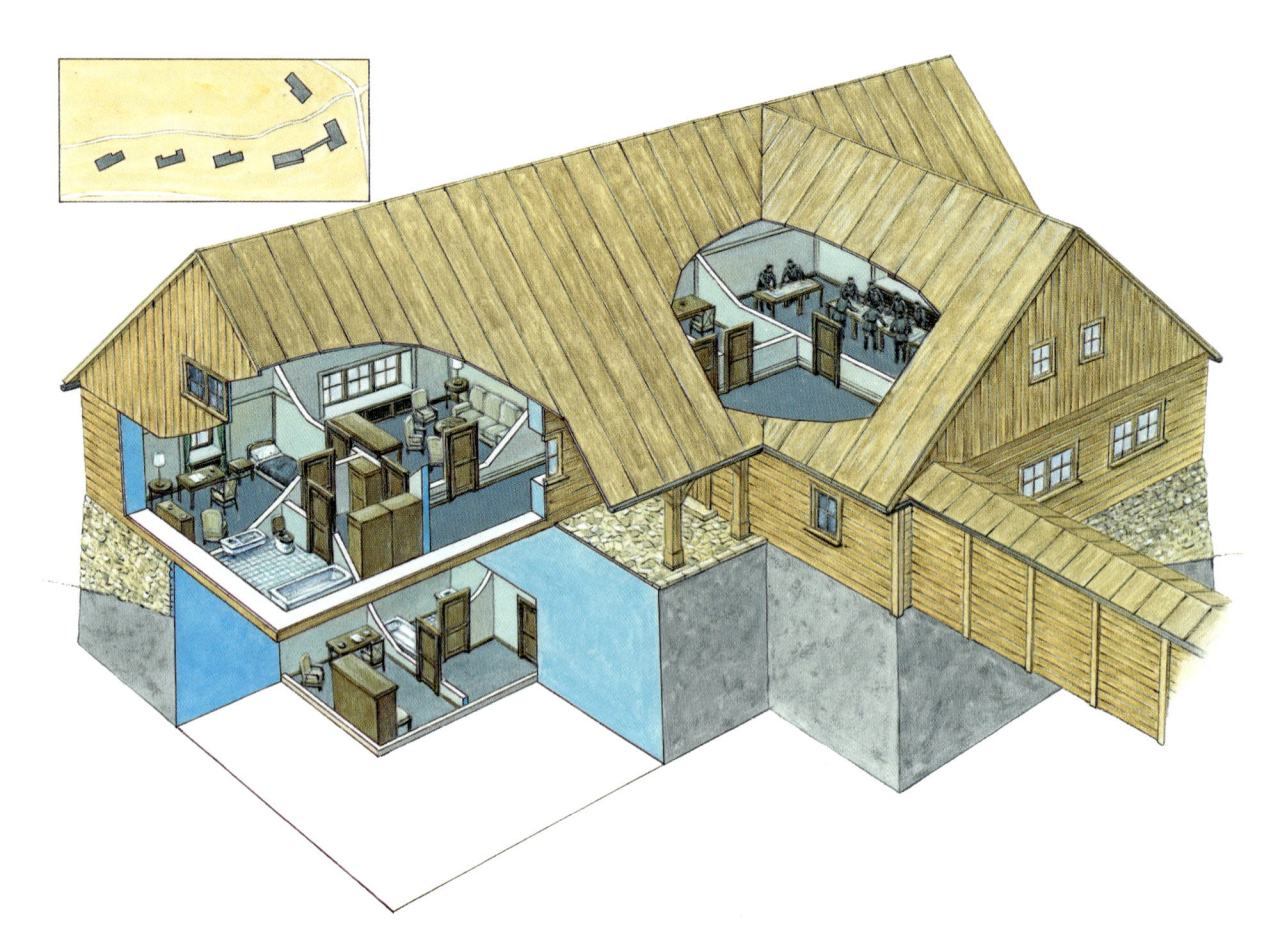

ABOVE: Adlerhorst, Bad Nauheim. On 11 December 1944 Hitler arrived at FHQ Adlerhorst, but rather than the splendour of the Schloß Ziegenberg, which had been renovated for his use, Hitler occupied one of the specially constructed fortified houses a kilometre to the rear near the village of Wiesental. Hitler's house consisted of a large bunker, the upper edge of which protruded just above the ground and was faced with natural stone. (Adam Hook © Osprey Publishing)

ANLAGE MITTE

Anlage Mitte was located east of Lodz near the town of Tomaszów and was split into three parts. The first, Anlage Mitte I, consisted of a 300m-long railway tunnel bored into the side of a mountain. A gallery leading off the main tunnel linked it to the machinery/pump house, which supplied fresh air, water and electricity. Outside the tunnel, a Teehaus (tea house) and huts to accommodate Hitler's personal retinue and security staff were erected. Beyond the tunnel a reinforced concrete 'tube' was constructed that was capable of housing Hitler's train. This was known as Anlage Mitte II. A gallery linked the tunnel to the machinery/pump house.

Anlage Mitte III consisted of a Type 102v Doppelgruppenunterstand. This was a standard bunker design used in the West Wall from 1939. It consisted of two rooms linked to the outside by two entrances, which were protected by a gas lock. In addition to the bunker there were two further concrete blockhouses, as well as six further wooden huts to accommodate OKH staff and security personnel.

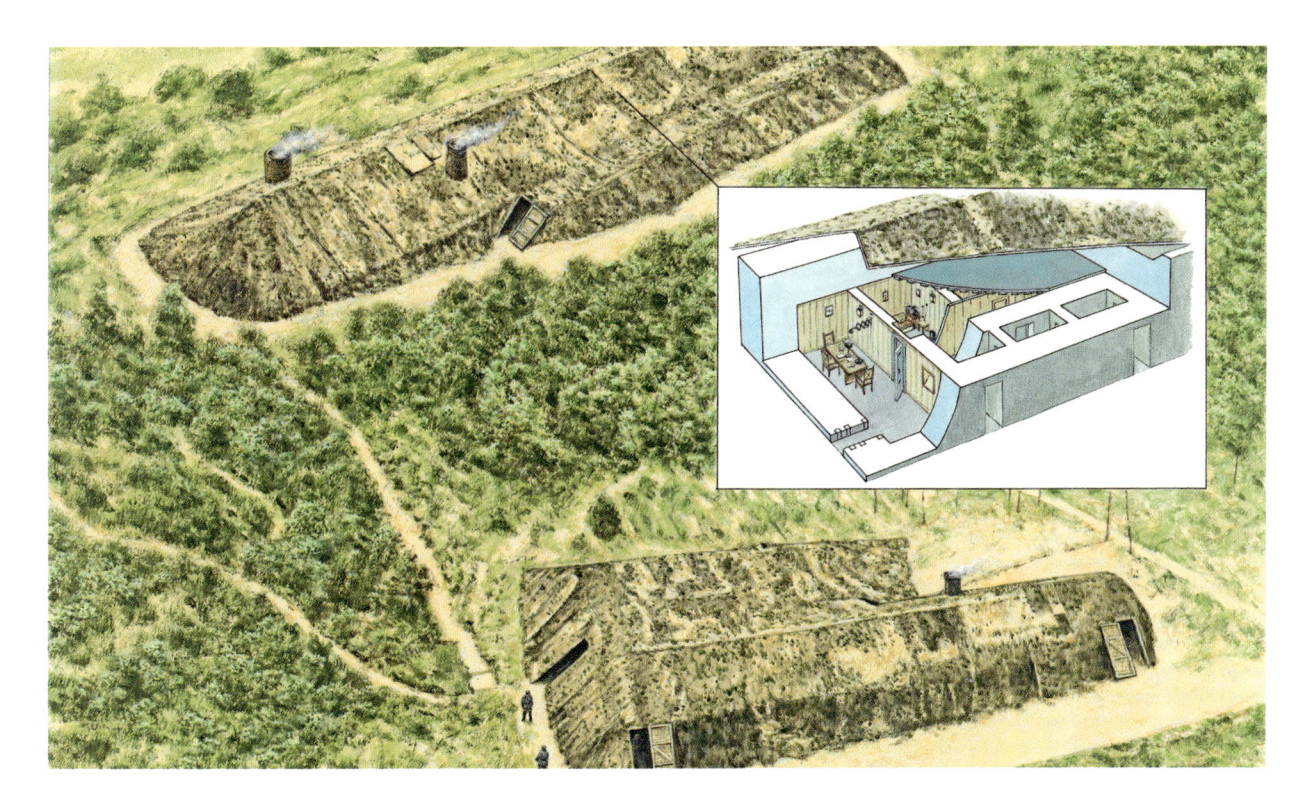

ABOVE: Felsennest, Bad Münstereifel. The main compound consisted of two bunkers and three barrack blocks, which were surrounded by a security fence and watchtowers and formed what was known as Sperrkreis I. The larger bunker was 16 x 8m and capable of accommodating 24 men in five separate rooms, but was adapted so that half served as Hitler's study and bedroom and the other half was used by his manservant Linge and his adjutant Schaub, as well as Keitel, Jodl and Schmundt. (Adam Hook © Osprey Publishing)

ANLAGE SÜD

Anlage Süd was split over two sites. At Strzyzów an existing railway tunnel that had been constructed by the Austrians before World War I was adapted to accommodate Hitler's train. Just outside the tunnel entrance a building to house pumps and generators was constructed and huts were provided for security staff, as a well as a Teehaus for Hitler.

A short distance to the north, at Frysztak, a reinforced concrete tunnel, similar to that at Anlage Mitte, was constructed. It was 7m high and almost 500m long, and was designed to house the Führersonderzug. It was serviced by a machinery/pump house and around the perimeter were located two large concrete shelters (Type 102v) and three pillboxes, each with three loopholes, which provided protection.

BÄRENHÖHLE

FHQ Bärenhöhle was located 9km west of Smolensk on the site of a former Red Army headquarters. Much of the infrastructure was reused or modified, but even so the OT and Russian labourers had to undertake a considerable amount of work to prepare it for

The entrance to Anlage Süd at Strzyzów. This is markedly different to the facility at Stepina. Rather than a man-made concrete shelter this was a tunnel bored into the hillside. Today it is sealed up, but is open to the public at certain times. (Neil Short)

its new role. A large reinforced concrete bunker was built for the Führer and more than 30 barrack blocks were erected to accommodate his staff; each was furnished with furniture and fittings 'liberated' from the Russians. The whole complex was enclosed by a perimeter fence almost 2km in length.

Water was supplied via two wells drilled 120m into the ground. Waste water was channelled to a sewage plant where it was treated and passed into the River Dnieper. Power was supplied from the civilian network, but diesel generators were installed to ensure continuity of supply should there be any disruption. The train station at Gniesdovo was upgraded with the platform lengthened to accommodate the Führersonderzug.

BRUNHILDE

At Diedenhofen (Thionville) in Lorraine some 15,300m^2 of tunnels of the Maginot Line were restored for use as a Führerhauptquartier known as FHQ Brunhilde. These tunnels would accommodate not only the Führer but also Heinrich Himmler (head of the SS) and the OKH, and were navigated, in part, by means of a narrow-gauge railway. Above-ground wooden huts were erected and two bunkers were built – one of which was similar in design to the Führerbunker at Wolfsschlucht II.

FELSENNEST

FHQ Felsennest was located in and around the village of Rodert, which lay in the so-called Luftverteidigungszone (Air Defence Zone) west of the West Wall. Sperrkreis I (Security Zone I) was located on a small wooded hill just to the south-west of the village. It consisted of a larger bunker with wood-clad walls and an adjoining hut. The bunker housed Hitler's study and bedroom and additionally was home to his personal staff Schaub and Linge as well as Generalfeldmarschall Wilhelm Keitel (head of the OKW). Adjacent was another hut and a smaller bunker where Generaloberst Alfred Jodl (Chief of the OKW Operations Staff), Hitler's three adjutants, Keitel's aide-de-camp and Dr Brandt, one of Hitler's personal physicians, were accommodated. A little distance away was a further hut where situation conferences were held. The whole of Sperrkreis I was surrounded by a fence with security towers. The village and surrounding countryside, some 30 hectares in total, was designated Sperrkreis II. A number of buildings in the village were commandeered by the Wehrmachtführungsstab (Wfst; Armed Forces Operations Staff) and were adapted for their use; these included offices, facilities for guests, a kitchen, garage and various air-raid shelters.

FÜHRERBUNKER (BERLIN)

The bunkers that were constructed beneath the Reich Chancellery were originally designed as air-raid shelters, but the incessant bombing forced Hitler and his staff to seek permanent refuge underground and these rooms were adapted for use as an improvised Führerhauptquartier. The so-called Vorbunker (lit. 'forward bunker'), from the earliest build phase, consisted of 12 rooms branching off a single corridor. In the final act of the war, a number of the rooms were given over to Joseph Goebbels (propaganda minister) and his family with the rest used to store, prepare, cook and serve food for the residents. From the Vorbunker a set of stairs led down to the Führerbunker. This was not only deeper underground, but also a significantly stronger construction with a roof almost 3m thick and walls over 2m thick. An armoured door protected the main access to the bunker. Beyond this were 20 or so small rooms reached by a long corridor. On the right of this corridor were a series of rooms that housed the engine room, ventilation equipment and the small telephone switchboard. It was also home to the medical room and a separate cabin for Hitler's personal physician. Farther down the main corridor, on the left, were Hitler's private rooms. The section of corridor that led to his apartments served as a waiting room and,

On around 6 March 1945, retreating German troops demolished the bunkers at FHQ Felsennest. Here, soldiers of the First US Army inspect the remains. The scale of the structure is clear from the GI standing amongst the rubble. (NARA)

by contrast with the rest of the bunker, was lavishly decorated with red carpet and paintings rescued from the Chancellery. From the corridor a small ante-room led to Hitler's study, which was furnished with a sofa, a radio and a desk, above which was a picture of Frederick the Great. A door led to Hitler's bedroom. This was again sparsely furnished with a bed, a safe and an oxygen cylinder. A further door led from Hitler's study to his dressing room and Eva Braun's bedroom/sitting room. Next to the ante-room was the cramped conference room where all the military briefings were held. At the end of the main corridor was a cloakroom and finally an exit with a flight of stairs that led out into the Chancellery garden.

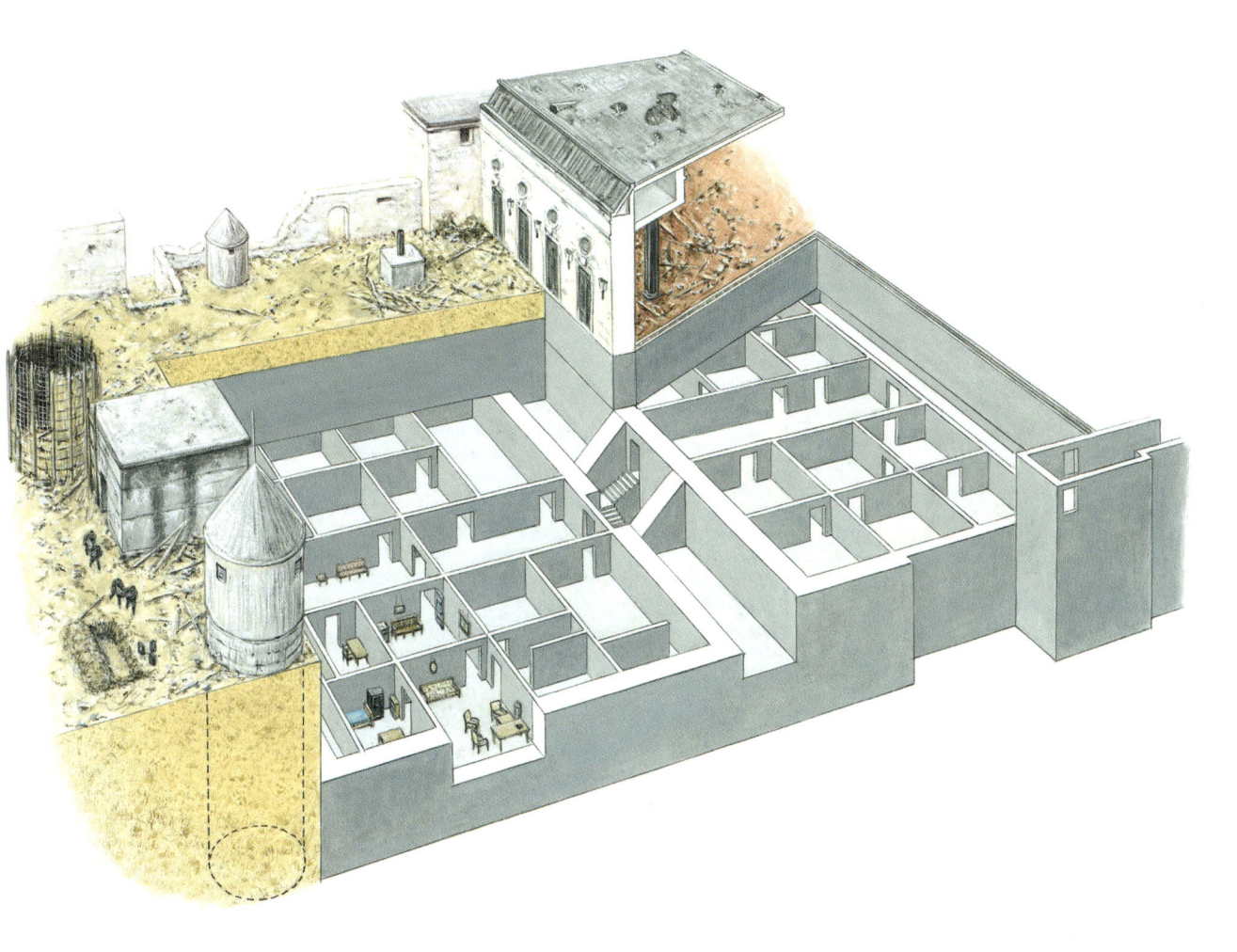

ABOVE: Berlin bunker. With the failure of the Ardennes Offensive, Hitler left FHQ Adlerhorst on 15 January 1945 and returned to Berlin. The city was much changed, having sustained months of heavy Allied bombing. The Reich Chancellery buildings were no longer safe, so Hitler and his staff retreated to the bunkers beneath. These had not been designed for permanent occupation but rather as a short-term refuge from isolated air raids. (Adam Hook © Osprey Publishing)

Hitler leaves his camouflaged bunker at FHQ Felsennest, followed by his adjutant Nicolas von Below. Just visible on the left is a camouflaged door that would have been closed to avoid detection by enemy planes. White hoops around the base of the trees helped people navigate around the site in the dark. (Topfoto)

HAGEN

FHQ Hagen (Siegfried) was located near the village of Pullach, south of Munich. It was built on an estate that housed Party functionaries and fell under the auspices of Martin Bormann. The Führerhauptquartier (which Hitler seemingly did not know about) consisted of seven wooden huts for accommodation and a further four huts, the roofs, walls and windows of which had been strengthened so that they provided protection against shell and bomb splinters. Two railway sidings that were linked to the main line via a branch line were constructed so that two Sonderzüge (special trains) could be accommodated.

A bunker for Hitler and his staff was built underground and was 70m long by 20m wide and approximately 11m high with a 3m-thick roof. It consisted of some 30 rooms, including work and conference rooms as well as rooms for the ventilation system, machinery, transformers and switches. Access was via a tower, which was fitted with both a lift and stairs. At the opposite end of the bunker a further flight of stairs formed an emergency exit.

OLGA

Some 200km north-east of Minsk, near the village of Orsha, was FHQ Olga. There were plans to build a series of bunkers and huts here, but when the site was abandoned the Führerbunker had not been completed.

RIESE

In November 1943 work began on FHQ Riese. The site chosen was south-east of Bad Charlottenbrunn in a mountainous and heavily forested area of Lower Silesia. Rather than a single location, Riese consisted of a series of underground facilities that were bored by specialist engineers. The exposed rock face was then sealed with concrete and faced with stone. The entrances were protected with armoured doors against bomb blasts. When completed, the tunnels would be capable of accommodating more than 20,000 staff including Hitler and his retinue, security personnel, the heads of the Army, Luftwaffe and SS along with their staffs, and the Reich foreign minister.

While work continued on the underground tunnels, in 1944 the nearby Schloß Fürstenstein was commandeered by the OT. Work started immediately on transforming it into a residence for Joachim von Ribbentrop (foreign minister) and his staff, with room also set aside for the Führer. From the castle, access was made to underground galleries that could be used in an air raid. It was also planned to have a bomb-proof siding for the Führersonderzug. When the war ended, the work at Riese, though extensive, was far from complete.

TANNENBERG

FHQ Tannenberg (Pine Mountain) was located between Baden-Baden and Freudenstadt on a 1,000m-high feature in the heart of the Black Forest called the Kniebis. The site was just off the Black Forest High Road and was on the site of an existing installation of the Luftverteidigungszone West (Air Defence Zone West). Two bunkers were constructed; one was for Hitler's use and the other, south of the road, was a Nachrichtenbunker (communication centre). In addition a series of wooden barrack blocks were built, one to accommodate Hitler and a further one to house Keitel and Jodl. There was also an officers' mess, a Teehaus, a hut for situation conferences (Lagehaus), barracks for Führerhauptquartier staff and security personnel, a guardhouse and a shower block. The whole of Sperrkreis I (Security Zone I) was protected by a barbed-wire fence. Unusually, Warlimont's OKW staff stayed in a local guesthouse a kilometre away.

WALDWIESE

FHQ Waldwiese was built around the village of Glan-Münchweiler, near Landstuhl, and consisted of a series of bunkers and huts. The Führerbunker was constructed in woodland to the east of the village, while a communications bunker was built in the village itself and was camouflaged with a slate roof and painted windows so that it looked like a normal dwelling.

WASSERBURG

FHQ Wasserburg was situated near Pskov on the River Welikaya and, like FHQ Adlerhorst, was based around a large mansion that was renovated to accommodate Hitler and his staff, including an officers' mess that was located in the mansion's central tower. Outbuildings were also adapted as accommodation and some of the Reichsarbeitsdienst (RAD; Reich Labour Service) huts were used as quarters for security personnel. Outside the mansion a standard Type 102v bunker was constructed for Hitler's use in the event of an air raid. A specially designed garage was also built, which was heated so that vehicle engines would start even in the hardest of winters.

Electricity was provided to the site from the power station at Pskov, which was stepped down through a newly built transformer. From here overhead cables connected the various buildings. Water was supplied to the headquarters from a natural spring, and was pumped into a large header tank that fed individual standpipes. A separate tank stored water to serve the system of fire hydrants. Waste water was channelled to the newly constructed sewage-treatment facilities. From here the treated water was pumped into the river. The access road to the site was resurfaced and around the facility 1,800m of 'Flanders hedge' was erected.

WEHRWOLF

In November 1941 work began on FHQ Wehrwolf, which was located in woodland just off the main route to Shitomir and 8km north of Vinnitsa. The facility consisted of a number of bunkers, blockhouses and huts all constructed by the OT.

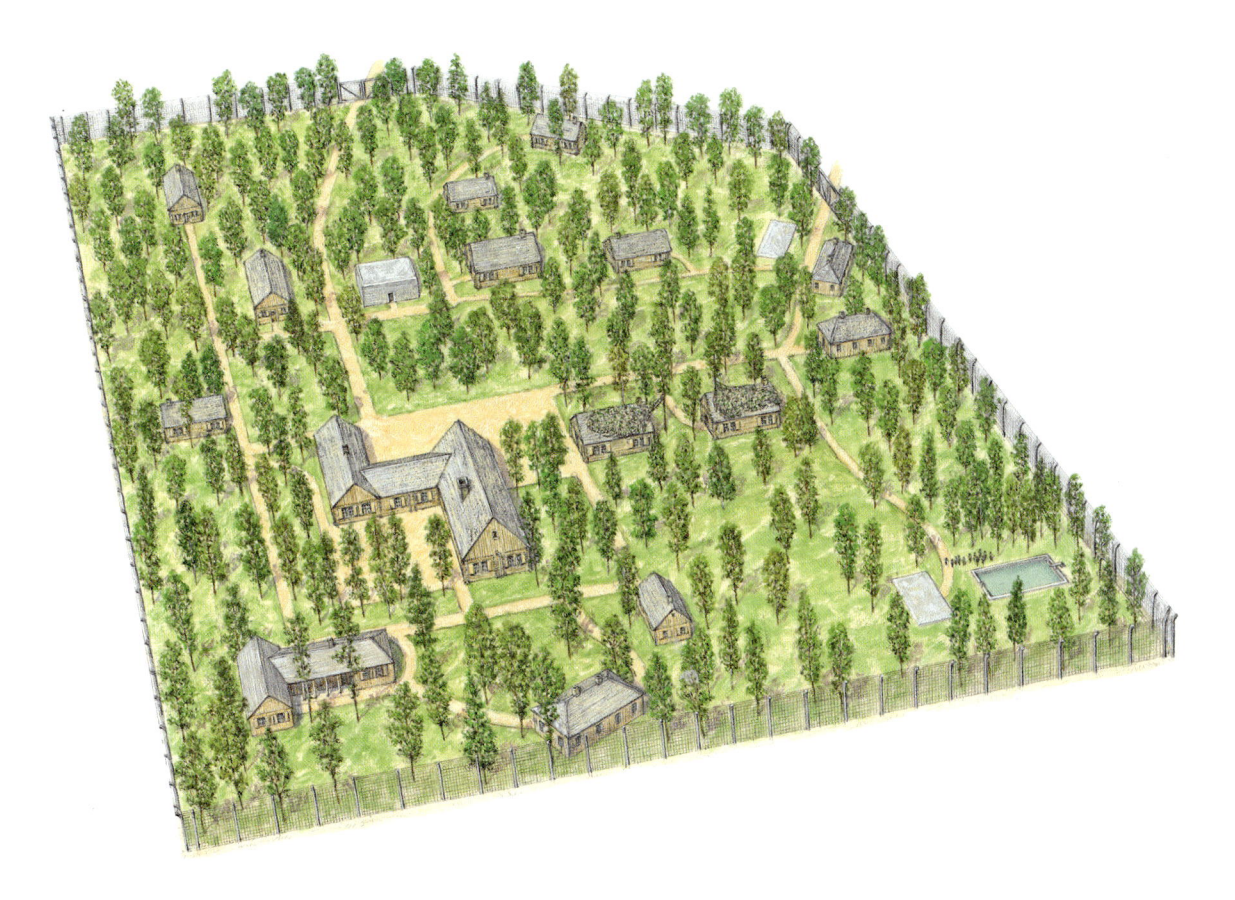

ABOVE: Wehrwolf, Vinnitsa. Hitler was resident at FHQ Wehrwolf from July until November 1942. Following a final visit in August 1943, his headquarters was taken over by Army Group South, but this proved to be only temporary and eventually FHQ Wehrwolf had to be abandoned. In December 1943 the buildings were demolished; the remnants of the concrete bunkers are still visible. (Adam Hook © Osprey Publishing)

A view of the hallway inside one of the blockhouses at FHQ Wolfsschanze. Timber was plentiful around Rastenburg and was used to line the walls. On the right wall a deckchair can be seen hanging. (Topfoto)

Sperrkreis I, where Hitler was housed, was located at the far end of the clearing where, according to Hans Baur, Hitler's personal pilot, 'Two bunkers were built, one for Hitler and his essential staff, the other for the rest of the workers on the base. They were planned only for protection in the event of bombings'. However, for day-to-day use Hitler and his staff were accommodated in 19 blockhouses constructed, at Hitler's behest, from non-treated timber, as on previous occasions Hitler had been badly affected by the fumes from the wood preservatives.

Water was supplied to the headquarters from two wells and was used for drinking and for more general use, including the filling of the swimming pool that had been specially built. Water for the fire hydrants was pumped from the River Bug, and this is also where the effluent from the sewage plant was pumped.

Hitler spent a considerable amount of time at Wehrwolf and it soon became clear that more room was needed, so in January 1943 work began on a second building phase that saw the construction of further blockhouses, huts, roads and paths. It also necessitated lengthening the perimeter fences from 6km to 7.6km. The site was extensively camouflaged with nets threaded with sea grass, and vegetation from the forest was also used. Some of the larger trees around the edge of the forest were adapted to serve as lookout towers, and, unusually, underground guard posts were dug for Hitler's security personnel.

WOLFSSCHANZE

FHQ Wolfsschanze was built in the Görlitz Forest in East Prussia. It straddled the road from Rastenburg (Ketrzyn) to Angerburg (Wegorzewo) and the rail line that ran broadly parallel. At the outset, work on the headquarters was undertaken in the utmost secrecy with the plans for the site initially referred to as a chemical works. Great efforts were expended on camouflaging the site with netting and fake trees and bushes located on the roofs. The Führersonderzug, when kept at Görlitz, was also camouflaged. Aerial photographs were taken to ensure that the camouflage was effective. The road and the train line through the site were closed to the public, as was the small station of Görlitz, which was now expanded so that it could accommodate the Führersonderzug and the trains of other visiting dignitaries.

The site itself was divided into a series of security zones. Sperrkreis I was located at the eastern end of the complex and was fenced with two entrances, one to the east and one to the west. This inner security zone was the nerve centre of Wolfsschanze and was where Hitler and his inner circle (Bormann, Göring and Keitel) were accommodated. Eventually it also included accommodation for Jodl and the WFSt staff, messes, accommodation for guests, Hitler's personal staff, security guards and liaison staff. It also had garages and a communication bunker, and was the location for the typists' office, which had its own fence to ensure the sensitive material processed there was not compromised.

In September 1943 a further security zone – Sperrkreis A – was established. A fence was constructed around the Führerbunker and the buildings in the immediate vicinity. Access to the area was closely controlled. Later, when Hitler's bunker was being strengthened, another security zone was established around the guest bunker where Hitler resided temporarily and an adjacent building – the Lagebaracke – and it was here that the unsuccessful July plot was perpetrated.

Work on the site was almost continuous from when the first sod was cut in 1940 to when Hitler left for the last time in November 1944, but was essentially divided into three phases: 1940–41, 1942–43 and 1944.

Phase 1

This consisted of concrete and brick hutments with steel shutters to protect the windows and included, in Sperrkreis I, accommodation for Hitler and his personal staff, Bormann, Keitel and security personnel as well as a mess, communication centre, garage

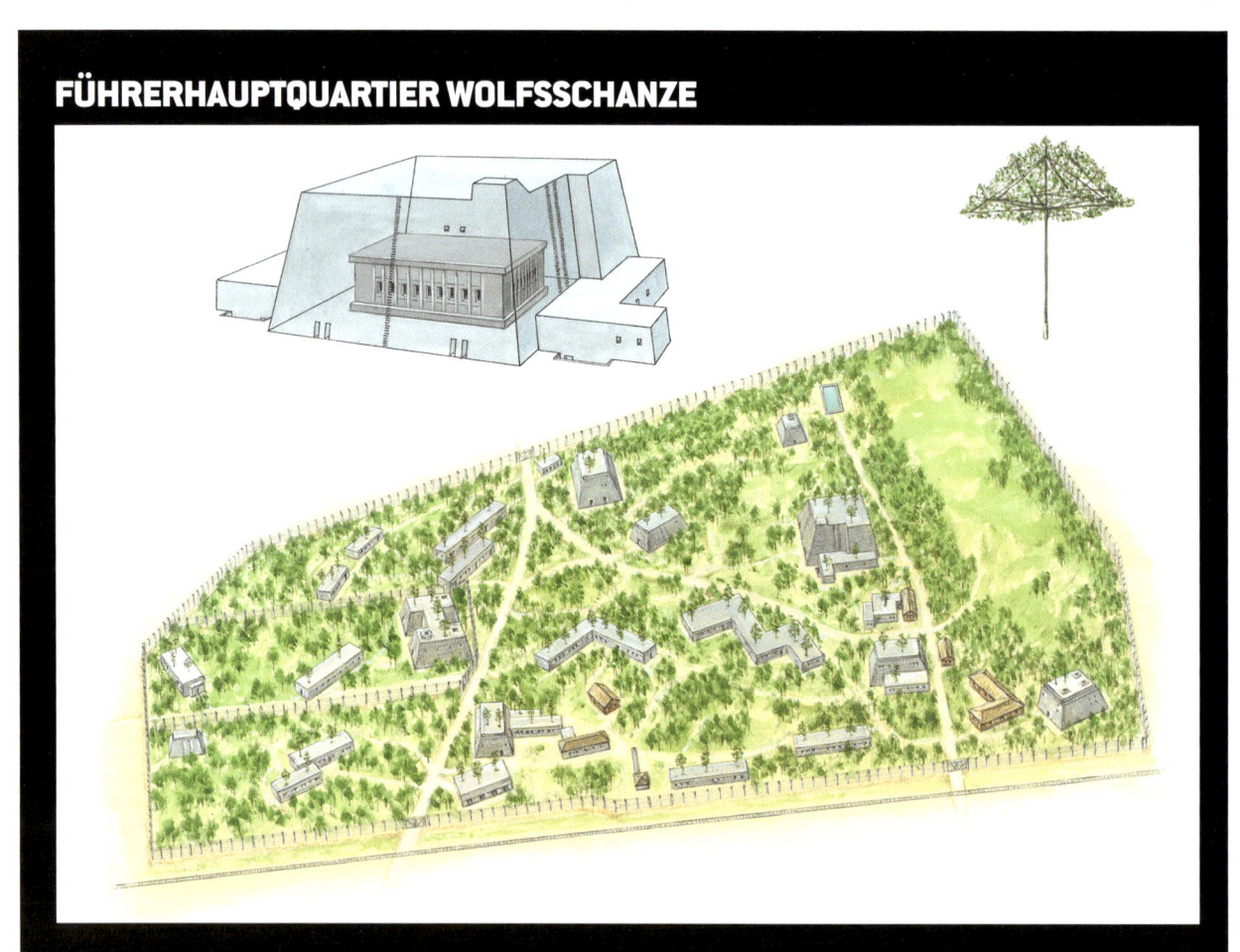

FÜHRERHAUPTQUARTIER WOLFSSCHANZE

Führerhauptquartier Wolfsschanze consisted of a series of security zones. The outer zone – Sperrkreis II – consisted of a barbed-wire fence reinforced with minefields, defensive emplacements and Flak positions that enclosed an area of approximately 2.5km². Within this zone was a further fenced-off area – Sperrkreis I – which is where Hitler's bunker was located as well as bunkers for Göring, Bormann and Keitel and accommodation for their supporting staff. The inner restricted zone also included guest accommodation, messes, a communications bunker, offices, garages and barracks for the guards. To occupy any free time there was also a cinema, a sauna and a Teehaus. In the autumn of 1943 a further security zone was introduced around the 'inner sanctum' that included Hitler's bunker, and was known as Sperrkreis A. At the beginning of 1944 work started on strengthening the various bunkers against air attack. While this work progressed a further security zone was established around the guest bunker, located to the west of Sperrkreis I. This was where Hitler stayed when he returned to Wolfsschanze in the summer of that year and is why the fateful situation conference on 20 July 1944 was held in the adjacent Lagebaracke – a fact that most likely saved Hitler's life. (Adam Hook © Osprey Publishing)

and heating plant. In addition, there were a number of wooden buildings, including a Teehaus, which Hitler used as a place of relaxation.

Phase 2

As the war dragged on it was realized that the accommodation would need to be extended. Initially wooden hutments were built, but later these were strengthened with the addition of concrete roofs and brick walls. Much of this accommodation was functional in purpose with offices for Jodl and Hermann Göring (head of the Luftwaffe), but also recreational buildings including guest accommodation, a second mess, a new Teehaus, a sauna and a cinema. Wooden annexes were also added to Keitel's and Hitler's bunkers – the latter being used as a study. Outside Sperrkreis I, south of the road, accommodation was provided for Kriegsmarine (Navy), Luftwaffe, foreign ministry, OT and SS liaison officers and their respective staffs.

Phase 3

In the final building phase, which began in February 1944, a number of key buildings were massively strengthened including Hitler's, Keitel's and Bormann's bunkers, the communication bunkers in both Sperrkreis I and II and the guest bunker. There was also a new bunker for Göring, a new general-purpose bunker adjacent to Bormann's and two further bunkers south of the road that were to be used by staff as an air-raid shelter.

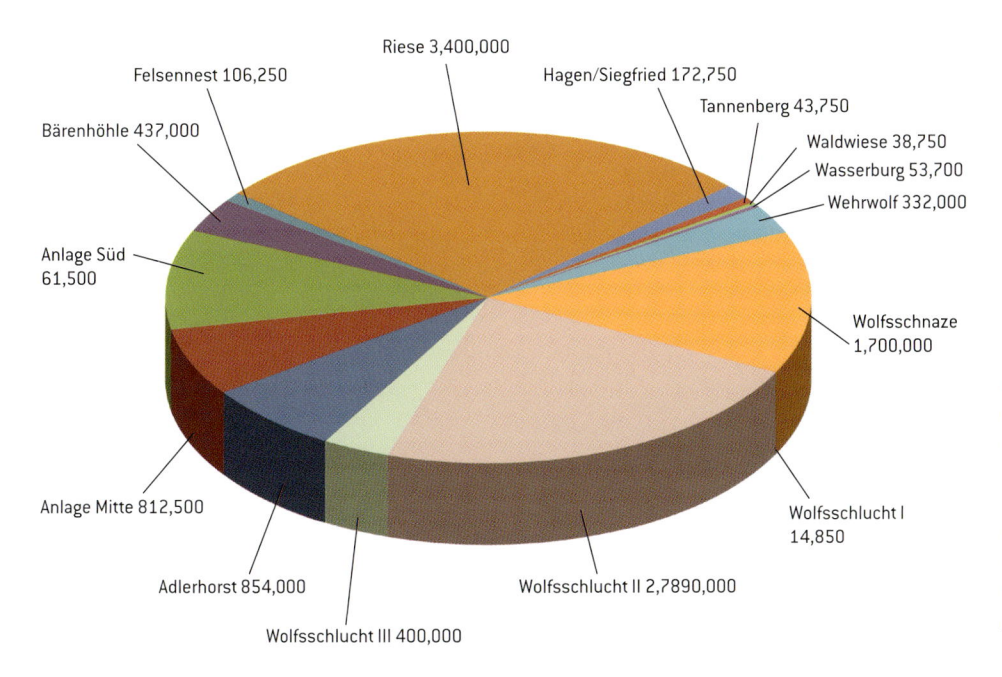

Riese 3,400,000
Felsennest 106,250
Hagen/Siegfried 172,750
Tannenberg 43,750
Bärenhöhle 437,000
Waldwiese 38,750
Wasserburg 53,700
Wehrwolf 332,000
Anlage Süd 61,500
Wolfsschnaze 1,700,000
Anlage Mitte 812,500
Wolfsschlucht I 14,850
Adlerhorst 854,000
Wolfsschlucht II 2,7890,000
Wolfsschlucht III 400,000

During the course of the war nearly 12 million working days were spent by the OT and other forced labourers constructing Hitler's various Führerhauptquartier. This pie chart shows that two thirds of the effort was expended on just three sites. (Neil Short)

Hitler had sketched out the design for the new bunker himself and wanted the existing structure encased in 3m-thick concrete. Then he wanted a further concrete jacket, some 5m thick, and in between the two he wanted a layer of sand that would serve to absorb any bomb blast. According to Speer, when complete, 'It looked like an ancient Egyptian tomb. It was actually nothing but a great windowless block of concrete, without direct ventilation, in cross section a building whose masses of concrete far exceeded the usable cubic feet of space'. He concluded his appraisal by noting that: 'It seemed as if the concrete walls sixteen and a half feet thick that surrounded Hitler separated him from the outside world in a figurative as well as literal sense, and locked him up inside his delusions.'

A further security zone for Warlimont's WFSt and headquarters commandant staff was constructed to the south-west of Sperrkreis I. The accommodation consisted of single-storey concrete and brick houses, but in 1944 was supplemented with an enormous Nachrichtenbunker to protect the telephone exchange. Adjacent to this and south of Sperrkreis I were buildings to accommodate OKM and OKL liaison officers and Ribbentrop's staff.

The entire site was surrounded by a further fence and was known as Sperrkreis II. It had three entrances: in the west, the east and the south – the latter linked the headquarters with the airfield at Rastenburg 6km distant. The entrances were guarded and further blockhouses and machine-gun posts were located around the perimeter along with Flak positions to guard against air attack. Extensive use was made of minefields and farther afield strategic road junctions were guarded.

WOLFSSCHLUCHT I

Wolfsschlucht I was based around the Belgian village of Brûly-de-Pesche. It consisted of six buildings, which were modified for their new role. The OT began work on 25 May 1940 with the vicarage, the village inn (renamed the Wolfspalast) and the school being converted into accommodation for Keitel, guest accommodation and an operations room respectively. The church tower was removed to disguise the structure and was 'put in a safe place' to be rebuilt again when the fighting was over. The main body of the church was used for offices and the nave partitioned off and used as a small cinema.

In addition to the conversion work a series of concrete bunkers and wooden buildings were constructed. In the forest a wooden chalet was built for Hitler, along with a Teehaus and a further wooden barrack block to house the OKW command staff (WFSt Section L). A small bunker (25m^2) was also built as an air-raid shelter. This could be accessed from either side and was fitted with steel gas-proof doors. A further bunker was planned near the Wolfspalast but was not completed. Next to it was a short aircraft

The OKW bunker at Wolfsschlucht II was later renamed 'Zucarello'. The road in front leads to the Teehaus. Hitler's bunker is to the right, out of the shot. (Neil Short)

landing strip. The garrison headquarters was located in a house on the road leading into the village. The whole site was secured with barbed wire.

WOLFSSCHLUCHT II

Wolfsschlucht II was constructed at the entrance to a rail tunnel between the villages of Neuville-sur-Margival and Laffaux; the idea being that the Führersonderzug could be safely parked in the tunnel, which had been fitted with armoured doors at the entrance, to protect against air attack.

The compound itself comprised six large bunkers and a mixture of other buildings, some of them with strengthened walls, roofs and windows. The Führerbunker consisted of a reinforced concrete air-raid shelter with walls some 3.5m thick, which was surrounded on two sides by an outer building that consisted of work rooms, a hall, kitchen, WCs and bath and shower rooms.

Adjacent to the Führerbunker was the OKW bunker, which was similar in set-up, with a massive air-raid shelter surrounded on three sides by an outer building consisting of more than 20 rooms and a further annexe with almost as many rooms again.

OVERLEAF: Wolfsschlucht, Brûly-de-Pesche. Hitler oversaw the second stage of the western campaign (Operation *Rot*, or red), which commenced on 5 June 1940, from the small Belgian village of Brûly-de-Pesche. The village consisted of six buildings and was perfect as a headquarters, nestling unobtrusively in the Forêt de Gondreux. (Adam Hook © Osprey Publishing)

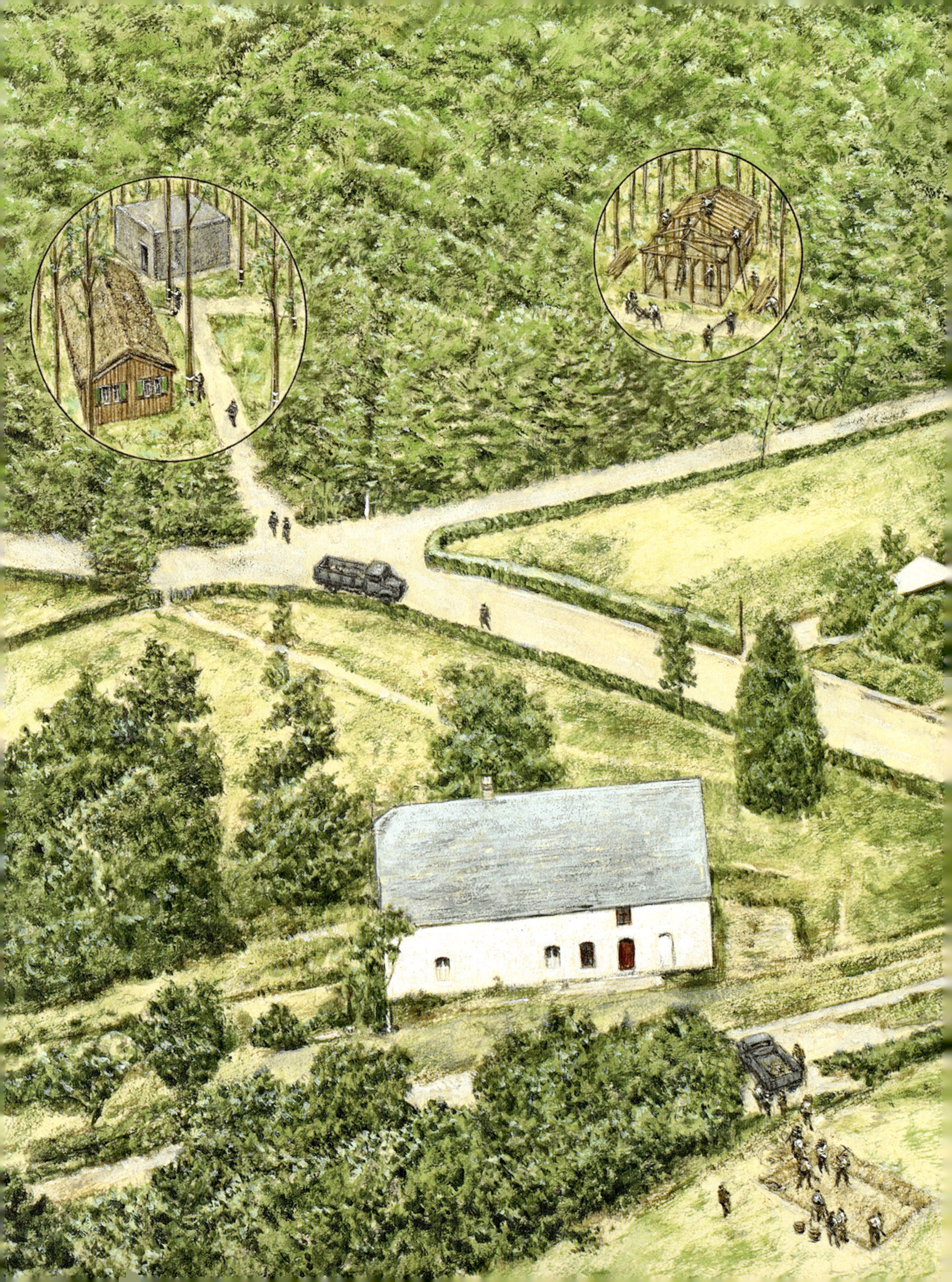

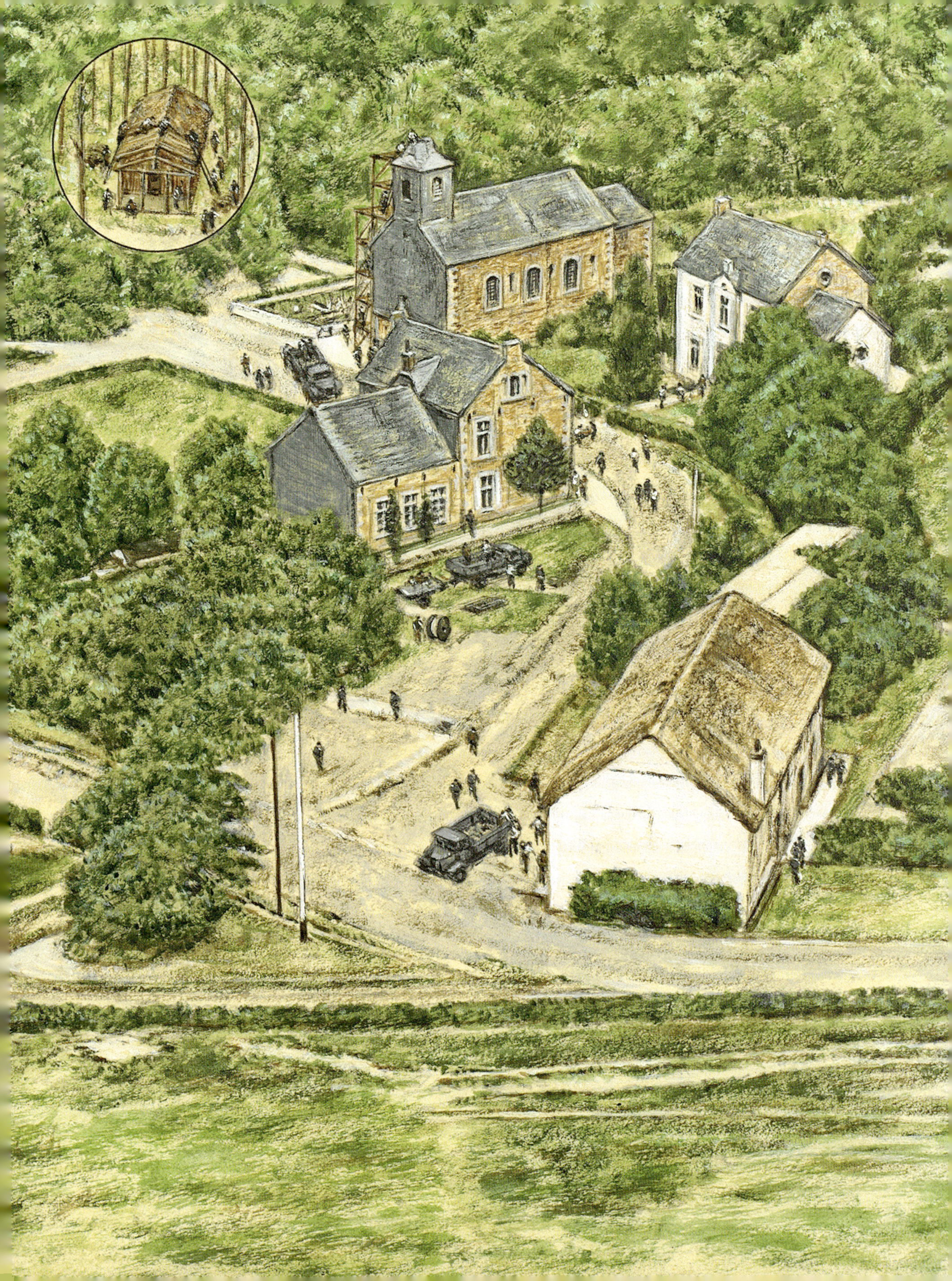

The original train station at Margival. Although Wolfsschlucht II is often quoted as being at Margival the actual Führerbunker is some 2km further up the track near the rail tunnel. Today the stop is still used, but not the station building. (Neil Short)

Finally, in this group was the largest of the buildings, which served as the staff department with offices, living quarters and a telephone exchange. In construction it followed the same format as the others, with outbuildings on three sides of a reinforced concrete bunker which was itself divided into four sections.

On the other side of the railway line was a smaller signals bunker with teleprinter and annexe. Farther down the railway line towards Margival was a guest bunker that was not dissimilar to the staff department bunker, but was divided into three sections. Finally there was a further bunker, which was on the opposite side of the track from Margival station. Internally this was divided into two and a garage was attached.

The main Führerhauptquartier buildings were surrounded by a belt of some 450 other positions, many of them anti-aircraft emplacements to accommodate heavy, medium and light anti-aircraft guns, rangefinders and searchlights.

WOLFSSCHLUCHT III

Although Hitler had ordered that only one Führerhauptquartier was originally necessary in France, a further facility was constructed 15km west of Vendôme. Once again it was built around a railway tunnel that was fitted with armoured doors to protect the Führersonderzug. At the north-east tunnel entrance a bunker was constructed for Hitler and another one for his staff. As at Wolfsschlucht II, a series of anti-aircraft emplacements were built to protect against air attack.

FÜHRERSONDERZUG

As the head of state, Hitler was entitled to use special trains provided by the Reichsbahn (German Railways). However, starting in 1937 Hitler ordered the construction of a series of new armoured coaches that were to be for his personal use only. These were completed by August 1939 and the special train was codenamed 'Amerika'. It consisted of a locomotive, two baggage cars (one at each end) and 11 carriages, painted dark green. The first of these was the Führer's Pullman carriage (No. 10206) – the 'Führerwagen' – which consisted of a series of compartments: two for Hitler, including a bathroom, and others for his personal staff to sleep and wash in. This was followed by

A view of the largest bunker at Wolfsschlucht II, which was later renamed 'Constance'. This long shot demonstrates how enormous the structure was. (Neil Short)

a Befehlswagen (command car), which was split in two. The forward half accommodated the conference room, including the map table, and the rear half housed the telephone exchange and signals centre. The third coach accommodated Hitler's personal bodyguards. There were then two dining carriages – one for the Führer and one for his staff, two sleeping carriages, a bathing carriage (with showers and hip baths), two carriages for Hitler's retinue (adjutants, personal physician, secretaries, cooks etc.) and a Pressewagen for Dietrich and his staff, which included a short-wave transmitter.

With the outbreak of the war the train was adapted for use as a mobile headquarters. Externally the main visible difference was the addition of two Flak wagons, armed with 2cm Flakvierling 38s, one at the front between the locomotives and the first car and the other at the tail of the train. Later in the war the locomotives were armoured to protect against air attack.

THE LIVING SITES

Hitler's time at the various Führerhauptquartiere was spent in the company of a small circle of individuals. The more senior figures like Goebbels, Göring, Himmler and Ribbentrop only tended to visit, having their own accommodation. The one exception

Wolfsschlucht II was protected from air attack by a series of Flak batteries. This position on the road between Margival and Laffaux was designed to take a light or medium anti-aircraft gun. The niches at the side were for ammunition. (Neil Short)

was Martin Bormann, Hitler's private secretary, who, like Hitler's staff, resided permanently with the Führer.

A number of Hitler's closest staff, like Julius Schaub, Hitler's chief personal adjutant, had been with him since the early days of the Nazi party. Other personal adjutants

The Church of Sainte Meér at Brûly-de-Pesche as it is today. In 1940 the upper section of the spire was removed to make it less conspicuous and the building itself was used by the OT. The church has since been returned to its former use and is still used for worship. (Neil Short)

joined his staff later and included Albert Bormann (brother of Martin, but whose relationship was so strained that they only ever spoke through intermediaries) and Otto Günsche, who was with the Führer until the very end and ignited the petrol to incinerate his chief and his wife after they had committed suicide. He was assisted by Erich Kempka, Hitler's driver, who provided the petrol for the cremation and Heinz Linge, his valet, who helped carry Hitler's body from the bunker. Also in the bunker at the end was Hans Baur, Hitler's personal pilot. Hitler's personal wellbeing, wherever he travelled, was catered for by his personal physicians – Dr Theodor Morell and Dr Karl Brandt – although the former arguably did more to worsen Hitler's condition with the medicines he prescribed than he did to ameliorate them.

During the course of the war Hitler had four secretaries – Gerda Christian (née Daranowski), Traudl Junge, Christa Schroeder and Johanna Wolf, the eldest of the group. Hitler was also supported by numerous military advisers and liaison officers, plus he was advised by senior OKW officers who also travelled with him and were accommodated in the various Führerhauptquartiere. Principal among these were Generalfeldmarschall Keitel (head of the OKW), Generaloberst Jodl (Chief of the OKW Operations Staff) and Jodl's deputy, General Warlimont.

These companions were with Hitler throughout the war and their lives in the various Führerhauptquartiere revolved around his schedule. This gradually changed and became

In June 1944 Hitler travelled to Wolfsschlucht II to discuss the Allied landings with his generals. They were protected from Allied air attack by the massive concrete roof of the Führerbunker. In the foreground is a red brick chimney. (Neil Short)

increasingly bizarre as Hitler's physical and mental state deteriorated. However, it broadly followed the same routine. For example, at FHQ Wolfsschanze, where he spent a good portion of the war, Hitler would get up late and have a simple breakfast (a glass of milk and some mashed apple) with his staff in No. 1 Dining Room. This would be followed at lunchtime by a situation briefing in Keitel's bunker, which would last approximately 90 minutes. Lunch was at 1400hrs and afterwards Hitler would deal with war-related issues, but not those involving the military – war production, for example.

On the opposite side of the track from Margival train station are a series of buildings that formed part of Wolfsschlucht II. Bunker 56 'Loano' was later adapted with the addition of a climbing tower for the training of commandos, which is visible at the top. (Neil Short)

HITLER'S FORTRESSES

From 1939 until the war's end, Hitler's Führerhauptquartier programme consumed over 1 million cubic metres of concrete. The pie chart shows that more than half of the concrete was used at just two sites. (Neil Short)

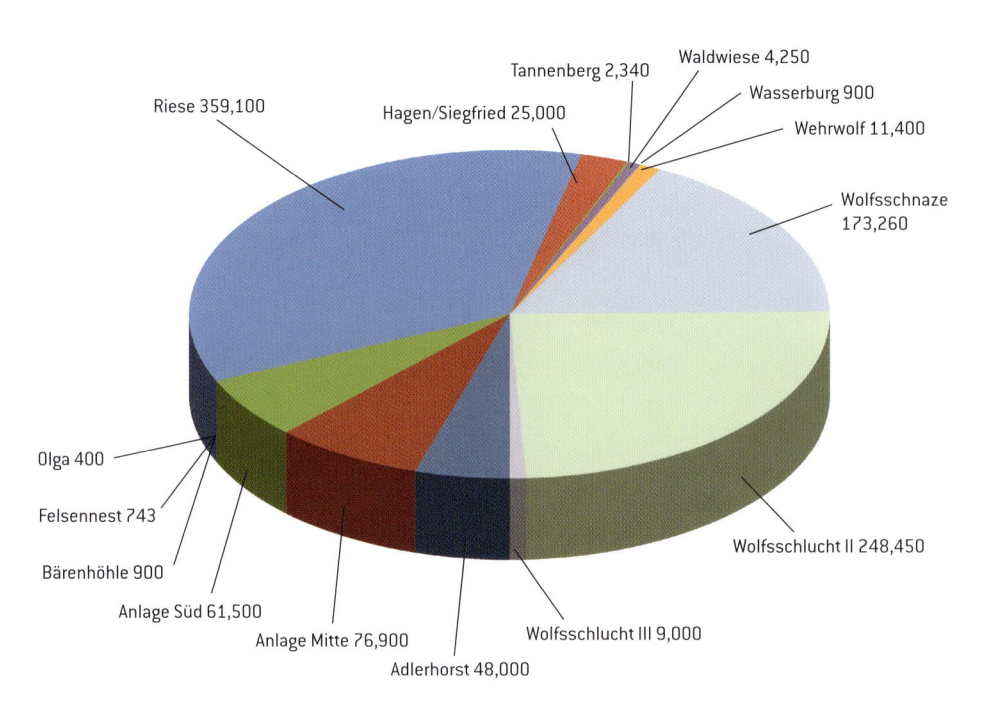

- Riese 359,100
- Hagen/Siegfried 25,000
- Tannenberg 2,340
- Waldwiese 4,250
- Wasserburg 900
- Wehrwolf 11,400
- Wolfsschnaze 173,260
- Wolfsschlucht II 248,450
- Wolfsschlucht III 9,000
- Adlerhorst 48,000
- Anlage Mitte 76,900
- Anlage Süd 61,500
- Bärenhöhle 900
- Felsennest 743
- Olga 400

At around 1700hrs Hitler would break for tea and cake before the next briefing chaired by Jodl at 1800hrs. This was followed by dinner at 1930hrs. Afterwards Hitler enjoyed talking to his immediate staff about non-war related subjects – informal gatherings that often went on into the early hours.

This relentless schedule and the accommodation that Hitler used did nothing for his health. At the start of the war Hitler was able to oversee operations from his personal train or from light and airy log cabins in the heart of the countryside. Indeed for much of the early fighting in France the weather was so benign and the threat from the enemy so insignificant that he was able to be outside for much of the time. However, on the Eastern Front he had to spend increasingly lengthy periods of time in concrete bunkers so as to reduce the threat from bombing and paratrooper attack, about which he became increasingly paranoid. He was also driven to seek refuge in his bunker by the heat and the mosquitoes.

Life was not unpleasant at FHQ Felsennest, where Hitler and his retinue took up residence in May 1940. Set in the heart of the Eifel (albeit Schroeder still complained of the clamminess in the bunker), and was helped by the various victories which were accompanied by celebrations. These, as Warlimont was quick to point out, were unheard of at a military headquarters. FHQ Wolfsschlucht I at Brûly-de-Pesche was also in a beautiful setting, although the accommodation was a little basic; to begin with there was no running water and Schroeder and Christian had to sleep in a pigsty that caught fire on the first night! With France defeated, Hitler's staff enjoyed a short respite from the claustrophobic atmosphere of headquarters life. But once the plans for the invasion of the Soviet Union had been finalized Hitler and his staff moved to FHQ Wolfsschanze in East Prussia. Initially the new headquarters was well received – the weather was fine and the surroundings beautiful, but as their stay lengthened perceptions changed. The daily routine became monotonous, and with so little to do (for the secretaries at least) that time dragged. If nothing else, the bunkers were cool and provided respite from the summer heat, and also afforded some sanctuary from the swarms of insects that were prevalent; Schroeder was badly bitten on her legs, which swelled up. The military were slightly better protected with their boots, their uniforms and hats, but even then they would often wear mosquito nets.

Life at FHQ Wehrwolf was a little better. The food was plentiful and good and security was not an issue (in the early days at least). As Warlimont noted, 'The civil population [around Vinnitsa] was still there both in town and countryside and in general appeared friendly. We used to walk unescorted through the woods and swim in the River Bug and there were never any incidents.' Small bunkers were provided for air raids, but Hitler and his staff were accommodated in wooden cabins or huts. On arriving

Life in the Führerhauptquartier carried on much as normal. Here, some of Hitler's courtiers celebrate the birthday of Oberstleutnant von Below, Hitler's Luftwaffe adjutant, at FHQ Wehrwolf in September 1942. The guest of honour can be seen with his back to the camera next to Johanna Wolf. (Topfoto)

at FHQ Wehrwolf the secretaries were full of optimism having survived so long in the dank, dark bunkers of the 'Wolf's Lair', but their hopes were dashed by what they found.

In the summer of 1942, Hitler moved his headquarters to Vinnitsa in the Ukraine, but he enjoyed no respite. Führerhauptquartier Wehrwolf was cold at night and stiflingly warm in the day and because of the mosquitoes Hitler and his staff were forced to take vile anti-malarial drugs. These factors combined to give Hitler migraines and he was quick to lose his temper. He longed for the relative comfort of Wolfsschanze and eventually he returned to East Prussia, but he was still plagued by the summer heat.

Things did improve gradually. Below noted on his return to FHQ Wolfsschanze in November 1942 that wooden annexes had been fitted to the bunkers which made them more habitable, and Hitler had a new study for conferences. Also a cinema was built and a Teehaus which made life bearable. But this improvement was short-lived. In February 1944 work began to strengthen the buildings against air attack. This was not complete when Hitler and his entourage were forced to return to FHQ Wolfsschanze in the summer of that year and the peace that was so jealously guarded was lost. Security was also compromised and indeed one of the construction workers was suspected of planting the 20 July bomb that injured Hitler and as a result the already stringent security was tightened further.

In spite of everything, the return to FHQ Wolfsschanze in the summer of 1944 was welcomed by some staff members. In July 1944 Karl Thöt, a stenographer, noted in his diary that, 'The whole site is resplendent with luscious greenery. The woods breathe a magnificent tranquillity.' In November 1944, Hitler left Wolfsschanze forever and after a short stay at FHQ Adlerhorst to oversee the Ardennes Offensive he returned to Berlin. Unable to sleep or work in the shattered grandeur of the Chancellery because of the constant air raids, Hitler descended into the Führerbunker – a surreal world that Speer described as the 'Isle of the Departed'. These were never designed for anything more than a short stay but now the Vorbunker and Führerbunker were pressed into use as an improvised headquarters. Light was supplied by naked light bulbs powered by a generator, which sometimes cut out, plunging everything into darkness. Fire hoses were laid along the corridors and served as improvised water mains. The ventilation system was overstretched, used as it was to provide fresh air for the bunker and the emergency dressing station under the Chancellery. With the thick smoke and dust outside it was sometimes turned off to avoid pumping noxious fumes into the bunker. The intermittent ventilation system, combined with fumes from the generator, cigarette smoke, fumes from alcohol and perspiration created an unsavoury mix for the residents of the bunker.

But the fetid air was a minor irritant when compared with the danger presented by enemy bombing, which caused bits of concrete to crumble from the walls; the roof of the Vorbunker was holed in a number of places, allowing water in. Still in spite of all this some occupants were still able to joke: 'Someone said Berlin was a very practical spot for headquarters, because soon we'd be able to travel between the Eastern Front and the Western Front by suburban railway.'

OPERATIONAL HISTORY

OPERATION *WEISS*

On 1 September 1939, the German training ship *Schleswig-Holstein*, anchored in Danzig harbour, opened fire on the Polish garrison stationed in the historic city and in so doing signalled the start of World War II in Europe. Concurrently Luftwaffe aircraft attacked Polish airbases and other strategic targets and German land forces crossed the border in accordance with the plans of Operation *Weiss* (White). Some 60 divisions attacked the much smaller Polish Army from Pomerania and East Prussia in the north and Silesia in the south, using the previously untested Blitzkrieg technique.

The campaign was planned and directed by the German Army, but was the realization of Hitler's strategy and he planned to keep a close eye on developments from his personal train – Führersonderzug 'Amerika'. On 3 September, with the declarations of war from Britain and France ringing in his ears, Hitler set off for Bad Polzin in Pomerania, arriving in the early hours of 4 September. For the next fortnight of the campaign the Führersonderzug shuttled along the eastern border of Germany, and Hitler, either in a convoy of vehicles or in a light aircraft, toured the front, seeing at first hand the awesome power of the Wehrmacht as it crushed the brave resistance of the inferior Polish forces.

On 17 September, Hitler returned to Berlin to ensure that he was well out of the way when the Soviets crossed into eastern Poland in accordance with the German–Soviet Treaty of Non-Aggression. But Hitler was not to be cowed for long and on 18 September he rejoined the Führersonderzug, this time as it headed for the historic city of Danzig, where the war had started and where the mainly German population was sure to give him a warm welcome – and so it did. Having set up his new headquarters at the Casino Hotel in Zoppot, he set off in a motorcade for Danzig, where he was greeted as a liberator.

The Casino Hotel served as Hitler's headquarters until 25 September when he returned to Berlin, and it was here that he received the news of the fall of Warsaw on 27 September and the end of organized resistance on 5 October. Yet in spite of the fact that the Poles had been crushed in a little over a month it was clear that there were a number of serious shortcomings in the way the operation had been executed. One of the most significant was that trains (and hotels) were not suitable to act as the Führer's headquarters. This deficiency had been recognized as early as 10 September when Rommel was dispatched to identify the location of a permanent headquarters in the west. Eventually Hitler chose FHQ Felsennest, in the heart of the Eifel, because it was located near the Ardennes – the Schwerpunkt (main emphasis) of the attack.

OPERATION *GELB*

On the night of 9 May 1940, the eve of the offensive in the west, Hitler boarded his train and set off from Berlin towards FHQ Felsennest. However, to avoid suspicion the train first headed north before swinging west and arriving at Euskirchen where Hitler alighted and headed for the village of Rodert, protected by a detachment of the Führer Begleit Bataillon (FBB; Führer Escort Battalion). He arrived at his Führerhauptquartier in the early hours of the morning.

The subsequent German attack prompted a rapid response from the French and British, who pressed north to meet the threat safe in the knowledge that their flank was protected by the impregnable Maginot Line and the impassable forest of the Ardennes. However, their faith was misplaced and German armour carefully edged along the narrow forest roads and massed on the east bank of the River Meuse. On 13 May lead elements crossed the river and thereafter the Panzers quickly advanced towards the Channel, reaching Abbeville on the coast on 20 May and in so doing cutting the line of retreat for the bulk of the British and French forces.

Indeed, so expeditious was the advance that Hitler asked that a suitable location be identified farther west so that he was better able to direct operations. An abandoned Maginot Line bunker near Maubeuge was identified as a possible location, but was considered too small. Instead a small village in Belgium – Brûly-de-Pesche – was chosen. With the local population resettled, the OT moved in and on 6 June 1940 Hitler arrived at the newly christened 'Wolfsschlucht'.

By this time Belgium had surrendered (on 28 May) and the British Expeditionary Force (BEF) had evacuated the bulk of its men in what became known as the 'miracle of Dunkirk'. The French Army continued to fight, falling back to the so-called 'Weygand Line' where they stubbornly resisted against German attacks. However, once this line was pierced there was nothing to stop the German advance and Paris was captured on 14 June, whilst the forts of the Maginot Line were systematically reduced from the rear. Three days later the German leaders were approached by the French seeking peace terms. Hitler was at Wolfsschlucht I when he heard the news from Walter Hewel, Ribbentrop's representative at the Führerhauptquartier, and the Führer could not disguise his delight – a scene that was captured on film.

The wrongs of the Paris Peace Settlement had been rectified. On 22 June France was forced to sign a humiliating armistice in the same railway carriage at Compiègne that had been used to take the German surrender in November 1918. To complete the humiliation Hitler took a whirlwind tour of Paris on 23 June but was back at Wolfsschlucht by mid-morning.

Hitler then moved to FHQ Tannenberg, one of the four headquarters that had been readied for the campaign in the west. From here he visited some of the battlefields of World War I where he had served as a Gefreiter and inspected some of the Maginot Line fortifications as well as visiting injured troops in hospital.

Hitler's next destination should have been FHQ Adlerhorst, where plans for the invasion of Britain were being prepared. However, a brave rearguard action and Hitler's decision to halt Rundstedt's Panzers on 24 May meant that the bulk of the BEF was successfully evacuated across the beaches of Dunkirk, and although lacking heavy weapons they represented a considerable threat to an amphibious attack. More significantly, Göring's Luftwaffe had signally failed to cow the RAF, which meant that any landing would not have air superiority – a factor that was vital for success. As a result Operation *Seelöwe* (Sea Lion) was postponed and eventually cancelled. Finally, on 5 July Hitler boarded the Führersonderzug and steamed to Berlin, where he received a hero's welcome. But what he did not realize was that the next time he visited his western headquarters it would be to direct operations to meet an Allied invasion, not launch his own.

Today the Führerhauptquartier codenamed Felsennest has become overgrown with trees and bushes, but it is still possible to visit the remains. Just in front of the tree line shown there is a track that runs from Waldstrasse in the village of Rodert to the various destroyed bunkers. (Neil Short)

HITLER'S FORTRESSES

ABOVE: Anlage Süd – Führersonderzug. The Polish Campaign was overseen by Hitler from his specially adapted train, Führersonderzug 'Amerika', as opposed to a permanent Führerhauptquartier. It was not ideally suited to the job but did give Hitler the flexibility he required to relocate his headquarters should Britain and France attack Germany from the west. (Adam Hook © Osprey Publishing)

THE BALKANS CAMPAIGN

With plans for the invasion of Britain cancelled, Hitler now concentrated all his energy on plans for the invasion of the Soviet Union and securing Lebensraum (living space) for the German people. However, his plans were interrupted by the difficulties of his main ally in the Balkans. On 28 October 1940, Italy had invaded Greece from bases in Albania, but the attack was repulsed and the Greek Army went on the offensive. Concerned by this reverse, but also keen to protect the Romanian oilfields and his southern flank in any attack on the Soviet Union, Hitler ordered plans to be prepared for an invasion of the Balkans. At the beginning of March 1941 the Italians renewed their attack but without success, and a month later the German forces launched Operation *Frühlingssturm* (Spring Storm) – the invasion of Yugoslavia and Greece. With no time to prepare a permanent headquarters, Hitler once again used Führersonderzug 'Amerika', with the WFSt on Sonderzug 'Atlas'. On 11 April 1941, five days after the start of the operation, 'Atlas' pulled into Mönichkirchen on the main line between Vienna and Graz. The village was chosen because of its location and because it was near a rail tunnel that could be used to shelter the train in the event of air attack. The station itself was small and was adapted with the erection of makeshift platforms and the establishment of a signals station. On the following day Hitler's train

The largest bunker at Wolfsschlucht II housed the staff department (and possibly the telephone exchange). The concrete bunker is just visible above the top of the outer building. (Neil Short)

HITLER'S FORTRESSES

Hitler's air-raid shelter at Wolfsschlucht I, in spite of the odd threat, was never used. This door led from the entrance into the body of the shelter. Directly opposite was a pistol port. It is worth comparing the modest proportions of this building with Hitler's bunker at FHQ Wolfsschanze. (Neil Short)

arrived and, aside from a few walks to a nearby hotel, this is where Hitler stayed for the whole of the short campaign – even celebrating his 52nd birthday there. On 26 April, with the Yugoslav and Greek forces defeated and the British and Commonwealth troops evacuating the Greek peninsula, Hitler entrained for Berlin where plans for the next, and most demanding, campaign were well advanced.

OPERATION *BARBAROSSA*

After a number of delays, Operation *Barbarossa* – the German invasion of the Soviet Union – was launched on 22 June 1941. The plan was simple: three army groups would advance on Leningrad, Moscow and the Ukraine respectively with the aim of destroying the Red Army. Generalfeldmarschall Walther von Brauchitsch was in overall command, but Hitler took a close personal interest and on 24 June arrived at FHQ Wolfsschanze in East Prussia.

At the end of August, with the campaign going well, Hitler now took time out to visit another of his headquarters on the Eastern Front – Anlage Süd – and held talks with Mussolini who had travelled east on his personal train. Their discussions complete, Hitler returned to FHQ Wolfsschanze where, at the end of September, he received news of the encirclement of Kiev. Convinced now that the Red Army was beaten, Hitler decided to make a final bid to capture Moscow in 1941. However, the hiatus had enabled the Muscovites to strengthen their defences around the capital and determined resistance brought the advance to a standstill. Subsequent attempts were made to renew the attack but bad weather and exhaustion meant that the advance had to halt just 30km from the city. With the enemy over-extended, the Red Army launched a surprise counter-attack that pushed the German forces back and ensured the safety of the capital.

One of the 'Type 102v' concrete shelters built near the rail tunnel at Stepina. This example was located adjacent to the tunnel and was fitted with two loopholes – one in each room and accessed through separate doors.
(Neil Short)

The failure to capture this key objective so incensed Hitler that on 19 December he relieved Brauchitsch of his role as Oberbefehlshaber des Heeres (Commander-in-Chief of the Army) and he assumed the role himself.

OPERATION *BLAU*

By the winter of 1941 Hitler's forces had reached Moscow, had all but encircled Leningrad and in the south had captured the Donets Basin. And it was in the south that Hitler's focus centred on the summer offensive planned for 1942. Because the offensive was so far removed from FHQ Wolfsschanze, a new site was identified near Vinnitsa in the Ukraine. From here Hitler could better direct operations towards Stalingrad and the Caucasus. In April 1942 Hitler issued the directive for Operation *Blau* (Blue), and on 28 June the first phase of the operation was launched. Soon thereafter (16 July) Hitler and his staff moved to FHQ Wehrwolf. Progress was good with Heeresgruppe A (Army Group A) advancing into the Caucasus and elements of Heeresgruppe B entering the city of Stalingrad in mid-September. Confident that his forces in the south would soon capture the city that bore the name of his ideological enemy, he departed Wehrwolf on 1 November for Wolfsschanze. In East Prussia he would be better able to direct operations personally against any Soviet winter

The main entrance to the Führerbunker at Wolfsschlucht II. Just visible above the door is the roof of the main concrete bunker. After the war the bunker was renamed 'Haut le Wastia'. (Neil Short)

offensive, which he confidently predicted would be launched on the northern or central fronts. His conviction could not have been farther from the truth. On 19 November, the Red Army launched a counter-offensive (Operation *Uranus*) that encircled the German troops fighting in Stalingrad. Hitler refused General Friedrich Paulus' request to break out and instead set about mustering a force to relieve the troops trapped in the pocket. The relief operation was launched but was unsuccessful and on 31 January 1943 Paulus (now a Generalfeldmarschall) surrendered, much to Hitler's chagrin.

With the German southern advance decisively stopped and the Red Army on the attack, Hitler reinstated Heeresgruppe Süd (Army Group South) and on 17 February 1943 returned to FHQ Wehrwolf to witness Generalfeldmarschall Erich von Manstein's spring offensive. At the end of February, 4. Panzer-Armee, under Generaloberst Hermann Hoth, advanced north from its position on the River Dnieper and, in spite of the thaw, recaptured Kharkov on 11 March.

OPERATION *CITADEL*

Hitler now began preparations for the German summer offensive and such was the air of optimism that permeated FHQ Wolfsschanze that plans were drawn up for a new headquarters – FHQ Olga – near Vitebsk. However, this optimism proved misplaced. On 5 July, Operation *Citadel* was launched and initially the two arms of the great pincer around the Kursk salient made good progress, but as the Soviets had had time to prepare deep defences and with good intelligence spelling out German intentions, the offensive stalled. This coincided with worrying developments in Italy, where the Allies had landed in Sicily on 10 July, and on 13 July Hitler cancelled Operation *Citadel*.

At the end of August the Soviets launched a series of offensives that pinched out the Orel and Kharkov salients. From this point forward the Red Army held the initiative, and Hitler and his generals ensconced in the bunkers of FHQ Wolfsschanze knew this. On 27 August, Hitler visited Manstein at FHQ Wehrwolf. Here he received a gloomy situation report; without reinforcements the Donets Basin would have to be conceded. Hitler promised to provide whatever units were available, before returning to Rastenburg that evening. This was to be Hitler's last visit to his headquarters in the Ukraine.

With no reinforcements available, Hitler reluctantly agreed that Army Group South should withdraw to the River Dnieper, but crossing points were limited and this meant that the broad front fractured. The Soviets took advantage of this, racing to cross the river using any means available and soon a number of bridgeheads had been created, which by December had developed into two significant bulges around Kiev and to the south around Cherkassy, Kremenchung and Dnepropetrovsk. On 28 December 1943,

Hitler ordered that FHQ Wehrwolf be demolished. In the north, the blockade of Leningrad was lifted at the end of January 1944 and Army Group North was forced back to the so-called Panther Line which ran along the River Narva, Lake Peipus and Lake Pskov. The Soviet offensive in the centre, although predictably heavy in terms of artillery, armour and infantry numbers, was hampered by adverse weather conditions and a general lack of preparation, and little progress was made save for the encirclement of six German divisions – many of which ultimately extricated themselves.

This concluded the winter offensive and at the end of February 1944 Hitler departed Wolfsschanze for his Alpine retreat at Berchtesgaden. The Soviets continued to apply pressure throughout the spring while at the same time planning for a major summer offensive. Hitler meantime had already stressed to his generals that the Eastern Front was a secondary concern. Territory could be conceded in the east but not in the west, where the Allied invasion was considered imminent. More immediately troops had to be sent from the Russian front to Italy to counter the Allied invasion of Sicily and Italy (which began on 3 September 1943). In April 1944 Hitler celebrated another birthday – the last 'normal' celebration he would enjoy – before his 'Fortress Europe' was hit with a further hammer blow with the landings in Normandy.

On 20 July 1944, Claus Schenk von Stauffenberg, a disillusioned young officer, planted a bomb at Hitler's East Prussian headquarters that was intended to kill the Führer. The bomb detonated, killing three, but Hitler survived, his life saved in part by the fact that the briefing was held in a temporary conference room, which absorbed some of the blast. (Topfoto)

D-DAY

For some time Hitler had been expecting the western Allies to open a second front in France. Now, on 6 June 1944, the invasion began. Hitler received the news while at Berchtesgaden. Initially he was convinced that this was simply a diversionary attack before the main invasion around the Pas-de-Calais, but as time passed this hypothesis carried less weight and in mid-June Hitler travelled to FHQ Wolfsschlucht II at Margival in France. Here he met Rundstedt and Rommel and was briefed on the situation. Hitler insisted that they maintain their positions and reiterated this at another briefing at Berchtesgaden on 29 June. But by now he had a far greater worry with the opening of the Red Army's summer offensive.

OPERATION *BAGRATION*

On 23 June 1944, the Red Army launched Operation *Bagration*, one of the largest land offensives of the war. The initial thrust was directed at Army Group Centre and was considered a feint by Hitler who instructed that the attack be held. However, in spite of the fact that Generalfeldmarschall Ernst Busch, the commander of Army Group Centre,

After the unsuccessful assassination attempt on 20 July 1944, Hitler made a radio broadcast to the nation to reassure the people that he was fit and well. His audience at FHQ Wolfsschanze consisted of his closest advisers, including personal adjutant Julius Schaub in front of the curtains. (Topfoto)

ASSASSINATION ATTEMPT, 20 JULY 1944

In the period after Hitler came to power several attempts were made on his life, none of which were successful. The failure of the conspirators led Hitler to believe that he was immortal and predestined to lead Germany to victory. However, this personal conviction did nothing to discourage his enemies and a further attempt on Hitler's life was planned for the summer of 1944. The man chosen to carry out the attempt was Oberst Claus Schenk Graf von Stauffenberg. A decorated officer who had been badly injured in North Africa, he was now a staff officer with access to Hitler at FHQ Wolfsschanze. The plan, codenamed 'Valkyrie', was simple. Von Stauffenberg would place a briefcase of explosives next to Hitler during one of his briefings and then make his excuses to leave. The bomb would explode, killing Hitler and his immediate circle of advisers. With the Führer dead the conspirators would cut communications to FHQ Wolfsschanze and seize key locations throughout the Reich. The bomb exploded as planned, but unbeknown to Stauffenberg, who had left the room and was now heading to Berlin, Hitler survived, receiving only minor injuries. The failure of the bomb to eliminate its prime target was partly due to the fact that von Stauffenberg had not had time to pack all the explosives in the case and partly because the briefing was held in a timber-lined barrack block rather than Hitler's reinforced concrete bunker, which was still being renovated. The explosion was thus much smaller than planned and the blast was dissipated through the hut's walls and windows. Hitler was badly shaken by the explosion and three of his staff were killed, but he was alive and with communication links still open he was able to confirm that he was safe and well and his supporters were able to quickly round up the conspirators, who were executed, often in a most gruesome fashion and filmed for the Führer's delectation. (Adam Hook © Osprey Publishing)

The former schoolhouse in Brûly-de-Pesche, which today is used as a youth hostel. In 1940 the building formed part of Wolfsschlucht I and was used as offices for Führerhauptquartier staff. (Neil Short)

committed all his reserves he was unable to stop the Soviet juggernaut. Hitler now realized that this was a major offensive and on 9 July he headed back to FHQ Wolfsschanze to direct operations. His eastern headquarters was still a building site, but the critical situation meant that it was vital that Hitler be close to the front to personally influence commanders in the field. But his presence could not turn the tide. Heeresgruppe Mitte (Army Group Centre) had all but collapsed and Generalfeldmarschall Walter Model, who had replaced Busch, now tried to make an orderly withdrawal. In this he was broadly successful but he could not disguise the fact that Operation *Bagration* had been a major success for the Soviets. The second phase exploited these successes as the Red Army advanced towards East Prussia and crossed the River Vistula. As Warlimont noted, 'The return to the field headquarters in East Prussia meant that we were for once – just as at the same period of 1941 – unwontedly close to the front.' Now, however, Hitler's armed forces were marching west not east, and, recognizing the enormity of the situation, Germany's allies toppled like a pack of cards: on 23 August Romania surrendered, on 2 September Finland signed an armistice and on 9 September Bulgaria did likewise.

In spite of these setbacks Hitler insisted, in October, that he would remain at FHQ Wolfsschanze until the crisis had been averted. Yet only a month later, on 20 November, with the concrete hardly dry, he left Rastenburg, ostensibly to oversee the imminent offensive in the west, but equally to avoid being cut off by the advancing Red Army.

As the tide of the war turned German forces were pushed back towards the borders of Germany and forward headquarters constructed for Hitler had to be demolished so that they did not fall into enemy hands. Here are some of the remains of FHQ Wehrwolf, which can still be seen in Ukraine today. (Topfoto)

ARDENNES OFFENSIVE

Although the situation at the end of 1944 was perilous, Hitler still managed to muster sufficient reserves to launch one last offensive in the west, which he hoped would deliver a decisive victory. The location he chose was the scene of his great triumph in 1940 – the Ardennes – which was weakly held by a mixture of new and recuperating US divisions.

On 10 December, Hitler arrived at FHQ Adlerhorst to direct the attack personally. The following day he briefed his commanders, explaining in a long speech the military and political imperatives for the attack. Finally, on 16 December 6. SS-Panzer-Armee, 5. Panzer-Armee and 7. Armee advanced. Their target was the port of Antwerp, which if captured would split the Allies' front in half. Initially progress was good with the enemy caught completely by surprise and cloud cover preventing the Allies interdicting the German ground forces.

Though initially caught off balance, the Allies soon recovered and rapidly instigated plans to counter the attack. In this they were undoubtedly helped by the fact that Hitler decided to exploit the advance of 5. Panzer-Armee too late, and by the time action was taken clearing skies exposed the German units to air attack, which further hampered the already fragile logistics operation.

By Christmas Day, the German bulge extended 95km at its deepest, but with supplies exhausted they could go no farther and on 3 January the Allies launched a counter-attack to pinch out the bulge. General Courtney Hodges' First US Army, which had borne the brunt of the attack, drove into the northern flank while General George Patton's Third US Army advanced to meet it at Houffalize. Heavy snow slowed the advance and the pocket was not closed until 16 January, by which time most of the German troops had escaped. But the damage done to the German Army and Luftwaffe was irreparable. His gamble having failed Hitler left FHQ Adlerhorst for Berlin on 15 January and prepared for the final Götterdämmerung.

After the war the Soviets tried to demolish the Führerbunker in Berlin, but with limited success. Here the observation/ventilation tower with conical roof and blockhouse above the exit lie on their sides. The photograph was taken in 1956. (Topfoto)

HITLER'S FORTRESSES

BERLIN

Although Hitler's adversaries saw Berlin as the ultimate symbol of Nazism, Hitler in fact spent relatively little time in the capital, preferring instead his field headquarters, principally FHQ Wolfsschanze or his Alpine retreat at Berchtesgaden. However, by the end of the war his choice of locations was severely limited and after the failure of the Ardennes offensive the Führer returned to Berlin. It was in the Reich Chancellery that he decided to see out the last days of the war, in spite of the protestations of some of his closest aides who wanted him to flee abroad or to Bavaria.

By 15 April Soviet forces under Konev, Rokossovsky and Zhukov had reached the River Oder, which at its nearest point was only 55km from the capital. Zhukov, who had been given the honour of capturing Berlin by Stalin, now set about launching a coup de main across the Seelow Heights, but in spite of a massive superiority in men and matériel his advance was held. At the behest of Stalin he now changed the point of the attack and swung north while Konev advanced from the south. The pincers closed around the beleaguered city on 25 April and the battle of Berlin began in earnest.

Russian troops indicate the probable site of Hitler's cremation in the Chancellery garden. (Getty Images)

Hitler now retired to the relative safety of the bunker under the Chancellery, but even this was not immune. Loringhoven recalled that, 'In the concrete block of the Führerbunker we felt the vibrations of the uninterrupted thunder of Russian artillery as it pounded the Chancellery. The ceiling of the Vorbunker, much less thick, was in danger of collapsing under the shelling.' German units within the city, supplemented by old men and boys of the Volkssturm (People's Army), bravely resisted the onslaught, but resistance was futile. Hitler was informed that the situation was hopeless and on 30 April Hitler and his new wife Eva Braun committed suicide in the bunker. Their bodies were carried out of the subterranean gloom into the small garden at the rear, where they were incinerated. Other bunker inhabitants variously committed suicide or made a break for freedom. Somewhat amusingly the bunker was captured by a group of Soviet female soldiers interested only in the wardrobe of the Führer's wife. Only later did intelligence officers reach the final resting place of the Führer to begin the long investigation into his death. On 2 May Generalleutnant Helmuth Weidling surrendered the city and on 7–8 May Germany unconditionally surrendered.

Hitler's command bunkers had, in their own way, aided the disintegration of his leadership. They formed discrete worlds of their own, in which Hitler could become increasingly detached from the world beyond the concrete walls. Those who entered from the outside were often struck by the surreal atmosphere, a bizarre court encased in a ferro-concrete structure. Yet merely viewing them architecturally, these buildings were robust defensive structures, physically protecting Germany's leadership while contributing little towards the protection of Germany's people.

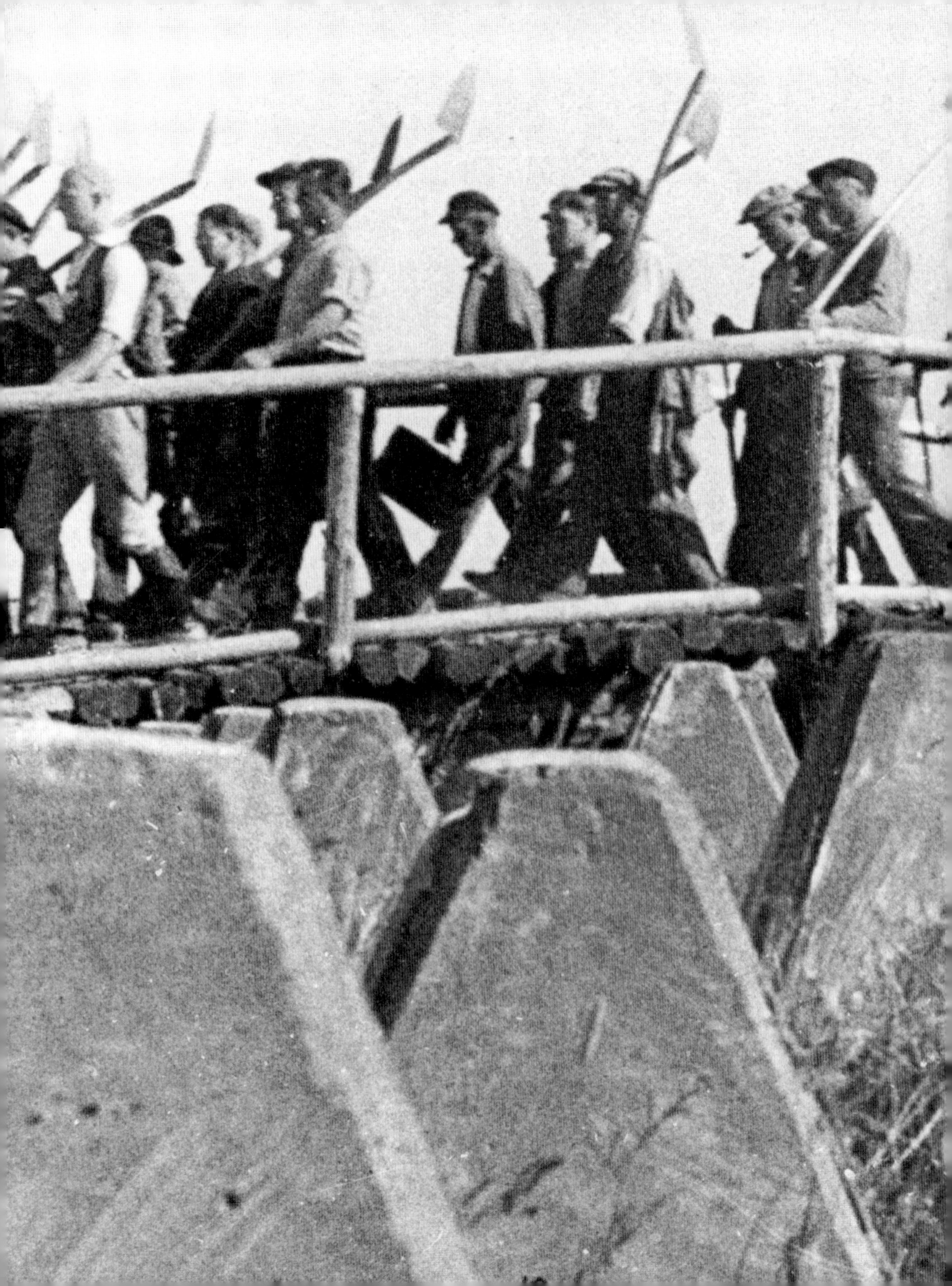

PROTECTING THE HOMELAND – GERMANY'S BORDER DEFENCES

LEFT: German civilians march to work on the West Wall in 1939, passing the infamous tank obstacles, dragon's teeth. (Scherl/SZ Photo)

In the immediate aftermath of World War I, Germany was a shadow of its former self. Exhausted by four years of war, it was subsequently compelled to accept the draconian peace terms agreed by the victorious powers at the Palace of Versailles in 1919. Germany's colonies were stripped away, as indeed was much of its territory; its armed forces were reduced drastically or scrapped completely. More specifically, Germany was forbidden from building or maintaining fortifications on the west bank of the Rhine or on the east bank to a distance of 50km. Allied Control Commissions enforced these restrictions, backed up by an army of occupation.

Yet by 1934, with Hitler in power and the country wriggling free from the Versailles restrictions, Germany had already taken steps to defend its western frontier with plans to construct the so-called Neckar–Enz and Wetterau–Main–Tauber lines. Because these defences were outside the demilitarized zone, there were no constraints on their construction. However, following Hitler's decision to reoccupy the Rhineland these plans were abandoned and work on what would be known as the West Wall began. Soon engineers were reconnoitring the area to establish the best locations for defences. But the fortifications Hitler planned were not designed to prevent a pre-emptive strike by France. After all, France had made her position quite clear with the building of the Maginot Line. The French military had adopted a defensive mentality; casualties on the scale suffered in World War I would not, indeed could not, be suffered again. France

The Siegfried Line of World War I was markedly different to its later, more famous namesake. This section of the line near Honnecourt taken in August 1917 shows that it was little more than an elaborate trench system. (Imperial War Museum, Q 45385)

PROTECTING THE HOMELAND – GERMANY'S BORDER DEFENCES

Although very little of the Kitzinger-Stellung was ever completed, a number of reinforced bunkers were constructed in 1943–44 in France well inland of the Atlantic Wall. These were mainly hardened headquarters bunkers like this example at Soissons. (NARA)

would only fight if attacked. Hitler's aim in building the West Wall – later known to the Allies as the Siegfried Line – was altogether much more sinister and revolved around his desire for Lebensraum in the east.

Hitler had from the outset expressed the opinion that for Germany to be a great power, her people needed living space. To the east the Slav peoples farmed vast tracts of land. Hitler planned to seize this land, relocate the population and give the farms to German settlers. His ambitions, however, were tempered by the spectre of war on two fronts. By building defences in the west it might be possible to deter France from invading Germany in support of her allies or, if France did attack, to enable much weaker forces to slow the advance while the campaign in the east was brought to a swift conclusion.

The job of building the defences and fulfilling this aim initially fell to the German Army. Using Regelbau (standard designs), many of which had been developed for the so-called 'East Wall' that protected Germany's border with Poland (see below), the Army contracted construction firms to build the defences, overseen by Army engineers. Despite the use of standardized models, which enabled the authorities to produce standard components and to better plan raw material requirements, progress on the 'Pioneerprogramm', as it was known, was slow. The Army first had to put in place the infrastructure to enable the building programme to commence, not the least of which was accommodation for the thousands of workers; and then there were difficulties with supplies of raw materials. By the spring of 1938 only 640 bunkers and pillboxes had

HITLER'S FORTRESSES

Map of the West Wall showing the main defences, the Luftverteidigungszone (West), and the Neckar–Enz and Wetterau–Main–Tauber Stellungen.

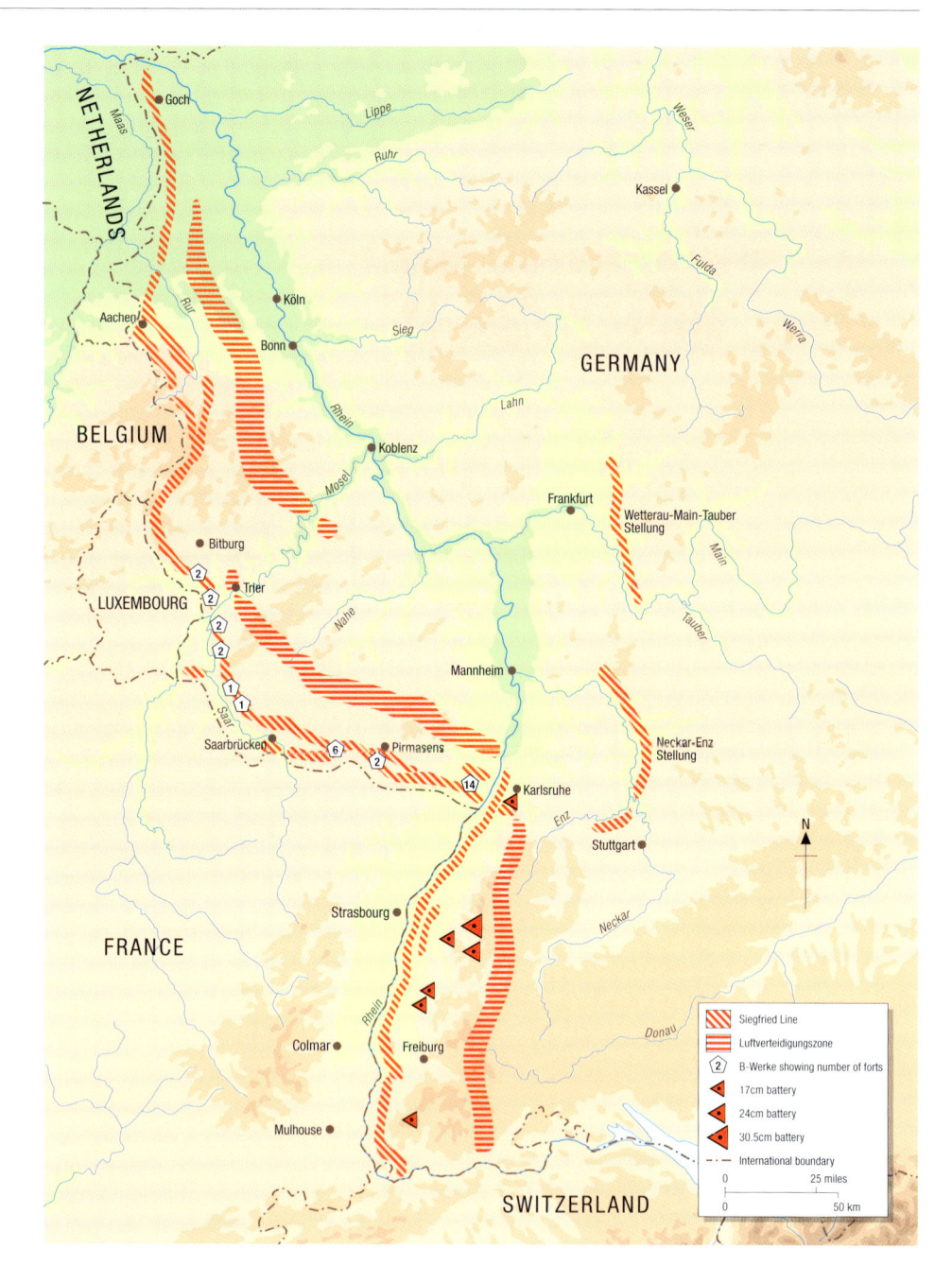

been completed and it was anticipated that the work would not be completed until 1948! Hitler, never one to conceal his feelings, was incensed (despite the fact that part of the reason for the delay was his failure to accord the work a high priority). In May 1938 he issued new building targets: 1,800 pillboxes and 10,000 bunkers were to be completed by 1 October 1938 – the date that he now planned to invade Czechoslovakia.

A motorcycle patrol passes through what appears to be a recently completed section of the West Wall. When this photograph was taken in late September 1939, Poland had all but capitulated, enabling regular German army units to be transferred to the west to man the lightly held defences. (Imperial War Museum, MH 13385)

As well as vastly increasing the number of structures and shortening the timescales, the Limesprogramm, as it was christened, also included the construction of Luftverteidigungszone (West), an air defence zone. This was situated to the east of the main defences and was designed to mount anti-aircraft guns, which would prevent enemy aircraft from reaching the German heartland.

By the time of the Munich crisis in September 1938, the majority of the defences had been completed. Determined to avoid war and horrified by the thought of an attack on such seemingly strong defences, France and Great Britain acceded to Hitler's demands. Emboldened by his success, Hitler, in October 1938, ordered the construction of more defences under the pretext that the western democracies, not Germany, threatened the peace of Europe. This phase was to see the strengthening of the defences around Aachen and the Saar, which in turn gave their name to the new schedule of defences: the Aachen–Saar Programm.

The final phase of the building programme began in late 1939 and continued into the spring of the following year. This saw the defences extended to the north to a point where the Rhine flowed into the Netherlands and provided a natural full stop to the defensive line. The defeat of France and the Low Countries saw work on the West Wall suspended until the autumn of 1944, by which time the Allies stood on the German border.

HITLER'S FORTRESSES

To complete a building programme on such a scale required an enormous amount of raw materials: gravel, sand, cement, iron and timber. It called for thousands of men and machines to dig the foundations, mix the concrete and bore the holes. Last, but not least, it absorbed vast sums of money to pay for the materials and the weekly wages of the engineers, construction workers and clerks. It is not surprising that the real cost of the Limesprogramm was estimated to be in excess of 1 billion Reichsmarks, a massive drain on German industry the cost of which far outweighed the benefits.

THE WEST WALL

PRINCIPLES OF DEFENCE

The debate over what form the German border defences should take reached back to the experience of World War I. The initial, sweeping advance of the German Imperial Army in the summer of 1914 was eventually halted by the Allies and the fighting settled down into a bloody stalemate. Both sides dug trenches stretching from the English Channel to the Swiss border and gradually the trench systems were strengthened to include deep shelters and concrete pillboxes to protect the infantry from the devastating

Every effort was made by the Germans to prevent the Allies gathering intelligence on the western defences. Here soldiers construct a screen to obscure the enemy's view, September 1939. (BArch, Bild 183-L22268/ unknown)

effects of artillery fire. Thick bands of barbed wire were erected and positioned to funnel attacking troops into pre-prepared 'killing zones'. Yet, in spite of these elaborate measures, there was still concern in some quarters of the German High Command that these defences were not strong enough to stop a full-scale Allied attack.

Oberst Fritz von Lossberg, Chief of Staff of the German 1. Armee, formulated a solution to the problem. He suggested a deepening of the existing defences with the introduction of a series of defensive zones. Immediately facing the enemy was the outpost zone. This was only lightly defended and was designed to slow the enemy attack. Once past this position the enemy would enter the battle zone, which was peppered with mutually supporting forts and strongpoints. Behind these positions were more trenches. Later Lossberg ordered a further line of defences, so that when complete the 'Hindenburg Line' was in places 8km deep. The theory behind the system of defence in depth was simple. As the enemy advanced through the zones it became weaker and weaker and was less able to maintain the momentum of the attack. More critically, as the attackers were drawn deeper into the maze of defences they moved beyond the range of their supporting artillery, leaving them dangerously exposed. Exhausted and isolated, the enemy was vulnerable to counter-attack by troops held in the rear, safe from enemy fire.

Although the Hindenburg Line ultimately failed to block the Allied advance, the principle of flexible defence in depth had been established. Thus, when the decision was taken to fortify the German border, Lossberg's idea was adopted. Clearly, the situation facing the military planners in 1936 was very different to that faced by their predecessors 20 years earlier. Then the frontline had been established and could not be changed without attacking or surrendering hard-won territorial gains. Now a defensive line could be built to take advantage of geographical features that would give the defender the upper hand in any future war. Hitler disagreed. He was determined that no part of German territory would be violated and insisted that as far as humanly possible the defences would follow Germany's national border. Equally contentious was the form that the defences should take. Two schools of thought emerged: one that favoured a linear defence system that stretched the entire length of the border; and another that propounded concentrating on more vulnerable sections of the border where the enemy was most likely to strike. At first, the idea of the linear defensive system, as favoured by Generalfeldmarschall Werner von Blomberg, Supreme Commander of the Wehrmacht, was adopted. Following Blomberg's resignation in February 1938, Hitler became the Supreme Commander. Typically, Hitler wavered between the two solutions. Initially he endorsed the linear defensive strategy, ordering an extension of the line along the border with Belgium and Holland. Later, however, he ordered the construction of thick bands of defences to protect Aachen and the Saar, both natural avenues of attack.

HITLER'S FORTRESSES

ABOVE: Typical bunker under construction. In the foreground workers put together the steel reinforcing rods that provide additional strength for the concrete dragon's teeth. Men pour the concrete from the mixers while others remove the shuttering after the concrete has hardened. To the rear more labourers work to construct one of the bunkers that will mount a machine gun to cover the entire stretch of teeth. (Chris Taylor © Osprey Publishing)

In spite of Hitler's personal interest, the defences of the West Wall were far from the impregnable barrier portrayed by Goebbels' propaganda ministry. Unlike the Maginot Line, which was begun in 1929 and was still under construction a decade later, the West Wall was built in indecent haste and suffered accordingly. Initially, the work was carried out by private building contractors, overseen by Army engineers. Many of the companies took advantage of the authorities' failure to introduce simple checks. Superior-quality materials supplied by the state were often misappropriated and substituted by inferior alternatives; deliveries of raw materials were often 'light'; and stories even abounded of government-supplied equipment being sold off. To make matters worse, Hitler's other

PROTECTING THE HOMELAND – GERMANY'S BORDER DEFENCES

ABOVE: A typical example of a West Wall personnel bunker located near Sevenig-bei-Neuerburg in the Eifel border region. This particular type was designed to accommodate two Gruppen – 20 infantrymen. (NARA)

LEFT: Some of the defences of the Hindenburg Line were very substantial and not that far removed from some of the more basic structures of the West Wall. This concrete and steel pillbox was built at Le Pave. The inscription reads, 'In greatest need was this built here, for a hero's death I greatly fear, 23.4.17 M.K.19'. (Imperial War Museum, Q 45391)

The pre-war West Wall served as the concrete spine of the new West-Stellung. This is a typical stretch of the West Wall with rows of dragon's teeth in the foreground covered by an armoured machine-gun cupola. These armoured cupolas were the only visible portion of a much more extensive bunker underneath. This particular example is a 40P8 Sechsschartenturm, a widely used cupola type armoured to A1 standards. (NARA)

massive public works programmes, like the Autobahnen, meant that raw materials were in short supply.

Hitler's failure to accord the work on the West Wall a high enough priority, and the need for the Army to put in place the basic infrastructure (roads, sleeping accommodation, etc.) before any work on the defences could start, meant that little progress had been made on the fortifications by May 1938. This infuriated Hitler and he now ordered an escalation of the scale of the programme and stipulated an October deadline. Unconvinced of the Army's ability to meet his demands, he placed Dr Fritz Todt in charge of the construction programme. Todt was a personal favourite of Hitler following his successful completion of the German motorway network and now he transferred his efforts and his labourers to work on the West Wall.

Many of the men of the OT and the RAD were conscripts who had little experience of heavy manual work and had been forced to leave their homes to work on the border defences. They now found themselves working long hours, often in difficult and dangerous conditions, for little pay. They were housed in rudimentary, prefabricated accommodation and enjoyed only a basic diet. Not surprisingly the poor working conditions, homesickness and lack of skills meant that the defences were often poorly or even incorrectly finished, with some positions requiring rebuilding.

PROTECTING THE HOMELAND – GERMANY'S BORDER DEFENCES

ABOVE: Many West Wall bunkers had been cannibalized for parts during the construction of the Atlantic Wall. This 423P01 armoured cupola on a bunker near Hollerath in the Eifel region near the Belgian Ardennes is missing the armoured plates for its machine-gun ports. Here it is inspected by a soldier of the US Army's 324th Engineer Battalion, 99th Division, on 8 February 1945. (NARA)

LEFT: The entrance to this bunker has been decorated with Nazi-inspired imagery. Above the door is a stylized swastika. Needless to say few bunkers were so ornately decorated. The shelter is fitted with a six embrasure armoured turret. (BArch, Bild 183-S53854/unknown)

The Air Defence Zone West (LVZ West) Flak positions were created in parallel to the West Wall in the late 1930s. Although under Luftwaffe control, these Flak batteries frequently played a prominent role in defence efforts in the 1945 fighting, like this emplaced 8.8cm battery in Neuss, part of the Brückenkopf Düsseldorf defences. Protected niches for the ammunition have been created using concrete sewer pipe. (NARA)

Although still responsible for tactical aspects of the construction programme, the Army had now been effectively usurped by the OT. This greatly angered the military High Command and caused friction between the two bodies. Instead of working in harmony to create a cohesive defensive line, the two blamed each other for the difficulties and delays. To make matters worse, from May 1938 onwards Hitler took a close personal interest in the project. He designed his own bunkers and on his numerous visits offered advice to local commanders. Unsurprisingly, the military increasingly lost faith in the worth of the West Wall. General Friedrich Wilhelm von Mellenthin, a corps commander inspecting the West Wall defences opposite the Maginot Line, was appalled by the state of the defences, noting that they 'were far from being the impregnable fortifications pictured by our propaganda'. Many senior German officers agreed with him – Rundstedt, commander of Heeresgruppe A for the western campaign, is said to have laughed when he inspected the defences.

By September 1944, furthermore, the German situation had changed markedly. The vulnerable northern flank was now exposed to enemy attack and the Allies sought to exploit the situation in the daring, but ultimately unsuccessful, attempt to capture the bridges at Eindhoven, Nijmegen and Arnhem. With the failure of Operation *Market Garden* the Allies were left with little choice but to fight their way through the main defences of the Siegfried Line. The prospect was not an enticing one. However, the years that had passed since Hitler boasted of the defences' invincibility had taken their toll. Little if anything had been done to maintain the structures, and many were now flooded or heavily overgrown. Still others had had all their fittings removed and either placed in storage or used in the Atlantic Wall.

More worryingly, the defences were alarmingly outmoded, the fighting of the previous five years having seen the development of more heavily armed tanks. Germany entered the war with the Panzer I armed with twin MG34 machine guns and now fielded the King Tiger with its impressive 8.8cm gun; and more powerful anti-tank weapons were available, many of them man-portable like the bazooka. The bunkers of

ABOVE: A typical bunker of the Limesprogramm. The most widely constructed model (3,471 were built) of the Limesprogramm was the Regelbau 10 (Standard Construction 10). The shelter could be accessed via two gas-proof entrance areas which were bisected by a crenellated embrasure that covered both doors. Both entrances led to the stand-to area which acted as living and sleeping quarters for both the crew and the resident rifle squad. (Chris Taylor © Osprey Publishing)

the West Wall had not been designed to withstand the impact of such weapons. Equally significant was the fact that the majority of the bunkers could not accommodate these new weapons. Certainly, the larger and more potent German anti-tank guns could not be mounted in the older Panzerabwehrkanone (PaK; anti-tank gun) shelters and so they had to be emplaced in the open. Improvised solutions to this problem were developed, but time, materials and labour were in short supply and it was unrealistic to think that they could fill this void.

In 1936, when the defences were first planned, the need to accommodate such powerful weapons was not even considered. The earliest and simplest shelters that were constructed were often provided with no more than simple loopholes. These could accommodate light machine guns, rifles and small arms and gave the defenders the added flexibility of taking their weapons outside and fighting in the open. Later models had steel or concrete apertures designed to accommodate particular weapons. The choice of which weapons were supplied for the respective shelters was based on the simple principle that each shelter could only mount the weapons for which it was designed. So, for example, pillboxes were fitted with either the older 7.92mm MG08 or MG34 machine guns. More elaborate bunkers were fitted with thick armoured cupolas with either three or six loopholes. These were mounted with one or two MG34

An American Sherman tank follows the path blasted by US Army Engineers during the fighting around Aachen in September 1944. The Americans tended to attack road blocks rather than sections of dragon's teeth because destroying the teeth was dangerous and time consuming. (Imperial War Museum, HU 75614)

machine guns that could be swivelled from loophole to loophole. The MG34 was the standard German machine gun of the period, but because of shortages it was not always possible to supply all the weapons required. For example, following the outbreak of war each pillbox in the Lower Rhine region could only be supplied with a single machine gun and elsewhere the position was similar. The situation was such that the old MG08/15, a lighter version of the MG08 with a pistol-style grip, shoulder stock and bipod, had to be deployed.

Other shelters were designed to accommodate anti-tank and anti-aircraft guns and artillery pieces. The anti-tank positions typically housed the 3.7cm PaK 35/36, one of the best anti-tank guns of the time and capable of piercing the armour of almost any tank then in service. Provision was also made for artillery in open and closed positions. Standard construction 18, for example, which was developed for the Limesprogramm, was designed to house the 7.5cm Feldkanone 16 neuer Art. A modernized version of the World War I gun, they were all later removed from the West Wall and used in the Atlantic Wall. Also as part of the Limesprogramm, shelters were constructed to house a number of large naval guns. Two 24cm and two 30.5cm guns were positioned so as to

In the final months of the war the West Wall was strengthened with a number of improvised fortifications. One of the deadliest was the use of Panther turrets mounted on concrete, steel or wooden shelters. This example was located near Niederwürzbach (Saarland) but is now on display at the West Wall Museum, Niedersimten. (Neil Short)

be able to bombard France. To the rear, in the Luftverteidigungszone (West), shelters were designed to mount machine guns in their role as a fallback position, but also to accommodate the famous '88' anti-aircraft gun which could be used against ground targets as well as aircraft.

The larger forts, or B-Werke, of the West Wall were more heavily armed. Each of the 32 examples, although unique, shared some common features. They were fitted with six loophole-armoured cupolas; a 5cm mortar that could fire 120 rounds per minute to a range of 600m; and for close-in protection a flame-thrower that was capable of rotating through 360 degrees. Peculiarly, each B-Werk was supposed to hold a double inventory of weapons, although it is not clear whether this was in fact the case.

ABOVE: A typical bunker of the Aachen-Saar Programm. The Aachen-Saar bunkers were strengthened compared to previous bunkers, with thicker walls and ceilings. The new designs were also far roomier and new storage areas for food and ammunition were introduced, as was a special room for an observer equipped with either a periscope or an observation cupola. (Chris Taylor © Osprey Publishing)

Following the defeat of Czechoslovakia, the German Army acquired a vast array of weapons, many of which were quickly pressed into service. The Czech 4.7cm anti-tank gun (originally built for the Czech-Sudeten defences) and the 8.35cm Flak were both used to bolster the West Wall, the guns having shelters specially designed for their use (Standard constructions 506 and 517 of the Aachen–Saar Programm).

In the summer of 1944 work to strengthen the West Wall began. Shelters were built to house both the standard and pivot-mounted 8.8cm PaK, which was more than a match for the relatively lightly armoured Allied tanks; and Panther tank turrets, with their deadly 7.5cm main gun, were mounted on concrete, steel or even, exceptionally, wooden bases. Still other anti-tank weapons were mounted on improvised frameworks and rushed to the front where they were located in open fieldworks.

Other, simple defences were also developed, like the 'Koch' shelter, named after the Gauleiter who supposedly developed the idea. It was simply a concrete tube dropped vertically into the ground and provided protection for a single infantryman. Also, numerous 'tobruk' shelters were built which could mount machine guns, mortars and other light weapons, including obsolete tank turrets. Named after the area where they were first extemporized, by the Italian Army, using concrete drainage pipes vertically emplaced, the tobruks were small emplacements. The German Army developed this concept, and the type became a common construction, being simple and cost effective. Versions were also incorporated into other types of bunker, as well as being of the stand-alone variety.

TOUR OF THE SITES

In front of the main fortifications a series of obstacles were constructed to block the enemy's advance. Thick bands of barbed-wire entanglements, held in place by stakes and strewn with anti-personnel mines, awaited the enemy infantry, while larger anti-tank mines were laid where tanks could traverse. More elaborate anti-tank defences were also constructed including Panzergraben (anti-tank ditches), various steel prefabrications, wooden poles rammed into the ground and, most famously, what were officially known as Höckerhindernisse ('dragon's teeth'). The latter were a series of concrete pyramids increasing in height from front to back and which resembled a set of sharp teeth, hence their nickname. Initially four rows of 'teeth' were constructed, but later five or even six rows were built to counter the threat posed by the much-larger and more powerful tanks that were being built. The last row of 'teeth' rose to 1.5m in height – not much less than the average height of a man.

When the defences were built, Germany was still at peace and it was therefore necessary to keep open the roads and tracks that ran through the 'dragon's teeth'.

Many pillboxes were fitted with thick armoured plates. Through the aperture in the centre an MG08 or MG34 could be fired. The huge bolts that were used to secure the plate to the concrete shelter are still visible. This example was probably used for firing practice and is now on display at the Wehrtechnische Studiensammlung, Koblenz. (Neil Short)

Various alternatives were developed, including steel gates and the so-called *Trägersperre*, a concrete structure built astride the road with recesses which could be fitted with steel H beams to bar access.

Behind these obstacles, hundreds of individual bunkers and pillboxes were built, but although different they all shared certain common features. Doors of varying types controlled access to the shelter and to the various rooms within the structure. These doors fell into two general types: armoured doors and gas-tight sheet metal doors (although latterly some wooden doors were fitted out of necessity). In total, some 192,725 doors were manufactured in the period up to 1941.

The armoured doors were cast in steel and constructed in different sizes; some were tall enough to enable a man to walk through upright, but more typically they were a little over 1m in height. The thickness of the doors ranged from 20–50mm and this influenced the weight, some doors weighing well in excess of 1,000kg. The armoured doors were secured from the inside by a simple lever lock and in peacetime could be secured from the outside with a bolt and padlock. Some of the doors were fitted with small apertures to enable the use of small arms and many of the external doors were fitted with a specially sealed escape hatch. This emergency exit could be used if the main door could no longer be opened. Interior armoured doors were fitted with felt or rubber seals to ensure that they were gas-tight. For practicality, the doors could be fitted to open on the left or the right by adjusting a few bolts.

The gas-tight sheet metal doors were prefabricated from two 2–3mm thick sheets of steel which sandwiched a number of steel struts that gave the door strength. Like some of the armoured doors, they were made gas-tight by the addition of rubber seals. The doors were typically 0.6–0.8m wide and 1.7–2.0m high and were sometimes fitted with a splinter-proof glass spy hole. To gain access to the armoured cupolas and observation posts, gas-tight hatches were fitted.

The interior and exterior gas-tight doors guaranteed the crew's safety when the bunker was completely 'closed down', but not when access was required. To ensure that troops could enter and leave the shelter during a gas attack without any impact on the crew remaining inside, a gas lock was built linking the main door and the interior doors. For this system to work it was essential that only one door to the gas lock was open at

After the war the victorious Allies systematically demolished many of the bunkers and pillboxes of the West Wall. This artillery fort at Kleinau was demolished in November 1948. The 136kg explosive charge completely shattered the structure and dislodged the armour plate. (Public Record Office)

HITLER'S FORTRESSES

ABOVE: A bird's eye view of the defensive system. By contrast with the Maginot Line, the defences of the Siegfried Line were built on the concept of defence in depth. The idea had been developed in the First World War and was now adopted for Hitler's impregnable West Wall. (Chris Taylor © Osprey Publishing)

any one time. A number of hand-operated ventilators were installed (depending on the size of the bunker) which drew air through a series of filters and removed any toxins. Each individual was required to spend half an hour cranking the handle to maintain the supply of breathable air. A simple valve system ensured that excess pressure was safely vented outside without allowing toxic gas to seep in. The inlets for the ventilators were generally located on the rear wall of the bunker and were protected against hand grenades and other explosive charges by a metal grille. To identify what, if any, gas was present, the incoming air was sucked through six filter tubes which reacted when exposed to different toxic gases. A colour chart could then be used to warn the crew of the type of gas and the concentrations present.

Emergency exit hatches were also fitted to many shelters. Made of steel, they measured 0.6 × 0.8m and could be opened from the inside by means of a lever lock. To prevent attackers from forcing their way through the hatch, the emergency escape was blocked with timber and brickwork that could only be removed from the inside.

An example of a very simple MG-Schartenstand built to B1 standards in the Aachen area as part of the original West Wall. These would contain a single machine gun, often an old MG08 from World War I. (NARA)

The adjoining shaft was filled with sand which had to be cleared prior to escape. The shaft varied in shape – circular, semi-circular or square – and in construction: sometimes pre-formed concrete, other times brickwork.

Fixtures and fittings within the various bunkers and pillboxes were, with the exception of the B-Werke, rudimentary. One of the most important pieces of equipment provided for the crew was a bed. Most of the larger shelters were fitted with bunk-beds in tiers of two or three. The frames were made of tubular steel with a wire mesh covering. On top were a sailcloth sheet, a separate mattress and a pillow. On one side the bunks were attached to the wall with a hinge and on the other side they were suspended by two chains secured to the ceiling. This arrangement meant that during the day the bunks could be folded against the wall to provide more space. The cots were just big enough for a man to lie down – 0.7m × 1.9m.

So that troops could eat their meals in relative comfort the sleeping quarters were supplied with at least one folding table which could normally seat six men. Simple folding stools were provided for the ranks and folding chairs for officers. It was not possible to use the bunk-beds and the table and chairs at the same time. Limited shelf space was provided for personal equipment and clothing bars were suspended from the ceiling so that the garrison could hang up their uniforms. A smaller bedside shelf was provided for personal effects. There was additional storage space for food and drink (on occasions in gas-tight containers), for weapons and ammunition, and for helmets and gas masks. Specialist shelters were additionally equipped with map tables, medical facilities, etc.

In addition to the larger items of furniture, the shelters were kitted out with a range of miscellaneous equipment including bins, brooms, washbowl and mirror. A stock of tools was also provided in each bunker to enable the crew to carry out simple repairs, to ensure that doors and embrasures were clear of obstructions – grass, shrubs, trees, etc – and, in the case of an emergency, to escape from the bunker. Tools included a spade, pickaxe, crowbar, wire-cutters, axe, scythe, hammer, chisels and various saws together with 3kg of nails.

Most shelters were not fitted with purpose-built toilet facilities. This was not a problem in peacetime when external field latrines could be used, but when the bunker was 'closed down' an improvised dry closet had to be used which consisted of a butt with an aperture. After use, turfs would be scattered on the excrement. One closet was provided for every eight men. The majority of bunkers were not provided with electric lighting, although some resourceful troops who manned the shelters during the Sitzkrieg (lit. 'sitting war', the German term for what the Allies called the 'Phoney War' of 1939–40) fitted their own simple electric light system. Where formal (or informal) electric lighting had not been installed, troops had to rely on standard-issue petrol and battery-operated lamps (or, exceptionally, candles) which could be placed in special recesses in the wall. The number provided reflected the number of rooms in the shelter and the use to which these rooms were put, so a map room or first-aid room would have more lamps than, for example, a fighting compartment.

For heating and the warming of food (no proper cooking facilities were provided in the basic bunkers) the structures were fitted with a stove (some larger shelters had two or even four stoves). The Wt 80K stove was constructed in such a way that when the shelter was under attack it could be made completely gas-tight – preventing noxious gases getting in and smoke getting out. Sealing the stove in this way could lead to a build-up of pressure within the unit and it was constructed in such a way as to withstand this. The chimney section was also fabricated in such a way that explosive charges dropped down the pipe could not reach the stove and explode.

Although facilities were basic, the intention was to make all fortifications in the Siegfried Line independently defensible for seven days as a bare minimum. The larger fortifications (the B-Werke) could be defended for much longer, while the simple Type D shelters, which had not been designed to accommodate the crew for lengthy periods of time, were only suitable as fighting positions and so were not fitted with a ventilation system, beds or furniture.

To enable the crew to remain in their shelter for this period of time, it was crucial that they had access to a supply of fresh water. Some shelters were fitted with wells or pumps, but most had to make do with a diverse range of containers from jugs to gas-proof containers. These had to be replenished from local sources, be they wells, springs or a local house. This was far from satisfactory and troops complained bitterly about the inconvenience and danger of having to collect water. Efforts were made to establish independent supplies for bunkers using pipe systems but it is unclear how far this work had progressed.

Another priority was food. Normally, troops stationed in the bunkers and pillboxes would be regularly supplied with food, but the shelters were additionally provided

Most major bridges along the major western waterways were fortified during the 1936–40 West Wall programme. This is a Brückensicherungsbunker (bridge security bunker) on the Saar near Dillingen, part of the heavily reinforced Saarpfalz defence sector. (NARA)

HITLER'S FORTRESSES

THE GERSTFELDHÖHE TUNNEL SYSTEM

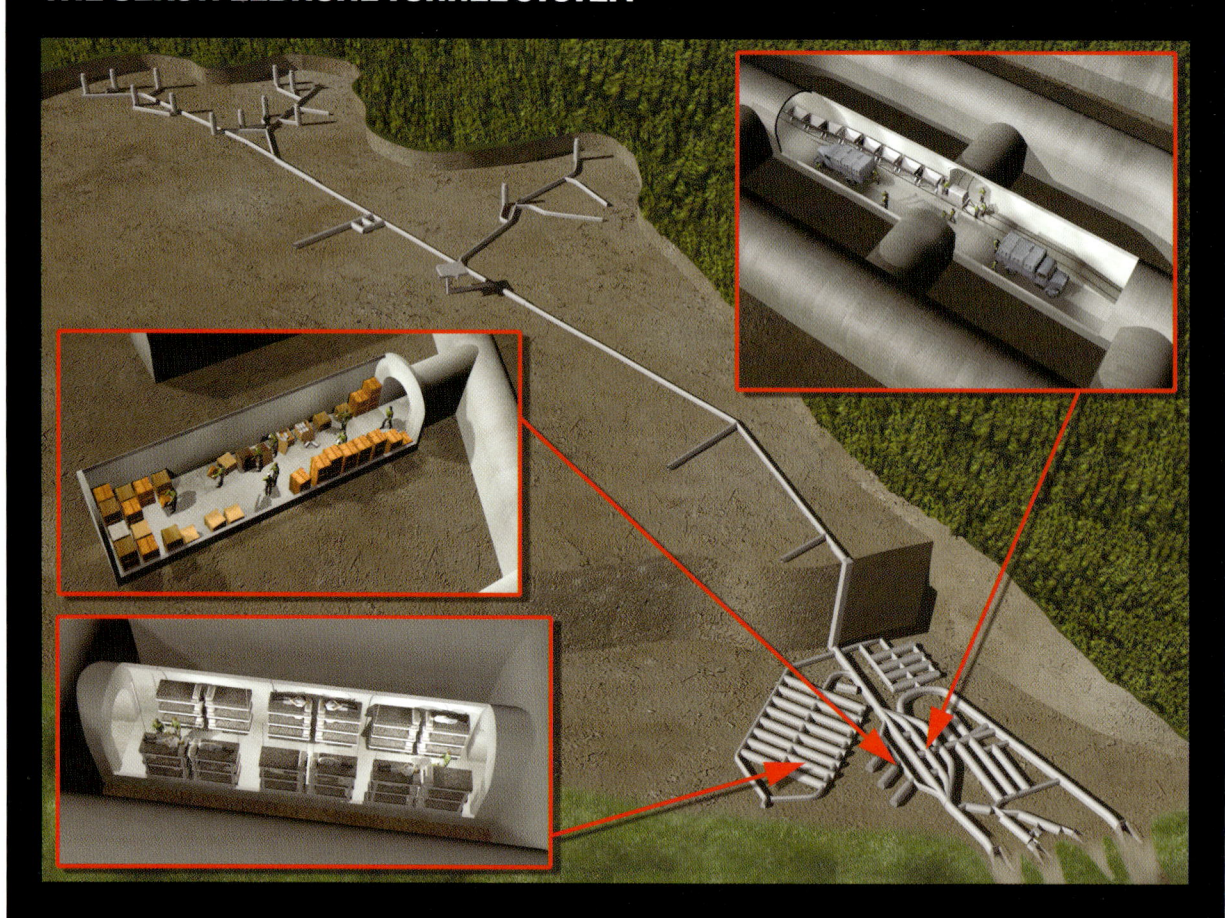

The Gerstfeldhöhe tunnel system at Niedersimten, near Pirmasens, was planned to be a key defensive installation of the West Wall. A series of interconnected bunkers and pillboxes were to be constructed that would dominate the Trulben valley, which was a natural avenue of attack from France. These positions in turn were to be linked by a 68m high elevator shaft to a further tunnel system that provided a safe haven for both the personnel and ammunition. A light railway was planned to run from the entrance at Niedersimten to the lift while another linked up the various fighting positions. By the time construction work was suspended following the defeat of France around 3 million Reichsmarks had been spent on the project. Work was restarted in 1944 but only on a very limited scale. Its main wartime contribution was to act as an air raid shelter for local residents and after the war served as a depot for US Army stores. Today the Gerstfeldhöhe is home to the West Wall Museum. One thousand metres of tunnels are open to the public with write-ups and exhibits. (Chris Taylor © Osprey Publishing)

with emergency stores. These included tins of meat and fish, processed cheese, crispbread, coffee, tea, sugar, salt and chocolate and were designed to sustain the men for a week.

OPERATIONAL HISTORY

During the 'Phoney War' of 1939 and 1940, the defences of the West Wall were largely untested, and following the fall of the Low Countries and the defeat of France the defences were mostly abandoned. Weapons and fittings were removed and placed in storage and incomplete bunkers demolished. All efforts now went into the building of the Atlantic Wall. Not until the summer of 1944 was serious consideration given to renovating the western defences. By this time the Allies had broken out of the Normandy bridgehead and were advancing across France. On 25 August, Paris was captured and Allied troops paraded down the Champs-Elysées.

A little over two weeks later, American forces were at the German border and were faced with only two obstacles – one man made and one natural – between them and victory. The latter obstacle, and arguably the more formidable of the two, was the River Rhine, which snaked from its source in Switzerland all along the German border and into the Netherlands before draining into the North Sea. Overcoming this obstacle, swollen with the autumn rains and with all the bridges sure to be destroyed by retreating German forces, would require a well-planned set-piece attack.

The Siegfried Line seemingly posed less of a problem. Built more than five years previously and abandoned in the interim, the defences were largely obsolete. The Allied High Command was bullish about the prospects of breaching the outmoded defences sooner rather than later. The reality was to prove very different. An overly cautious

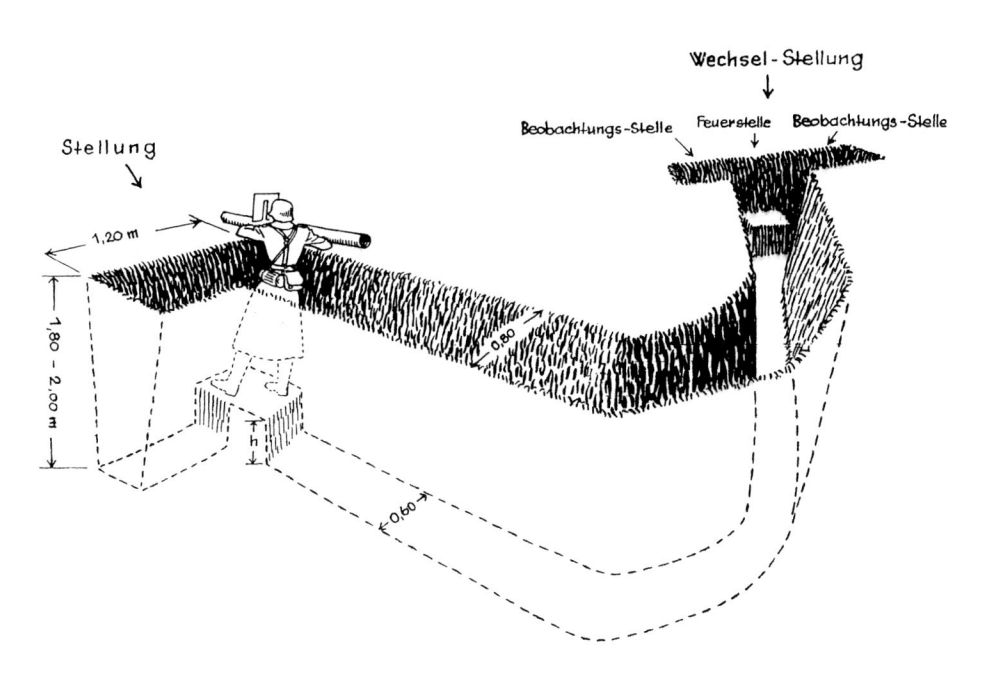

An illustration from a Heeresgruppe G pamphlet showing the recommended layout of a Panzerschreck anti-tank position, consisting of a foxhole on the left for the rocket-launcher crew, and a Wechsel-Stellung (reserve-position) trench to the right, which also accommodated the team's Beobachtungs-Stellen (observation posts). (NARA)

approach of the commanders of the First US Army, which was in the vanguard of the American advance, allowed German resistance on the line to gather and harden, and stop the Allied push. General Patton was left kicking his heels in the south, starved of petrol and ammunition as the meagre supplies were given to the British and American forces further north in what was seen to be the main theatre of operations.

The German High Command's so-called 'miracle of the west' had begun. It would be wrong to suggest that this was purely due to the western defences; logistical difficulties also played a part, as did a continuing lack of adventure among senior American commanders. General Charles Corlett, advancing on General Joseph Collins' left, delayed his attack until he had sufficient supplies of ammunition and fuel and the weather was suitable for tactical air support. As such, it was not until 1 October that Corlett ordered the 30th Infantry Division and the 2nd Armored Division forward.

This brief respite was not wasted, however. General Leland Hobbs, commander of the 30th Infantry Division, took this rare opportunity to withdraw his troops from the line in rotation for two days of intense training in the art of attacking fortified positions. The investment paid off, and the US attack towards Aachen punched through the West Wall defences in that sector; on 21 October the city's garrison capitulated, much to Hitler's chagrin.

Elsewhere, the Americans enjoyed less success, and the West Wall proved brutally resistant in sectors. The 28th Infantry Division alone, attacking the Monschau corridor

In some of the more major construction projects, like the tunnel system at Niedersimten, it was planned to construct a light railway. Small diesel engines, like the example shown, would transport men and munitions from the delivery point to the fighting positions. (Neil Short)

in October–November, suffered more than 6,000 casualties without breaking the German line. The bloody reverse suffered by the Allies in the autumn of 1944 had been due in no small part to the defences of the West Wall. However, although the fortifications around Aachen were undoubtedly strong, it was not the most formidable part of the line. This was located to the south around the Saar and lay between Patton's Third Army and the German heartland.

Before attacking the main defences of the Siegfried Line there was the small matter of the 'Siegfried Switch Line' which ran from the River Moselle in an easterly direction to Orscholz and which provided its alternative name – the Orscholz Switch Line. It was designed to prevent France outflanking the main defences of the West Wall and was built in a similar fashion to its larger cousin. When the tanks of Patton's 10th Armored 'Tiger' Division reached the line in the second half of November, Patton gave little credit to such defences and confidently predicted that given the supplies he would '… go through the Siegfried Line like shit through a goose'. The truth was somewhat different.

One of the most common configurations of Panzersperre was this timber type, with the shoulders constructed of a timber box filled with stone or earth and a removable set of horizontal logs forming the centre of the barrier. Here, an M10 3in GMC (Gun Motor Carriage) of the 645th Tank Destroyer Battalion crunches through a Panzersperre in Lembach on 14 December during the attack by the 45th Division in the Low Vosges. (NARA)

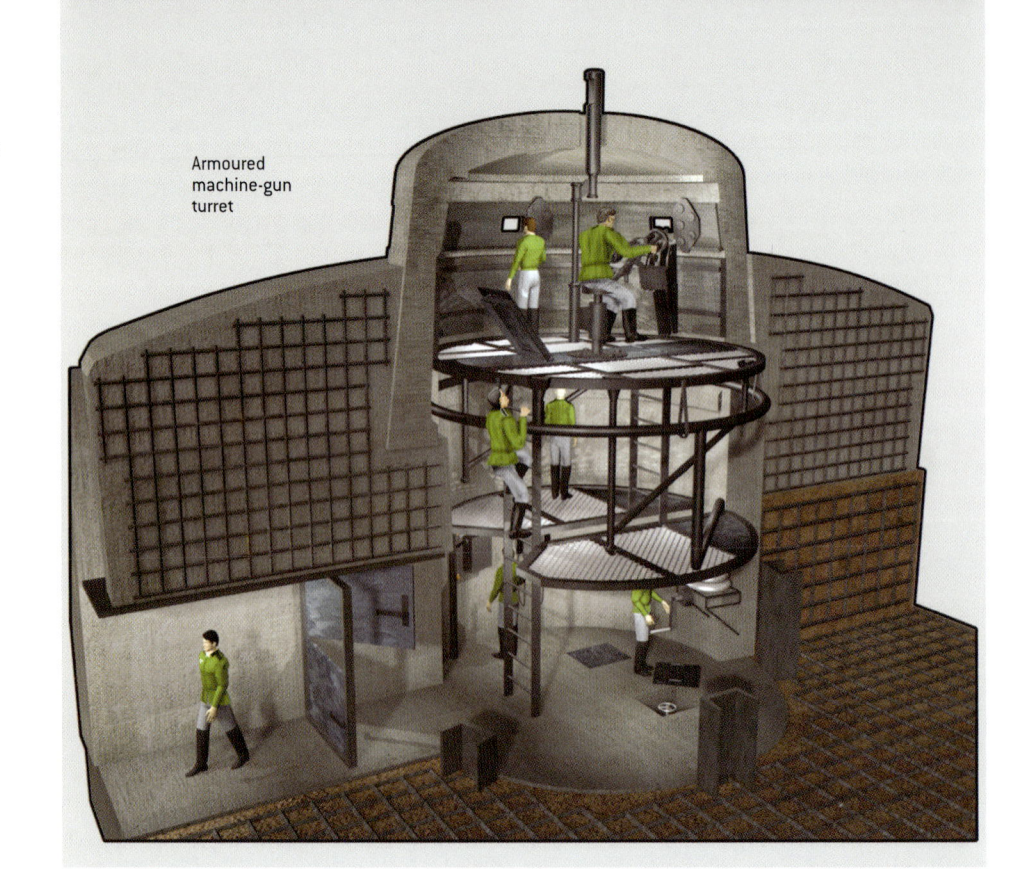

HITLER'S FORTRESSES

Katzenkopf B Werk. One of the most interesting features of the Pionierprogramm was the so-called B-Werk (the name originates from the construction thickness 'B'). Thirty-two bunkers of this type were started in the period 1937–38.

First Storey
1. Armoured turret
2. Small cloche
3. Artillery observation turret
4. Mortar
5. Flamethrower
6. Entrances

Second Storey
1. Pit
2. Ammunition room
3. Ammunition room
4. Entrance to corridor leading to armoured turret
5. Kitchen
6. Provisions store
7. Rest room
8. Corridor
9. Rest room
10. Flamethrower supply room
11. Stair shaft to tunnels
12. Staircase
13. Liquid fuel store
14. Corridor
15. Toilet with wastewater construction
16. Washroom
17. First-aid room
18. Machine room
19. Ammunition room
20. Water store
(Chris Taylor © Osprey Publishing)

Flamethrower

M19 Automatic Mortar

Armoured machine-gun turret

PROTECTING THE HOMELAND – GERMANY'S BORDER DEFENCES

First storey

Second storey

Tunnel to armoured turret

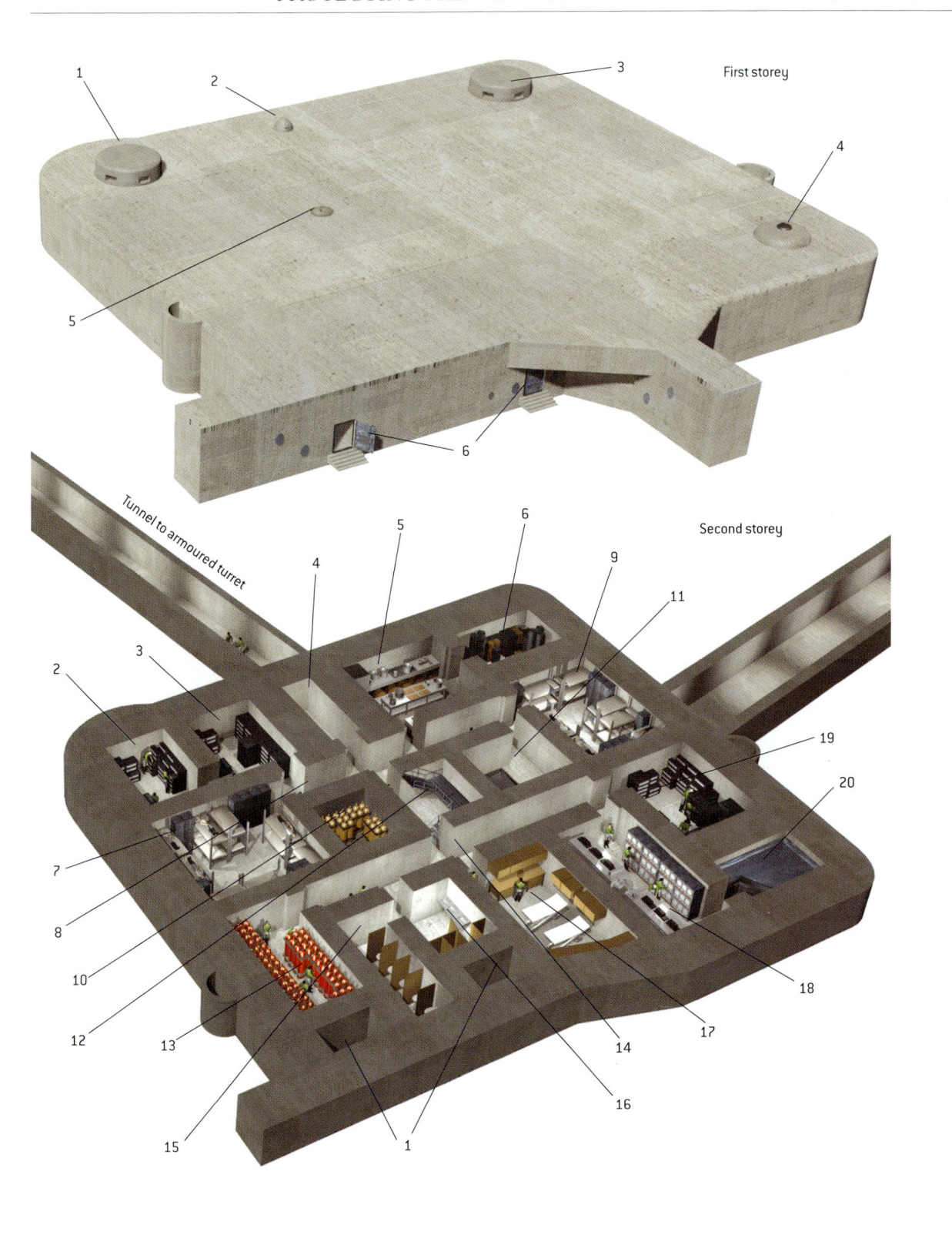

A significant number of Flak guns were assigned to the Rhine PaK front. Some, like this one, were surplus Luftwaffe weapons that were issued to Festung-PaK-Abteilungen with a Behelfslafette cruciform mount. Unlike the normal cruciform mount, this inexpensive frame was designed for fixed use only, and the gun was no longer mobile after it was deployed. This example saw combat in the fighting for the Cologne bridgehead in early March 1945. (NARA)

On 21 November, the men of the 'Tiger' Division were ordered to attack the Orscholz Switch Line. Supremely confident in the ability of his division to succeed, the division's commander decided not to use elements of the 90th Infantry Division that had been placed at his disposal and instead attacked alone. Faced with an unexpectedly ferocious defence, he soon realized the error of his ways and reversed his earlier decision, but by the time reinforcements arrived the opportunity of a breakthrough had disappeared and the defences held.

Further to the south the bulk of the 90th and 95th Infantry Divisions managed to cross the River Saar at the start of December and captured a number of pillboxes. This unexpected coup was short-lived. On 16 December, Hitler launched his counter-attack in the Ardennes and offensive operations in the Saar were suspended. Operations launched in the north along the Monschau corridor towards the River Roer dams on 13 December were similarly curtailed by Hitler's sudden strike.

As it transpired, the ill-conceived Ardennes offensive, or the Battle of the Bulge as it was popularly known, was a blessing in disguise for the Allies. It undoubtedly caused a great deal of anxiety in its early days but as the tide of the battle turned it became clear that the German High Command had now used the last of its reserves of men, tanks, ammunition and fuel and that little remained between the Allies and final victory.

At this point it is worth hypothesizing as to the outcome of the fighting for the Siegfried Line if the 250,000 men sacrificed in the Ardennes counter-attack had been used to man the western defences. The American GIs on the ground were no fools. When faced with an occupied bunker they would scout around for an easier route forward and, more often than not, would find one since few of the positions were manned. Had this not been the case the attempts to break the Siegfried Line might have been far more costly than they were – and they were sanguinary struggles in their own right. The advance might also have been considerably slower. Air power was of little use against the heavily fortified and dispersed pillboxes, which meant that each pillbox had to be reduced individually; a time-consuming business. Indeed, if the Siegfried Line had been properly manned it is conceivable that the political map of Europe might have been very different, with the Red Army conquering most of Germany. By mid-December the Allies had breached the Line but were unable to exploit the situation. With the onset of winter the Allied High Command was considering suspending large-scale offensive action and waiting until the spring to resume its attack. The Ardennes offensive changed all that. Not only did it result in total failure, but it also resulted in large sections of the West Wall being either undermanned or unmanned.

The bleak scenario faced by the German Army was in stark contrast to that of the Allies. Nevertheless, it was with more than a little trepidation that the soldiers of the 76th Infantry Division crossed the River Sauer on 7 February 1945 to attack one of the most densely fortified sections of the Siegfried Line along the German border with Luxembourg.

This nervousness might have contributed to the decision to launch a company-sized attack, preceded by a 15-minute barrage, against a single pillbox manned by a section of riflemen with two machine guns. In the mêlée that followed the officer leading the attack was hit, as were a number of his men including the individual tasked with depositing the satchel charge of explosives at the bunker door. Despite these difficulties the pillbox and its defenders were eventually captured. The 76th Infantry Division could now put its mind to the more daunting task of how it was going to storm the Katzenkopf position that barred its way to the Rhine. The Katzenkopf was one of the largest bunkers built by the German engineers and was constructed inside a hill that dominated the small town of Irrel, near Trier. Although not bristling with weapons – one of Hitler's criticisms of such positions – it certainly posed a significant challenge to anyone who was foolhardy enough to attack it, boasting in its arsenal machine guns, a mortar and a retractable flamethrower.

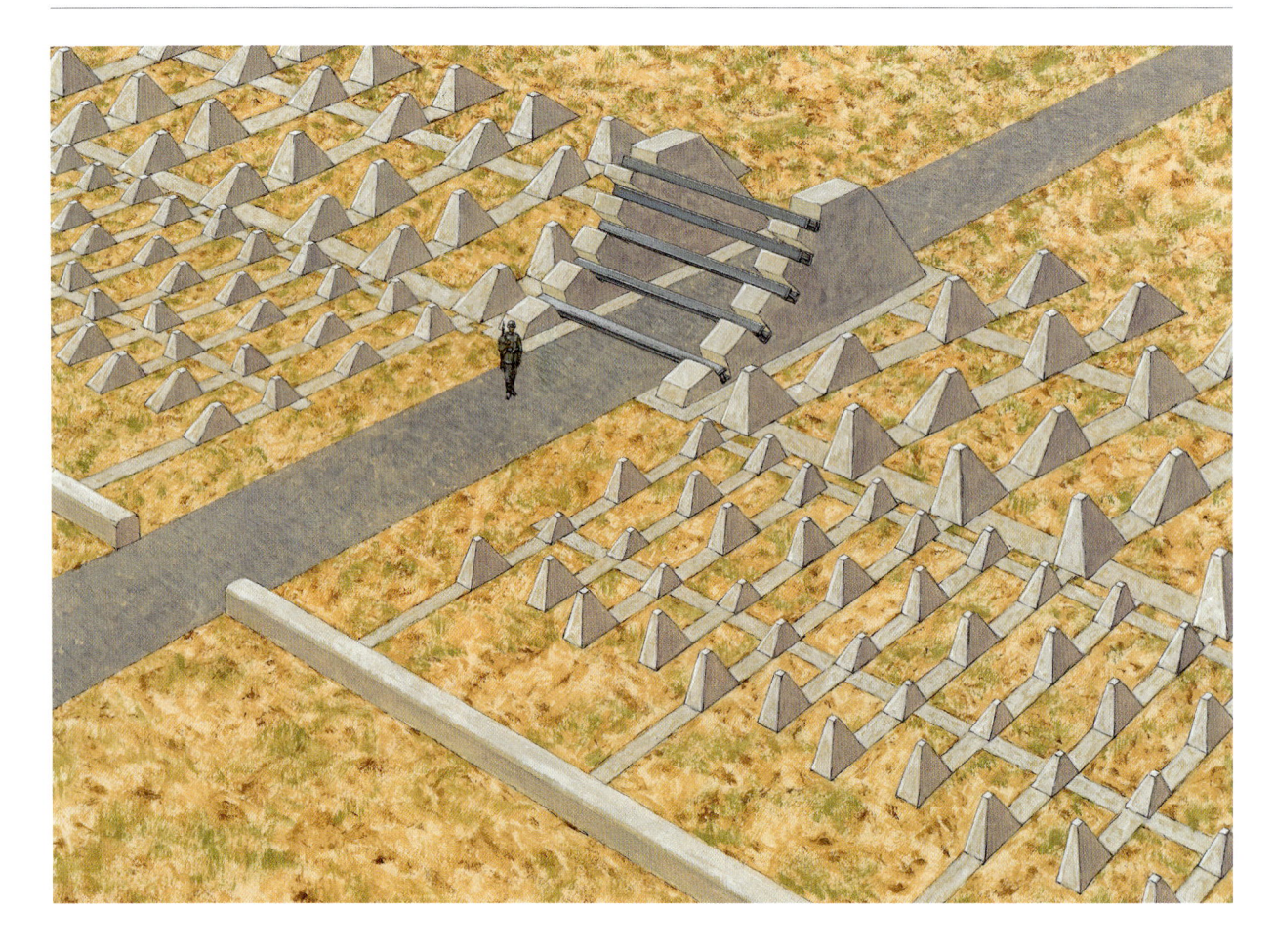

ABOVE: Dragon's teeth anti-tank obstacle. These were generally emplaced as connected fields of obstructions, not as individual obstacles, and they had a distinctive pattern of lower obstacles followed by higher obstacles in order to encourage enemy tanks to attempt to surmount the low obstacles at the edge of the field, which would cause them to become stuck on the higher obstacles deeper in the field. (Adam Hook © Osprey Publishing)

In light of the previous debacle the men tasked with taking the fort were understandably very nervous. But as events transpired their worries were ill founded. The preliminary barrage was enough to convince the majority of the defenders that there was little point in fighting on and they slipped away into the darkness. Thus the Allies, without a fight had captured one of the most powerful works of the Siegfried Line.

On 7 March 1945, the First US Army captured a railway bridge at Remagen over the Rhine. The positions of the Siegfried Line that were still held were now of little strategic importance and the troops were gradually withdrawn, in spite of Hitler's insistence that every position should be defended to the last. The Siegfried Line had been defeated and Patton's prediction realized, albeit much later than he had anticipated.

DEFENCE OF THE RHINE

The Rhine has been Germany's traditional defensive barrier in the west since Roman times. In the autumn and early winter of 1944–45, the Wehrmacht conducted an extensive fortification effort in the foreground of the Rhine, consisting of the rejuvenation of the derelict West Wall fortifications, the incorporation of parts of the Maginot Line, and the construction of numerous new defensive lines. This was known as the West-Stellung (West Position).

This defence system has been surrounded by confusion and obscurity. It is often confused with the West Wall. While large parts of the West Wall were incorporated into the new fortification scheme, the new defensive lines covered areas not previously reached by the West Wall, and considerably amplified the depth of the defences. Another source of confusion is the nickname 'Siegfried Line', which has been loosely used over the years to refer both to the 1940 West Wall and to the far more extensive defences of

Several Rhine bridges were protected from air attack by the secret new Flakwerfer 44 Föhngerät, which fired a salvo of 35 7.3cm unguided rockets, depending on volume of fire rather than accuracy for its effect. This example served with 3./Flak Ausbildungs-und-Erprobungs Batallion 900 in Erpel near the Ludendorff Bridge at Remagen, where it was captured along with the bridge. Behind it is a US Army M16 anti-aircraft halftrack of the 634th AAA Battalion (Automatic Weapon) guarding the bridge area. (NARA)

HITLER'S FORTRESSES

1944–45. The Siegfried Line misnomer stemmed from Hitler's 28 April 1939 Reichstag speech in which he described the new West Wall as 40 times stronger than the old Siegfried-Stellung fieldworks of 1918. Due to a misunderstanding, the British press began referring to the West Wall fortifications as the Siegfried Line in 1939–40. When Allied forces reached the old West Wall in September 1944, the German defensive positions were again called the Siegfried Line.

The 1944–45 West-Stellung programme differed considerably from the earlier West Wall. Due to the poor weather, as well as the lack of material and skilled labour, few new concrete bunkers were constructed. The old West Wall served as the concrete spine of the new West-Stellung and additional defensive lines were layered around it using fieldworks reinforced with obstacles and gun emplacements. Special emphasis was placed on anti-tank defence in the form of numerous anti-tank obstacles as well as dense anti-tank-gun positions. Instead of a thin and brittle string of obsolete concrete bunkers, the West-Stellung offered defence in depth. Construction of the West-Stellung was mainly carried out by labour drafts from the cities along the Rhine. It was an enormous civic undertaking, exceeding 400,000 labourers by October 1944.

The West-Stellung was a significant enhancement to the Wehrmacht campaign in the west in the autumn of 1944, serving to reinforce the declining combat effectiveness of German infantry units while at the same time providing a shield behind which the Army could hoard its elite Panzer units for the planned December offensive in the Ardennes. The West-Stellung proved far less effective in February–March 1945 when the Allies began their final offensive to the Rhine. No fortification system could compensate for the crippling losses suffered in the failed Ardennes campaign, and the new defensive lines were quickly overwhelmed by the Allied onslaught. A further defence scheme on the east bank of the Rhine, the Rhein-Stellung, was largely stillborn and was overrun before completion in March–April 1945. This book contains a comprehensive description in English of the 1944–45 West-Stellung fortification programme.

CREATING THE WEST-STELLUNG

The 20 July 1944 bomb plot against Hitler had originated with the leaders of the Ersatzheer (Replacement Army), so to squash any future mutinies Reichsführer-SS Heinrich Himmler was placed in charge of homeland defence, becoming Chef der Heeresrüstung und Befehlshaber des Heimatheeres (Chief of Army Mobilization and Commander of the Home Army). In early August 1944, Himmler called together a meeting at Kaiserslautern with the leaders of the western border Wehrkreise (military districts) and their staffs along with the Gauleiter (Nazi party district leaders) to announce that Hitler had entrusted him with the organization of the defence of the western German border. Himmler's Kaiserslautern meeting started the process of creating a new series of defensive lines along Germany's western borders. On 5 August 1944, the fortification staffs of the western Wehrkreise met in Wiesbaden under Generalleutnant Rudolf Schmetzer to plan the construction programme. Schmetzer had been the fortification inspector of OB West until early 1944, and had been heavily involved in the Atlantic Wall effort. The plan called for a defence zone which was to include the Netherlands, with special emphasis on the immediate erection of a defensive line from Antwerp via Maastricht to Aachen, called the Brabant-Stellung. This line was planned to exploit the Albert Canal by reinforcing it with fieldworks.

OPPOSITE: This Pantherturm I on an OT-Stahlunterstand Type D was being emplaced by Festungs-Pionier-Kommandeur XIX, 5km west of Bonn along Highway 56, but was captured by the US Army before it was finished in 1945. This example uses the Ostwallturm, which was based on the Panther tank turret but with thicker roof armour and other changes. A second steel box containing the crew quarters would be positioned underneath the fighting compartment box seen here, and the entire assembly buried, leaving only the turret exposed. (NARA)

HITLER'S FORTRESSES

West-Stellung, February 1945.

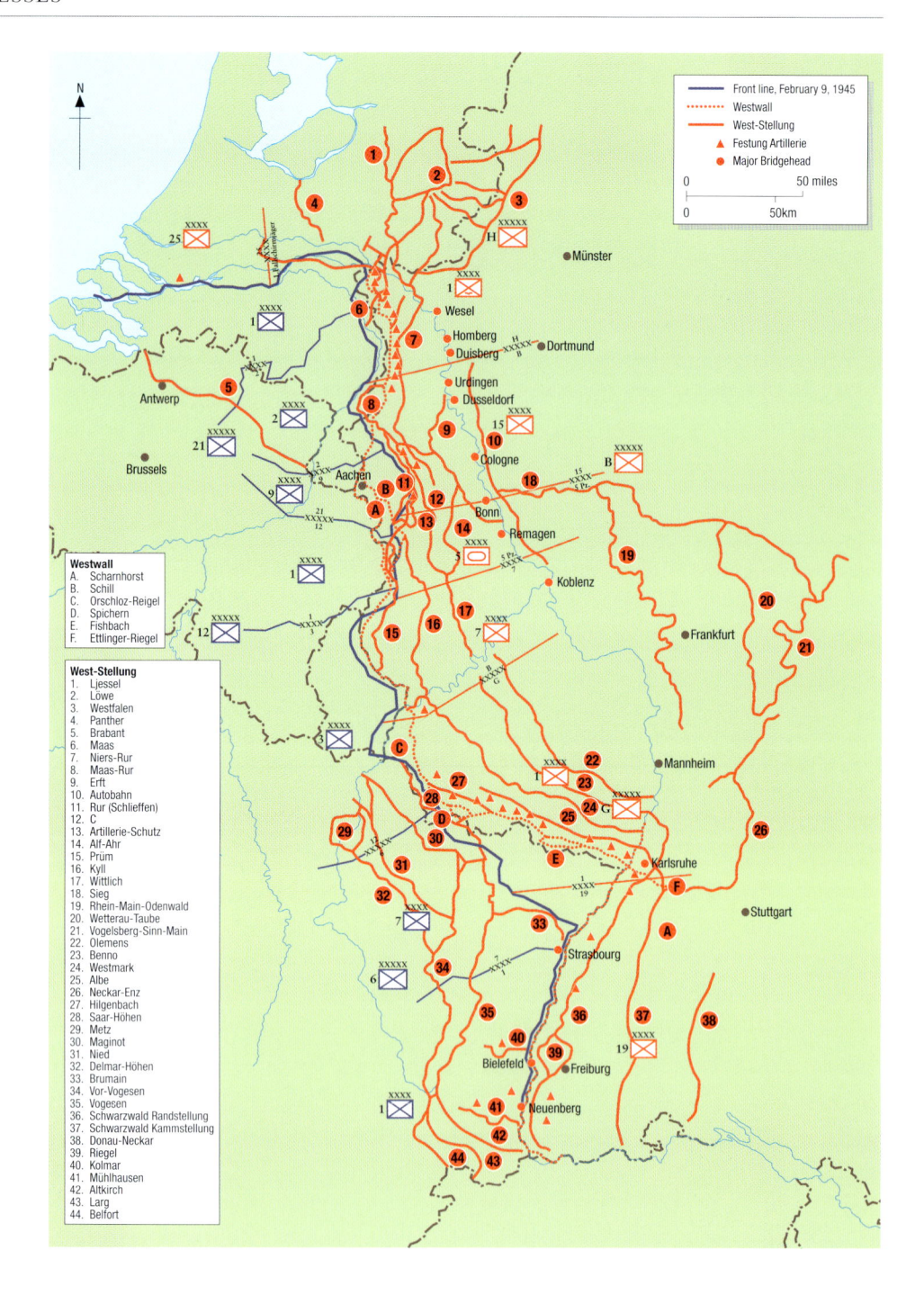

Westwall
A. Scharnhorst
B. Schill
C. Orschloz-Riegel
D. Spichern
E. Fishbach
F. Ettlinger-Riegel

West-Stellung
1. Ijessel
2. Löwe
3. Westfalen
4. Panther
5. Brabant
6. Maas
7. Niers-Rur
8. Maas-Rur
9. Erft
10. Autobahn
11. Rur (Schlieffen)
12. C
13. Artillerie-Schutz
14. Alf-Ahr
15. Prüm
16. Kyll
17. Wittlich
18. Sieg
19. Rhein-Main-Odenwald
20. Wetterau-Taube
21. Vogelsberg-Sinn-Main
22. Olemens
23. Benno
24. Westmark
25. Albe
26. Neckar-Enz
27. Hilgenbach
28. Saar-Höhen
29. Metz
30. Maginot
31. Nied
32. Delmar-Höhen
33. Brumain
34. Vor-Vogesen
35. Vogesen
36. Schwarzwald Randstellung
37. Schwarzwald Kammstellung
38. Donau-Neckar
39. Riegel
40. Kolmar
41. Mühlhausen
42. Altkirch
43. Larg
44. Belfort

The formal start of the West-Stellung can be traced to Hitler's Directive Nr. 61 of 24 August 1944. This divided the task of creating the West-Stellung between the Gauleiter and the Wehrkreise:

The positions should be constructed in such a way that an uninterrupted system of tank obstacles is created first of all, preparations are made for a demolition zone ahead of the positions, and a continuous and deeply echeloned system of fortifications is built up, which should constantly be reinforced at the most important points. The Metz-Diedenhofen [fortified zone] and sectors of the Maginot Line will be incorporated into our position, the existing installations rebuilt, and those which will not be used should be destroyed.

Hitler amplified his intentions for the West-Stellung with another directive on September 1944, which ordered an extension of the West Wall to the Ijsselmeer in the Netherlands. Construction of the West-Stellung was to be carried out using a levy of the local population as well as the RAD and the OT. Hitler ignored his earlier disapproval of rear defensive lines, but he retained a visceral antipathy to any talk about defences on the eastern side of the Rhine owing to its association with Army defeatism.

The Wehrmacht's growing dependence on fortified lines was a tacit recognition of the severe deterioration of German infantry units after the summer 1944 debacles in both the east and the west. The Wehrmacht was able to recover from 'the void' in September 1944 by transferring tens of thousands of Luftwaffe and Kriegsmarine personnel into the Army after their aircraft and ships were idled by the growing fuel shortages. This sudden infusion of troops helped to stem the tide of defeat and was the wellspring of the 'Wunder am West Wall' (Miracle on the West Wall) in September 1944 when the Allied advance through Belgium was finally halted. Although the young Luftwaffe ground crews and Kriegsmarine sailors were often well motivated, they were thrown into combat with little or no specialized infantry training. Under these conditions, a hurriedly assembled infantry battalion was much more effective when fighting from carefully prepared defensive fieldworks and bunkers than in open-field combat. Furthermore, the 1944 defeats had chewed up much of the Army's vital tactical leadership, especially the NCOs and junior officers so critical in close-quarters combat. It was much easier for inexperienced NCOs and junior officers to control green troops in trenches. Conditions in the infantry continued to deteriorate through the autumn and into the winter of 1944–45 as the pool of Luftwaffe and Kriegsmarine troops was exhausted, leaving little recourse but to absorb regional militias and Volkssturm into the defence effort.

In 1944–45 the Allies enjoyed a substantial firepower advantage over the Wehrmacht both in terms of field artillery and air power. Field fortifications provided a measure of relief for the German infantry. The West-Stellung substantially enhanced the firepower of the Feldheer (Field Army) by the addition of the numerous machine-gun positions and anti-tank guns beyond divisional holdings, as well as the long-range firepower of the fortification artillery. The role of the West Wall in halting the Allied advance in the autumn of 1944 encouraged the Wehrmacht to attempt to repeat this success in other sectors by extending fortification lines along the Rhine.

One reason that the 1944–45 fortification programmes are not well known is that they were created by the Heimatheer (Homeland Army), not the better-known field army tactical formations. The German Army had a separate Ersatzheer, responsible for raising and training units for the field armies. Engineer offices of the Ersatzheer had managed the previous West Wall programme, and were responsible for much of the 1944–45 programme as well. Germany was divided into 19 Wehrkreise; three of these districts (V, VI, and VII) covered the western border on the Rhine and so figured prominently in the West-Stellung programme.

Construction of the West Wall had been managed by three principal commands: the Festungsdientstelle Düren (Düren Fortification Sector) under Wehrkreis VI, the Kommandantur der Besfestgungen Eifel-Saarpfalz (Eifel–Saar-Palatinate Fortification Command) under Wehrkreis XII and the Kommandantur der Befestigungen Oberrhein (Upper Rhine Fortification Command) under Wehrkreis V. By the summer of 1944 there were six fortification commands (Kommandantur der Befestigungen) in the west: the Dutch Coast (Küste), Lower Rhine (Niederrhein), Eifel, Saar-Palatinate (Saarpfalz), Upper Rhine (Oberrhein) and Vosges (Vogesen). During the autumn of 1944 the sector commands were reduced to five by merging the Dutch Coast and Lower Rhine offices, and most were redesignated as Höhere Kommando der Befestigungen (Senior Fortification Commands). These sector offices coordinated the efforts of the district military engineers, the OT paramilitary construction agency, local Nazi Party offices and private contractors.

The subordinate defence sectors of the West Wall were managed by a Festungs-Pionier-Kommandeur (Fortification Engineer Command), which was equivalent to a brigade headquarters. These were composed of a Festungs-Pionier-Stab (Fortification Engineer Staff) equivalent to a regimental engineer staff, usually with two Abschnittsgruppen (Sector Groups), which were equivalent to battalion staffs. The number of commands and staffs in each district fluctuated depending on the workload and, in some cases, commands or staffs from interior Wehrkreise were transferred to the Rhine districts to assist with the West-Stellung effort. The main function of these organizations was planning, surveying and overseeing the construction of the fortifications. The actual construction work was done by other organizations.

Since 1942, the Nazi Party Gauleiter as Reichsverteidigungskomissare (RVK; Reich Defence Commissars) were responsible for civil defence. In August 1944, Himmler announced plans to expand their responsibilities more broadly to homeland defence. The RVK were responsible for the Operationsgebiet (operational zone) 20km behind the front, while the Army controlled the 'Combat Zone'. Under the 19

July 1944 Führer Directive, construction of fortifications inside Germany was assigned to the RVK, although supervision remained in the hands of the Wehrkreis fortification staffs. Party involvement in the West-Stellung would prove to be a source of endless frustration for the Army. The Gauleiter had no engineering experience and tended to view the construction programmes as simply another way to curry favour with party leaders in Berlin.

The task of coordinating the fortification programmes of the Ersatzheer with the tactical needs of the field army was undertaken by the OB West's Kommandant Festungsbereich West (Commander for Fortification Affairs West). Hitler's 9 September 1944 directive transferred command of the West-Stellung, including the West Wall, from the local Wehrkreis commanders to OB West, and temporarily subordinated the border Festungs-Pionier commands to the field command, effective from 11 September 1944. As a result, the OB West fortification department was elevated to the Oberkommando Festungsbereich West (High Command for Fortification Affairs West) and General Karl Kitzinger was appointed its commander, effective from 5 October 1944. It was based in Bad Kreuznach.

The OT had been the primary state bureau for the creation of the West Wall, Autobahnen and the Atlantic Wall, but the OT was not especially prominent in the construction work on the West-Stellung in the autumn of 1944. The rout of the Wehrmacht in France in the summer of 1944 had led to a massive loss of OT engineers and workers in France and Belgium, and it was in the process of rebuilding in the autumn of 1944. Hitler directed the OT to other high-priority projects, especially those connected with the reconstruction of German industry in the face of relentless Allied bombing attacks. The OT was also responsible for a massive programme to create underground factories for key German military industries. Although not prominent in the West-Stellung effort, the OT did sometimes provide engineers and workers where specialized skills were needed, such as in the construction of major concrete bunkers.

WEST-STELLUNG DESIGN

The West-Stellung programme had barely begun when the US Army began approaching the outer edge of the old West Wall in mid-September 1944 on the approaches to Aachen. This was part of the Düren Fortification Sector, one of only two West Wall sectors with a double set of defensive lines. By the end of November 1944, about half of the original West Wall bunkers were still operational after many had been lost in the Aachen fighting.

The September 1944 plan for the West-Stellung envisioned a substantial expansion of the old West Wall to provide defence in depth through a series of secondary lines and

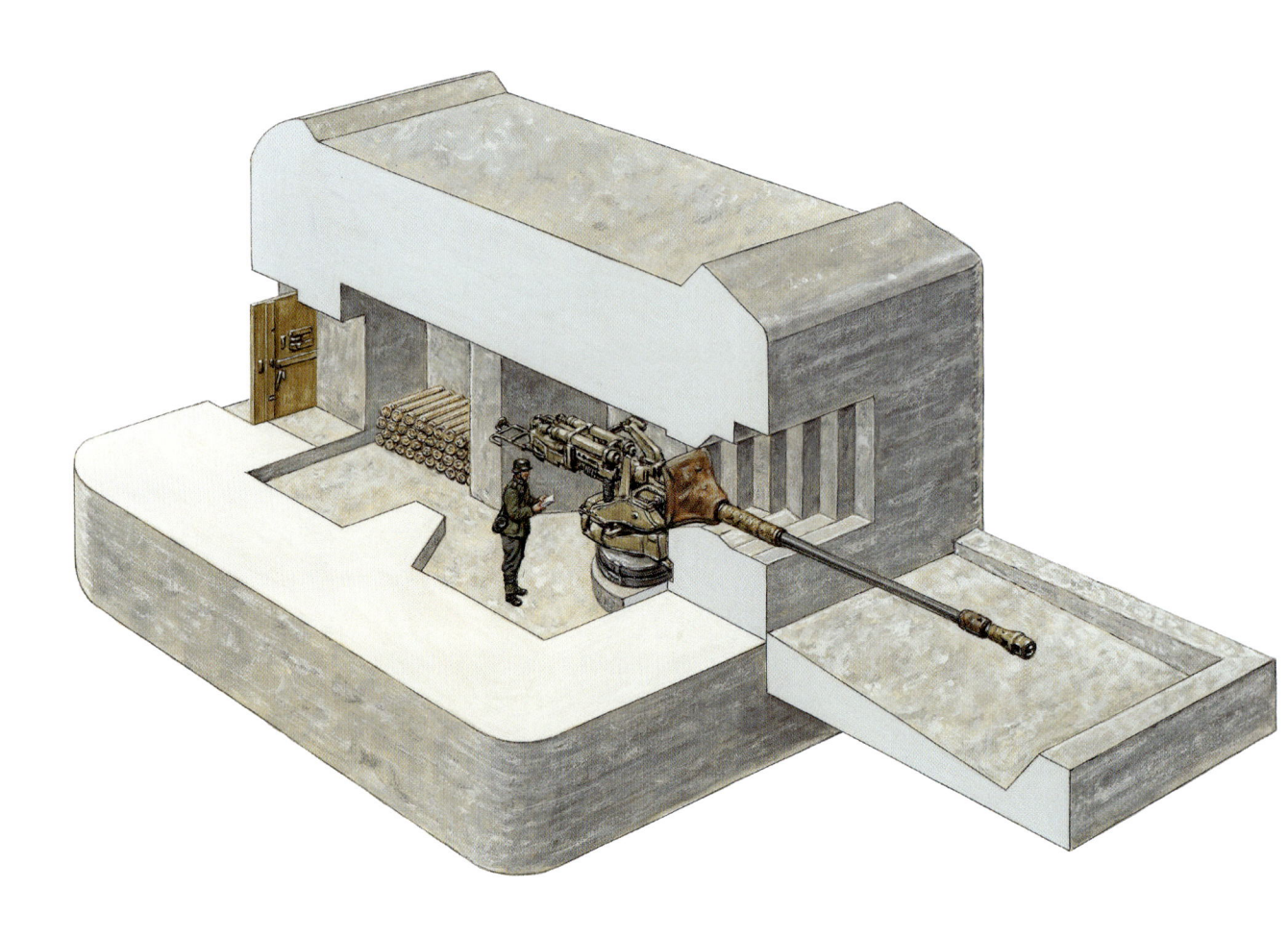

ABOVE: Regelbau Nr. 703 Schartenstand für 88mm PaK 43/3 auf SKL IIa, Festungs-PaK-Verband XI, Panther-Stellung, Netherlands, 1945. The design of the Rgl. Nr. 703 is simple, consisting of a fighting chamber for the gun and crew and two ammunition closets behind. A concrete apron was often poured in front of the embrasure to prevent loose earth or dust from being kicked up by the gun blast. (Adam Hook © Osprey Publishing)

blocking positions. The plan included the construction of 3,636 combat pillboxes and casemates, 7,999 underground bunkers, 847 observation posts and 270 command posts with funding of 310 million Reichsmarks. By the third week of September 1944, the workforce had mushroomed to over 400,000, including about 300,000 German civilians and 65,000 foreign labourers, plus various soldiers, OT workers and other groups. The initial allotment of concrete was about 50,000m³ per month, and this was gradually expanded to over 500,000m³ to cover the construction through early 1945. To put this in some perspective, this was about 15 per cent as much concrete as had been used in

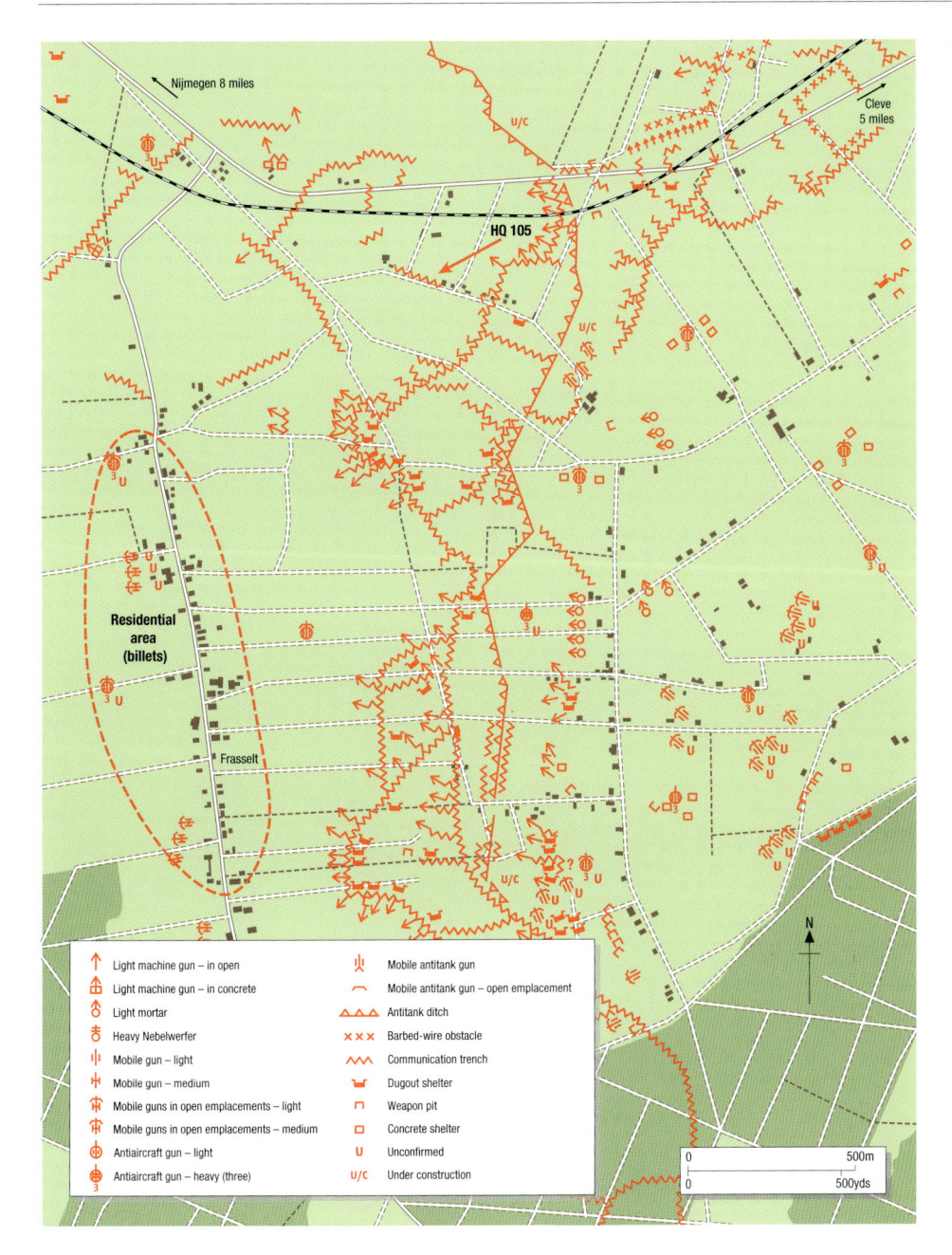

PROTECTING THE HOMELAND – GERMANY'S BORDER DEFENCES

Battalion defence sector, Scharnhorst-Stellung, Reichswald, February 1945.

the four-year West Wall programme of 1936–40. Another major aspect of the West Wall enhancement was the improvement of anti-tank positions, since tanks and other AFVs had become a far more central focus in land combat tactics in the decade after the West Wall's original conception in the mid-1930s. Hitler issued a 'Sofort Aktion Panzerabwehr' (Immediate Action Tank Defence) directive to give additional priority to this issue,

109

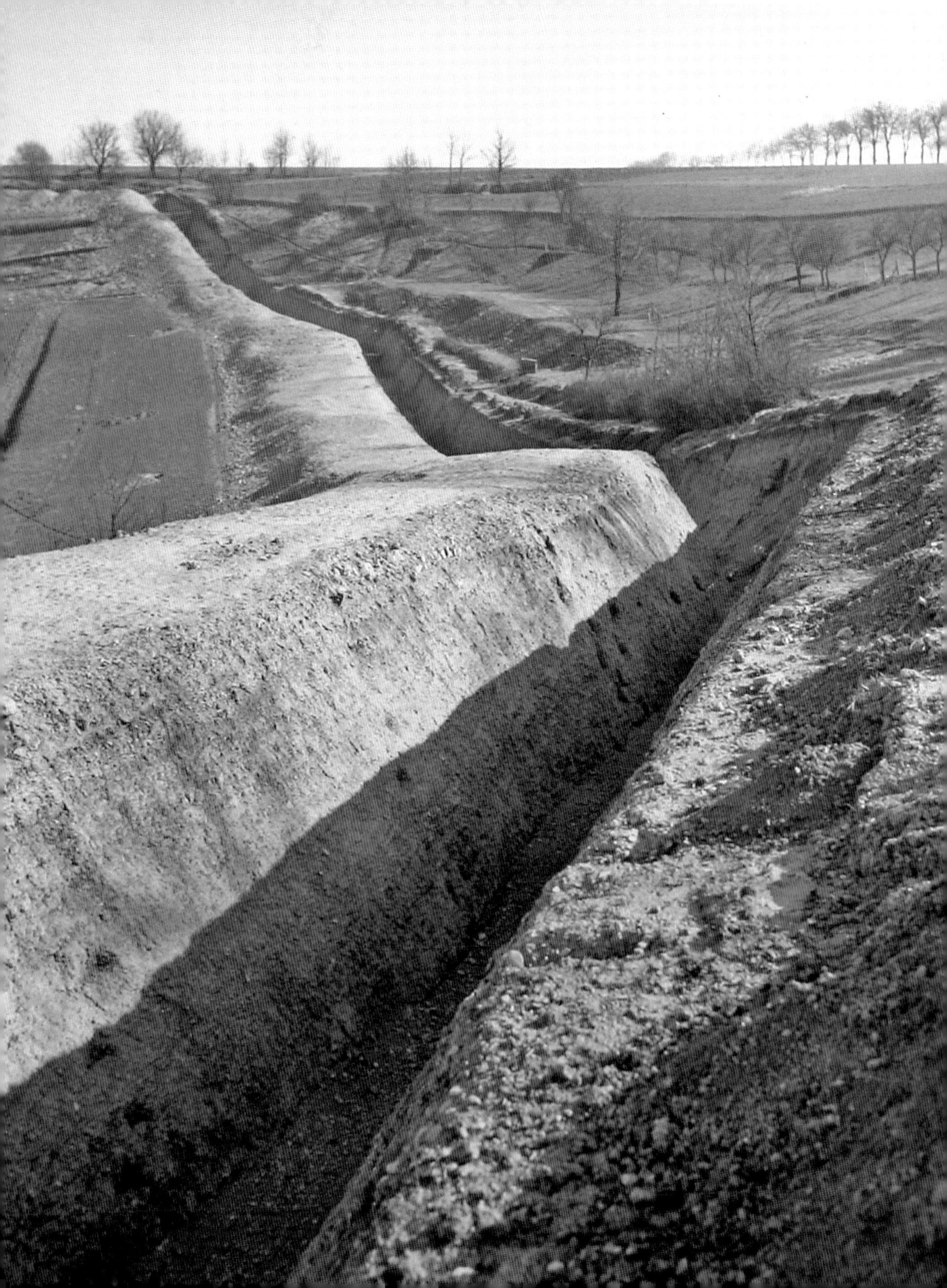

which is covered in more detail below. Besides conventional anti-tank guns, the advent of anti-tank rockets such as the Panzerfaust and Panzerschreck was integral to the new fortification plans. The new weapons provided fresh opportunities for infantry to go tank-hunting. There was a tactical synergy between these infantry weapons and anti-tank obstacles. Anti-tank obstacles such as dragon's teeth, mines, road barriers and anti-tank ditches could slow the tanks and force them into predictable channels where they could be destroyed at close range using the new anti-tank rockets.

OPPOSITE: One of the most common elements of the West-Stellung created with civilian labour was the many miles of Panzerabwehrgraben anti-tank ditches, like this barrier near Piramasens in the Saarpfalz region photographed on 22 March 1945. (NARA)

ARMING THE WEST-STELLUNG

The West Wall had been thoroughly stripped of weapons for the Atlantic Wall programme, and so there was a desperate need for weapons. At the beginning of October 1944, the three border Wehrkreise had about 1,940 machine guns, but the existing bunkers required 5,120. In September 1944, all Luftwaffe, Kriegsmarine and OT units east of the Rhine were ordered to turn in 100 per cent of their machine guns and 90 per cent of rifles; those between the Rhine and the West Wall were to give up 50 per cent. The principal types of machine guns allotted to the West-Stellung were the World War I MG08 and the newer MG34. Some Luftwaffe MG151s were adapted to the fortification role and a programme was begun to permit the use of the common MG42 machine gun in embrasures originally designed for the MG34, which had a smaller barrel.

As we have seen, the West Wall rejuvenation's most pressing need was for anti-tank guns. The existing West Wall PaK bunkers had been configured around the 3.7cm PaK 36 or in later cases, Czech 4.7m guns. These were obsolete but in any case often had been removed. In September 1944, Oberst Hermann Öhmichen from the Generalinspekteur der Panzertruppe office was assigned to determine if the existing West Wall anti-tank bunkers could be rearmed with 7.5cm guns. A survey of about 700 West Wall anti-tank bunkers found that about 200 weren't worth the effort since their guns were intended for short-range flanking fire. Of the remainder, about 335 were potential candidates for conversion to 7.5cm PaK 40 guns. Ideally, the bunkers needed a new armoured embrasure for the gun; these were difficult to manufacture, transport, and install so in the event only about 100 bunkers were rearmed with the 7.5cm PaK 40. Since the old West Wall bunkers could not easily accommodate the larger guns a series of new gun bunkers were developed, patterned on the types used in the Atlantic Wall such as the Regelbau 703 Schartenstand (Construction Standard 703 Embrasure Bunker) for the 8.8cm gun.

A novel source of anti-tank weapons for the West-Stellung emerged after Allied strategic bombing of German Panzer factories made several hundred guns redundant. Hitler became enamoured of the concept of quickly turning these into improvised

OVERLEAF: Betonfundament für SKL IIa mit 8.8cm PaK 43/3 Jagdpanther, Festungs-PaK-Verband XIV, Ruhr-Stellung, February 1945. This is a typical example of a fieldworks gun pit for a Pantherkanone. It consists of a simple earthwork pit, wide enough to permit easy gun traverse and with enough room for the crew and ammunition, with a concrete pad constructed in the centre. (Adam Hook © Osprey Publishing)

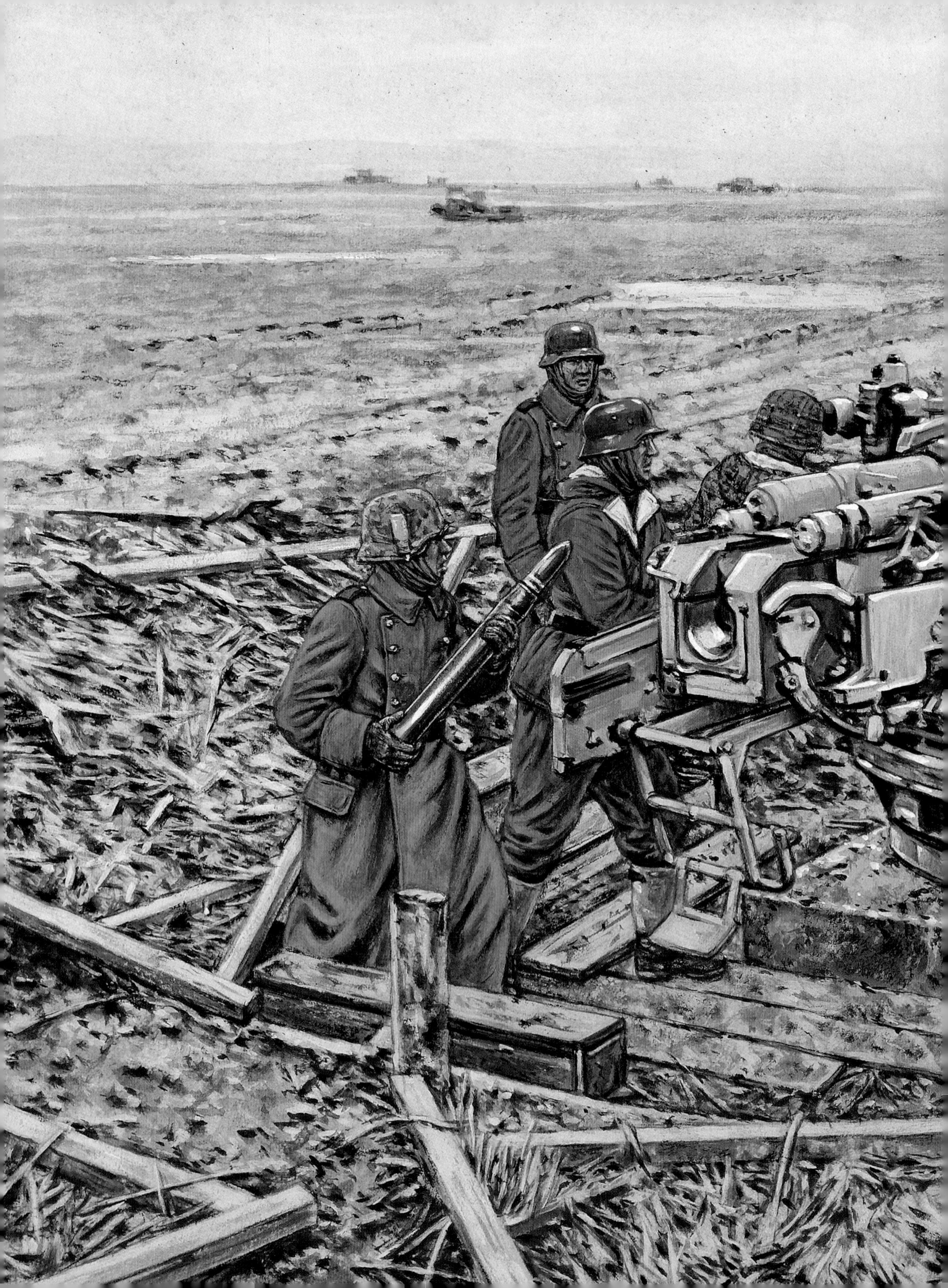

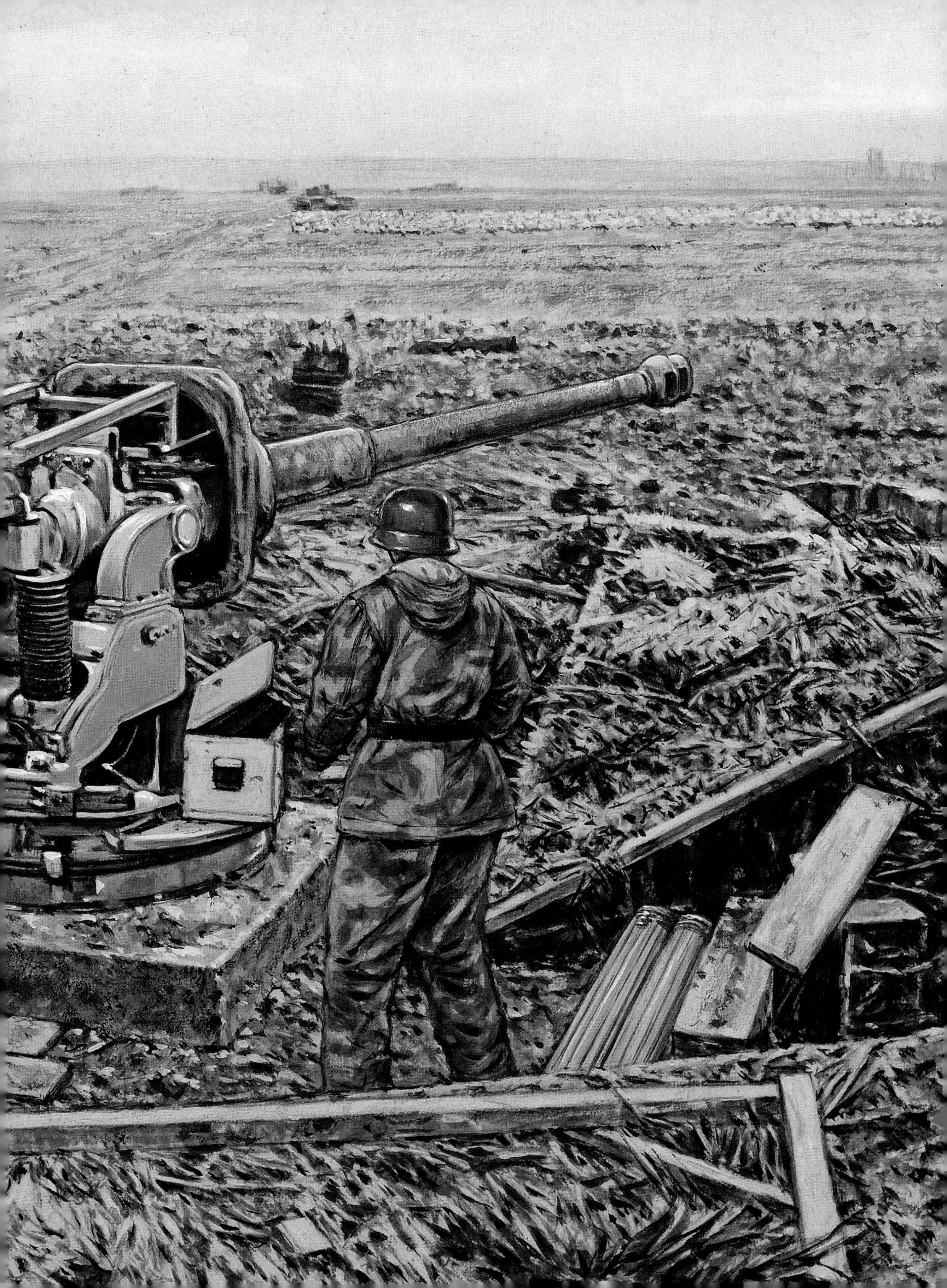

The West Wall bunkers in Steinfeld were camouflaged to look like ordinary rural buildings. This German propaganda photo was taken on 3 January 1940 and shows an artillery bunker armed with a World War I vintage FK 16 7.7cm gun in Steinfeld, camouflaged to resemble a barn. (NARA)

anti-tank guns to create a defensive belt behind the main line of resistance to stop any Allied tank penetrations. These weapons were assigned to special Festungs-PaK-Verbande (fortification anti-tank units), and a 16 September Führer Directive specifically forbade the deployment of these units in the frontlines. These new formations were raised in the border Wehrkreise and varied in size, some only consisting of a staff to administer existing gun batteries, while others were relatively large with several new gun companies, each with a dozen anti-tank guns.

In the rush to arm these new formations, a variety of simple pedestal mounts, or Sockellafetten (SK-L), were hastily designed and manufactured by Rheinmetall-Borsig's plants in Düsseldorf and Unterlüss. Ideally, these could be bolted to pads inside the new PaK bunkers, but the difficulty of creating enough new bunkers meant that they were usually deployed in open revetments. This had obvious shortcomings, so later batches of guns were mounted instead on a simple cruciform steel mounting, the Behelfskreuzlafette (improvised cruciform mount), which could be repositioned if necessary. Some Festung troops nicknamed these new weapons Pantherkanonen (Panther guns), even though none came from Panther tanks.

By late 1944 about 2,000 pedestal guns had been ordered, including 400 5cm KwK 39/1 Bordkanone aircraft guns, 700 short 7.5cm L/24 guns (KwK 51 and KwK 67), 250 long-barrelled 7.5cm PaK 40s, 450 Kwk 43/3 Jagdpanther 8.8cm guns and 50 8.8cm Kwk 43 King-Tiger guns with plans to complete them by mid-March 1945. In addition, more than 500 regular 7.5cm PaK 40 guns on the normal wheeled carriage were earmarked for mounting in bunkers and special fieldworks. Not all of these weapons were directed to the West-Stellung, as a similar fortification effort was underway in eastern Germany to deal with the threat of the Red Army; most of the short-barrelled 7.5cm guns were earmarked for the east while the 8.8cm guns were allocated to the west.

The first large-scale deployment of the fortification anti-tank guns took place in October 1944 in the construction of the Vosges and Belfort Gap defences, when an initial allotment of 58 Pantherkanonen was made. The Panther-Stellung in the Netherlands also received some of the early shipments of these weapons. By the end of November 1944 over 80 of the Jagdpanther guns had been deployed on concrete pads, but over 30 were lost when the Vosges defences were overrun. The loss of Strasbourg on 25 November 1944 put the Allies firmly on the Rhine and greatly alarmed Hitler. This prompted a Führer Directive on 28 November 1944 calling for a crash programme for anti-tank defence (the Sofort-Aktion Panzerabwehr directive). Hitler insisted that the Upper Rhine and Saar fronts receive special attention, with at least 100 Jagdpanther guns going to the Saar defensive line from Merzig to the Rhine and 90 more along the Upper Rhine.

The anti-tank guns were not evenly spread along the West-Stellung, but concentrated in the most vital sectors. For example, during the construction of the Panther-Stellung in the Netherlands in September 1944, five batteries of 8.8cm guns were provided. During the reinforcement of the Ruhr-Stellung in January and February 1945, about 160 8.8cm guns were emplaced. About 300 anti-tank guns were emplaced during the Upper Rhine defence effort in late 1944 to early 1945, mainly in the Germersheim–Karlsruhe area. Besides the dedicated pedestal guns, the defensive lines were amplified by the use of surplus anti-aircraft guns, especially the ubiquitous 8.8cm Flak and captured Soviet 85mm guns.

One of the principal problems in reinforcing the Rhine defences was the shortage of heavy artillery. The disastrous summer 1944 campaign had led to the loss of nearly all

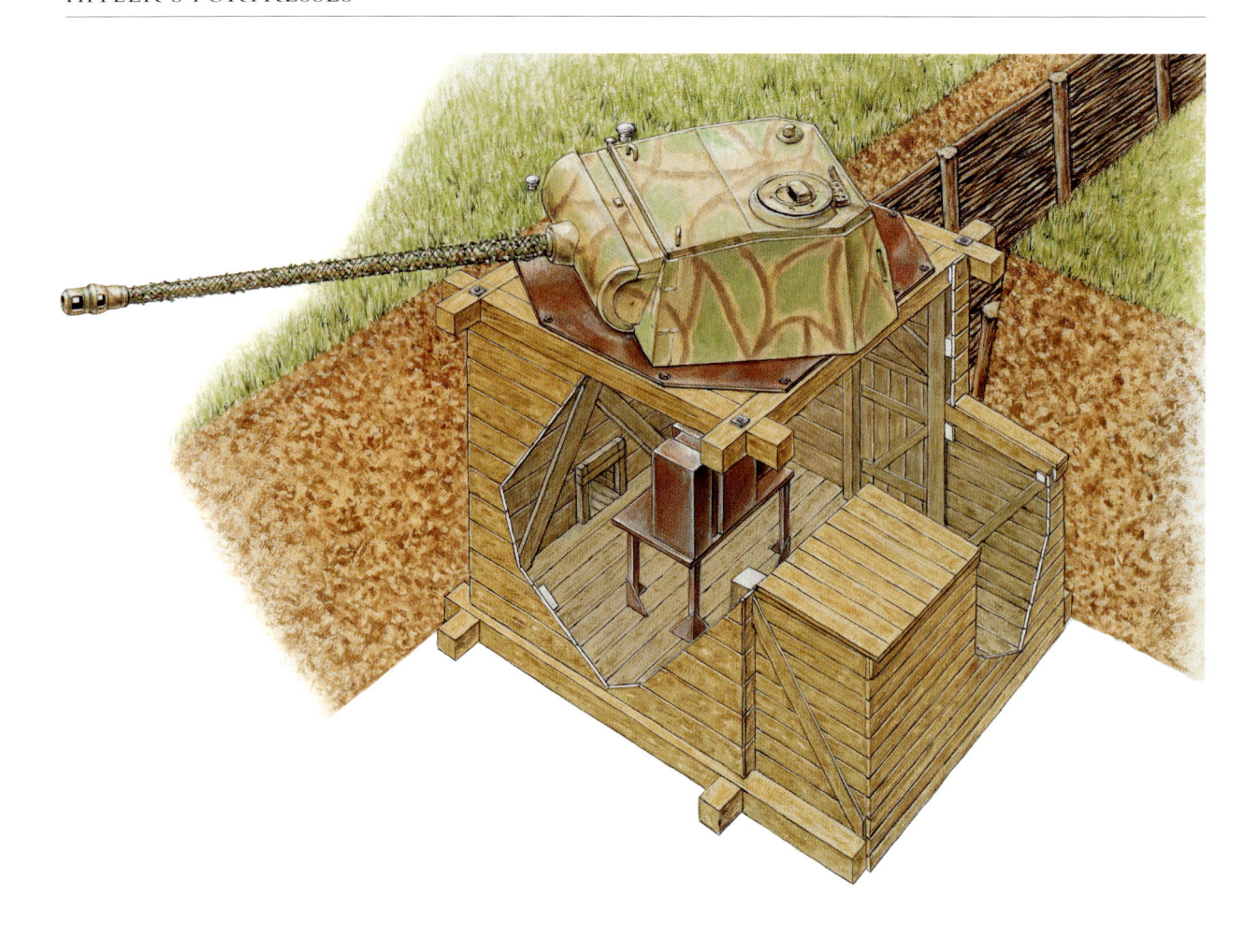

ABOVE: Holzstand für Pantherturm, Festungs-PaK-Verband XII, Saarpfalz, March 1945. Lack of time and resources led to the use of improvised wooden substructures (Holzunderstände) for many of the Pantherturme that were emplaced in early 1945, also nicknamed as *Schnelleinbau* or 'fast construction'. These timber structures were deep enough to provide elementary crew quarters including a heater, as well as a niche in the rear for ammunition storage. (Adam Hook © Osprey Publishing)

of the 4,900 field guns deployed in France and the Low Countries, as well as the 3,800 large-calibre guns positioned on the Atlantic Wall. Besides these many field guns, the Atlantic Wall had also consumed vast amounts of anti-tank guns in the 3.7–5cm range. An October 1944 survey in the border Wehrkreise located 932 field guns of 41 different types; this inventory was reinforced by guns from districts further inside Germany. These weapons armed the Festungs-Artillerie-Abteilungen (fortress artillery units) that were gradually assigned to the West-Stellung. By early 1945 there were 35 of these deployed along the West-Stellung, substantially reinforcing local firepower. Indeed, in the most heavily contested sectors of the West-Stellung the Festungs-Artillerie often doubled or tripled the artillery firepower available to infantry divisions. In spite of their designation, very few of these batteries were deployed in concrete fortifications as there were only 256 artillery casemates in the West Wall; by 1945 the designation essentially meant that the formation had no organic transportation and so was immobile.

RHINE PANZER-STELLUNG

The problems of fortifying the pedestal guns and the vulnerability of the guns mounted in open revetments prompted consideration of other alternatives. Surplus French tank turrets had been widely used on the Atlantic Wall, and a design based on the Panther tank turret had been developed in 1943. The Pantherturme proved to be a better anti-tank fortification than bunkers since the gun and crew were far better protected than when in bunkers with open embrasures, they offered complete traverse compared to the limited traverse from bunkers, and they were small and inconspicuous targets. There were two sources of Panther turrets: they were either cannibalized from damaged or worn-out tanks, or custom-produced Ostwallturme (East Wall turrets) with thickened roof armour. There were plans to produce a hundred Ostwallturme a month by late 1943, but the low priority afforded to fortification work meant that this plan was reduced to only 15 a month by the end of January 1944. The Pantherturm was deployed initially in Italy in April 1944 and proved to be highly effective in the defence of the Gothic Line. Although better known for its role in Italy, the Pantherturm was much more extensively used in the Rhine-Stellung, though with far poorer results.

The original configuration, called the Pantherturm I, was deployed on a pre-fabricated two-storey underground steel structure developed by the OT to speed construction in remote locations. A total of 143 were manufactured in this configuration, of which 119 were allotted to the west. As an alternative, a conventional reinforced concrete bunker was designed in May 1944, called Regelbau 687. There were significant problems building these complicated structures in remote mountain areas such as the Vosges and on the Rhine plains due to cold and wet weather. A simpler underground timber bunker was developed locally among the Rhine-Festungs Pioniere in November 1944.

In the Vosges defensive line, 49 Pantherturme were allotted by November 1944. However, the Allied offensive struck before any of the turrets were completed, and only two concrete bunkers had been poured. At least one turret and some other components were lost. In the Aachen area, work started in September 1944 with plans to deploy 40 Pantherturme with 17 on concrete bunkers and the rest on steel. Three fortification companies were deployed in this sector to man the turrets: Festungs-Pantherturm-Kompanien 1201, 1202 and 1203. Due to the intense fighting with the US Army along the Ruhr-Stellung, 20 of the steel sub-structures were overrun prior to installation and the programme was stalled. As a result, the programme shifted its focus and planted the turrets further east along the new Erft-Stellung. A combination of the weather and combat conditions delayed the progress of the programme. At least two turrets were hastily emplaced on the Ruhr-Stellung in late January 1945, but one quickly flooded. By mid-February only one was ready for combat and the other 30 sites under construction were overrun during Operation *Grenade* in late February 1945. The seven surviving turrets were ready for action by early March 1945, though some were missing components. One was hastily emplaced in Siegburg in the suburbs south of Cologne.

The Pantherturm could also be deployed on a Regelbau 687 concrete bunker. This is the original trial bunker at the Hillersleben Proving Ground and it uses a recycled Panther Ausf. A turret rather than the dedicated Ostwallturm. (MHI)

The Saar region was the third area to receive the Pantherturme, starting in late December 1944. These were built in two clusters, a group of 11 for Festungs-Pantherturm-Kompanie 1204 in the Hardt mountains north of Saarbrücken and 20 more for Festungs-Pantherturm-Kompanie 1205 covering the Wissembourg Gap (Weissenburger Senke, or Zabener Senke) on the west bank of the Rhine. When Operation *Undertone* was launched on 15 March by the Allied 6th Army Group, 23 of the 31 turrets were combat-ready. Details of their combat history are lacking and they were quickly overrun in the late March 1945 fighting.

After the failure to deploy the Pantherturm in Alsace, Festungs-Pionier-Kommandeur I shifted its attention to the eastern bank of the Rhine as part of the Black Forest fortification effort. A total of 30 Pantherturm IIs were emplaced on wooden sub-structures in March 1945 in spite of lingering problems with the supply of parts. They were manned by Festungs-Pantherturm-Kompanien 1207 and 1208 but there is little evidence regarding their combat use in the 1945 fighting against the French 1ère Armée.

Besides the Pantherturme, a large number of obsolete PzKpfw I and PzKpfw II turrets were modified for fortification use. Improved PzKpfw I turrets were designated as Festungs-Panzer-Drehturm 4803 and 143 were assigned to the west. Festungs-Pionier-Kommandeur XIX allotted 55 of these to the Eifel and 40 for the Lower Rhine, but only 44 had been completed by February 1945. The larger PzKpfw II turrets were modified, becoming the Festungs-Panzer-Drehturm 4804, substituting a 3.7cm gun. A total of 60 of these were deployed in the west, often mounted on Regelbau 238 bunkers; at least 25 were lost by February 1945. Another armoured turret used in the Rhine defensive lines was the MG-Panzernest, a small armoured steel pillbox first deployed in Italy and Russia in 1943 as a means to quickly build up a defensive position. It was small enough to be towed into position using a normal transport truck, and after a shallow pit was dug it could be emplaced by a few men with no special equipment. A total of 50 MG-Panzerneste were shipped to the West-Stellung, all for the Armeeoberkommando 19 (AOK 19; Army High Command 19) sector on the Upper Rhine, but many were lost in November 1944 when the Vosges defences were overrun.

RESISTING THE ALLIES

This section surveys the Rhine defences from north to south, and how they coped with the Allied push from the west. In the north, Heeresgruppe H had been added on 10 November 1944 to take over responsibilities for most of the Netherlands opposite Montgomery's British-Canadian 21st Army Group and thereby freeing up the

HITLER'S FORTRESSES

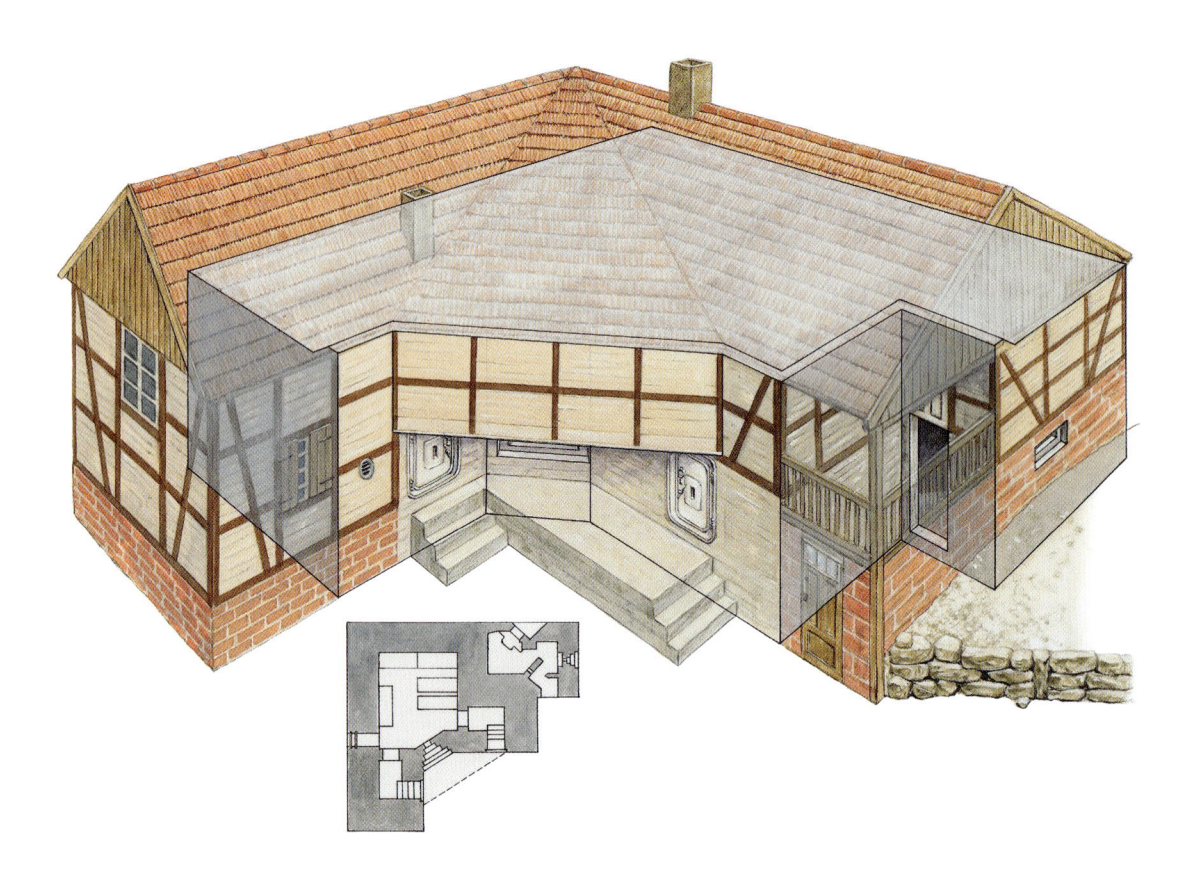

ABOVE: Unterstand 230/10, Einheit Wagner, 905. Volksgrenadier-Division, Steinfeld, March 1945. When the Wissembourg Gap was fortified as part of the West Wall in 1938–39, the village of Steinfeld received an especially elaborate treatment. This particular type of bunker design was one of the most common in the West Wall, with over 3,000 constructed. It was intended to accommodate a standard squad/section (Gruppe) of ten men and also included a fighting compartment (Kampfraum) with two machine-gun posts. (Adam Hook © Osprey Publishing)

neighbouring Heeresgruppe B to prepare for the Ardennes offensive. Heeresgruppe B was the largest of the three army groups in the most critical sector, from the Lower Rhine near the Netherlands through the Eifel and along the Rhine through the Saar as far as Trier; it faced General Omar Bradley's American 12th Army Group. Heeresgruppe G's sector started at Trier in the Saarpfalz and ran through Alsace and the Black Forest to the Swiss border, facing General Jacob Devers' Franco-American 6th Army Group.

Lower Rhine defences: Heeresgruppe H

In the wake of the Operation *Market Garden* attack towards Arnhem there was some concern that the British 21st Army Group was intending to break into Germany by a northern route, and so a new defensive line, the Panther-Stellung, was created in October 1944 to block a northward drive along the eastern side of the Ijsselmeer. In the event, the Panther-Stellung protected against a contingency that did not occur. The 30 September 1944 Führer Directive ordered the construction of a second defensive line behind the Dutch West Wall extension between the Ems and the Rhine on the German side of the frontier.

During December 1944 and January 1945, the Ardennes battles to the south provided Heeresgruppe H with the time to deepen defences for an anticipated British winter offensive out of the Nijmegen area south-eastward towards Wesel on the Rhine. The West Wall was not strong in this area so attention focused on a sequence of north–south blocking positions: the Kellenriegel through the Reichswald, followed by the Niers-Ruhr-Stellung stretching from Kleve southwards towards München-Gladbach (now called Mönchengladbach). The defensive lines played a significant role during Operation *Blockbuster*, the February–March 1945 Rhineland offensive. The final defensive positions in the Rhine foreground were a series of bridgehead defences near the main Rhine cities. Brückenkopf Wesel was constructed in the bend on the western bank of the Rhine. This was reached by the First Canadian Army on 10 March 1945 and reduced in conjunction with the neighbouring Ninth US Army.

The most extensive Heeresgruppe H bridgehead was the Erweiterter Brückenkopf Duisberg-Düsseldorf (Reinforced Bridgehead Duisberg-Düsseldorf), which was intended to shield the Ruhr industrial zone. This consisted of an outer defensive line stretching from the Rhine near Dinslaken down past Krefeld and finally to Düsseldorf. Inside this outer belt, each of the four major river-crossing areas received their own defensive lines: Brückenkopfen Homberg, Duisberg, Ürdingen and Düsseldorf. The Ruhr bridgehead line stretched across the boundaries of both Heeresgruppen H and B. This was struck by the Ninth US Army's Operation *Grenade*, starting on 23 February 1945, which penetrated the Düsseldorf bridgehead by 1 March and reached the Rhine on 5 March. The final blows in this sector were Operations *Varsity* and *Plunder*, a combined airborne and river-crossing operation on 24 March, which broke through the Rhine defences around Wesel.

Lower Rhine and Eifel defences: Heeresgruppe B

Heeresgruppe B had the most extensive and complicated defensive line in north-western Germany. This sector was especially important since it blocked access to the Ruhr industrial region and shielded the preparations for the planned Ardennes offensive. It was the site of the most intensive fighting along the former West Wall in the autumn of 1944, dubbed the Siegfried Line Campaign in official US Army histories.

This area included most of the old Festungsdientstelle Düren of the West Wall and stretched from the Düsseldorf bridgehead southward to the Trier Flankenstellung (flanking position) on the Germany–Luxembourg border. Aachen was shielded by two layers of West Wall defences: the initial Scharnhost-Stellung, which started at the border, and the Schill-Stellung east of the city. This sector was the initial focus of Bradley's 12th Army Group attacks towards the Rhine. The initial border defensive line was breached almost immediately and the city was taken in October 1944. After capturing Aachen, the First US Army had attempted to push up through the Stolberg Corridor past the Hürtgen Forest to seize the Roer dams. As soon as the West Wall was penetrated in September extensive efforts began in order to create new fortification lines to prevent the rest of the West Wall from being rolled up on either flank. This started with a complicated series of switch positions in the southern portion of the defensive line near Monschau and the Hürtgen Forest. The new Ruhr-Stellung, sometimes called the Schlieffen-Stellung, was created along the Roer near Düren and continually reinforced in October–November 1944. One of the major impediments to the construction of defences in this area was the unusually rainy autumn weather and the shallow water tables near the many rivers. On the other hand, the Wehrmacht was able to flood some lowlands deliberately as a means of blocking and channelling the US attacks.

Immediately behind the Ruhr-Stellung was the C-Stellung, which stretched about 80km from the Cologne suburbs to Wittlich, where it bifurcated into the Kyll- and Wittlich-Stellungen. A major PaK front was created behind the Ruhr-Stellung with roughly 160 8.8cm guns on concrete pads. Behind the C-Stellung was the Erft-Stellung from Düsseldorf to Bad Godesberg, and within this defence sector were three large bridgeheads: Brückenkopfen Düsseldorf, Köln (Cologne) and Bonn. To further strengthen the defence, several major blocking positions were also erected: the Rheindahlen-Riegelstellung north of München-Gladbach and the Euskirchen-Riegelstellung west of Bonn.

The Eifel region opposite the Ardennes in Belgium had an extensive section of the West Wall still intact, and this had been reinforced sequentially by the Prüm-Stellung and Kyll-Stellung along these rivers. These lines came under attack in February 1945 after the failure of the Ardennes offensive and the subsequent push by Hodges' First US Army and Patton's Third US Army into the Eifel region. As a result, a third line, the Wittlich-Stellung emanating off the C-Stellung, was under construction in March 1945, but it was overrun before completion. This was the sector where the first major breach of the Rhine defences occurred when the First US Army captured the Ludendorff Bridge at Remagen on 7 March. The unexpected capture of this bridge provides evidence of the inherent problems in the German 1945 defence scheme. Hitler's directive to 'stand-fast on the West Wall' tied the main forces in the sector to an overextended and vulnerable defensive line. When the US 9th Armored Division penetrated the defensive line, it was able to race to the bridge much faster than the German infantry divisions in this sector could react. There was exceptionally poor coordination between the field army and the Ersatzheer rear-area formations in the sector, and the bridge had not been completely prepared for demolition. The bridge was shielded by a completely inadequate garrison of Landesschützen and Volkssturm men, who failed to contest the American advance.

The Saarland: Heeresgruppe G

The southern flank of Heeresgruppe B where it met Heeresgruppe G on the Moselle was the Trier-Flankenstellung, a traditional fortification zone for many centuries because it was the guardian of the Moselle Gate, which commanded access to the heart of Germany. The Saar-Palatinate region south-east of Luxembourg had been a traditional invasion route into Germany via the Moselle Gate, and so had an extensive array of classic fortification zones. Aside from Aachen, this was the only section of the West Wall with a double defensive line that covered Saarbrücken. Following France's defeat in 1940 Germany once again absorbed Lorraine and Alsace into the Reich, along with it the fortification zones that had been modernized by the Kaiser's army in 1870–1918 around Metz and Diedenhofen (Thionville). The Metz fortresses blocked Patton's Third Army for most of October and November 1944. German fortification efforts in this sector in 1944 were focused on amplifying the extensive West Wall fortifications along the old 1918–40 border with additional new defensive lines.

The defence in the Saarpfalz sector was awkwardly reinforced by the Maginot Line fortifications on the former French side of the border. The Maginot Line forts were not ideal for protecting the German frontier since obviously they were oriented in the other direction, but many weapons had full traverse and numerous infantry shelters were useful regardless of the original intent. German engineers conducted an extensive survey of these fortifications in 1941 and conceived a scheme to reorient the defences to protect the German frontier; these studies remained on paper. The only major change was the addition of underground cabling linking the old French communication system into neighbouring German networks. In 1944 Hitler ordered another survey to determine which complexes could be useful and he ordered that any that were ill-suited to incorporation into the German defensive lines should be blown up. Like the West Wall, the Maginot Line was cannibalized for weapons and components for the Atlantic Wall. The Maginot Line forts in this area were partly reoccupied by the Wehrmacht in November 1944. The Maginot Line from Metz to Hagenau saw extensive fighting in December 1944 during the Seventh US Army's drive into the Low Vosges, with the Bitche ensemble around this old fortress city resisting the initial US attacks.

With the start of the Ardennes offensive on 16 December 1944, Heeresgruppe G conducted a diversionary offensive, Operation *Nordwind*, which started on 1 January 1945. Some Maginot bunkers that had fallen into American hands in the Hagenau sector were attacked and recaptured in this offensive. When the offensive was crushed in late January 1945, AOK 1 was deployed along the Maginot Line with the old West Wall behind it. There were extensive West Wall fortifications around Saarbrücken and in the

This is a view of the Krab MG-Panzernest in the vertical position, showing the machine-gun embrasure in the front. This is a captured example sent back to the Aberdeen Proving Ground for technical evaluation, probably from those captured in Alsace in November 1944 during the Vosges campaign. (APG)

INFANTRY-SECTION TRENCH, 1945

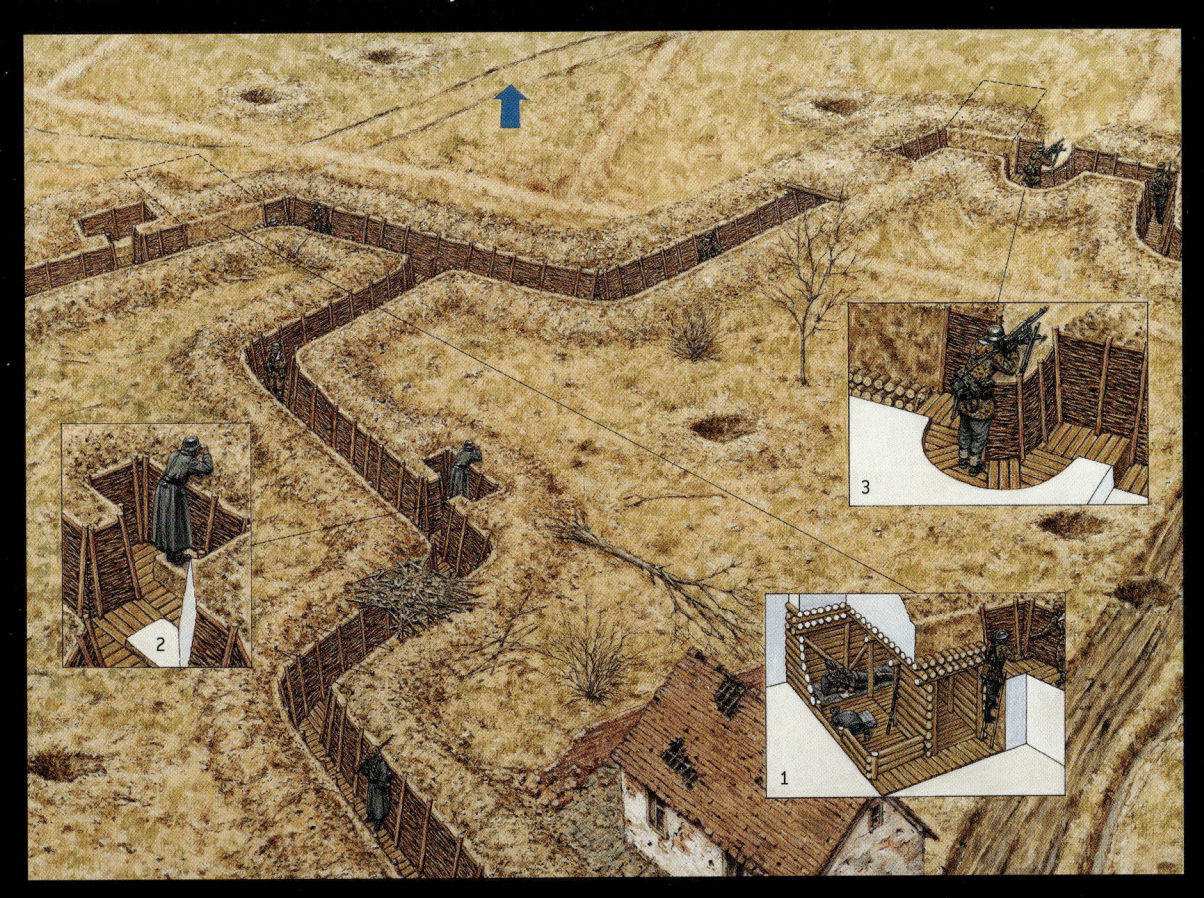

This illustration is based on a Heeresgruppe G booklet issued to troops in 1944–45. This is a typical trench (Graben) for a Gruppe (section/squad), in which a 1944 Volksgrenadier rifle platoon would have one NCO and eight enlisted men. The zigzag shape was to limit the avenues of fire should enemy troops enter the trenches. The section frontage was typically 30–40m and it would be part of a larger platoon and company position. Two Holzunterschlupfe für 3 Männer (three-man wooden bunkers; see inset 1) are built into the front of the line for temporary shelter; deeper in, the positions would usually be more substantial with larger timber bunkers (B-Stellen aus Rundholz) for resting in. This section contains two Führung-Stellungen (command positions; see inset 2), the forward one for the assistant squad leader, to serve as the main section observation post, and one slightly deeper in the position for the squad leader, to permit him to oversee the position. These positions typically could accommodate up to three men. On the right side of the position is a dedicated stand for light or heavy machine guns (Feuerstellung für leichtes oder schweres Maschinengewehr). This typically included a platform for mounting the MG42 tripod in cases where a heavy machine gun was in use (see inset 3). (Adam Hook © Osprey Publishing)

Wissembourg Gap, and these had been substantially improved under the West-Stellung programme. Due to the heavy casualties suffered in the *Nordwind* offensive, AOK 1 was poorly prepared to resist the inevitable American assault. Forces were so thin that the Maginot Line and West Wall defences were manned at a level well under half of the intended strength, with single divisions holding areas of frontline meant for two.

The attack against AOK 1 in the Saar came from two directions: an assault by Patton's Third US Army from the west and by General Alexander Patch's Seventh US Army from the south. The push into the Saar began against the Orscholz-Riegel on 13 January 1945, hoping to crack open the West Wall defensive line. The US infantry gradually ground through the weakly manned German defences, and by mid-February were able to take the Trier defences from behind, helped in no small measure by its anaemic Volkssturm defence. This gained access behind Saarbrücken's double West Wall defensive line, which AOK 1 engineers attempted to close with blocking positions fortified with Pantherturme and 8.8cm anti-tank guns.

In the south, the dense line on the Alsatian plains south of the Wissembourg Gap was still located along the trace of the Maginot Line, with a reinforced West Wall behind. These defences were every bit as dense as those in Festungsdienstelle Düren, which had held up the US Army for many months in September 1944 to February 1945, but the troops behind the defences were substantially weaker. Once the US offensive began on 12 March 1945, the AOK 1 positions quickly became untenable. Hitler had imposed a 'stand-fast or die on the West Wall' directive, and German units that obeyed were quickly infiltrated and trapped as the US forces raced to the Rhine. The Wehrmacht defences in the Saarpfalz were overrun in a week's time, dubbed the 'Rhine Rat Race' by US troops. Once past the fortification lines, the bridgehead defences on the west bank of the Rhine were completely inadequate due to the lack of sufficient troops, numbering a handful of infantry battalions on a front more than 40km wide. During the last week of March 1945, the Rhine was breached from Frankfurt to Mannheim by VIII Corps in the Rhine Gorge south of Koblenz, north of Oppenheim by XII Corps, at Worms by XV Corps and at Mainz by XX Corps.

Alsace: Heeresgruppe G

The fourth Rhine defence sector, the Upper Rhine under the control of Wehrkreis V, was shielded on the west bank of the Rhine by the Vosges mountains in Alsace. Prior to 1940 Alsace had been heavily fortified by France as part of the Maginot Line, but these fortifications played little role in the 1944–45 defence schemes. A plan to reinforce this sector had been discussed at a meeting in Wiesbaden on 5 April 1944 with the various fortification staffs, and a defensive line was planned by the Vosges survey staff (Erkundungsstab Vogesen) of the Kommandantur der Befestigungen Oberrhein. Berlin showed little enthusiasm for the scheme and resources were limited because of the heavy commitment of the OT to the Atlantic Wall.

The situation changed dramatically in August 1944 with the Operation *Dragoon* landings in southern France and the subsequent retreat of Heeresgruppe G up the Rhône Valley towards the Upper Rhine Valley. The April 1944 plans were dusted off and the small survey staff was enlarged into the Höhere Kommando der Befestigungen Vogesen (Vosges Senior Fortification Command). Fortification work began in the Vosges using a labour draft, starting on 1 September 1944. Hitler held out high hopes for the Vosges as an impregnable defensive line and the fortification plan was formally supported by a Führer Directive on 27 September 1944. The Vosges defences were intended to consist of three distinct elements. An initial defensive line, variously called the Vor-Vogesenstellung (Vosges Foothills Line) or Vogesen-Randstellung (Vosges Perimeter Line) was located on the western slopes of the High Vosges mountains. These were primarily focused on sealing key mountain passes providing access to the Rhine Valley. It was reinforced by the Vogesen-Stellung (Main Vosges Line), also called the Vogesen-Kammstellung (Vosges Ridge Line), deeper in the Vosges mountains. No army in modern times had succeeded in attacking over the Vosges, so this defensive line was expected to be highly effective. The major concern was the Belfort Gap in the south. This was the traditional route into the Rhine Valley and allowed an attacker to advance into the Upper Rhine basin, avoiding the formidable barrier of the Vosges mountains. The Belfort Gap defences consisted of three sequential blocking positions – the Belfort-, Mühlhausen- and Kolmar-Riegelstellungen – and two substantial bridgeheads – Brückenkopfen Neuenberg and Breisach. The city of Strasbourg was declared a Festung, and received an extensive defensive belt. This sector was held by AOK 19.

The Allied 6th Army Group attacked the Vosges defences in late October, before they had been completed. The Seventh US Army overcame both Vosges mountain defensive lines and debouched onto the Alsatian plains in mid-November 1944, while the French 1ère Armée penetrated the Belfort Gap and reached the Rhine on 19 November 1944.

The comprehensive and unexpected failure of the Vosges defences created a crisis in Berlin since it posed the first opportunity for the Allies to cross the Rhine. As a result, Hitler issued his 28 November Directive, freeing up precious anti-tank guns and other scarce resources to bolster the Rhine defences. The commander of the 6th Army Group, Lieutenant General Jacob Devers, intended to bounce the Rhine near Rastaat in late November, but was ordered instead to continue northward on the west bank into the Low Vosges to relieve pressure on the flank of Patton's Third US Army.

While these schemes unfolded on the western side of the Rhine, engineers of Wehrkreis V began the first extensive fortification effort on the eastern bank of the

HITLER'S FORTRESSES

The Krab MG-Panzernest was designed as a quick way to emplace a machine-gun pillbox with minimal engineering support. The armoured cupola was delivered upside down with a wooden towing limber connected to a machine-gun embrasure in the front. After a suitable trench was dug, the crew would simply tip over the contraption into the hole. These examples were intended to be deployed in the Vogesen-Stellung near the Saales Pass, but were captured by the Seventh US Army in November 1944 before they could be deployed. (NARA)

Rhine. The West Wall in this area was located immediately along the eastern bank of the Rhine and was modernized as the Oberrhein-Stellung (Upper Rhine Line) with additional anti-tank-gun defences. In contrast to the Heeresgruppen H and B defences further north, Hitler permitted an extensive fortification effort in the Black Forest on the eastern side of the Rhine due to the unexpected Allied threat on the Rhine in that area. This sector was the only one in Germany with an existing deep defensive line, the Neckar-Enz-Stellung east of Karlsruhe and the Wetterau-Main-Tauber-Stellung (WMTS) following those rivers to the east of Frankfurt. These two programmes had begun in 1934 and pre-dated the better-known West Wall as a means to block a French attack. The late 1944 defensive programme was called the Hochrhein-Stellung (High Rhine Line) and consisted of a sequence of defensive lines in the mountains east of the Rhine, starting with the Schwarzwald-Randstellung (Black Forest Perimeter Line), followed by the Schwarzwald-Kammstellung (Black Forest Ridge Line). Deeper still

PROTECTING THE HOMELAND – GERMANY'S BORDER DEFENCES

AMERICAN TECHNIQUES FOR ASSAULTING FORTIFIED POSITIONS

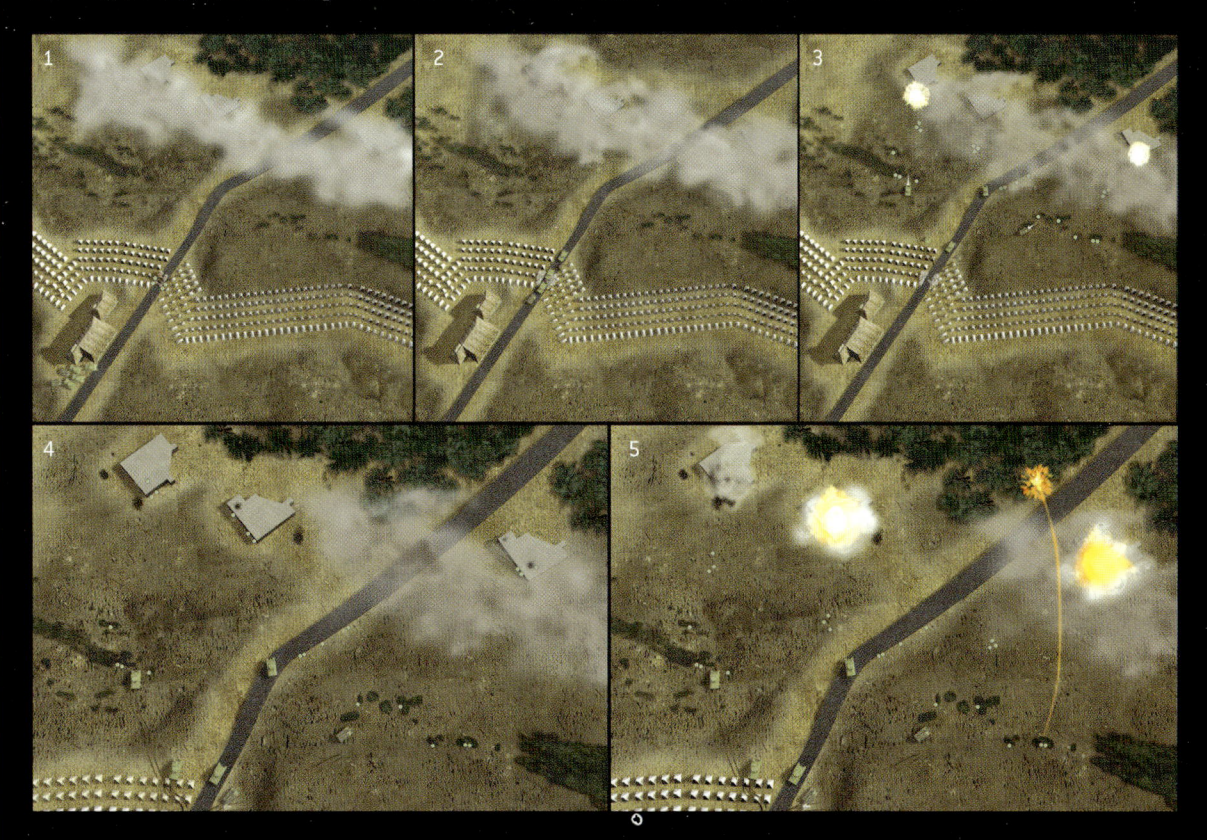

1) Artillery and mortars firing high-explosive shells are used to suppress the pillboxes covering the dragon's teeth, or smoke is fired to obscure the defenders' view. Engineers then blast or dismantle the 'gates' that block the roads. 2) Infantry, engineers and armour move forward, covered by direct fire from artillery and mortars. Once the infantry platoon and engineer sections are in place and the armour in a position to offer direct fire support the barrage is lifted. 3) Tanks, tank destroyers and self-propelled guns engage the pillboxes targeting the apertures and doors. This barrage allows the infantry and engineers to get in close to their target. 4) Following a signal the direct fire is lifted and the assault teams attack covered by fire from men of their own unit. The assault teams use pole charges through the damaged apertures or doors, or place beehive charges and/or TNT on the roof, to demolish the structure. 5) With the structure destroyed a signal is given (sometimes a coloured flare) to inform other assault teams they can now attack their targets.

With the pillbox destroyed the next in line would be unsupported by interlocking fire and would be attacked from this exposed side. As experience grew it was found to take about an hour to reduce each enemy position. Unlike their countrymen in the Pacific, the infantrymen in the European Theatre of Operations found flamethrowers to be of little use against pillboxes; the defenders would simply move to another room when under assault by such a weapon. (Chris Taylor © Osprey Publishing)

A typical log anti-tank roadblock, part of the Kyll-Stellung near Kyllberg, Germany being surmounted by troops of the US 318th Infantry Regiment, 80th Division on 9 March 1945. (NARA)

were the Donau–Neckar-Stellung (Danube–Neckar Line) from the Swiss border to Pforzheim, and, deeper still, the Schwäbische-Albstellung (Swabian-Alb Line). Besides the work along the Rhine, the 8 October 1944 Führer Directive ordered the construction of defences along the Swiss border starting north of the Swiss city of Basel and continuing down along the northern shores of Bodensee to Friedrichshafen. Work on this Alemanen-Stellung was conditional on the completion of the Vogesen-Stellung, and on 5 February 1945 construction was discontinued to free up its 11,000 workers to aid in the Upper Rhine fortification effort.

The main problem with the Upper Rhine defence scheme was not the fortification effort, but the battered state of the Army in this sector; AOK 19 was decimated in the Colmar Pocket in late January 1945 and its remnants retreated over the Rhine in February 1945 in a very depleted state. Patch's Seventh US Army, instead of jumping the Rhine at Rastatt as planned in November 1944, finally crossed the Rhine near Worms on 26 March alongside Patton's troops. The French 1ère Armée took on the task of clearing the Black Forest. Lacking sufficient engineer assault equipment, 2e Corps d'Armée avoided the heavily fortified bridgehead defences around Karlsruhe and crossed the Rhine instead between Mannheim and Karlsruhe, starting on March 30. The defensive belt shielding Karlsruhe was avoided and the city was attacked from the north; its Volkssturm garrison was routed on 4 April. The Neckar-Enz-Stellung was outflanked from the north by the Seventh US Army above Heidelberg, and then penetrated by both American and French units during the first week of April. The French operations isolated the bulk of AOK 19 in the Black Forest, and it was enveloped and gradually overcome later in April with the new Hochrhein-Stellung lines mostly outflanked from the north.

THE RHEIN-STELLUNG

With the failure of the Ardennes offensive in January 1945 the threat greatly increased that the Allies would break through the West-Stellung and cross the Rhine. In spite of his earlier antipathy to constructing defences on the eastern bank of the Rhine, on 15 February 1945 Hitler ordered the construction of a new Rhein-Stellung from Emmerich to Karlsruhe. This was intended to shield the Ruhr industrial region and was to be amplified by an obstacle zone 30km in depth extending in the line Münster–Hamm–Hagen–Remscheid, with the strongest sector between Emmerich and Königswinter. Correspondingly, construction on the west bank of the Rhine was to be stopped. In reality, the sodden late-winter weather and the start of Allied offensives along the Ruhr in late February 1945 prevented much work on the Rhein-Stellung from ever being completed. The only area with comprehensive defences was the Black Forest, as mentioned above. Most of the other defensive lines on the eastern bank of the Rhine were rapidly overrun by Allied forces in March 1945 before they were completed.

BORDER DEFENCES ON THE EASTERN FRONT

A consideration of Germany's border defences would be incomplete without some reflection on those developed in the east. These fortifications did not quite reach the advanced state of the West Wall or the Atlantic Wall, and most of the heavy construction took place within the 1930s. During the war years on the Eastern Front, Germany was surging ahead on the offensive (1941–42), or fighting a collapsing defensive action with limited resources. Both of these conditions, plus Hitler's ambiguous mindset when it

HITLER'S FORTRESSES

came to defensive warfare, meant that the defences in the east could never stop the Soviet juggernaut bearing down on the Führer's empire. Unlike the experience on the West Wall, there would be no 'miracle on the East Wall'.

Work on permanent defences on Germany's eastern borders began in the early 1930s, even before Hitler came to power. The concentration of these defences was, naturally, along the German–Polish border, the major works being the Oder Line and Pomeranian Line. In addition, East Prussia – the most geographically isolated piece of German real estate – also began investment in defensive lines during the early 1930s, focused principally in the Heilsberg Triangle and the Samland Fortress.

The positions developed prior to Hitler's taking the German chancellorship in 1933 were of limited strength. They often consisted of tank obstacles and barbed-wire

Another example of a well-camouflaged machine-gun bunker is Stand 230/10 in Steinfeld. The machine-gun embrasure is evident in the niche below the overhang, with an armoured door on the other side. (NARA)

obstacles accented by individual troops shelters and machine-gun bunkers, the latter being of a two-level construction with multiple crenels to enable the bunker crew to deliver an all-round defence. Yet the watery and convoluted landscape of the German–Polish frontier meant that, with intelligent siting, the defences would have presented a potential invader with a serious challenge. The designers made maximum use of the landscape. For example, dams and weirs were fortified with bunkers and machine-gun posts, protecting important locations on key waterways.

Once Hitler was in power from 1933, the defences in the east – as with those in the west – received a sudden injection of investment. Much of the focus of this investment was known as the Oder–Warthe Bend (OWB), otherwise known as the East Wall. As the name suggests, the OWB ran from the River Oder in the south through to the River Warthe in the north. Work on this line began in earnest in 1934–35. Once again, the OWB maximized the value of waterways and natural features

An infantryman from the 14th Armored Division looks over the trenches outside Steinfeld following the fighting there in late March 1945. Although the commander had intended that the infantry in the town fight from these trenches, in fact they mostly remained in the bunkers during the fighting. (NARA)

Obsolete PzKpfw I turrets were recycled for fortification use by adding a thicker front armour plate as the Festung-Panzer-Drehturm 4803. A total of 143 of these were deployed in the West-Stellung, mainly in Festungsdientstelle Düren along the Roer. This particular example was captured by the US Army 30th Division during the fighting near Niederzier, part of the Ruhr-Stellung north of Düren, on 26 February 1945. (NARA)

in its defences. Rolling or sliding bridges, for example, were developed as a means of opening or closing river or stream crossings according to the tactical situation. During the second half of the 1930s, furthermore, the OWB began to receive far more substantial (both in terms of quality and numbers) fortified positions. The smaller 'C-Type' bunkers, known as 'Hindenburg Stands', were two-level rectangular brick and reinforced concrete bunkers, with the lower level serving as a personnel quarters and the upper level featuring embrasures for heavy machine guns. A field or anti-tank gun was kept in a garage in the bunker, to be wheeled out into action when necessary. In 1935, however, the OWB received numerous heavier and better protected 'B-Werke' bunkers, armed with machine guns, flamethrowers, mortars/grenade launchers and, in some instances, a 3.7cm anti-tank gun. Garrison facilities were also more substantial, and the bunkers were self-sufficient in terms of power and sanitation. The bunkers had muscular armour – the 'B-neu' version, for example, had concrete walls 2m thick, turret armour of 250mm and general armour plate of 200mm. In the important central sector of the OWB, these bunkers were also gathered together in mutually supporting groups known as Wehrgruppen (defence groups), the individual positions being connected by substantial tunnel networks. Later in the 1930s, Wehrgruppen were also established at other points along the OWB.

Thus it was that the OWB received heavy investment between 1934 and 1938. Indeed, there were even plans for huge 'A-Werke' bunkers that mounted 10.5cm artillery, although these were never realized in actuality. In fact, although the OWB received major attention and money, by 1938 many of the bunkers had not received actual weapons, a fact that angered Hitler during a visit that year. Indeed, Hitler's emerging offensive plans for Poland meant, in many ways, that the OWB was largely redundant, thus investment trailed off at the end of the 1930s.

The need for a strong defence would seem very different by the end of 1942, as Germany's collapse on the Eastern Front began in earnest. From 1943 onwards Hitler became fond of declaring areas as 'fortresses', often with scant regard for the reality on the ground. After the German defeat at Kursk in August 1943, he begrudgingly gave permission for the construction of a proper defensive network on the Eastern Front, termed the Panther–Wotan Line. On paper, the Panther–Wotan Line looked like an impressive barrier against the Soviets, starting from the Estonian Baltic in the north and roughly following the line of the Dnieper to the Black Sea. Hitler optimistically viewed the line as the point at which Germany could win a war of attrition against the Red Army. The generals on the ground knew better, with some (such as General Georg von Küchler) even refusing to refer to the line, so it did not give his soldiers grounds for unwarranted optimism. Construction of the line began around September 1943, and several thousand small bunkers (mostly log and earth structures) were built, augmented by anti-tank obstacles and prepared fields of fire for anti-tank weapons and artillery. The weakest section of the line was that covering Heeresgruppe Süd, and overall the Panther–Wotan Line possessed only about half the construction manpower required to fortify the entire line properly.

The Panther–Wotan Line was never adequate for the scale of the threat it faced. Despite the undoubted skill of the German forces in conducting a defence, the Red Army punched through the line during 1944, albeit at heavy cost. Hitler's army was committed to an awful, inexorable retreat back into the heart of the Third Reich, and lines on maps were quite incapable of preventing that reality.

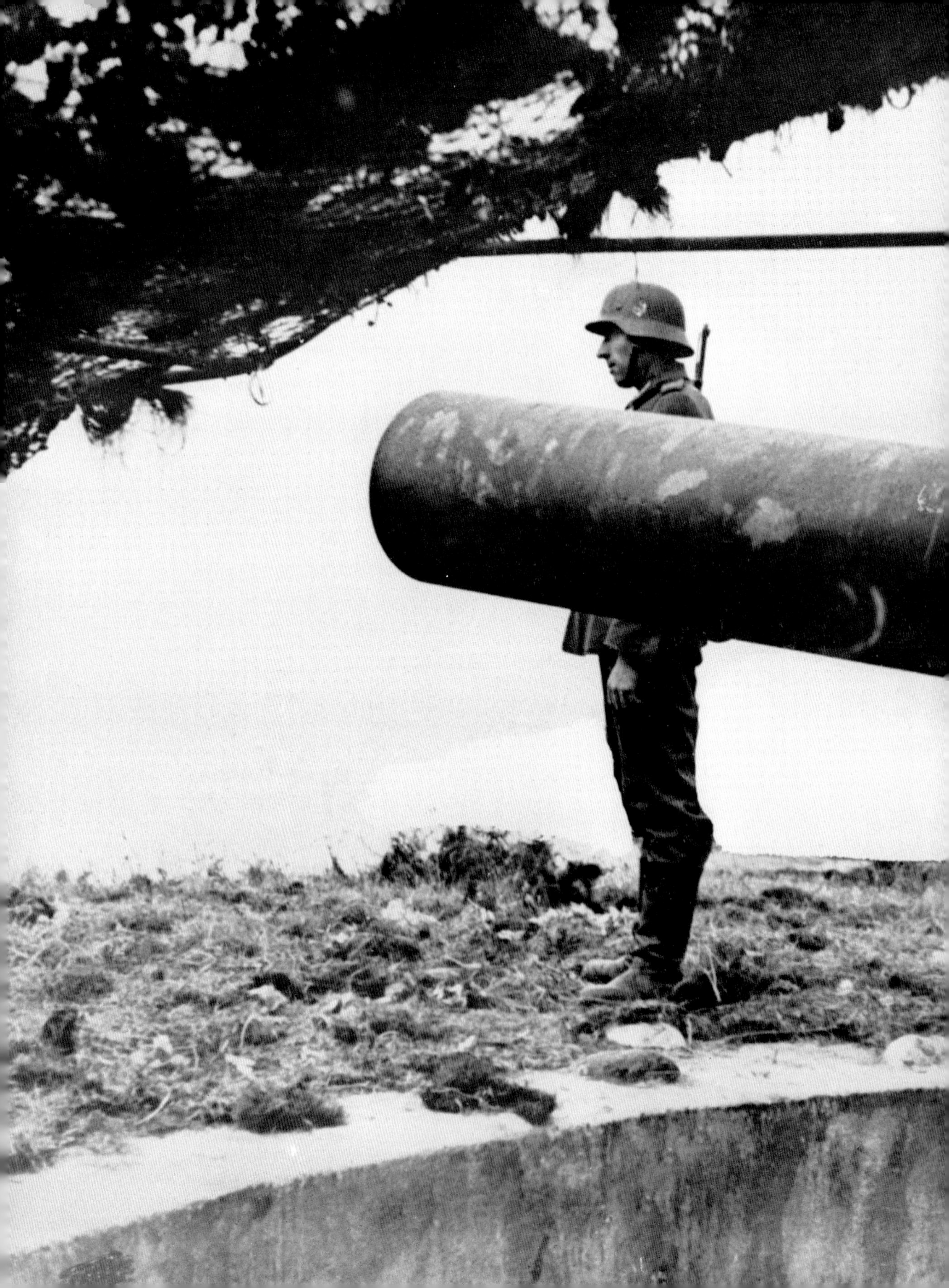

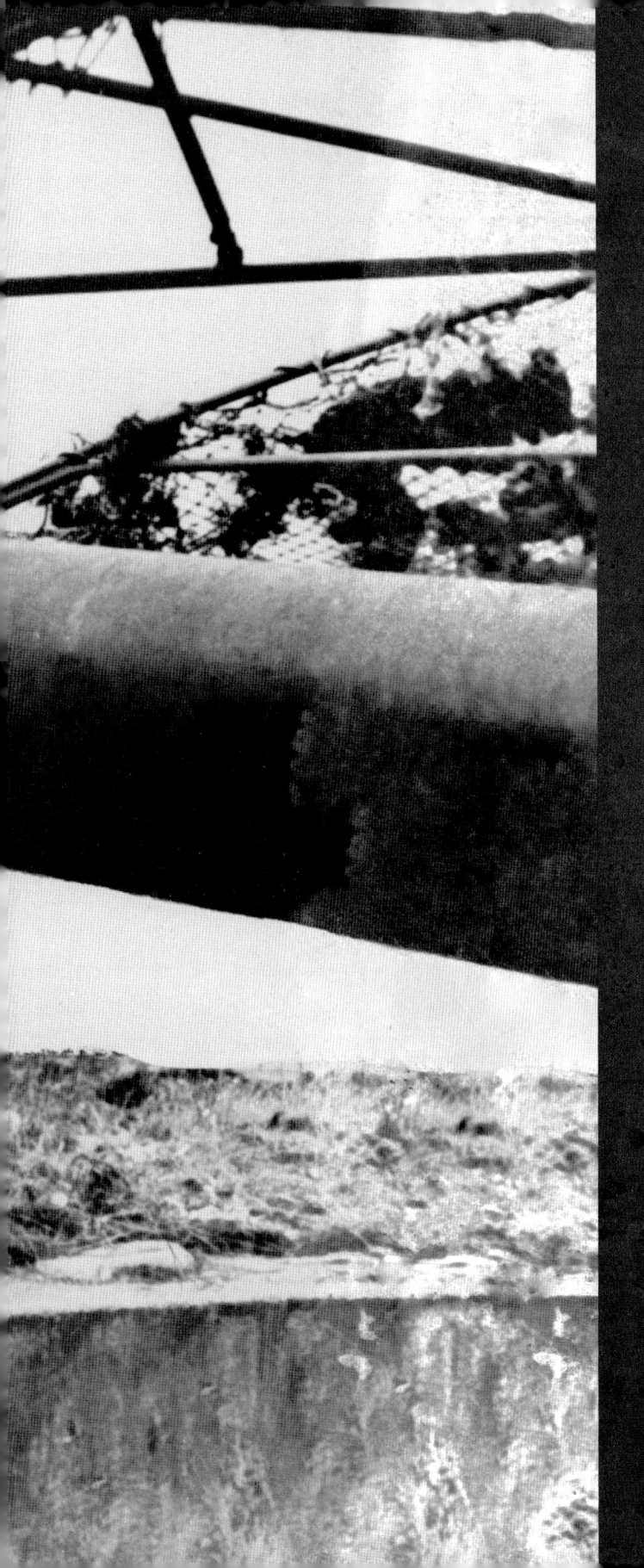

DEFENCE OF THE PERIPHERY — THE ATLANTIC WALL

LEFT: A German soldier stands guard at an Atlantic Wall artillery bunker during World War II. (Topfoto)

The Atlantic Wall was the largest fortification effort in recent European history, rivalled only by France's Maginot Line. The portions in France consumed over 17,000,000m³ of concrete and 1,200,000 tonnes of steel and cost some 3.7 billion Reichmarks. To put this in some perspective, the steel consumption was about 5 per cent of German annual production and roughly equivalent to the amount used in annual German tank production.

If the Atlantic Wall had been carefully designed and skilfully integrated into Germany's strategic planning, it might have been worth its considerable cost. But it was created on Hitler's whim, built in haste with little coordinated planning, and fitted uncomfortably with the Wehrmacht's tactical doctrine. Hitler ordered its construction in response to British raiding along the English Channel and as a barrier to an anticipated Allied invasion. Wehrmacht commanders had little influence on this scheme, and a debate raged until D-Day over the best way to resist the inevitable Allied amphibious assault. The overstretched German war economy was unable to match Hitler's dream of 'Fortress Europe', and the Atlantic Wall was never fully completed. The Wehrmacht commander in France, Rundstedt, later derided the Atlantic Wall as an enormous propaganda bluff.

On D-Day, the Atlantic Wall was strongest where the German leadership expected the Allied invasion, the 'Iron Coast' of the Pas-de-Calais opposite Britain. The Allies wisely chose to avoid this heavily defended area and struck instead where the Atlantic

The army preferred heavy railway guns over massive fixed guns for long-range firepower. This is a Krupp 203mm K(E) of battery EB.685 stationed near Auderville-Laye in the Cherbourg sector shortly after its capture in June 1944. (NARA)

Wall was weaker in lower Normandy. The D-Day assault overcame the Atlantic Wall in less than a day. Other stretches of the Atlantic Wall, especially near the Channel ports, were involved in later fighting but proved no more effective.

THE ATLANTIC WALL IN FRANCE

DESIGN AND DEVELOPMENT

Coastal defence had been assigned to the Kriegsmarine since the reforms of Kaiser Wilhelm in the late 1880s. This mission focused on the defence of Germany's ports along the North Sea and Baltic coasts. By the time of World War I, German naval doctrine saw coastal defence as a series of layers beginning with warships and submarines at sea as the initial barrier, followed by coastal forces such as torpedo boats and small submarines as the inner layer, and eventually fixed defences such as minefields and shore batteries as the final defensive layer. Fortification played a minor role. During World War I, this doctrine was found inadequate when Germany occupied Belgium. The Kriegsmarine did not have the manpower nor resources to create an adequate defence along the coast of Flanders, and the dominance of the Royal Navy in the English Channel undermined the traditional tactics, since German warships stood little chance of challenging the British on a day-to-day basis. The Kriegsmarine was obliged to turn to the Army to assist in this mission, particularly in the creation of gun batteries along the coast to discourage British raiding or possible amphibious attack. These gun batteries were employed in elementary Kesselbettungen (kettle positions), so named for the pan-like shape of the fortification. The Kriegsmarine began to pay more attention to the need for fortification in the late 1930s after Germany's re-militarization under Hitler's new Nazi government. One of the first major coastal fortification efforts took place on the islands in the Helgoland Bay, along the North Sea coast.

At the start of World War II, the Kriegsmarine retained the traditional coastal defence mission. There was no dedicated coastal defence force, but rather the mission was simply one of those assigned to the regional naval commands. The North Sea coast was defended with a scattering of coastal batteries and newly installed naval Flak units, but there was little modern fortification construction prior to 1939. Following the defeat of France in the summer of 1940, the Wehrmacht began preparations for an amphibious assault on Britain, Operation *Seelöwe* (Sealion). On 16 July 1940, Hitler issued Führer Directive No. 16, which called for the creation of fortified coastal batteries on the Pas-de-Calais to command the Straits of Dover and to protect the forward staging areas of the German invasion fleet.

Since it would take time to erect major gun batteries, the first heavy artillery in place was Army railroad guns that began arriving in August 1940. To provide these with

HITLER'S FORTRESSES

The Atlantic Wall.

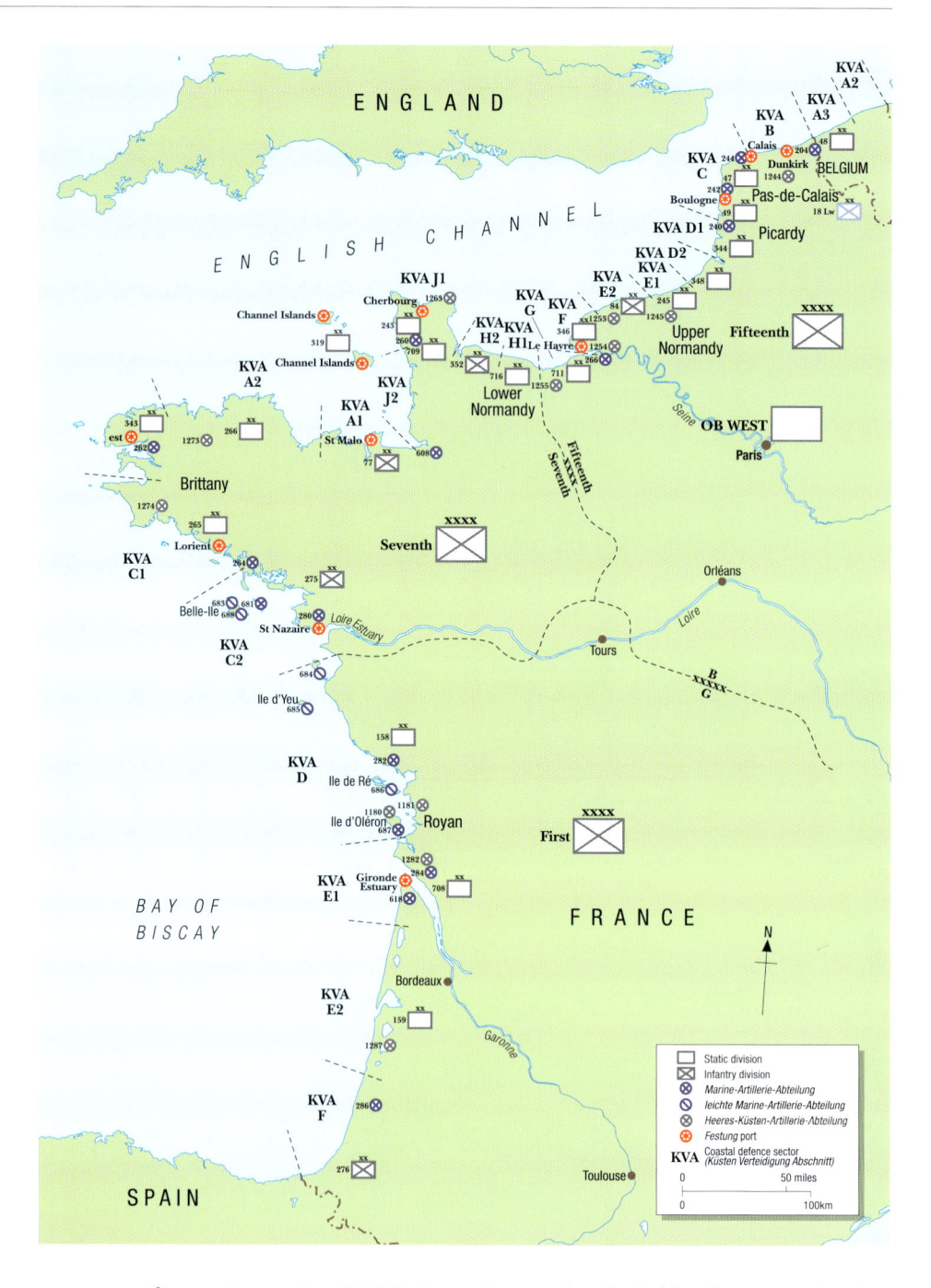

a measure of protection against British air attack, several cathedral bunkers (Dombunker) were created near the coast at Calais, Vallée Heureuse, Marquise and Wimereux. At the time, the Army had nine railroad artillery regiments with a total of 16 batteries and the Kriegsmarine had a pair of 15cm railroad guns known as Batterie Gneisenau. The Army created a coastal artillery command to manage this new mission and the Army artillery along the English Channel was put under the command of Army Artillery Command 104. There was some dispute between the Army and Kriegsmarine over the direction of the coastal artillery, with an eventual compromise being reached that the Kriegsmarine would direct fire against naval targets while the Army would direct fire against land targets and take over control once the invasion of Britain began.

Following the arrival of the railroad guns, both the Army and Kriegsmarine began to move other types of heavy artillery to the Pas-de-Calais. The Kriegsmarine obtained some of these by stripping existing coastal fortifications, while the Army obtained some weapons from the West Wall border fortifications or from field army heavy artillery regiments. Four powerful batteries were constructed, starting in 1941, which actually

A good example of a kettle gun emplacement typical of the initial construction in 1940–42, still part of the Cherbourg defences in June 1944. The gun is a Saint-Chamond 155mm K220(f), a French World War I type widely used in the Atlantic Wall defences. Most but not all of the kettle emplacements were rebuilt with full casemates by 1944. (NARA)

MKB Graf Spee of 5./MAA. 262 in Lochrist near Brest was armed with the Krupp 28cm SKL/40 M06 originally built for the old Brauschweig class of warships and previously located on one of the Friesian islands off the northern German coast before being transferred to Brittany in 1940. Three of the four guns were in open pits like this one, and only one in a large casemate. (NARA)

had the range to reach Britain near Dover and Folkestone. These included the Lindemann, Todt, Friedrich August and Grosser Kurfürst batteries. The artillery concentration in the Pas-de-Calais pre-dated the Atlantic Wall and was in reality an offensive deployment intended to support the invasion, and not a defensive fortified position. Even though not a true part of the Atlantic Wall, these batteries would come to symbolize Fortress Europe due to their frequent appearance in propaganda films.

The role of the Pas-de-Calais artillery batteries gradually evolved due to changing German war plans. As the possibilities for Operation *Seelöwe* dimmed in the winter of 1940, the role of the batteries gradually shifted to the naval interdiction role, challenging British shipping in the Channel. The railroad guns were gradually removed, especially once Hitler shifted his attention to Operation *Barbarossa*, the invasion of Russia scheduled for the summer of 1941. Construction of some of the large gun batteries initiated in the summer of 1940 continued, but without any particular priority and

DEFENCE OF THE PERIPHERY – THE ATLANTIC WALL

most of the larger Pas-de-Calais batteries were not completed until well into 1942. The only area to receive special attention was the Channel Islands, which attracted Hitler's personal interest. He wanted the islands to be heavily defended to prevent their recapture by Britain and, in October 1941, authorized the heavy fortification of the islands as a key element to this process.

Coastal defence began to attract the attention of the Wehrmacht's occupation forces in France due to Britain's initiation of commando raids along the Norwegian and French coasts. In February 1941, the Army began proposing a policy directive which argued that a unified defence of the coast be established, with the Army rather than the Kriegsmarine taking the lead role. This attempt was rebuffed by the OKW, which left the Kriegsmarine in charge of coastal defence artillery and the Luftwaffe in charge of Flak protection of the coast, including naval Flak batteries. Until the invasion of the Soviet Union in June 1941, there was a general policy against extensive fortification of

The heights of Mont de Coupole, located to the south-east of Wissant, provided an ideal observation point between Cap Gris-Nez and Cap Blanc-Nez for the heavy artillery batteries nearby. As a result, the hilltop is dotted with observation bunkers like this one. (Steven J. Zaloga)

HITLER'S FORTRESSES

ABOVE: 28cm K5E railway gun Dombunker. Among the first type of fortifications built along the French coast was the Dombunker (cathedral bunker), so-called because of its resemblance to the arched shape of Gothic cathedrals. These were intended to protect three batteries of 28cm K5E railroad guns deployed to the Pas-de-Calais in the summer of 1940 and construction began in September 1940. (Lee Ray © Osprey Publishing)

the French coast for fear that it would confirm that the Wehrmacht's intention had shifted from the invasion of Britain to the invasion of Russia.

British commandos staged attacks against the Lofoten Islands off the northern Norwegian coast in March and December 1941. These prompted another Führer Directive on 14 December 1941, which ordered the construction of a 'new West Wall'. This order recognized that the Western Front was seriously short of troops due to the war in Russia, and it was proposed to substitute fortification for manpower. Light fortifications were authorized along endangered coastlines and permanent strongpoints at key points. Priority was given to the Norwegian coast, which Hitler felt was more vulnerable to such raids. Second priority went to the French coast, followed by the Dutch coast and Helgoland Bay in that order. Hitler also ordered the reinforcement of the coast defence with Flak batteries that were assigned the dual role of anti-aircraft defence and potential use against landing craft. As a consequence of this order, the OB West, Generalfeldmarschall Erwin von Witzleben, began to designate some of the key French ports as Festungsbereichen (fortified areas) to assign priorities for the eventual fortification effort. The Kriegsmarine was primarily responsible for the defence of the port itself, but the Army was assigned the task of ensuring landward defence against possible airborne attacks.

British commando raids continued in early 1942, including the daring raid on Bruneval to secure a Würzburg radar. With the Wehrmacht bogged down in Russia, it seemed likely that the Western Front would remain on a defensive footing for some time to come. The evolving strategic situation led Hitler to issue Führer Directive No. 40 on 23 March 1942, which laid the groundwork for the Atlantic Wall. The directive provided few specifics about the actual nature of the fortification, and it reaffirmed earlier priorities, with Norway and the Channel Islands being singled out for special attention. The ink was hardly dry on the new directive when it was followed a few days later by the dramatic raid on St Nazaire by British Commandos, which managed to severely damage the vital dry docks there. This led Hitler to refocus the attention of the earlier directive, with a new emphasis on the defence of ports to prevent a repeat of the St Nazaire raid. The first serious planning meeting for the Atlantic Wall occurred in May 1942 at Wehrwolf, the Führer Headquarters at Vinnitsa, and attending the meeting was the new Reichsminister for Armaments, Albert Speer, who had taken over the OT following the death of Fritz Todt in an airplane crash in February. The OT was responsible for nearly all of the major fortification and military construction programmes in France and the neighbouring countries, including the gun batteries on the Pas-de-Calais, the new U-boat bunkers on France's Atlantic coast and the fortifications on the Channel Islands. The Wehrmacht's Festungs-Pionier Korps (Fortress Engineer Corps) under the Inspector of Engineers and Fortifications was responsible for designing and supervising the construction of fortifications by OT.

Serious construction efforts on the Atlantic Wall began in June 1942, and this was the first time that concrete consumption for the new fortifications exceeded that for the U-boat pens. In 1943–44, OB West designated several port areas as Festungen, including Dunkirk, Calais, Boulogne, Le Havre, Cherbourg, St Malo, Brest, Lorient, St Nazaire, the Gironde estuary and the Channel Islands. The US invasion of French North Africa in November 1942 prompted the German forces to occupy Vichy France, adding another coastal region to the list. The Mediterranean coastal fortifications were

HITLER'S FORTRESSES

Batterie Lindemann, Pas-de-Calais. The casemate consumed some 17,000m³ of concrete and the gun was mounted in a fully armoured Schiessgerüst C/39 turret, directed by a massive fire-control bunker based on the S100 type, which included a large Lange optical rangefinder and was supported by a Würzburg See-Reise FuMO 214 surface-search radar located nearby on Cap Blanc-Nez, as well as several other observation and range-finding posts.
(Lee Ray © Osprey Publishing)

DEFENCE OF THE PERIPHERY – THE ATLANTIC WALL

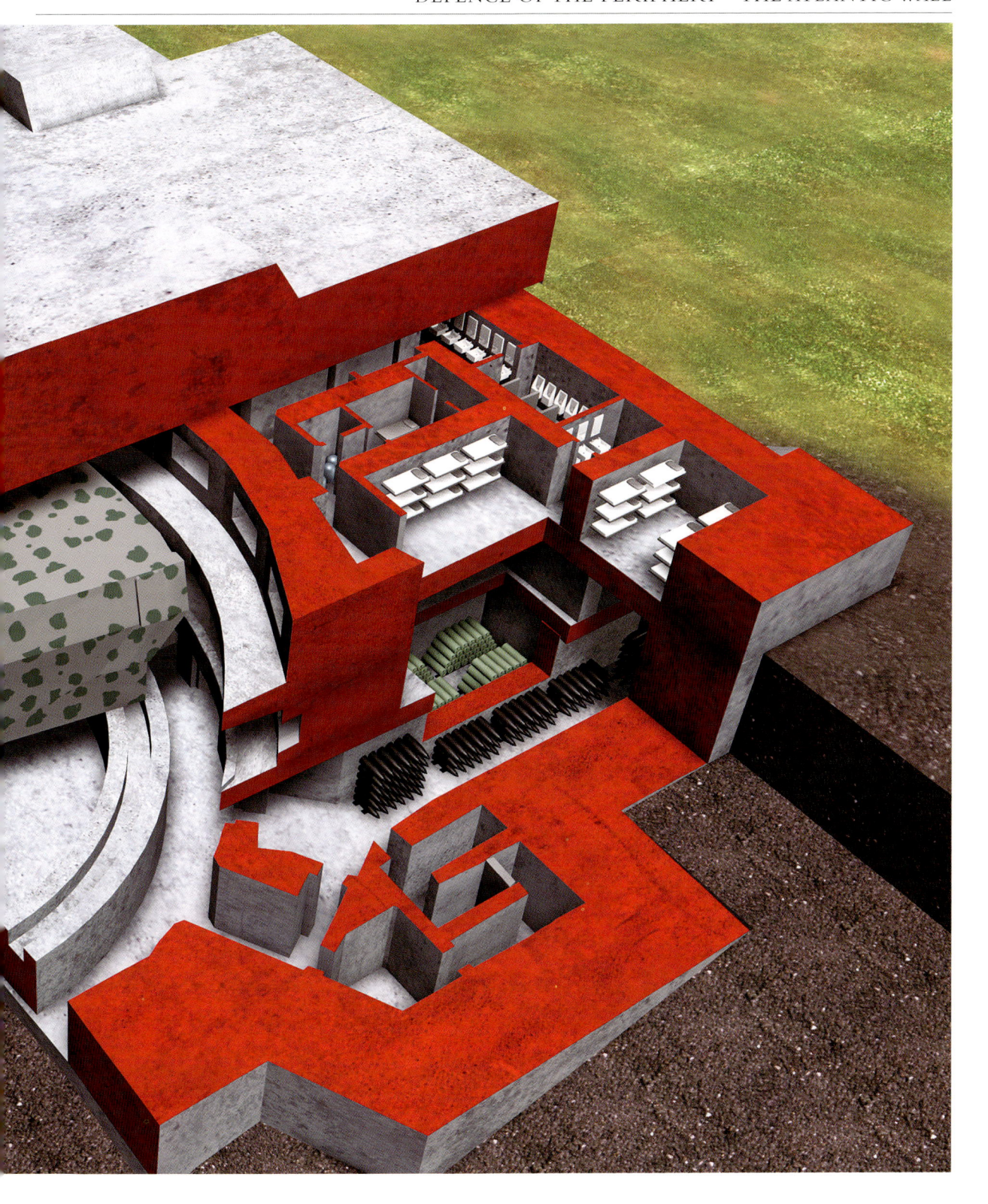

Among the massive coastal artillery casemates on the Pas-de-Calais was Turm West of MKB Oldenburg MAA. 244, armed with a 240mm SK L/50, originally a Tsarist 254mm gun captured in 1915 and re-chambered by Krupp. The two casemates of this battery were specialized SK designs built to the heavy Standard A with 3m-thick walls and ceilings. In the foreground is one of the associated H621 personnel shelters. (Steven J. Zaloga)

dubbed the Südwall (South Wall) and are outside the scope of this book. In the event, the Mediterranean ports of Marseilles and Toulon retained the lesser and earlier designation as 'fortified areas', as did some Atlantic ports such as La Rochelle and Bayonne. The Festung ports were to be fortified on both the seaward and landward sides and were to be provisioned to be able to hold out for at least three months.

KRIEGSMARINE AND ARMY

From a coastal fortification standpoint, the most significant defences were provided by coastal artillery units. There were three principal types, the Marine-Artillerie-Abteilung (MAA), the leichte Marine-Artillerie-Abteilung (leMAA: light naval artillery battalion) and the Marine-Flak-Brigade (MaFl-Br). Each naval artillery regiment consisted of several gun batteries, each battery deployed at a single coastal artillery post with several guns, a fire-control bunker and associated defensive and support positions. There were 14 regiments along the Atlantic Wall in France plus two more (MAA. 604 and 605) on the Channel Islands. The light naval artillery battalions were peculiar to the Atlantic coast islands and were hybrid formations consisting of a few gun batteries and a few companies of naval infantry for island defence. The Navy Flak brigades, as their name implies, controlled major port anti-aircraft sites. There were three of these: III. MaFl-Br at Brest; IV. MaFl-Br at Lorient; and V. MaFl-Br at St Nazaire.

One approach to coastal defence rarely used on the Atlantic Wall in France was the shore-based torpedo battery. The Kriegsmarine was made painfully aware of the capabilities of such batteries with the loss of warships in the 1940 Norwegian campaign, and developed a shore-based version of the standard TR 53.3 Einzel launcher from the S.Boote torpedo boat, which fired the 533mm G7a torpedo. However, these weapons were expensive and not as well suited to the open coastline of France as the constricted fjords of Scandinavia. The only significant use of shore-based torpedo stations in France was around the harbour of Brest where batteries were installed in 1942 near Crozon Island at Fort Robert and Cornouaille Point.

One style of camouflage for the shoreline casemates was trompe l'oeil painting, intended to make the bunker look like a harmless civilian home. This example is certainly more elaborate than most, complete with a cart in the false garage. This Canadian soldier is looking into the gun embrasure of the casemate, which had been covered with a false wooden cover now on the ground. (NAC PA-131229 Ken Bell)

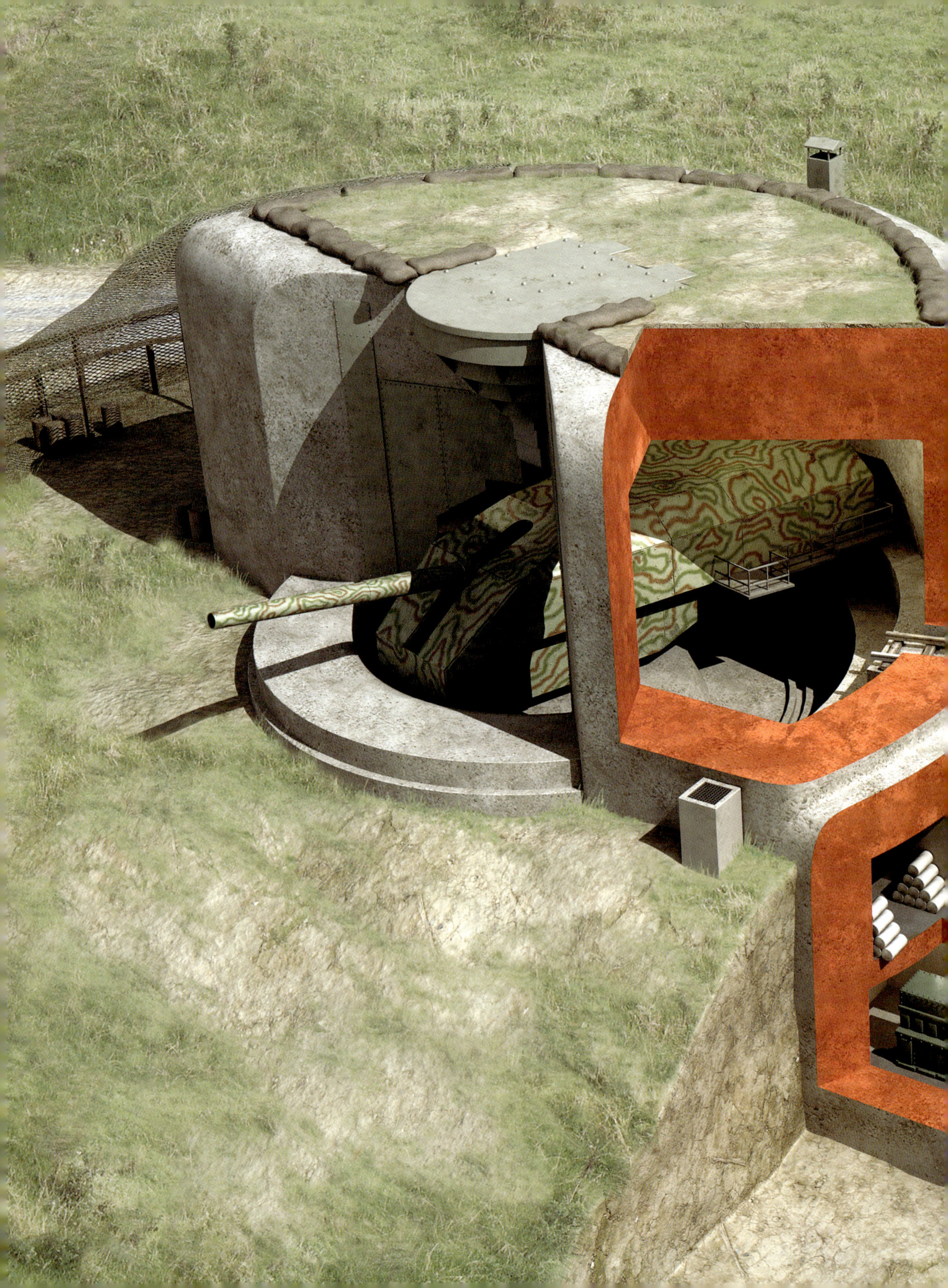

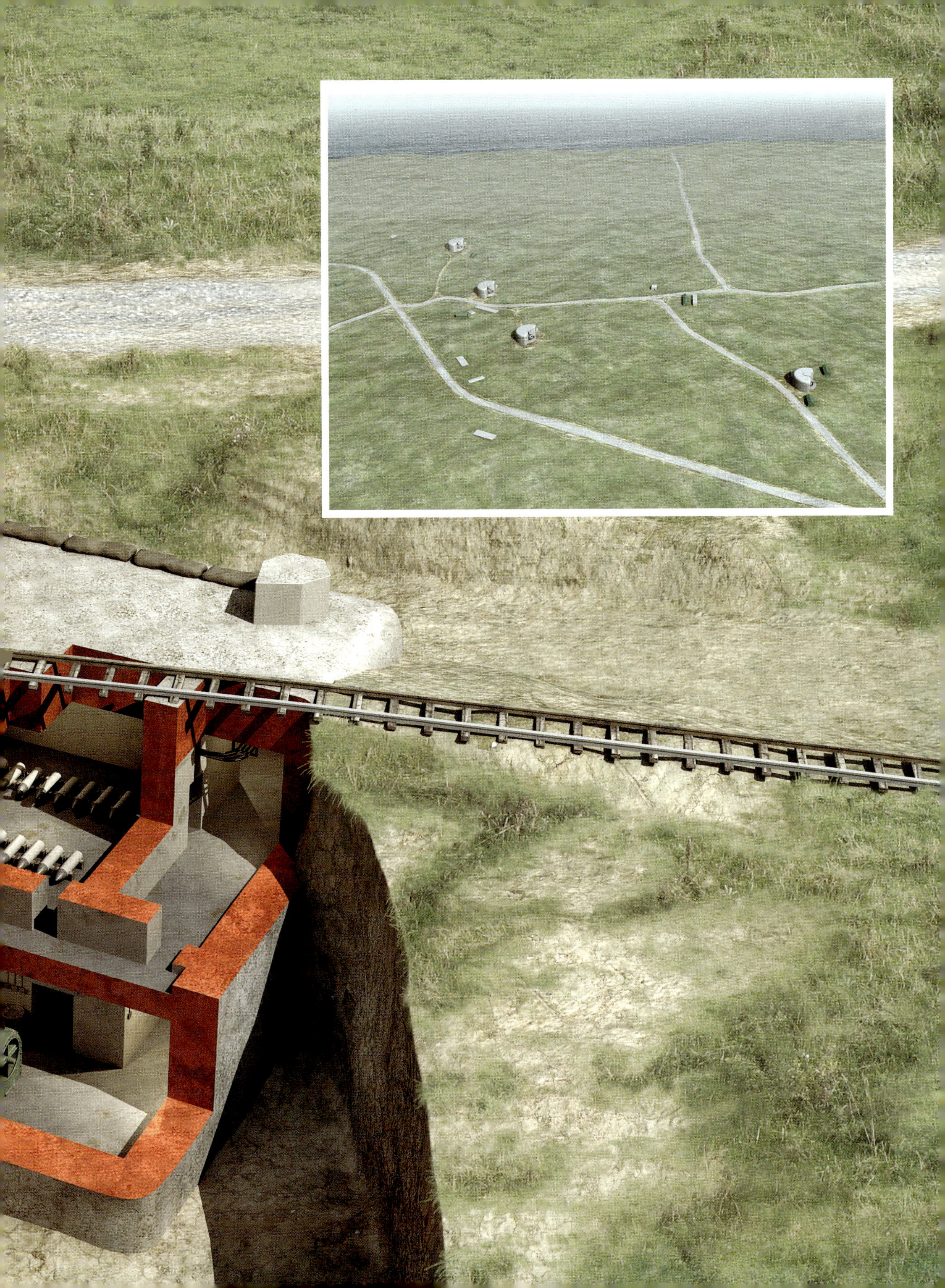

PREVIOUS SPREAD: Batterie Todt. Construction of Batterie Siegfried began in August 1940, armed with four 38cm SKC/34 in B-Gerüst C/39 turrets, near the village of Haringzelles. The battery was located close to the sea and within sight of Cap Gris-Nez where several supporting observation posts were located. The four turrets were of a special design consisting of a main circular gun casemate with a smaller multi-storey bunker for ammunition and support located to the left of the gun pit. (Hugh Johnson © Osprey Publishing)

Until 1943, the areas between the ports were much less heavily defended than the ports. The naval coastal artillery batteries tended to be clustered around the key ports, leaving significant expanses of coastline without any protection. These were gradually covered by Army coastal artillery batteries deployed along the coast like 'a string of pearls' to provide a basic defensive barrier. Coastal artillery was viewed as an excellent expedient since a single battery could cover about 10km of coastline to either side of the battery. In addition, the resources needed were fairly modest since most of the batteries were created using captured French, Russian or other weapons. As in the case of other defences, the Army's coastal batteries were most heavily deployed along the Pas-de-Calais and Upper Normandy in the 15. Armee sector, with an average density of one battery every 28km, while in the 7. Armee sector from Lower Normandy around the Cotentin Peninsula, the density was only one battery every 87km. The 15. Armee had nearly double the density of artillery of the other two sectors, averaging nearly one gun per kilometre. This certainly did not live up to the propaganda image of the Atlantic Wall. German tactical doctrine recommended a divisional frontage of 6 to 10km, implying a density of about five to eight guns per kilometre, substantially more than average Atlantic Wall densities.

Although the coastal artillery batteries were an economical way to cover large areas of coastline with minimal coverage, they could do little against commando raids. The task of patrolling the coastline was assigned to the infantry divisions stationed near the coast. These sectors consisted of divisional Küstenverteidigungs-Abschnitte (KVA; coast defence sectors), further broken down into regimental Küstenverteidigungs-Gruppen (KVG), battalion-strength Stützpunktgruppen (strongpoint groups), company-sized Stützpunkte (StP; strongpoints) and finally platoon-sized Widerstandsnester (WN; resistance points). Since the Kriegsmarine received the bulk of the construction work in 1943, these positions were often little more than field entrenchments with a small number of fortified gun pits and personnel shelters. Except on the Pas-de-Calais, there was little fortification of the infantry coastal defences until 1944. The bunkers and defensive positions were intended to compensate for the severe shortage of troops. German tactical doctrine recommended that an infantry division be allotted no more than 6–10km of front to defend, but the occupation divisions in France were frequently allotted 50 to 100km of coastline, sometimes even more in the remoter locations of Brittany or the Atlantic coast.

The allotment of fortifications was by no means uniform along the coast. In 1943, the Wehrmacht was deployed in three major formations: the 15. Armee from Antwerp westwards along the Channel coast to the Seine estuary near Le Havre; the 7. Armee from Lower Normandy to Brittany; and the 1. Armee on the Atlantic coast from the Loire estuary near Nantes to the Spanish coast near Bayonne. Of the three main sectors in France, the 15. Armee on the Channel coast received a disproportionate share of the fortification, and the 7. Armee much of the remainder. Of the 15,000 bunkers envisioned under the 1942 plan, 11,000 were allocated to the 15. and 7. Armeen and the rest to the Atlantic coast of France, the Netherlands, Norway and Denmark. By way of comparison, the 1. Armee sector, which covered the extensive Atlantic coast facing the Bay of Biscay, was allotted only 1,500 to 2,000 bunkers.

The initial role of coastal artillery was to stop the invasion force before it reached the shoreline. The configuration of the coastal artillery batteries was a subject of some controversy between the Army and Kriegsmarine. The Navy had traditionally viewed shore batteries as being an extension of the fleet, and so deployed the batteries along the edge of the coast where they could most easily to take part in naval engagements. As had become evident from attempts to repulse the Allied amphibious landings in the Mediterranean Theatre, one of the Allies' main advantages was heavy naval gunfire. As a result, a growing focus of the Navy's Atlantic Wall programme was to deploy enough coastal artillery to force the Allied warships away from the coast and thereby undercut this advantage. Naval coastal batteries were patterned on warship organization. The four to six guns were deployed with a direct line of sight to the sea, and connected by cabling to an elaborate fire-control bunker, which possessed optical rangefinders and plotting systems similar to those on warships to permit engagements against moving targets. The Army derided these batteries as 'battleships of the dunes' and argued that their placement so close to the shore made them immediately visible to enemy warships, and therefore vulnerable to naval gunfire. In addition, the proximity to the shore also made the batteries especially vulnerable to raiding parties or to infantry attack in the event of an amphibious assault.

The Army's attitude to the coastal batteries was based on the premise that they were needed primarily to repulse an amphibious attack, not engage in naval gun duels. As a result, the Army was content to place the batteries further back from the shore, though some were located along the shore if it gave them particularly useful arcs of fire. For example, this was the case with shorelines edged with cliffs, since a coastal battery deployed on a promontory could rake the neighbouring beaches with fire, avoiding the cover of the cliffs. The Army fire-control bunkers were far less elaborate than the naval bunkers, possessing rangefinders and sighting devices but usually lacking plotting devices for engaging moving targets. The Army placed more emphasis on wire or radio connections with other Army units, depending on artillery forward observers to assist in fire direction against targets that were beyond line of sight. The Kriegsmarine complained that these batteries were incapable of engaging moving ships.

Besides their differences about coastal artillery tactics, the Kriegsmarine and Army had very different views on the ideal technical characteristics of the coastal guns.

The Kriegsmarine preferred a turreted gun that could survive in a prolonged gun duel with a warship. A few actual warship turrets were available and were emplaced in areas that had a rock-bed deep enough to accommodate the sub-structure of the turret: a turret from the Gneisenau near Paimpol in Brittany, two turrets from the cruiser *Seydlitz* on Ré Island and the 38cm gun turret from the French battleship *Jean-Bart* near Le Havre. Since armour plate was at a premium and fortification too low on the Reich's priority list, it was impossible to manufacture steel turrets for coastal artillery. This led to the development of casemates to protect the gun against most overhead fire, with a limited armoured shield around the gun itself. Such configurations limited the traverse of the gun compared to a turret. This would later prove to be a fatal flaw when the attack came from the landward side since the embrasure seldom permitted more than 120 degrees of traverse, limiting the gun's coverage to seaward targets. The Kriegsmarine was aware of this problem but since its primary mission was to deal with the seaborne threat, the issue was brushed aside.

During 1943, fortification engineers began to experiment with an advanced type of reinforced concrete using wire under stress instead of the usual steel reinforcing bars. This promised to be significantly lighter, leading to plans for a fully traversable concrete turret to get around the limitations of traverse in fixed casemates. An experimental example was completed outside Paris in early 1944, and the first concrete turrets began to be built on the Atlantic Wall, starting with one near Fort Vert to the east of Calais. However, the technology appeared too late in the war to be widely used.

The Army did not favour fixed guns like the Navy and preferred to use conventional field artillery. This was based on the premise that the batteries could be moved from idle sectors to reinforce the defences in sectors under attack. The Army pointed to previous examples of British amphibious attack, such as Gallipoli, where the amphibious assault became a protracted campaign. At first, the Army preferred to use simple kettle mounts patterned on the World War I style, which were simply circular concrete pits with protected spaces for ammunition. The gun itself was completely exposed, but the gun pit was supported by fully protected crew bunkers, ammunition bunkers and a fire-control bunker. This was the predominant type of Army coastal battery configuration on the Atlantic Wall from 1942 into early 1943. However, as Allied air activity over the French coast increased in intensity, the vulnerability of these batteries to air attack became the subject of some concern. Intuitively it seemed that the Navy's casemates offered better protection from air attack than the kettle positions. However, based on actual combat experiences, some of the fortification engineers argued that this was not the case. The confined casemate tended to concentrate the blast of any bomb that landed near the gun opening, and it was found that guns in open pits were almost invulnerable to air attack except for the very rare direct hit on the gun itself. In the wake of the Dieppe raid, however, the policy shifted to full protection of the Army coastal batteries in casemates. These resembled the Navy casemates except that they generally had a large garage door at the rear to permit easy removal of the gun for transfer to other sectors if needed.

The Army fortification engineers had established protection standards during the West Wall programme based on steel-reinforced concrete (Beton-Stahl). Category E fortifications were based on walls and ceilings 5m thick, but this standard was uncommon and used mainly for strategic command posts such as the Führer bunkers. The highest level for tactical fortifications was A, which used a 3.5m basis, and this was confined to large, high-priority structures such as the U-boat bunkers and some key facilities such as the heavy gun batteries on the Pas-de-Calais and special military hospitals. Most Atlantic Wall

ABOVE: Marine Peilstände und Meßstellen 2 (MP2) (Naval artillery direction and range-finding tower) at Corbiere, Jersey. Despite their rather forbidding external appearance, there was actually very little inside these towers. They sat on cliff tops overlooking the sea and were constructed to house and protect artillery observers operating a system that was soon abandoned due to fundamental flaws in its philosophy. (Chris Taylor © Osprey Publishing)

HITLER'S FORTRESSES

fortifications were built to the B standard, which was 2m thick, proof against artillery up to 210mm and 500kg bombs. Many minor bunkers, such as the ubiquitous tobruks, were built to the slightly lower B1 standard of 1 to 1.2m, since these structures were partially buried. The designers attempted to minimize the amount of steel necessary in construction, so aside from the steel reinforcing bars (rebar), steel plate and especially steel armour plate was kept to a minimum. A standardized family of small armoured cupolas, doors and firing posts had been developed during the West Wall programme and these were used on the Atlantic Wall as well. Most personnel bunkers and other enclosed bunkers built in 1942–43 were also provided with protection against gas attack both by systems to seal the structure from outside air, as well as filtration systems. Obviously, this was not possible with large gun casemates, but the associated crew bunkers typically had gas protection.

The Festungs-Pionier Korps in Berlin designed a family of standardized bunkers for typical applications. Some of these were based on the earlier West Wall programme, but the majority were newer designs. The original West Wall fortifications had been designated in the OB or Vf series for Offene Bettung (open platform) or Verstärkt feldmäßig (reinforced field position). Although some of these designations were retained during the construction of the Atlantic Wall, a new series of designations emerged. There is some disparity in how these designs are identified so for example, the '611' bunker design is variously called Bauform 611 (Construction Plan 611); R611 (Regelbau 611: Construction Standard 611) or H611 (Heer 611: Army 611) to distinguish Army bunkers from Air Force (L: Luftwaffe) and Navy (M: Kriegsmarine) bunker designs. There were about 700 of these standard designs of which about 250 were used on the Atlantic Wall. It should be mentioned that these designs were often modified in the field to better match local terrain contours. Besides the standardized designs, there were localized variations of standard plans as well as entirely new designs, sometimes identified with an SK suffix for Sonderkonstruktion (special design).

OPPOSITE: One of the more common types of obstacles deployed in 1944 was a simple post obstruction enhanced by adding a Teller mine on top to blow a hole in the bottom of landing craft. In reality, such mines failed as often as not due to the effect of frequent submersion in seawater, symptomatic of Rommel's slap-dash obstacle program, which argued that 'something was better than nothing'. (NARA)

PRINCIPLES OF DEFENCE

Like many of Hitler's personal passions, the Atlantic Wall was a half-baked scheme. The gnat bites by British commandos along the French and Norwegian coast provoked Hitler into a massive construction completely out of proportion to its tactical value. Hitler had a visceral enthusiasm for monumental fortification after his experiences as a young infantryman in the trenches in World War I. Ironically, it was the Wehrmacht that had demonstrated the futility of linear defences against the combined power of mechanized firepower and air attack. Furthermore, the Atlantic coast was so long that it was impossible to create any defence in depth with the Atlantic Wall, inevitably resulting in a weak and vulnerable configuration.

HITLER'S FORTRESSES

Rheinmetall 150mm C/36 destroyer gun in coastal mounting. One of the most common naval guns used in Kriegsmarine Atlantic Wall gun batteries was the 15cm Torpedoboots Kanone (Tbts K) C/36. This destroyer gun had been developed by Rheinmetall in the early 1930s, and these weapons were usually deployed in the normal Tbts LC/36 mount which employed a conventional armour splinter-shield covering all of the gun except the rear. (Adam Hook © Osprey Publishing)

DEFENCE OF THE PERIPHERY – THE ATLANTIC WALL

HITLER'S FORTRESSES

When Rundstedt was appointed to head OB West in the spring of 1943, he ordered a comprehensive inspection of the Atlantic Wall defences which took place from May to October 1943. The problem was not so much the uncompleted Atlantic Wall as the continuing drain of resources out of France to the Russian Front. The infantry divisions stationed in France were second-rate static divisions, which were hardly adequate for positional defence. The continued decline in troop quality in 1943 was somewhat offset by continuing fortification of the coast, since it was widely believed by German commanders that the poor-quality troops would be more likely to resist from the safety of bunkers than from exposed field positions.

Under the circumstances, OB West attempted to meld accepted tactical doctrine with the Atlantic Wall fortifications. The resulting tactics were dubbed 'crust–cushion–hammer'. The Atlantic Wall was the crust that would stop or delay the initial Allied invasion and give the Army time to move its mobile reserves into action. The cushion was the coastal region immediately behind the Atlantic Wall, which would be covered by proposed 'Position II' defences. This was a half-hearted attempt started in November 1943 to provide some defence in depth to the Atlantic Wall through a series of field emplacements. Since there was not enough concrete, construction was limited to earthen defence works.

This Rheinmetall 15cm SKC/28 in a coastal C/36 mount with non-standard gun-shield was one of four guns of MKB Landemer, 6./MAA. 260, positioned in an M272 casemate, part of StP 230 in Castel-Vendon to the west of Cherbourg. (NARA)

In the event, Position II never emerged as a serious defensive programme due to Rommel's insistence that the emphasis be placed on the initial 'crust' of the Atlantic Wall. The 'cushion' of the coastal belt also served as a buffer zone since the Panzer commanders did not want to conduct operations near the beaches within the range of Allied warships, based on the lessons of the Mediterranean Theatre, where Panzer attacks were repeatedly demolished by naval gun fire. The 'hammer' was the OB West reserve, primarily Panzer Gruppe West under the command of General Freiherr Leo Gehr von Schweppenburg.

With the threat of an Allied invasion of France increasing, even Hitler realized that the Western Front could no longer be ignored. His first action in the autumn of 1943 was to appoint Rommel to command the new Heeresgruppe zur besonderen Verwendung (Army Group for Special Employment; later Heeresgruppe B) to direct the invasion front. Hitler also authorized Führer Directive No. 51 on 3 November

The St Chamond 155mm K420(f) gun was adapted for coastal defence with a special armoured mount to fully enclose the embrasure. This example is mounted in an H679 casemate of MKB Gatteville of 7./HKAR. 1261 near Cherbourg. (NARA)

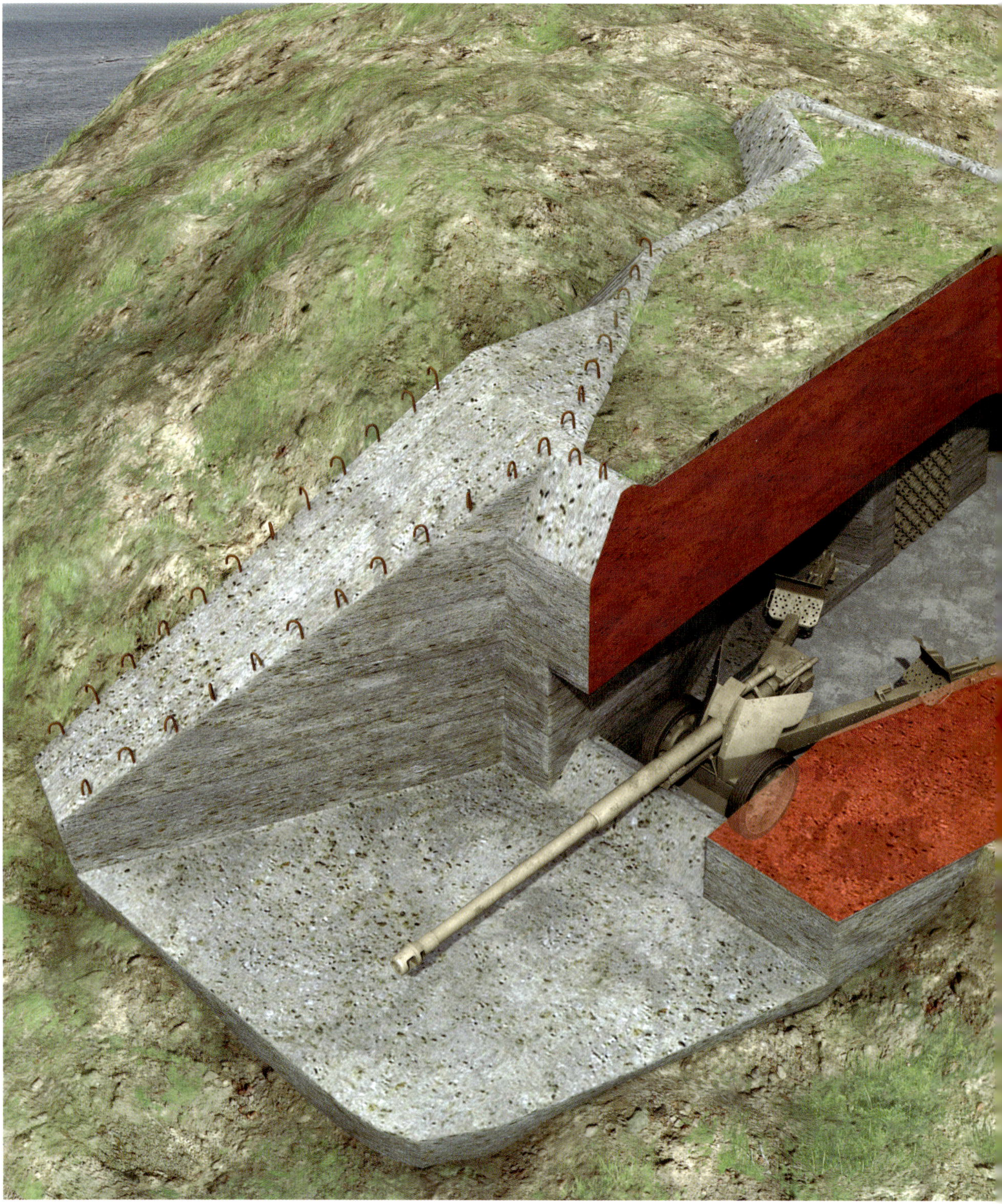

DEFENCE OF THE PERIPHERY – THE ATLANTIC WALL

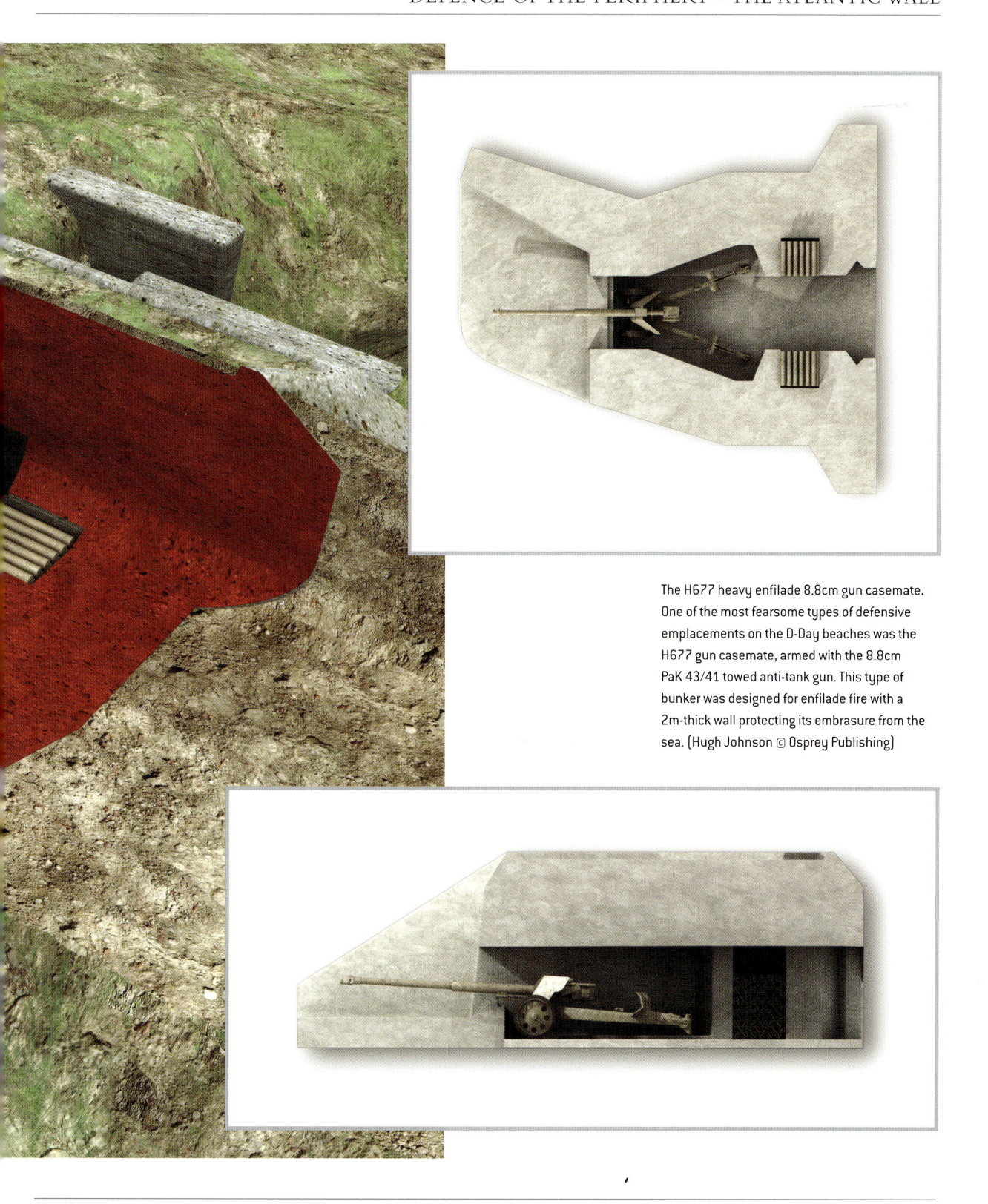

The H677 heavy enfilade 8.8cm gun casemate. One of the most fearsome types of defensive emplacements on the D-Day beaches was the H677 gun casemate, armed with the 8.8cm PaK 43/41 towed anti-tank gun. This type of bunker was designed for enfilade fire with a 2m-thick wall protecting its embrasure from the sea. (Hugh Johnson © Osprey Publishing)

163

HITLER'S FORTRESSES

1943, which on paper at least reoriented the strategic priorities for resources and ordered that additional steps be taken to reinforce the Western Front due to the likelihood of Allied invasion sometime in 1944.

Rommel approached his new assignment with characteristic vigour and began a tour of the defences starting in Denmark in December 1943 and working his way down the French coast in early 1944. He came to this new command with a different perspective than most senior Wehrmacht commanders, having spent the past few years fighting the Allies in the Mediterranean Theatre rather than the Red Army on the Russian Front. His last assignment had been the command of German forces in northern Italy. While this did not directly involve him in combating recent Allied amphibious assaults in Italy, he had been involved in the debates over the best approaches to repel the Allied landings. In the case of both Sicily in July 1943 and Salerno in September 1943, the Wehrmacht in Italy had followed the accepted doctrine

Some bunkers were camouflaged to blend into their surroundings like this observation bunker along the seawall in Le Havre. (NARA)

but it had failed to crush the landings. In both cases, the Allied landings were initially unopposed, but Panzer forces were promptly mobilized and the beachhead attacked in force. In both cases, the mechanized attacks were stopped cold by a combination of tenacious Allied infantry defence stiffened by a suffocating amount of naval gunfire. During the course of his inspections along the Atlantic Wall, the Allies launched yet another amphibious attack against Anzio in January 1944 and, once again, the German mechanized counter-attacks in February 1944 failed with heavy losses. This only served to reinforce his doubts about the current tactics for dealing with Allied amphibious attacks.

From a tactical standpoint, Rommel rejected the current doctrine and argued that instead of defence in depth with the Panzer divisions kept in reserve away from the beaches, all available resources should be moved as close to the likely landing areas as possible. He believed that the Italian campaign had demonstrated that if the invasion could not be stopped immediately, it could not be stopped at all. He also questioned whether the Allies would actually strike at a port. A landing some distance from a port could lead to the eventual envelopment and capture of the port. In spite of Rommel's considerable influence with Hitler, his views were not widely accepted by senior German commanders in France. The debate over the best approach to deploying the Panzer divisions continued right up to D-Day and was not settled to the satisfaction of either side in the debate.

From the perspective of the Atlantic Wall, Rommel's leadership had several important consequences. Rommel invigorated efforts to defend the beaches between the major ports, especially along the Pas-de-Calais and Normandy.

By early 1944, the Kriegsmarine had received the bulk of OT's resources and the ports had been well fortified. More attention had to be directed to the Army's shoreline defences. Besides enhancing the fortifications along the coast, Rommel suggested that more attention had to be paid to extending defences out on the beaches. His own experiences in the desert campaign had convinced him of the value of mine warfare and obstacles. Rommel argued that by creating obstructions along the coast, amphibious landing craft would be prevented from reaching the shelter of the shoreline. In combination with enhanced beachfront fortifications, this would create a killing zone along the shoreline. Instead of landing near the protective seawalls so common on the Channel coast, the infantry would have to disembark hundreds of metres from shore, exposed to prolonged fire as they attempted to reach the sanctuary of the shoreline. In contrast to his arguments about defensive tactics, Rommel's recommendations for improved coastal defence were welcomed by Rundstedt and the other senior commanders who felt that the Army had been too long neglected in the Atlantic Wall construction compared to the Kriegsmarine.

Rommel's intervention came at an opportune time for the fortification programme. The pace of construction of the Atlantic Wall had fallen off from its highpoint in April 1943 to its lowest point in January 1944 when less than half as much construction was completed. While some of this decline was seasonal, other factors were more important. On the night of 16/17 May 1943, the RAF had breached several of the River Ruhr dams, flooding a portion of Germany's industrial heartland and knocking out hydroelectric power generators. Speer pledged to Hitler that the OT would clean up the mess as quickly as possible, and so resources were drained out of the Atlantic Wall programme through much of the summer of 1943. Hitler's new fancy in the autumn of 1943 was the forthcoming V-weapon programme, and a major construction effort was begun by the OT in Normandy and the Pas-de-Calais to create launch sites for the missiles, further undermining the fortification effort. Finally, the pre-invasion Allied air campaign was aimed at crippling the French rail and road networks, and through the late winter and early spring of 1944, OT workers were diverted from fortification programmes to assist in rebuilding the railroads.

To compensate for the shortages of OT construction workers, in 1944 the Wehrmacht began to assign some of the construction work to infantry divisions along the coast. Each of the infantry corps had a Festungs-Pioneer-Stab (Fest.Pi.Stab: Fortification Engineer Staff) assigned to it. These were organized somewhat like a regiment with three attached battalions, but these were administrative units, not tactical formations, and their principal role was to plan and direct the construction of fortifications within their sector. In the late winter and spring of 1944, they were assigned additional troops, often Ost battalions of Soviet volunteers, to help carry out construction work.

The primary work assigned to the infantry troops was to assist in creating the shoreline defences. Since resources were very limited, most of this work involved either the transfer of obstacles from idle defensive works in occupied Europe, or the creation of improvised obstacles using local resources. 'Cointet' obstacles, also called Belgian gates or C elements, were large steel-frame devices manufactured in the 1930s to block Belgian frontier roads. 'Czech hedgehogs' (Tschechenigelen) – static anti-tank obstacles made from angled iron girders – were collected from Czech forts in the Sudetenland as were similar obstacles found elsewhere in occupied Europe. Similar obstructions were made from scrap metal and concrete including concrete tetrahedrons. One of the simplest forms of anti-craft obstruction was an angled pole, often topped by a Teller mine. During his tour of the defences in February 1944, Rommel was shown a local technique at Hardelot-Plage using fire hoses to dig holes for these stakes quickly, and this technique was widely disseminated through France. Some of this work was too hasty and ill conceived. When some officers decided to test the effectiveness of the stakes using a British landing craft captured at Dieppe, they were shocked to find that

H667 KLEINSTSCHARTENSTAND FÜR 5CM KWK

The H667 was the most common anti-tank gun casemate built on the Atlantic Wall, with some 651 constructed in 1943–44, of which 443 were built on the French coast. These were designed to provide better protection than the common Vf600 open gun pits widely used for the pedestal-mounted 50mm gun. This weapon consisted of obsolete KwK 39 and KwK 40 tank guns mounted on a simple pedestal (Sockellafetten) with a spaced armour shield added in front. During 1944, some of these guns were re-bored to fire 7.5cm ammunition. Since the gun was mounted on a fixed pedestal, there was no need for a rear garage door as was so characteristic of other Atlantic Wall gun casemates. Instead, the casemate had a simple armoured door at the rear, protected by a low concrete wall. This bunker, like the H677, was designed to be placed directly on the beach. It was oriented to fire in enfilade along the beach, not towards the sea. The design incorporated a thick wall on one side or other to shield the embrasure from naval gunfire. The interior was very elementary, large enough for only the crew and a few containers of ammunition. (Lee Ray © Osprey Publishing)

the craft simply ploughed through the obstructions with little trouble. As a result, the more substantial Hemmbalk (beam obstruction) was designed resembling a large tripod.

The most effective anti-craft device was a Kriegsmarine mine called the Küstenmine-A (KMA; Coastal Mine-A), which consisted of a concrete base containing a 75kg explosive charge surmounted by a steel tripod frame with the triggering device. Although cheap and effective, they became available too late to be laid along the entire coastline. They were first laid along the Channel coast from Boulogne south towards Le Havre since this sector was considered the most likely to be invaded, and this phase was completed in early June 1944. The next area to be mined was the Seine estuary around Le Havre, which was to begin on 10 June, but this never took place due to the invasion. Because of shortages of the KMA mine, the Army developed cheap expedients, the most common of which was the Nussknacker (nutcracker), which consisted of a French high-explosive artillery projectile planted in a concrete base with a steel rod serving as the activating lever. Nearly 10,000 of these were manufactured and deployed in 1944.

Another change in fortification plans in early 1944 was the decision to place all field artillery of the static divisions on the coast under concrete protection, based on the lessons from the Salerno campaign. These casemates were not especially elaborate and were simple garage designs such as the H669 and H612. This programme began in earnest in January 1944.

OB West was very concerned about the possibility of Allied airborne attacks, and several steps were taken to deal with this threat. Large fields near the coast were blocked with poles and other obstructions to prevent glider landings, though in practice this proved to be flimsy and ineffective. In some low-lying coastal areas such as the fields behind Utah Beach and the fields south-west of Calais, the Wehrmacht flooded the fields to complicate exit from the beach. However, many German tactical commanders were reluctant to flood valuable crop fields as local units often depended on local produce to feed their troops and this placed a limit on the extent of deliberate flooding.

TOUR OF THE FRENCH SITES

The Atlantic Wall consisted of so many strongpoints, gun batteries and other fortified positions that it is impossible in this short survey even to list them all. Instead, some typical examples of defensive positions will be described.

Naval coastal artillery

The Kriegsmarine coastal artillery batteries varied in composition depending on the type and number of guns. Some of the naval artillery regiments were composed primarily of heavy batteries. A good example of this was MAA. 244 located on either side of Calais. This unit included six heavy batteries averaging three guns per battery. A typical example was MKB Oldenburg, located immediately east of Calais in Moulin Rouge. This battery was armed with a pair of 240cm SKL/50 guns, which were Czarist 254mm guns captured in 1915 and re-chambered by Krupp. Originally installed in 1940 in open gun pits as part of the Operation *Seelöwe* build-up, the batteries were substantially improved starting in 1942 with a pair of massive casemates, along with two H621 personnel shelters, a H606 searchlight stand and numerous supporting bunkers. The neighbouring regiment to the west, MAA. 242, had some of the most famous naval batteries including Batterie Todt. Positioned along the high ground of Cap Gris-Nez and Cap Blanc-Nez, this regiment had an extensive array of observation bunkers on the promontories, as well as radar surveillance stations. These two regiments constituted the densest and most powerful assortment of naval coastal batteries on the Atlantic Wall. This heavy concentration was in part due to the strategic decision to heavily fortify the Pas-de-Calais, but the batteries also served to interdict Allied shipping in the Channel.

Most of the other major Festung ports had a similar concentration of naval artillery, though often of less imposing size. A typical battery was MKB Vasouy, the 9. Batterie of Marine-Artillerie-Abteilung 266 (9./MAA. 266) located along the south bank of the River Seine opposite Le Havre on the outskirts of Honfleur. The battery's mission was to cover the mouth of the River Seine. Its basic armament consisted of four 15cm Tbts.K.L/45 guns, essentially a coastal version of the standard 15cm destroyer gun with an effective range of 18km and a rate of fire of 1.5 rounds per minute. These were enclosed in four M272 Geschützschartenstände (gun casemates) arranged in a line a few hundred metres from the river's edge. This type of casemate was fairly typical of Kriegsmarine designs but not especially common in France, with only six along the Channel coast and 21 elsewhere including Norway, Denmark and the Netherlands. This particular type was first built in April 1943 and required 760m^3 of concrete. The guns were directed from a M262 Leitstand für leichte Seezielbatterie (fire-control bunker for light naval battery) located on a rise on the left of the battery position, connected to each of the four gun casemates by buried electrical cable. Although typical of Kriegsmarine fire-control bunkers, it was not a particularly common type, with only four on the French Channel coast and ten more in the Netherlands. Like most naval fire-control bunkers, it had two storeys with an observation post in the lower level, and an optical rangefinder post on the upper level. Inside the bunker was a control room where the target was plotted and the aiming data sent to the gun casemates. The battery had a single munitions bunker on the other end of the battery site, and two personnel bunkers immediately behind the gun casemates. In 1944, the battery was entirely surrounded by barbed wire, and there were four tobruks armed with machine guns for site defence.

Army coastal artillery

Fortified Army coastal artillery batteries came in three main varieties, the dedicated Army coastal artillery regiments (Heeres-Küsten-Artillerie-Abteilung/-Regiment; HKAA/HKAR) deployed in 1942–44, the fortified divisional artillery battalions and the railway artillery batteries. The Army coastal artillery regiments could be found along many sections of the coast but they were not evenly spread. So, for example, naval batteries dominated the Pas-de-Calais, while Army batteries dominated lower Normandy, including HKAR. 1260 located along the D-Day beaches and HKAR. 1261 on the eastern Cotentin coast to the south-east of Cherbourg. Some of the batteries in these regiments were originally naval batteries such as 3./HKAR. 1261 in St Marcouf and 4./HKAA. 1260 at Longues-sur-Mer, which were absorbed into the

Tank turrets mounted on tobruks were a common feature of the Normandy defences and this example of a 'U'-pattern tobruk with World War I Renault FT tank turret was located near one of the breakwaters in Grandcamp harbour between Utah and Omaha Beach. (NARA)

DEFENCE OF THE PERIPHERY – THE ATLANTIC WALL

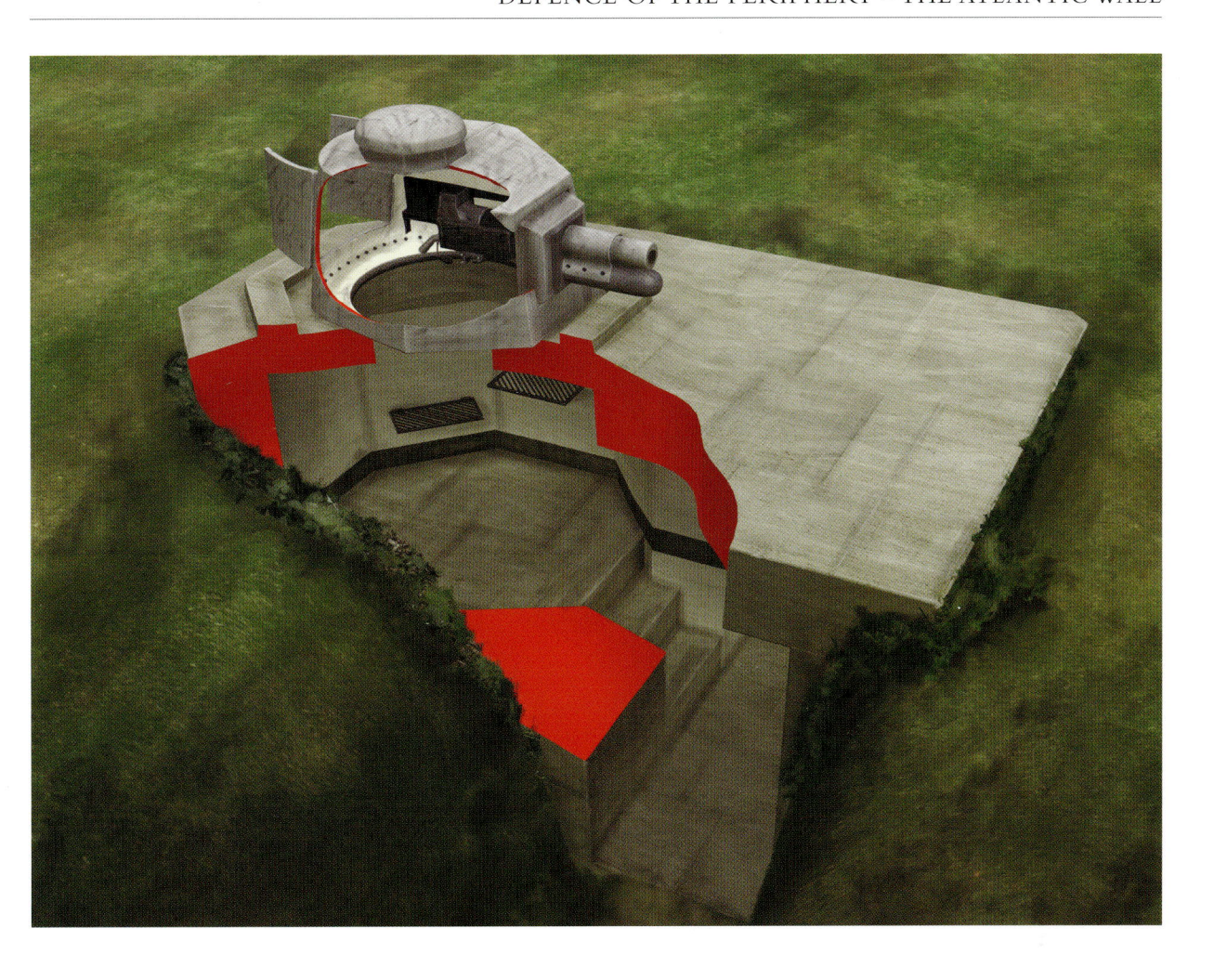

ABOVE: This plate depicts the turret taken from a French FT-17 tank, captured in great quantities by the German Army in 1940, mounted on a tobruk bunker. Such practice appears to have been a synthesis of Italian and Soviet techniques, the bunkers evolving from tobruk pits, which were named for the area where they were first extemporized by the Italian Army, using concrete drainage pipes vertically emplaced. (Chris Taylor © Osprey Publishing)

Army regiments in 1943 to create a unified command. The most extensive of these was HKAR. 1261, which had ten batteries stretching from St Martin-de-Varreville near Utah Beach along the Cotentin coast to La Pernelle on the outskirts of Cherbourg. In general, these batteries were not as well equipped to deal with moving naval targets as the naval batteries, lacking radars or plotting rooms in their forward observation bunkers. This regiment had some of the best of the Army gun casemates, usually including at least partial armoured shields for the guns. For example, its 7. Batterie located in Gatteville in H679 casemates had their 15.5cm K420(f) guns behind a traversable

This H677 casemate armed with the formidable 8.8cm Pak 43/41 anti-tank gun formed the core of the WN29 strongpoint near the harbour in Courseulles-sur-Mer and is seen several days after D-Day after Canadian troops had established an anti-aircraft position on top with a 20mm cannon. (Ken Bell, NAC PA140856)

armoured shield that completely covered the embrasure; the 2. Batterie in Azeville had lighter 10.5cm K331(f) guns, and these had an armoured shield which partially covered the embrasure. These dedicated coastal batteries tended to have an extensive array of support bunkers, including personnel shelters and ammunition bunkers.

In contrast to the dedicated coastal artillery batteries, the fortified divisional artillery batteries tended to have simpler garage casemates without specialized armoured protection for the embrasure since their weapons were towed field artillery pieces. Supporting bunkers were often less extensive due to the relatively late date of construction of many of these sites, which did not begin in earnest until January 1944.

The degree of fortification was quite uneven so for example, the famous Merville Battery attacked by British paratroopers on D-Day had a selection of bunkers comparable to that of dedicated coastal artillery batteries due to the early date of its fortification. Many divisional artillery battalions were not fortified at the time of the D-Day landings.

The Army's railroad artillery batteries fell out of favour after the 1940 bombardment campaign as rail-guns were withdrawn to other theatres. The Dombunker construction programme was not extended beyond the Pas-de-Calais, and the remaining railroad gun batteries such as those on the Cotentin Peninsula near Cherbourg did not have dedicated bombproof shelters.

Army infantry strongpoints

Infantry platoon and company strongpoints followed no particular pattern and tended to be constructed on the basis of available concrete supplies, available fortification weapons, and the terrain features of the coast where they were located.

In general, the infantry fortifications on the Atlantic Wall were not as comprehensive as those on the West Wall built along the German frontier in 1938–40. There were two reasons for this, the first of which was the lack of time and supplies to complete any comprehensive fortification of the entire French coastline. The second reason was tactical. Rundstedt and many German commanders were leery of extensive infantry fortification, as they feared it would lead to rigid tactics based around fixed sites. The commanders did not want the infantry cowering in their bunkers while the Allies flowed past the defences, but expected them to get out of the bunkers when necessary and use conventional infantry tactics. As a result, OB West favoured the use of a generous number of fortified machine-gun, mortar and anti-tank positions, but most of the infantry would fight from normal slit trenches. Personnel bunkers were provided for shelter during naval bombardment, but not for fighting.

The 4. Kompanie, Infanterie-Regiment 919, 709. Infanterie Division, provides an example. This company was deployed along the Cotentin coast from St Martin-de-Varreville to Ravenoville, a distance about 4km wide. This sector was a few kilometres to the north of Utah Beach on D-Day. Since German tactical doctrine recommended that a company defend a sector 400 to 1,000m wide, this sector was about four to ten times wider than would be assigned to an unfortified company in normal field conditions.

This company was commanded by Oberleutnant Werner, numbered about 170 men and was deployed in three strongpoints: WN10, WN11 and StP 12. Of the three strongpoints, WN10 on the right flank was by far the largest and most amply equipped. The WN11 strongpoint in the centre was primarily the company headquarters. It had minefields on either side and its principal bunkers facing the beach included two tobruks with 37mm French tank turrets, an artillery observation bunker, two machine-gun entrenchments and a 50mm gun in a Vf600 gun pit. Bunkers within the strongpoint included a mortar and a machine-gun tobruk, and five personnel and munitions bunkers. The northernmost strongpoint, StP 12, was small but heavily fortified and included four tobruks with 37mm French tank turrets, a H612 enfilade casement with 75mm gun, a modified H677 casemate with 50mm gun and a large H644 observation bunker with armoured cupola.

ABOVE: Strongpoint WN10, Les Dunes de Varreville. WN10 was a fairly typical infantry resistance nest containing a mixture of reinforced concrete bunkers and earthen entrenchments. This was one of three inter-related strongpoints manned by 4. Kompanie, Infanterie-Regiment 919, 709. Infanterie-Division, and located to the north-west of Utah Beach, covering an area 600m wide and 300m deep. (Chris Taylor © Osprey Publishing)

As can be seen from this description, several types of bunkers were very common in these infantry strongpoints. By far the most common were the tobruks, which were not a single type of bunker but rather a generic term for a wide range of small defensive works characterized by a small circular fighting position, hence their official designation as *Ringstand*. The German version was more elaborate than the Italian original since it generally included one or more compartments for the protection of the crew and for ammunition stowage. They were most often used to create a machine-gun position, but another common variant was a variety of mortar pit for either the battalion 81mm mortars or the company 50mm mortars.

A third common application was to mount the turret from French Renault FT, Renault R-35 or Hotchkiss H39 tanks on the tobruk, all armed with a version of the short 3.7cm tank gun. Another widely used fighting position was the Vf600 gun pit, typically fitted with the 5cm anti-aircraft gun. This was a six-sided open concrete emplacement with semi-protected cavities for ammunition stowage around its inner perimeter. The 5cm anti-craft gun was an adaptation of the obsolete 5cm tank gun mounted on a simple pedestal with a shield added for crew protection. Both the short (KwK 38) and long (KwK 39) versions of the gun were used and a number of these guns were re-bored to fire 7.7cm ammunition. An interesting hybrid of the tobruk and Vf600 was the Michelmannstand, developed by Colonel Kurt Michelmann, the commander of Festungs-Pionier-Stab 27 responsible for fortifying Dieppe and upper Normandy. This was a prefabricated reinforced concrete machine-gun pit that could be rapidly emplaced on beaches or other areas in lieu of more conventional and time-consuming construction techniques. Although it resembled a shrunken Vf600, its tactical application was closer to that of a tobruk.

THE FRENCH SITES AT WAR

The gun batteries along the Pas-de-Calais took part in a desultory campaign of bombardment against the English coast around Dover starting in 1940 and continuing well into 1944. This resulted in a continuing campaign of counter-bombardment from British batteries as well as a prolonged air campaign against the 'Iron Coast' gun batteries. Although the air campaign was not especially effective in disabling the fortified casemates, the battery sites soon took on the appearance of a lunar landscape due to the many bomb craters. There was also some exchange of fire between coastal batteries and British warships over the years and the heavy gun batteries along the Pas-de-Calais frequently fired upon coastal shipping in the Channel.

The Allied campaign against the coastal batteries was intensified in 1944 and extended to upper and lower Normandy and parts of Brittany in April 1944 as part of the run-up to the D-Day invasion. The campaign was intentionally conducted also at sites other than the D-Day beaches to keep the Wehrmacht guessing where the actual landings would take place. The bombardment campaign had very mixed results, in some cases effectively neutralizing batteries such as the Army coastal battery on Pointe-du-Hoc, in other cases failing to have any appreciable effect on the battery such as at Merville, while other instances had mixed success such as Longues-sur-Mer, where the gun casemates were intact but their performance degraded due to the destruction of the cabling between the fire-control post and the guns.

The D-Day landings in lower Normandy on 6 June 1944 quickly overwhelmed the defences. The coastal batteries with very few exceptions had been disabled before the landings and, even in the case of the few batteries that engaged the landing fleet such as the St Marcouf, Azeville and Longues-sur-Mer batteries, they were quickly suppressed. The only defences that posed a significant problem were those at Omaha Beach, and this was due primarily to the presence of more defences, more and better troops, and a more challenging defence configuration due to the bluffs along the beach compared to the other D-Day beaches.

This 5cm anti-tank gun in an H667 casemate proved to be one of the most effective elements of the WN65 strongpoint covering the E-1 St Laurent draw. It was finally silenced by 37mm automatic cannon fire from a pair of M15A1 multiple gun motor carriage half-tracks of the 467th AAA Battalion. (NARA)

DEFENCE OF THE PERIPHERY – THE ATLANTIC WALL

ABOVE: Tobruks were the most common type of fortified position along the Normandy coast, and existed in a wide range of styles. One version of the tobruk commonly seen on the Normandy beaches was the Panzerstellung, equipped with a tank turret. These were sometimes based on the standard Vf67v tobruk as seen here, but also on modified types including a common but non-standard U-shaped tobruk. (Hugh Johnson © Osprey Publishing)

Once the D-Day landings took place, there was no immediate evacuation or weakening of other portions of the Atlantic Wall since senior German commanders remained convinced for several weeks that the Normandy landings were only a feint and that other landings would occur elsewhere along the coast. Elements of the Atlantic Wall defences were involved in continual combat through June as the US First Army advanced up the Cotentin Peninsula, culminating in the VII Corps attack on Cherbourg in late June 1944. Although Cherbourg had been ringed with defences as part of the Festung policy, in reality these defences were not adequate to stop the US Army. The outer crust of Cherbourg defences served to delay the US advance, but they were comprehensively breached within a few days of intense combat. The defences in Cherbourg itself were mostly oriented seaward and so played little role in the city fighting. Indeed, the traditional French fortified defences around the port played as much a role in the defence as did the newer Atlantic Wall defences, such as Fort Roule in the centre of the city and the fortified harbour. The heaviest fortifications, such as the numerous Navy coastal artillery batteries, played little or no role in the fighting since their ferro-concrete carapace limited the traverse of their guns to seaward targets. This experience would be repeated in the subsequent battles for the Channel ports, where most of the work on the Atlantic Wall fortifications proved to be in vain due to this fatal shortcoming.

ABOVE: The Vf600-SK 5cm gun emplacement. One of the most common gun emplacements along the Normandy coast was the open gun platform for the 5cm pedestal-mounted gun. This type was variously called the OB 600 (Offene Bettung = open platform) or Vf600 (Verstärkt feldmäßig = reinforced field position). In its basic Vf600v form, it was an octagonal concrete gun pit about 4.15m wide generally with recesses for ammunition stowage in the four front and side walls. (Hugh Johnson © Osprey Publishing)

Further fighting ensued along the Atlantic Wall after the breakout from Normandy in late July that unleashed the Allied advance along the coast towards the Pas-de-Calais and towards Brittany. St Malo at the junction between lower Normandy and Brittany was the scene of an intense urban battle made all the more difficult for the US Army by the traditional walled fortifications of the port. The assault on St Malo by the 83rd Division began on 5 August and took nearly two weeks of fighting, finally being overwhelmed on 17 August. Even then, German defenders held out on the offshore fortifications of Cézembre until 2 September. The port of Brest was one of the most heavily fortified along the Atlantic Wall and US armoured spearheads began probing its defences on August 7. The city was gradually surrounded and a full-blooded attack began on 25 August by VIII Corps of Patton's Third Army. Although the fortifications and gun positions of the Atlantic Wall defences played some role in the defence of Brest, for the most part they were not especially useful for the defenders except in some limited sectors. Once again, traditional French fortifications such as Fort Montbarey and Fort de Portzic proved more troublesome than the newer and much smaller Atlantic Wall bunkers, most of which were oriented seaward. As in the case of Cherbourg, the German garrison was eventually overwhelmed, but in the interim, the Kriegsmarine managed to demolish the harbour facilities. As a result, the US Army decided against a direct assault on St Nazaire or Lorient, preferring to simply bottle up the German garrison rather than sacrifice large numbers of infantrymen for a shattered port. The same would be the case along the Bay of Biscay, with fortified ports such as Royan and La Rochelle holding out until May 1945. To reduce the number of US troops assigned to this siege, in the autumn of 1944 newly raised French units were gradually assigned this mission.

Operation *Astonia*: Festung Le Havre

While the US Army was dealing with the fortified ports in Brittany, Montgomery's 21st Army Group was advancing northward toward upper Normandy, the Picardy coast and, eventually, the Pas-de-Calais. The honour of taking Dieppe was given to the Canadian 2nd Division and the city fell without a major fight on 1 September. The second major port in Normandy, Le Havre, was invested by the British I Corps, starting on 3 September. To soften up the defences before the ground attack, the Royal Navy monitor HMS *Erebus* began bombardment along the coast on 5 September, but was forced to withdraw by the heavy concentration of coastal artillery west of the city. These positions included the only heavy gun battery in the city, a 38cm turreted gun from the French warship *Jean-Bart* located at Clos de Ronces and supported by the Goldbrunner battery of 3./HKAR.1254 with three 17cm K18 guns, two of which were in H688 casemates. Besides these batteries, there were several other batteries in the immediate vicinity that took part in some of the subsequent engagements. The *Erebus* returned on 8 September, but was

HITLER'S FORTRESSES

LONGUES-SUR-MER GUN BATTERY

The Longues-sur-Mer gun battery is illustrative of coastal artillery in Normandy. This bunker had the most modern fire-control system of any of the batteries in this sector. It was electrically powered and fed the aiming data directly from the control bunker to the individual gun casemates. This was a two-storey bunker with range-finding and observation equipment, and a target-tracking centre located in the lower chamber. It was connected by landlines to the four M272 gun casemates. The four gun casemates were armed with 15cm C/36 single-mount Torpedoboots Kanonen (destroyer guns), built by Skoda in Pilzen, with a maximum range of 19km. There were ammunition rooms behind the gun chamber, one to contain the powder charges and the other to contain the ammunition. The casemate was protected to Class B standards with walls and roof 2m thick and construction consumed 760m^3 of concrete. (Hugh Johnson © Osprey Publishing)

again forced back by heavy gunfire from the German coastal batteries. Prior to the start of I Corps' main attack, Operation *Astonia*, on 10 September, the *Erebus* returned but this time was accompanied by the battleship HMS *Warspite*, which demolished the offending batteries with its 15in guns. The two ships then conducted a six-hour bombardment against other coastal fortifications and defences. The battle for Le Havre by two infantry

DEFENCE OF THE PERIPHERY – THE ATLANTIC WALL

ABOVE: H633 bunker for M19 automatic mortar. The H633 Kampfstand für M19 Maschinengranatwerfer was specifically developed for the West Wall, but by the time that production began in 1940, the requirement had ended. Instead, most were eventually used on the Atlantic Wall, and some 79 were installed in the H633 and H135 bunkers, with 48 on the French coast. The entry way was protected by an armoured machine-gun embrasure and led to the usual gas lock prior to access to the living quarters. (Chris Taylor © Osprey Publishing)

divisions supported by the specialized armour of the 79th Armoured Division lasted only two days in no small measure due to the demoralization of the isolated garrison.

Operation *Wellhit*: Festung Boulogne

While Operation *Astonia* was under way, Canadian forces had begun to probe the outer defences of both Boulogne and Calais. The Canadian 3rd Infantry Division was assigned Operation *Wellhit*, the assault against Boulogne and the associated German fortifications in the neighbouring hills. In light of the experiences at Le Havre, the specialized armour of the 79th Armoured Division was also used to support the Canadians, especially

One of the more elaborate mounts for the 5cm pedestal gun was the R600, which had the usual hexagonal gun pit on the top of the structure, but included an alert room and ammunition storage in a chamber below. Normally, this casemate would have been buried in the edge of a coastal dune, but this example on the beach at Wissant has been left stranded by coastal erosion since the war, exposing its interesting shape, including the pair of rear stairways to the gun pit above. (Steven J. Zaloga)

Churchill Crocodile flamethrower tanks and Churchill AVRE (Armoured Vehicle Royal Engineer) fitted with heavy petards. Festung Boulogne had three major concentrations of fortifications: a trio of coastal batteries near Pointe de la Crèche on the coast north of the city, a set of defensive bunkers and a gun battery from 4./AR. 147 on Mont Lambert on the main road into the city from the east, and a series of coastal guns and bunkers on the heights to the south of the port around Le Portel. Besides the defences of the city itself, Operation *Wellhit* also contained a subsidiary attack on German positions around La Trésorerie overlooking the city to the north-east, which contained the substantial naval battery of Batterie Friedrich August of MAA. 240 with three 30.5cm SKL/50 guns in massive casemates. Operation *Wellhit* began on 17 September, including an attack by the North Shore Regiment on La Trésorerie and two brigades assaulting toward Mont Lambert. Mont Lambert was not overcome until 18 September after engineers had blasted the final bunkers with explosive charges. The gun casemates of Batterie Friedrich August were stubbornly defended by nearby Flak positions armed with 2cm cannon, but the position was finally overwhelmed on the second day of fighting using PIAT anti-tank launchers and grenades. The Canadians fought into the city and captured the old citadel, but then were faced with the problem of clearing the numerous bunkers on the heights south of the city around Le Portel. These positions had been a constant source of fire through the fighting, with one battery of Flak guns alone having fired some 2,000 rounds in the three days of fighting. This position was finally overwhelmed but fighting for the other bunkers on the high ground continued through 22 September when the garrison finally surrendered. Canadian troops had begun to attack the bunker complexes of La Crèche, but the garrison surrendered before a full-scale attack was launched.

Operation *Wellhit* led to the capture of about 10,000 German troops at a cost of about 600 Canadian casualties through the use of proven combined tank–infantry tactics that succeeded in the face of a significant number of bunkers and heavy gun emplacements. The capture of the port took six days instead of the planned two days, but the operation involved only about a third of the troops used at Le Havre. The Churchill Crocodile flamethrower tanks proved to be especially useful and an after-action report recorded that most German bunkers surrendered at the first sign of a flamethrower tank. The AVRE tanks were not particularly effective as their petard launcher, although powerful, could not penetrate the 2m reinforced concrete of the bunkers, and this weapon was no more effective than any other tank gun in penetrating the embrasures and armoured doors of the fortifications, if anything being shorter-ranged and less accurate. The aerial bombardment that preceded the attack was not effective in suppressing the bunkers and hindered tank operations in Boulogne due to the craters and rubble. In subsequent operations, such as Calais, the emphasis was shifted to the use of fragmentation bombs to limit the cratering. The fighting demonstrated the limitations of the Atlantic Wall fortifications since the vast majority of defences were oriented seaward. The heavy gun casemates limited the arc of fire of the guns and, as a result, most batteries were unable to take part in the fighting. The few batteries that did have suitable orientations, such as the dual-role Flak batteries designed for enfilade fire along the port, were responsible for the majority of Canadian casualties.

Operation *Undergo*: Festung Calais

Although consideration was given to simply bypassing Calais in favour of devoting the troop strength to the clearing of the Scheldt estuary leading to Antwerp, in late September Montgomery was persuaded to deal with Calais due to the havoc that its strong gun positions could cause to Allied shipping in the Channel. On the night of

The most potent fortification to take part in the D-Day fighting was the Crisbeq battery of 3/HKAA. 1261 located near Saint-Marcouf. Only two H683 casemates for its four Skoda 210mm K39/40 guns were completed by D-Day. After engaging in prolonged gun duels with Allied warships off Utah Beach on D-Day, the battery was the scene later of intense ground combat, which earned its commander, Oberleutnant zur See Ohmsen, the Knight's Cross. (NARA)

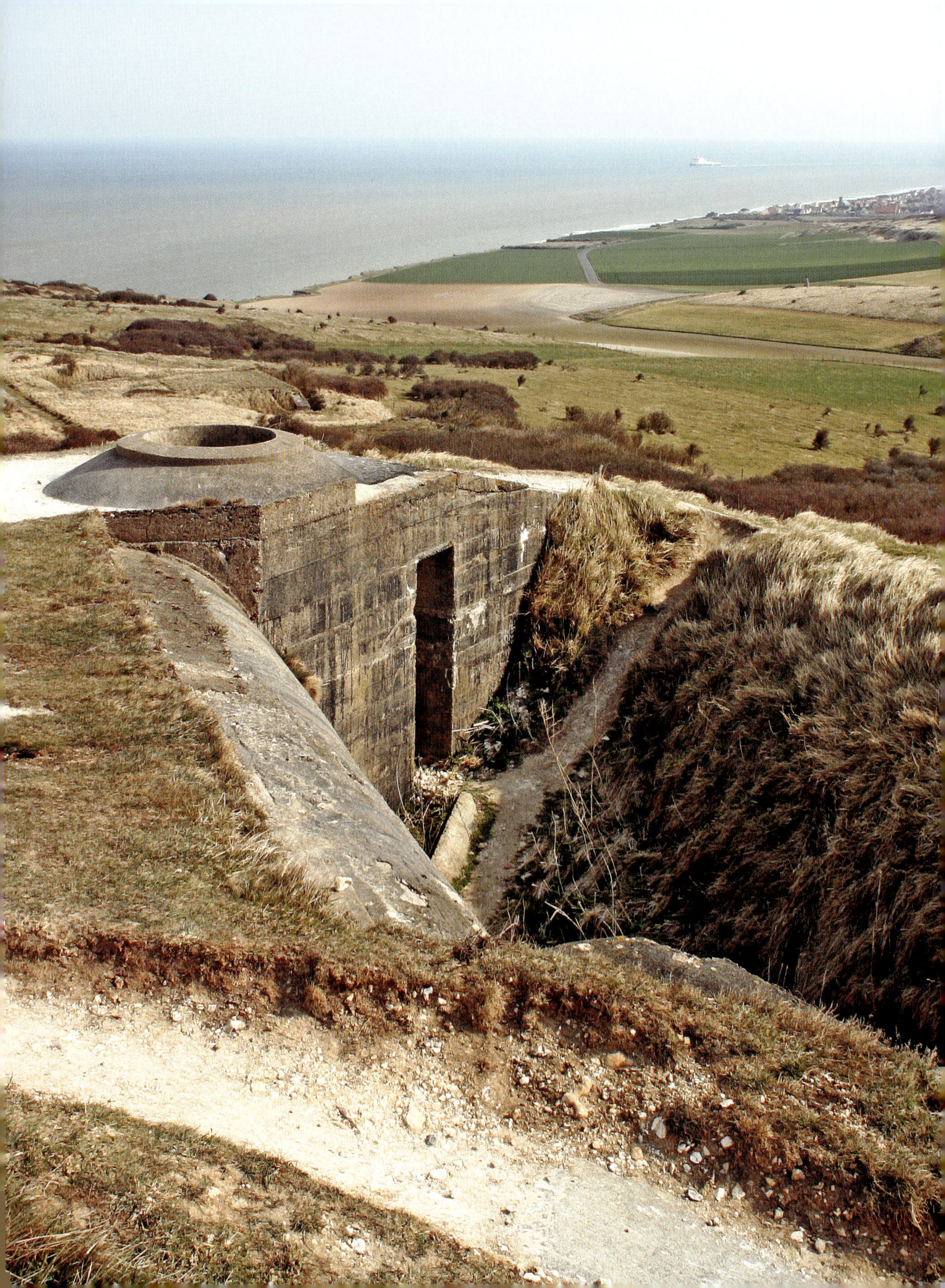

9/10 September, the Regina Rifles took the fortified port town of Wissant and overran the bunkers on Mont Coupole, which offered excellent observation of the Cap Gris-Nez and Calais region.

Operation *Undergo* was again assigned to the Canadian 3rd Infantry Division, supported by the 6th Assault Regiment RE of the 79th Armoured Division with their specialized armour. After a series of delays, the attack began on 25 September with heavy tank and artillery support. Batterie Lindemann could offer little resistance as its guns were pointed to sea, and the garrison surrendered at noon on 26 September. Within two days, the two Canadian brigades had cleared through most of the defences to the south-west of the city, while at the same time routes of escape to the east were cut off. Once again, the old French fortifications such as Fort Lapin proved to be more formidable than the scattered German bunkers, and it was taken only after a determined Canadian infantry assault backed by Churchill Crocodile flamethrowers; the same process was repeated at Fort Nieuley. A temporary truce was called on 29 September to organize the evacuation of civilians still in the city.

While the 7th and 8th Brigades were busy in Calais, the 9th Infantry Brigade was assigned to clear the fortified belt along Cap Gris-Nez including the Batterie Todt with its four massive 38cm guns. By this stage the Canadians had a well-orchestrated scheme for dealing with the bunkers; all four of the main German batteries were overcome in a few hours fighting on 29 September and 1,500 prisoners taken at the cost of 42 casualties, with only five killed.

The evacuation of the civilians from Calais only served to further undermine morale within Festung Calais. When the truce ended on 30 September, the defence simply collapsed and the garrison formally surrendered at 1900hrs.

In spite of the enormous numbers of heavy gun bunkers and coastal defences, the landward defences were completely inadequate to hinder a determined attack, especially considering the lack of sufficient infantry in the Festung Calais garrison. The garrison did manage to thoroughly wreck the harbour, and it took more than three weeks to rehabilitate the port.

Unlike Calais and Cap Gris-Nez, Dunkirk lacked long-range gun batteries so Montgomery decided to contain the port rather than waste time and troops capturing it. The Festung Dunkirk garrison numbered about 12,000 troops. Both sides engaged in periodic artillery skirmishes, and evacuation of the civilian population occurred during a truce on 3–6 October. The Czechoslovak Armoured Brigade replaced most of the Canadian troops cordoning the city after the truce. After the German garrison staged a raid on the night of 19/20 October, Operation *Waddle* was conducted on 28 October to discourage further actions, the last major military action of the siege. The garrison offered to surrender on 4 May 1945, and the town was finally liberated on 6 May.

OPPOSITE: The R621 personnel bunker has a tobruk machine-gun pit on one side for observation and defence. This particular type of bunker was the most common type along the Atlantic Wall in France with over 1,000 built including the related R501. This one is part of StP Düsseldorf on the eastern slope of Cap Blanc-Nez, overlooking Sangatte and the Eurotunnel to the right. (Steven J. Zaloga)

THE CHANNEL ISLANDS

The Channel Islands were the only part of the British Isles occupied by the German forces, from late June 1940. On 20 October 1941, Hitler – ever paranoid about a possible British attempt to reclaim the islands – ordered their transformation into fortress islands. Under this direction, the Channel Islands actually became one of the most formidable elements in the Atlantic Wall chain, as well as one of the most underutilized. As in the West Wall, the purpose of the defences was to offer an integrated response to any enemy attack, whether from the sea or air or, as was more likely, both. However, unlike the West Wall there could be little in the way of defence in depth; the restricted physical area saw to that.

COASTAL DEFENCES

An enemy approaching the Channel Islands from the sea would first be engaged by the coastal artillery batteries, able to range to some 38km in the case of the heaviest battery on Guernsey, Batterie Mirus. This fire would be directed from the HQ of Seeko-Ki, an abbreviation for Kommandant der Seeverteidigung Kanalinseln (Naval Commander Channel Islands), a command set up in June 1942 which, from October 1942, was responsible for the tactical command of Army coastal artillery and Army divisional batteries firing on seaborne targets, as well as the harbour command and defence flotillas in the three principal islands, in addition to naval artillery.

The control of firing on sea targets was initially to be established by triangulation from a planned series of Marine Peilstände und Meßstellen (naval artillery direction and rangefinding towers). These were multi-storeyed affairs, with each floor controlling a separate artillery battery; the location of the target was ascertained by taking compass bearings on it from two adjacent towers, the known distance between them thus forming the base of a triangle that, together with the established angles, enabled a simple trigonometric calculation to locate the target's exact position. The drawback to such a system was that it could not easily handle multiple targets; it would have been difficult, perhaps impossible, for an observer in one tower to ascertain that he was taking a bearing on the same target as his opposite number in the neighbouring tower. In the event, the prescribed number of towers was not constructed, and the system was superseded by direct gun laying with stereoscopic rangefinders by individual batteries.

The coastal defences were deployed to comply with the principle that any force that managed to effect a landing was to be met at the earliest opportunity and destroyed or repulsed. The defences constructed at Vazon Bay, on the north-west coast of Guernsey, can serve as an example of the coastal defences that proliferated on the three main Channel Islands. Described in pre-war tourist literature as possessing a 'fine sandy beach'

BATTERIE MIRUS

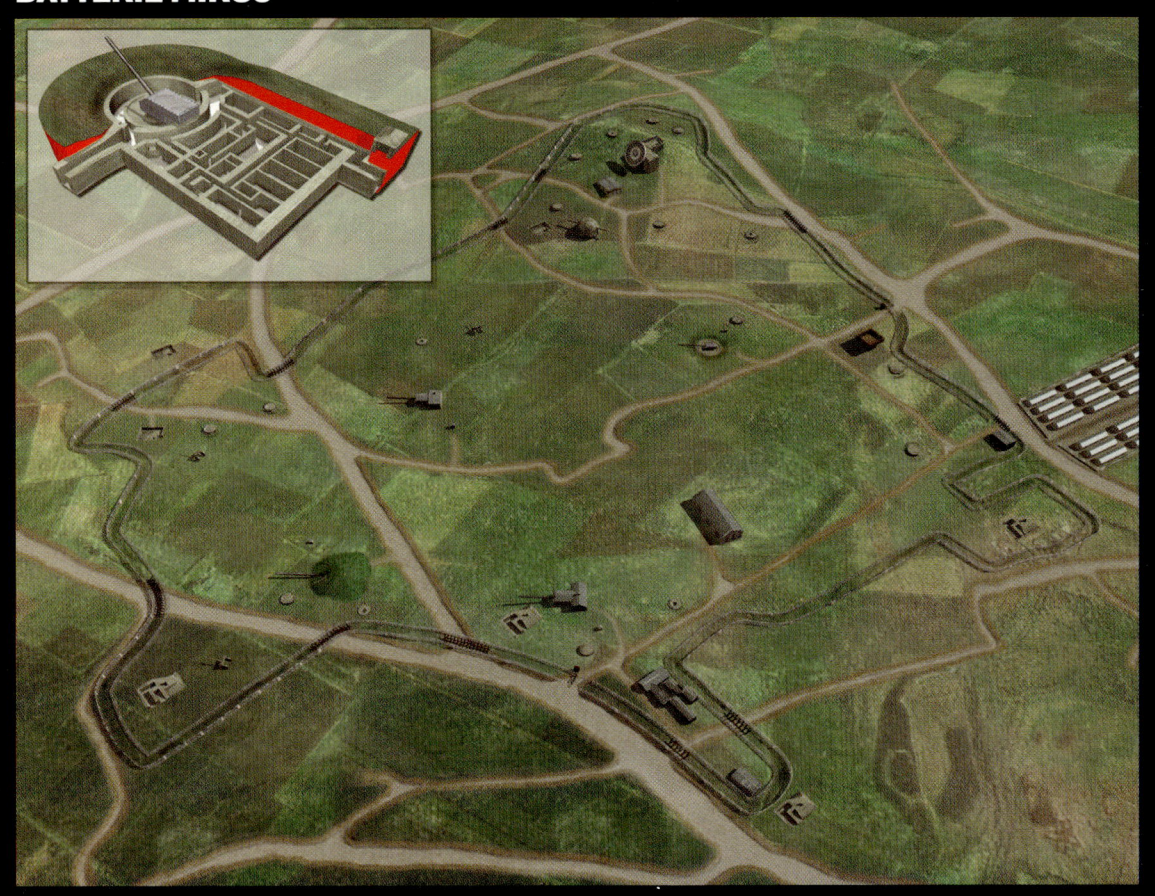

Located at Le Frie Baton on the north-west coast of Guernsey, Mirus was the largest-calibre battery to be installed in the Channel Islands. The four emplacements each had their own ammunition stores, plant rooms and crew accommodation for 72 men. Each weapon consisted of a 30.5cm gun in a single armoured turret. The turrets of Guns 1 and 3 were disguised as cottages whilst Guns 2 and 4 were draped in camouflage netting – Gun 2 has been depicted without this. The perimeter was marked and protected by barbed-wire entanglements and continuous belts of mines, with two entrances – the main entrance, off the Les Paysans Road, towards the bottom of the artwork, and an eastern entrance adjacent to the barrack-type buildings of Lager Westmark. Just inside the western entrance was a parking area and the guardroom, together with a stone farmhouse, which formed the admin office. The battery mess was located in the large building to the north of the entrance complex. The Leitstand (command bunker) was largely subterranean, with only the optical rangefinder and observation cupola visible, which would have been hung with camouflage material, but no amount of netting could have disguised the antenna of the Würzburg radar installation. Nine light 2cm Flak positions protected the battery, seven of which were within the perimeter and two outside. The three reserve ammunition bunkers, unlike most other bunkers on the site, were constructed at ground level, and were camouflaged as houses with pitched roofs and cosmetic windows and doors. Infantry defence was provided by some 17 field emplacements reinforced with concrete, five of which contained mortars and the rest machine guns, and three field guns that are recorded as having been deployed within the battery perimeter. (Chris Taylor © Osprey Publishing)

HITLER'S FORTRESSES

with a 'low-lying road' just inland, Vazon Bay presented an ideal landing ground for an amphibious force, and was therefore heavily fortified in line with Hitler's directive. Primarily these fortifications consisted of a network of emplacements to provide flanking fire and defences against tanks.

The principal armaments of the coastal defences were 10.5cm guns, manufactured by Schneider and originally designed in 1913 as field artillery for the French Army. Single casemated 10.5cm guns, with a maximum range of some 12km, formed the core of the two Vazon Bay strongpoints, Stützpunkt Rotenstein, constructed around the obsolete Fort Hommet, and Stützpunkt Reichenburg, based around Fort Richmond and Fort le Crocq, on the two promontories that flanked the bay. At least four of these guns were able to bear on any seaborne force that approached or entered the bay, and all were contained in fortress-standard bunkers, with a roof and external walls of ferro-concrete. Also present were five casemates, again of fortress standard, equipped with anti-tank weaponry, which had been removed from Czechoslovakia when that state had

The Dieppe raid led to an intensive programme to protect coastal batteries with steel-reinforced concrete casemates like this Bauform 671 armed with a 15cm C/36 destroyer gun and currently preserved as part of the Domain Raversijde museum. (Steven Zaloga)

come under German control following the annexation of the Sudetenland in 1938. These guns were originally designated as 4cm Kanon vz.36 but were re-designated by the Germans as the 4.7cm Festungspanzerabwehrkanone 36(t), abbreviated to 4.7cm PaK 36(t), the 't' designating *tschechisch* (Czech). When in a fortress mounting they shared a coaxial ball mounting with a Czech machine-gun, the MG37(t).

Also featuring in the Vazon Bay defences were two Sechsschartentürme (sometimes rendered as Mehrschartentürme) für schweres Maschinengewehr (six-loopholed, or multi-loopholed, turrets for heavy machine guns). These were essentially thick – 270mm – armoured-steel cupolas mounted on a fortress-standard bunker that was largely underground with, as the name suggests, six (or multiple) loopholes for giving a wide arc of fire to twin MG34 heavy machine guns. In practice some of these loopholes were blanked off, as when they were built into sloping terrain for example. Though the sources are somewhat confusing and tend to differ, it seems that by 1944 there were four of these cupolas on Guernsey, eight on Jersey and two on Alderney.

Of note is the 5cm Maschinengranatwerfer M19 (automatic mortar), which was only manufactured in small quantities with fewer than 100, some sources say 98, being produced from 1937 to 1938. They were first installed in the West Wall. The M19 was, like the MG cupola, housed on a subterranean bunker constructed to fortress standard, and was a true fortress weapon, being designed to operate whilst almost entirely invisible to any attackers. The weapon fired through an aperture in a thickly armoured horizontal plate, and was aimed with a periscope sight that could be extended through a similar hole, both protected with an armoured cover when not firing. Loaded manually with clips containing six rounds, these weapons could discharge one round per second, over ranges 30–750m, and were considered to be shattering in their effect. For emergencies the loading system could be switched to automatic and the rate of fire doubled. This, however, was believed to place undue strain on the weapon, as well as swiftly depleting the ammunition supply of some 4,000 rounds. Four of these weapons were deployed on Guernsey, one on Jersey and two on Alderney.

Four tobruk pits also defended Vazon Bay. They could be easily adapted to take a variety of weaponry, including, in the case of three of the four in question here, a tank turret. Tobruk pits were usually constructed to a lesser specification than fortress standard, being designated as reinforced field order installations, with a roof and external walls of up to 1.2m-thick ferro-concrete. Apart from tobruks, the most common installations in this category were personnel shelters, mortar pits, observation posts and artillery emplacements, though it was often the case that this category of construction was found alongside fortress-standard works as at Vazon Bay. Reinforced field order installations were normally built by Army construction units rather than by the OT.

HITLER'S FORTRESSES

This is a superb example of the open-kettle-style gun pits typical of the Atlantic Wall in 1940–43, armed in this case with a war-booty Cockerill 120mm mle. 1931 Belgian field gun. This is part of the Batterie Saltzwedel neu/Tirpitz of 6./MAA. 204 from 1941 until April 1944, and now preserved at the Domain Raversijde museum. (Steven Zaloga)

For night-fighting, Stützpunkt Rotenstein was equipped with two searchlights housed in fortress-standard bunkers. These were essentially garages for the light, which was mounted on a trolley on narrow-gauge railway tracks, and deployed by pushing it out to a prepared position. Unterstände (shelters) were stand-alone personnel bunkers and generally came in two sizes, designated as Gruppenunterstände (group shelters) or Doppelgruppenunterstände (double-group shelters), which were designed to provide protection for groups of 10 and 20 men respectively. They were often subterranean with their roofs at ground level, and were of fortress or reinforced field order standard, as were bunkers for ammunition and other stores. Hitler, as always interested in the minutiae of such matters, had specified that personnel shelters were only to be used as protection against heavy artillery fire and aerial bombardment, and that the troops must otherwise remain outside their protection in order to fight. With what can now be viewed as an ironic twist, given that the last months of his life were spent leading a troglodyte existence, he added that 'whoever disappears into a bunker is lost'.

DEFENCE OF THE PERIPHERY – THE ATLANTIC WALL

THE LUFTWAFFE COMMAND BUNKER, ST ANNE, ALDERNEY

This complex formed the HQ of the Luftwaffe on Alderney, and this rendition shows what it might have looked like before the addition of another storey containing a water tank, thus giving rise to its popular designation of the 'Water Tower'. The bunker contained communications equipment, including a telephone exchange and the Enigma machine depicted in the insert, as well as ventilation plant and air filtration systems, a kitchen/crew room, ablutions, offices, stores, a radar centre and defensive positions armed with the MG42 machine gun. The radar antenna atop the tower is for a Freya air surveillance radar, one of the earliest types of German radar, the first sets being ordered by the Luftwaffe in 1937, and one that through continuous improvement became one of the most ubiquitous with some 2,000 units delivered during the war. Being a fully steerable, smaller, and thus mobile, system, and giving better resolution, the Freya radar has been adjudged as more sophisticated than its British counterpart, in 1940 the fixed Chain Home system. However, it had a maximum range of only 160km, and an effective range of around 100km, and could not accurately determine altitude. It was thus inferior to Chain Home in those respects. Freya also formed an important component in the 'Kammhuber Line', the integrated air defence created by General Josef Kammhuber to protect the Third Reich from Allied bombing. A series of radar stations with overlapping coverage were layered from Denmark to the middle of France, each covering a zone about 32km long (north–south) and 20km wide (east–west). Each of these zones contained a Freya radar and a number of searchlights, and were assigned a primary and backup night fighter. (Chris Taylor © Osprey Publishing)

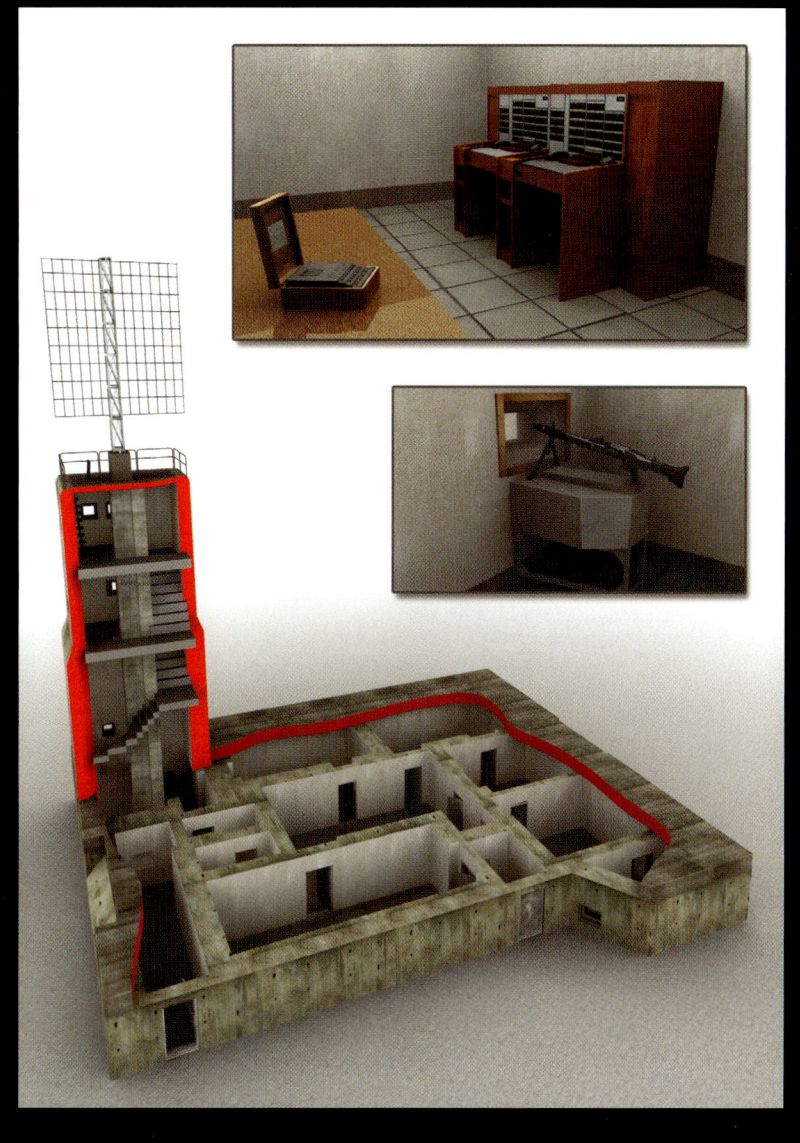

HITLER'S FORTRESSES

The Schwimmende Balkenmine was an improvised anti-craft mine consisting of a half-dozen Teller mines strapped to a wooden raft. These were anchored off the invasion beaches to concrete bases or to other obstructions. In the background is one of the ubiquitous Czech 'hedgehog' obstructions. (MHI)

Aside from the two fortress-standard machine-gun cupolas, two other reinforced field order emplacements for machine guns were constructed for the defence of Vazon Bay, the one within WN Margen being mounted on the seawall. Granite sea-defence walls feature prominently throughout the Channel Islands, having been constructed during the 19th century in order to mitigate coastal erosion. Though their architects and builders could never have foreseen such an eventuality, they also make first-rate barriers to vehicles attempting to exit the beach; in other words they provide excellent anti-tank defences.

Not discernible on the map are the networks of trenches and foxholes that proliferated along the edge of the bay, where the infantry would fight after emerging from their bunkers. Also not shown is the ubiquitous barbed wire, kilometres of which were wrapped around the island.

The Channel Islands were heavily sown with mines; over 100,000 in total had been laid by 1945. Some 54,000 are recorded as having been placed on Guernsey by April 1944, and it can safely be assumed, though no reliable records have been located, that a good number of these featured in the defences at Vazon Bay. An additional device sown on the beaches to discourage invaders was the Abwehr-flammenwerfer (Defence-Flamethrower) 42. This was an emplaced flamethrower, another idea adapted from Soviet practice after the German Army had encountered such devices in the defence zone around Moscow. Basically it was a metal tank of 30cm diameter and 53cm height, rather similar to a modern day cooking-gas cylinder, filled with some 30 litres of thickened flammable liquid, and buried in the ground up to its neck. Inserted into the top of this tank was an electrically activated 'pressure cartridge', and, welded into place, a tube that could be bent at a desired angle. One end of this tube sat close to the bottom of the cylinder, whilst the other, to which was attached a nozzle and electrically fired fuse, was pointed in the required direction. Upon activation by a remote operator, the pressure cartridge forced the contents up through the tube and out of the nozzle where they were ignited. The flame had a maximum range of around 50m and a maximum spread of around 15m, and endured for a few seconds.

Apart from the hazards of mines and flamethrowers, beach exits were physically blocked, both by means of barbed wire against infantry and Igel (hedgehog) anti-tank devices. Some sources also speak of these devices, which were also found on the foreshore providing a defence against landing craft, having shells fixed to them, which were designed to detonate on impact. Other anti-tank obstacles, constructed from railway line embedded in concrete, blocked many roads and tracks leading inland, where a second series of bunkers, designated Einsatzstellung (operation position) and usually of reinforced field rather than fortress standard, were to be found. Normally manned only during alerts, these commanded strategic points such as crossroads and contained

HITLER'S FORTRESSES

The Batterie Saltzwedel neu/Tirpitz of 6./MAA. 204 on the western side of Ostend was armed with pintle-mounted 10.5cm SKC/32U submarine guns in Bauform 671 casemates starting in April 1944. This well-preserved example is part of the Domain Raversijde museum; the embrasure is covered by a window to protect it from the weather. (Steven Zaloga)

anti-tank weapons and machine guns. In short, mounting an amphibious attack across the beach at Vazon Bay, or of course any other point on the coast of any of the Channel Islands, was likely to be a desperately hazardous enterprise.

AIR DEFENCES

Aerial attack figured in Hitler's directive for the Channel Islands, where he had stated that 'strongpoints must be created with searchlights sufficient to accommodate such anti-aircraft units as are needed for the protection of all important constructions'. The Führer specified that the islands must be able to defend themselves without help from the Luftwaffe based on the French mainland, and accordingly the anti-aircraft defences assigned to the Channel Islands were immensely powerful. By 1944 there were 16 mixed medium/light Fliegerabwehrkanonen (anti-aircraft guns, generally best known by their German acronym: Flak) batteries, plus around 83 light batteries, deployed on the Channel Islands and operated by the Luftwaffe.

There were four mixed batteries on Alderney, each deploying six 8.8cm and three lighter weapons, either 2cm or 3.7cm guns, together with 18 dedicated light batteries deploying two or three light weapons. Altogether these Flak batteries mounted nearly 100 guns, which is a formidable defensive array for an island of only some 800 hectares. However, these air force-controlled weapons were augmented by a further 17 2cm guns, including four-barrelled weapons known as Flakvierlinge, manned by Army and Kriegsmarine personnel to defend the coastal artillery sites.

Jersey contained six mixed batteries deploying 36 8.8cm and around 12 light guns, as well as some 25 light Air Force batteries. In addition there were complements of Army and Kriegsmarine anti-aircraft gunners, making a total of around 165 guns.

One of the solutions to the threat of British midget submarines was to deploy these Rheinmetall-Borsig R300 rocket-propelled depth charge launchers to Norwegian and Danish ports in 1944–45. (NARA)

The Belgian coast had a relatively heavy concentration of railroad guns for its heavy artillery. This is the 28cm Kurze Bruno station in Bredene with E.696. (A. Chazette)

Guernsey likewise had six mixed batteries and an even larger number of light batteries, some 30, making a total of around 175 dedicated anti-aircraft guns. Two of the mixed batteries, at L'Ancresse Bay and Torteval, were built to fortress standard; that is the weapons were mounted on concrete bunkers, whilst one at St Germain, above Vazon Bay, was partially constructed in this way. The others were mounted in field emplacements. Each of the mixed batteries was provided with a Würzburg Dora radar for fire control and, in addition to the dedicated Flak weapons, machine guns on anti-aircraft mountings abounded.

TUNNELS

An essential element of any defensive system is the allocation of reserves, in terms both of supplies and of equipment and personnel. Both Jersey and Guernsey have a number of valleys, which proved attractive in providing underground shelters for these reserves.

Tunnelling into the hillsides gave up to 36m of solid rock protection from aerial bombardment; it was intended that the tunnels should be lined with concrete. A number of tunnels were planned and excavated on Alderney also.

Designated as Hohlgangsanlage (generally translated as cave passage installations), abbreviated to Ho, 16 of these sites were planned for Jersey, 41 for Guernsey and nine for Alderney. The larger of these works were designed to have two entrances, but not all were of this type and fewer were actually completed as designed; for example, of the 16 planned for Jersey, only a minority were completed by 1945. The remainder had been started and worked on, and may have been usable to some degree.

Thus reconfigured, the Channel Islands became one of the most heavily fortified places in the world. However World War II was a war of manoeuvre, and the Channel Islands were simply avoided by the Allies in terms of major assaults. Yet more of Hitler's resources had been poured into concrete and metal for no great purpose.

THE ATLANTIC WALL IN THE NORTH

Although France, of course, would be the place where the Atlantic Wall was most vigorously tested under combat, the system of defences also stretched well north of France's coastline. This section, therefore, discusses the coverage from the Belgian coast eastwards to the Netherlands and Denmark, and north to Norway. In the case of the countries covered here, the mission was more complex than that in France. Coastal defences in Belgium were the same as those in neighbouring France and part of the same anti-invasion scheme. But for the rest of this region, the Atlantic Wall was a response to more diverse threats posed by the Royal Navy.

Norway was the first country to see extensive deployment of coastal artillery, provoked in large measure by early British commando raids. Allied deception operations through the war attempted to convince the German military that an invasion of Norway was part of Allied strategy, in hopes of tying down German forces. There was a revival of Norwegian defences in the late summer of 1944. The loss of critical U-boat bases in France forced the Kriegsmarine to deploy its surviving force to Norwegian harbours such as Trondheim, invigorating Royal Navy actions to these northern waters and provoking renewed defence efforts. When the Red Army pushed the Wehrmacht out of Finland via the arctic Finnmark region of Norway, coastal defences were reinforced to protect the troop convoys streaming down along the coast from arctic waters.

Although the threat of amphibious invasion on the Dutch coast was slight due to the terrain, the important ports of Rotterdam and Amsterdam and their access to the key rivers leading into the German industrial heartland guaranteed serious fortification

HITLER'S FORTRESSES

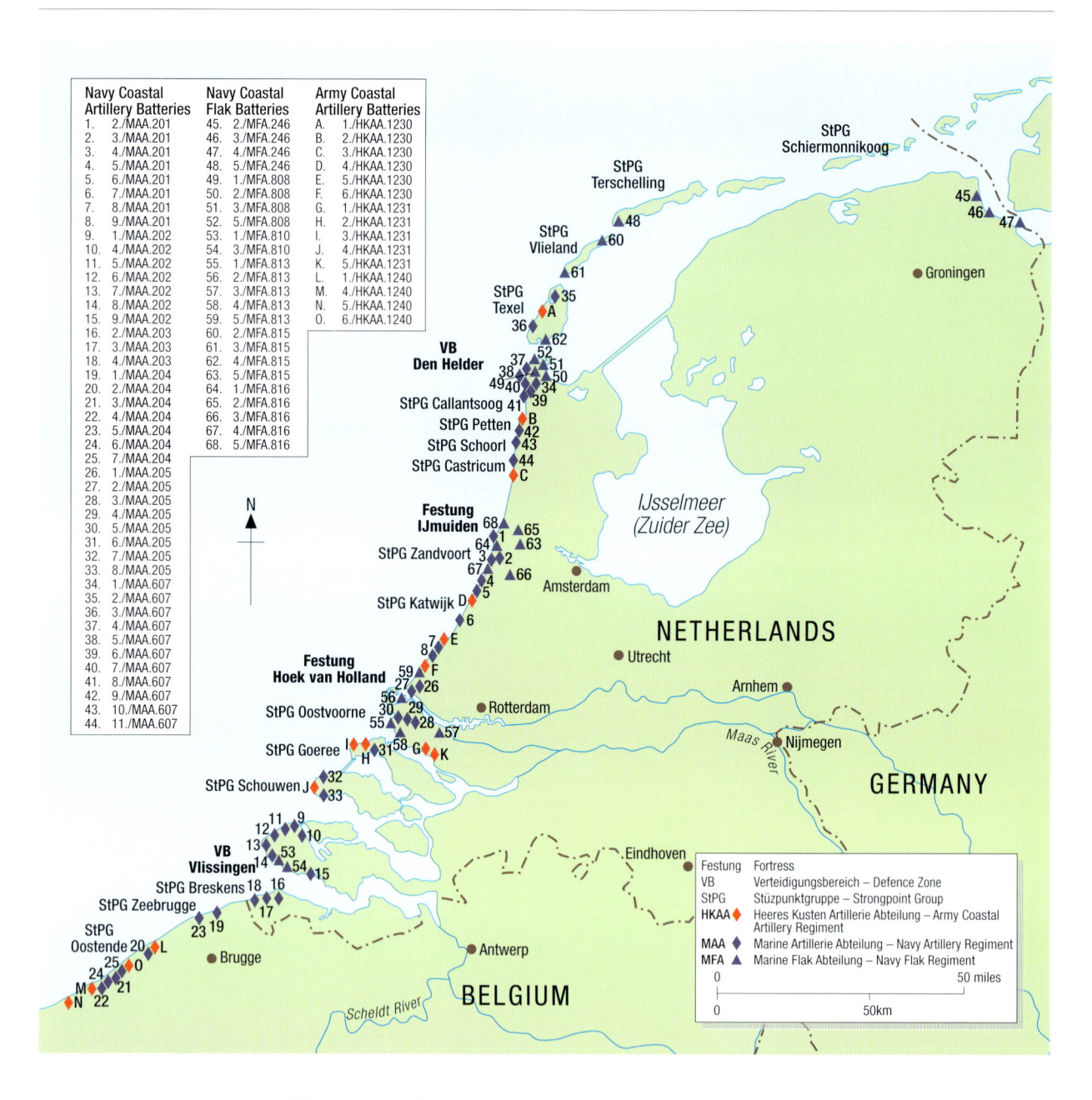

Atlantic Wall fortifications on the North Sea.

efforts. Denmark presents a different case altogether, with its defences oriented primarily to keeping the British fleet out of the Baltic, with strong gun positions to cover the narrow straits.

Of the regions covered in this section, only the Netherlands saw extensive combat. The Atlantic Wall along the Dutch coast became involved in the autumn 1944 fighting to open the approaches to Antwerp. The fiercest of these battles took place on Walcheren,

DEFENCE OF THE PERIPHERY – THE ATLANTIC WALL

where British amphibious forces paid a heavy price to overcome a concentration of fortified guns. Norway remained a backwater for most of the war, the arctic north seeing some combat in the autumn of 1944 during the withdrawal of German forces from Finland. Denmark was spared any extensive land combat and its Atlantikwall defences were never tested. Curiously, Norway and Denmark became models for the final evolution of German coastal defence doctrine, serving as the proving grounds for several new types of weapon including guided torpedoes, underwater acoustic sensors and infrared detectors.

The Blitzkrieg victories in the spring and early summer of 1940 presented the Wehrmacht with the substantial new challenge of defending an extended coastline from the Arctic Circle of northern Norway, down the Atlantic coast to the North Sea towards the Skagerrak, some 3,800km. The four occupied countries in the northern

BELOW: M178 fire-control post, Seezielbatterie Heerenduin, WN 81, IJmuiden, The Netherlands. Kriegsmarine coastal gun batteries included a fire-control post (Leitstand) to identify, track and designate targets for the battery. Three-storey posts like this one had a range-finder post on the top, an observation deck in the front, and working space on the lower level. (Adam Hook © Osprey Publishing)

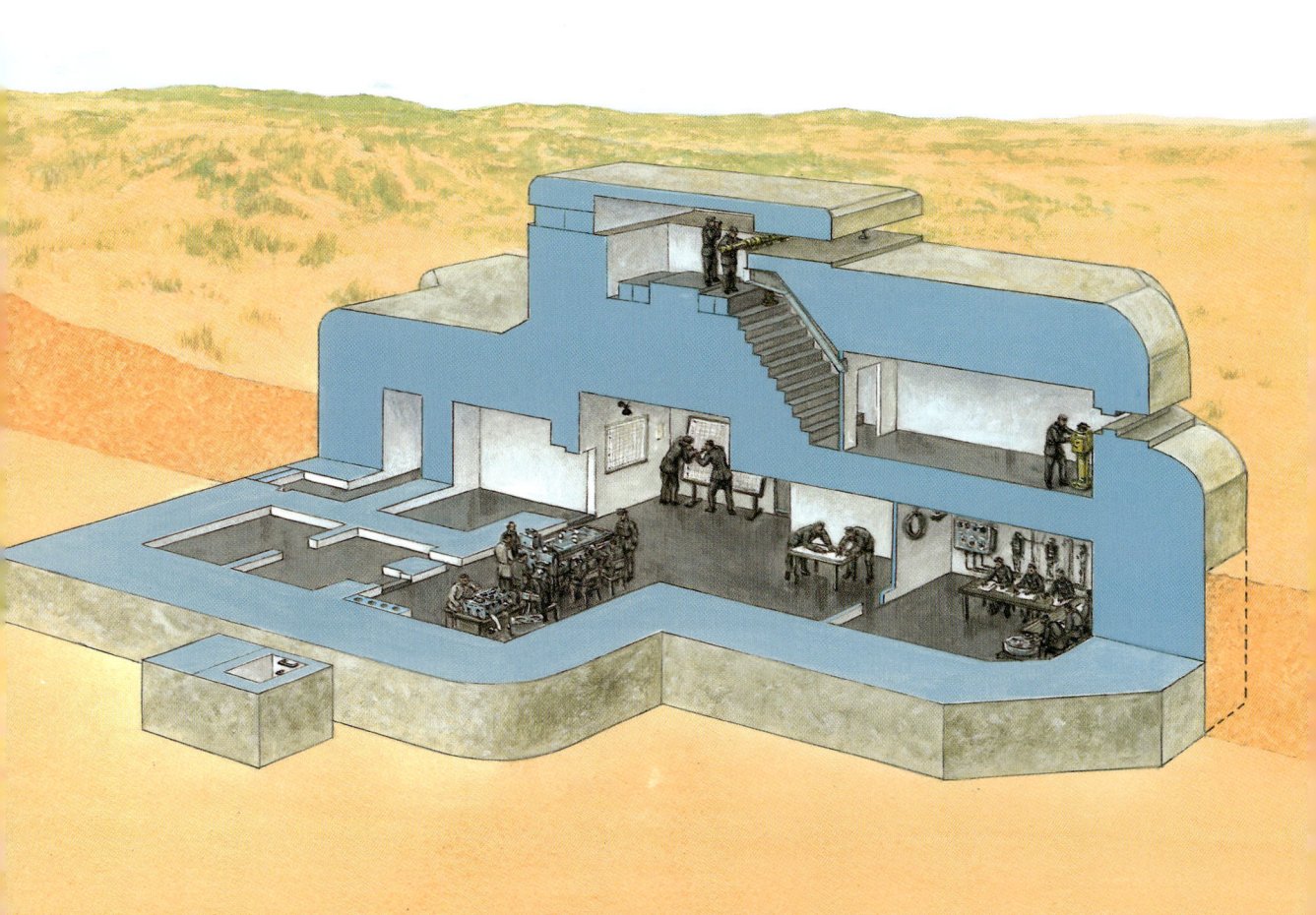

sector – Norway, Denmark, Belgium and the Netherlands – already had modest coastal artillery defences. The only coastal defences that played a role in the 1940 campaign were the Norwegian defences in the Oslo Fjord where the German cruiser *Blücher* was sunk on 9 April 1940 in a duel with two fortified batteries. As the Wehrmacht deployed for occupation duties, these existing coastal defences formed a thin crust for what would later emerge as the Atlantic Wall.

As the coastal fortification issue became more significant in 1941, the priority for the fortification programme was Norway, the French and Belgian Channel coast, the Dutch coast and the German Bight, in that order. The emphasis on Norway was a recognition that Norway presented an especially difficult defensive challenge due to its extensive coastline, as well as the importance of the coastal convoys along the Norwegian coast that were bringing vital materials to the German war industry from the mines in northern Norway. The coastal artillery positions had two principal missions: protection of German coastal shipping, and defence against enemy raids. The initial New West Wall construction was on a very small scale and focused on reinforcing the coastal artillery positions by providing select batteries with personnel bunkers for their crews along with protected ammunition bunkers. With the August 1942 Atlantic Wall directive, however, the focus was now shifted to the French and Belgian Channel coast. Of the 15,000 bunkers in the programme, 11,000 were allocated to the AOK 7 and AOK 15, which covered from the western Netherlands through Belgium to Normandy. The AOK 1 on the Atlantic coast of France was allotted 1,500 to 2,000 bunkers and the remaining bunkers were authorized for the Netherlands. This shift in priority was in part due to the imminent completion of much of the fortification work on the Channel Islands, but more importantly to the growing threat of Allied invasion. Infantry defences along the Atlantic Wall tended to be thickest where the likelihood of invasion was greatest, so coastal infantry positions were densest in Belgium and the Netherlands, while relatively thin in Denmark and Norway.

THE NORTHERN SITES

Belgium

During the Great War, the Kriegsmarine's coastal artillery force experienced its first large-scale deployment away from home waters along the Belgian coast. Some 225 guns were deployed, shielding the canal exits that led to the U-boat harbour in Brugge (Bruges). The success of the U-boats in commerce raiding around Britain precipitated the legendary Royal Navy raids of March 1918 against Zeebrugge and Ostend. After the war, little of the 1918 defences remained, having been spiked by the German troops prior to their withdrawal and scrapped after the war. Belgium had a modest array of coastal defences in the inter-war years including the excellent Vickers 94mm pedestal gun, and these were initially occupied by German troops in 1940 before more elaborate defences were organized.

The German coastal artillery forces deployed in Belgium between 1940 and 1944 were substantially less than those between 1914 and 1918. Zeebrugge lost its strategic importance, as the longer-ranged U-boats were based out of harbours in France rather than in the more confined waters of Belgium. The Atlantic Wall in Belgium was largely an extension of the Channel defences in the neighbouring Pas-de-Calais region of France under AOK 15 control. As a result, the defence sectors here were numbered and named in the AOK 15 fashion as KVA.A (Küstenverteidigungs-Abschnitt-A: Coast Defence Sector-A). Each KVA roughly corresponded to a divisional sector, and was further divided into three regimental sectors (KVA.A1 to A3).

The Navy guns in Belgium were an unusually motley selection including Tsarist 3in field guns rechambered by the Poles in 1926 for standard French 75mm ammunition, as well as more conventional naval guns. The predominant Army coastal weapon was the K418(f), better known by its French designation of 155mm GPF. The most powerful weapons in Belgium were not the fixed batteries, but rather four railroad gun batteries. The most common weapon was the 17cm K(E), which was a gun taken from the World War I Deutschland class and remounted on rail carriages, and there was also a battery with the powerful 28cm Kurze Bruno. As in the neighbouring AOK 15 sectors in France, the Belgian coast had a denser concentration of infantry positions than in the neighbouring Netherlands because of its role in defending against an expected Allied amphibious invasion. In the summer of 1944 it was occupied by the 712. Infanterie-Division, 89. Armee Korps. Since the Belgian coast was only 58km long, the Atlantic Wall construction there consumed only 510,420 metres^3 of concrete – less than 5 per cent of the total.

The Netherlands

Coastal defences in the Netherlands constituted about a tenth of total Atlantic Wall fortification activity in 1942–44. The Netherlands was never especially high on the list of probable Allied invasion points, since the low-lying land behind the coastal dykes could be readily flooded and made impassable. The Dutch ports at Rotterdam and Amsterdam and their access to key waterways leading into the German industrial heartland ensured a significant fortification effort on the Dutch coast. A secondary reason for heavy defence of the Dutch ports was their role in basing S-boat torpedo boats, which were very active in the naval campaigns in the North Sea.

A number of substantial S-boat shelters were built in Dutch harbours to defend this force against RAF bomber raids. The majority of the Dutch coastal defences were

HITLER'S FORTRESSES

Adjacent to the IJmuiden Kernwerk was WN.81, which included Seezielbatterie Heerenduin of 4./MAA. 201, armed with four 17cm SKL/40 naval guns in M272 casemates. The centrepiece was this M178 naval fire-control post. (Steven Zaloga)

subordinate to the Wehrmachtsbefehl in den Niederlanden (WBN; Armed Forces Command in the Netherlands). The exception was the Scheldt estuary region around Breskens and Vlissingen; it was subordinate to the neighbouring AOK 15 which controlled German Army units in the Pas-de-Calais and Belgian coast.

There were four primary defence zones in the Netherlands, two designated at the highest level as Festung and the other two as Verteidigungsbereich (defence zone). The single most heavily fortified area was the Hoek van Holland (Hook of Holland) due to its strategic importance. Aside from including the cities of The Hague and Rotterdam, this estuary and port area offered access to the two most important rivers in this area of northern Europe, the Maas (Meuse) and the Rhine. Nearly a quarter of the major

ABOVE: 10.5cm SK C/32, Marine Flak Batterie West (3./MFlA.810), Stützpunkt Edelweiss, Nolledijk, Vlissingen, The Netherlands. The 10.5cm SK C/32 was one of the most common Kriegsmarine Flak weapons, and had originally been designed by Rheinmetall-Borsig for small warships. There were two configurations of steel cupola: the rounded type seen here, and a similar design built of welded flat sheet steel. (Adam Hook © Osprey Publishing)

fortifications built in the Netherlands during the war were located in this sector. The defence was based around the New Waterway, the late 19th-century canal connecting Rotterdam to the North Sea. The centre of the defences was its Kernwerk on the south bank of the canal near the site of today's Europort.

The second Festung in the Netherlands was IJmuiden. While this small fishing port would hardly seem to merit such a designation, the fortified area served to cover the entrance of the neighbouring North Sea Canal which led to Amsterdam and the IJsselmeer (Zuider Zee). The Kernwerk was based on Forteiland, a Dutch fortified island at the entrance of the canal. This Festung also included a heavy concentration of naval Flak batteries for air defence, along with fortified radar stations.

The northernmost of the major Dutch fortified zones was VB Den Helder. This site had strategic significance as a major port at the tip of North Holland, controlling naval access into the IJsselmeer. The fourth major defence sector was VB Vlissingen (Flushing), which controlled access to the Scheldt estuary and the port of Antwerp. This defence sector included a substantial arsenal of naval batteries facing the North Sea, as well as additional batteries to control the Scheldt. On the southern bank of the Scheldt estuary was Stützpunktgruppe (Strongpoint Group) Breskens, a substantial defensive position in its own right with a significant Landfront. Although these defensive positions were originally under WBN control, in September 1942, they were transferred to the neighbouring AOK 15 command as part of the Channel Coast defence effort. With the advance of Canadian and British forces in August 1944, the AOK 15 responsibility was shifted further up the coast, taking control of strongpoints up to Oostvoorne. With the liberation of Antwerp in September 1944, the Scheldt estuary suddenly took on greater importance, since without control of the Scheldt the port was virtually useless due to the threat of the substantial German coastal defences. Due to this change in importance, this sector was redesignated as Festung and played a significant role in the brutal October–November 1944 engagements which will be covered in more detail later.

Besides the usual coastal artillery batteries, the Netherlands had an unusually heavy deployment of Kriegsmarine Flak batteries. These were most often dual-purpose 10.5cm naval guns that had a secondary role of coast defence. The widespread deployment was in part due to the need to defend Dutch harbours from RAF attacks, but the Netherlands was in the path of Allied heavy bombers heading towards Germany. So the batteries were used both in harbour defence and against the bomber streams. In 1943 alone, the naval Flak batteries fired 13,253 rounds of 10.5cm and 26,914 rounds of 2cm ammunition. The Flak batteries played an important role in defending Dutch harbours as they were available in sufficient quantity to make air attacks costly. For example, on 17 January 1945 a raid by 30 Beaufighters of 16 Group into the Den Helder anchorage led to the loss of six aircraft.

Norway

The enormous length of Norway's coastline was a formidable challenge to establishing any sort of comprehensive defence line. The Norwegian coast extended from the Skagerrak to the North Cape on the Arctic Ocean, a distance of 2,532km though the actual coastline was a daunting 25,148km if measured along the numerous fjords. Much of the coast was mountainous and undeveloped which presented enormous difficulty in moving any large construction equipment into place for fortification purposes. On the other hand, the rocky coastline also permitted the construction of defensive works by digging into the rockbed to minimize the need for extensive amounts of steel-reinforced concrete.

The enormous length of the Norwegian coast forced the Wehrmacht to divide the country into three defence sectors each with a Kriegsmarine command and corresponding Heer command. The Navy's sectors were Admiral der Westküste headquartered in Bergen, Admiral der Nordküste based in Trondheim and Admiral der Polarküste in Tromso. In turn, these sectors were divided into regional sea commands (Seekommandanten/Seekos). The Heer units were subordinate to AOK Norwegen (Norway Army High Command), though after January 1942, the Kirkenes sector fell under AOK Lappland (later AOK 20 Gebirgs) which was responsible for the Finnish front. At peak strength the Army had five corin Norway, including one in the Kirkenes sector not under AOK Norwegen command, but by 1945 this had been whittled down by the transfer of one corps to other fronts.

German fortification work in Norway initially began in mid-1941 with the construction of reinforced submarine bunkers in Trondheim. OT created the Einsatzgruppe Wiking to specialize in construction work in Scandinavia. Fortification efforts in the more remote northern areas were considerably hampered by the lack of road and rail lines, and prompted an ambitious German programme to construct a supporting transportation network to link German occupation forces. A further incentive to create a road and rail network in the north was Hitler's scheme to create a major German port in the Trondheim area with facilities for a quarter of a million German military and civilian personnel. The enormous demands of these construction schemes consumed most of the early supplies of reinforced concrete and slowed any

A 'battleship of the dunes', the Seezielbatterie Schveningen-Nord of 8./MAA. 201 armed with 15cm SKC/28 naval guns. In this view, the multi-tier S414 fire control post can be seen in the foreground as well as three of the Bauform 671 gun casemates beyond. (Steven J. Zaloga)

HITLER'S FORTRESSES

Batterie Fjell, MKB.11/504, Bergen, Norway. Among the most impressive Atlantic Wall fortifications were two turrets from the battlecruiser *Gneisenau* emplaced in Norway at Örlandet and (as seen here) at Fjell.

1. S446 command bunker
2. R633 bunker
3. Transformer bunker
4. Defence bunker
5. Crew quarters
6. Main entrance bunker
7. Main turret
8. Western access
A. Shell handling room
B. Charge handling room
C. Main ammunition trunk
D. Auxiliary ammunition hoist trunk

(Adam Hook © Osprey Publishing)

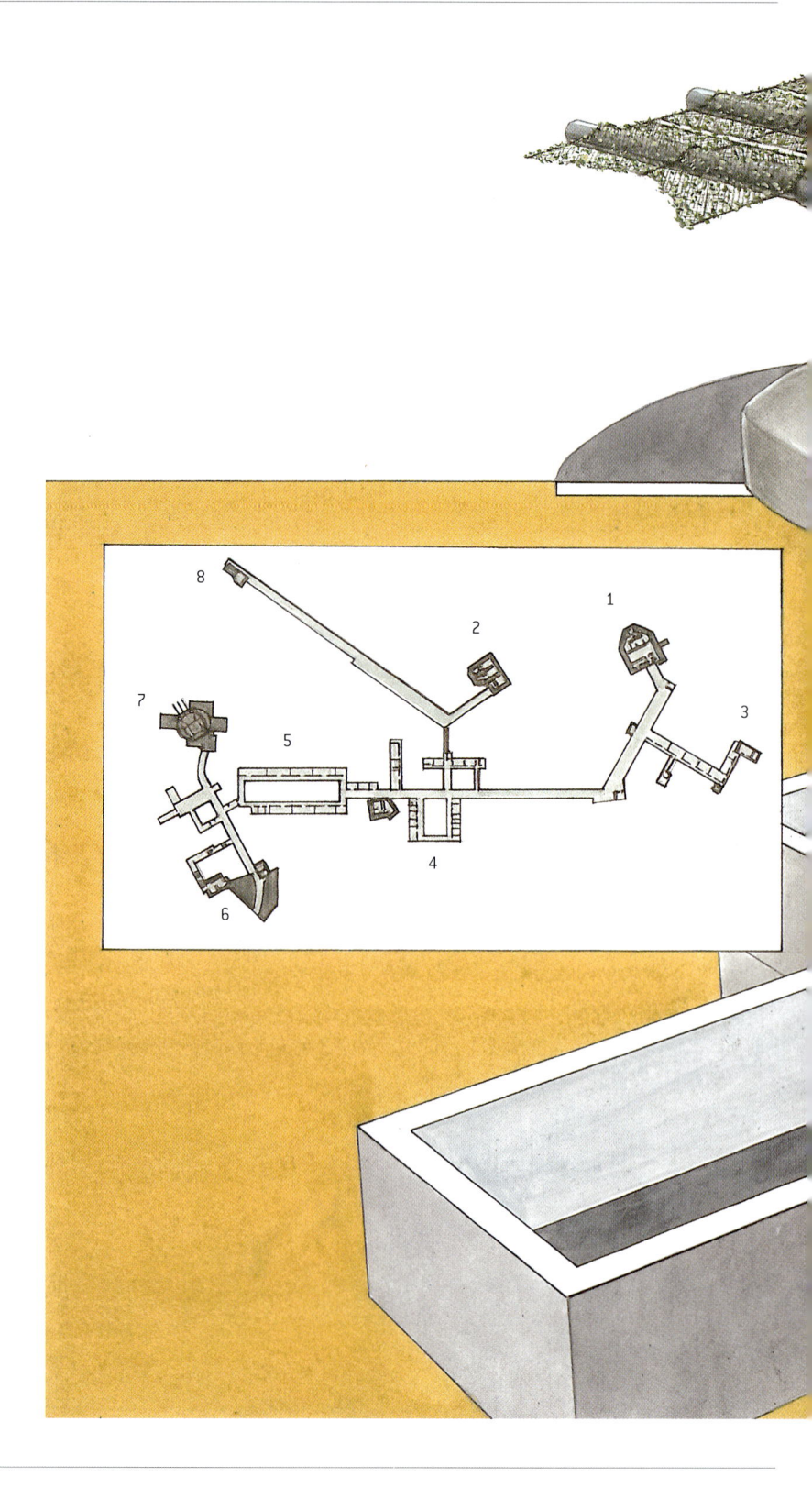

DEFENCE OF THE PERIPHERY – THE ATLANTIC WALL

coastal defence fortification. Local units were obliged to make do with improvisations, including the use of rock to create expedient defences and to use caves and tunnels for ammunition and personnel shelters. In comparison with the Atlantic Wall in France, Norway was very weakly provided with reinforced concrete shelters. So while there were over 2,000 gun casemates in France, there were only about a hundred in Norway.

The initial steps to defend the Norwegian coast began late in 1940 with Kriegsmarine plans to absorb 13 existing Norwegian coastal batteries, add additional batteries from captured Norwegian Army artillery, and reinforce these batteries with additional artillery to increase the total to 44 Navy coastal batteries. The difficulties of moving construction supplies to many of the more remote coastal positions forced the naval coastal batteries to deploy in open field emplacements in many locations. As a minimum, attempts were made to provide a concrete platform with pintle mount for medium coastal guns and to provide some form of protected ammunition and crew shelter. The British coastal raids in March 1941 infuriated Hitler and triggered a scheme to increase the Norwegian coastal batteries with 160 Army coastal batteries.

The vast majority of coastal artillery pieces deployed to Norway were war-booty rather than standard German field artillery or naval guns; about 1,100 guns were eventually deployed in Norway. In comparison, there were about 2,200 guns deployed on the Atlantic Wall in France.

By 1944, the Wehrmacht in Norway eventually deployed a total of 12 naval coastal artillery battalions and 11 Army coast artillery battalions. By far the most spectacular coastal artillery in Norway were the three dozen heavy naval guns, usually surplus warship weapons, assigned to critical defensive assignments. The most powerful of these weapons were the 'Adolfkanonen', a set of 40.6cm guns originally intended for the never-completed H-class battleships. They were installed in the islands shielding Narvik and were intended to cover all sea approaches to this port. The Vara battery near Kristiansand on the Skagerrak was mounted in similar single-gun turrets in an S169 kettle position; a set of massive casemates was under construction but not occupied at the end of the war. Although of less impressive size, many other surplus warship turrets were deployed in Norway including eight 15cm SKC/28 guns in twin C/36 turrets intended for the incomplete *Graf Zeppelin* aircraft carrier.

The value of torpedo batteries in the defence of Norway's numerous fjords was made painfully apparent to the Kriegsmarine on 9 April 1940 when the cruiser *Blücher* was sunk by two 28cm torpedoes from the Oscarborg fort in Oslofjord. The Norwegian Navy had begun establishing torpedo batteries as early as 1890, mounted in concealed underwater launchers. These batteries were positioned to cover passageways that were 5,000m wide or less. Besides taking over several Norwegian batteries and using

DEFENCE OF THE PERIPHERY – THE ATLANTIC WALL

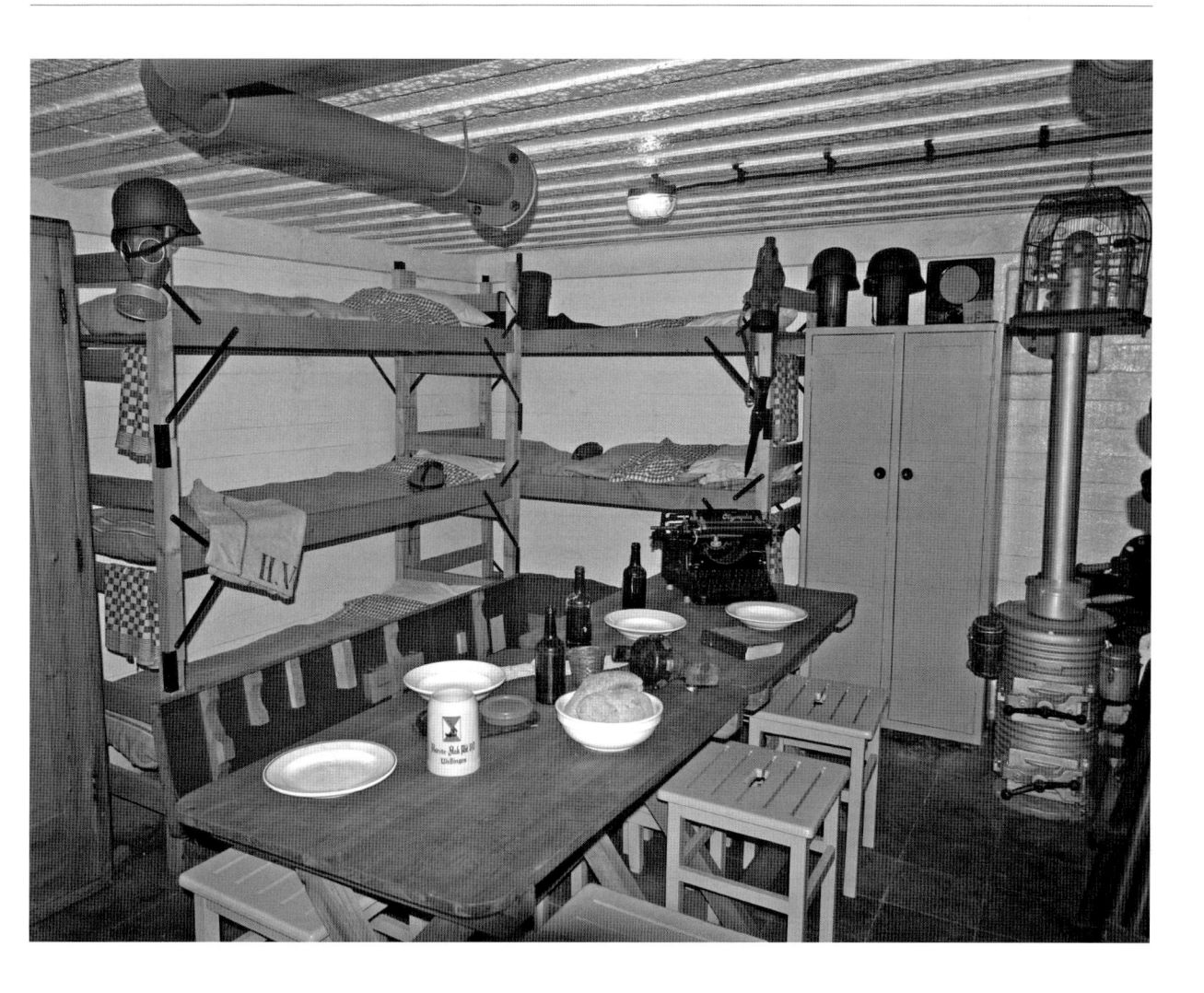

Norwegian Navy equipment to create others, the Kriegsmarine installed their own batteries, eventually totalling 17 shore batteries. In contrast to the original Norwegian batteries, the German batteries typically used destroyer-type triple launch tubes mounted on the surface in a concrete building with a fire-control post located nearby, often supported by a searchlight. A typical battery consisted of three officers and 40 men, and was subordinated to the coastal artillery battalion in the area. In addition to the shore batteries, two floating batteries were deployed in Bergen.

Denmark

Denmark was the most obscure portion of the Atlantic Wall. Denmark had very modest coastal defences prior to the 1940 invasion, mainly centred on Copenhagen's harbour. As a short-term expedient, in the summer of 1940 the Wehrmacht deployed 15 Navy

Life in a German coastal bunker was cramped. This is the preserved interior of a Bauform 502 of StP Lohengrin in Vlissingen and this small room would have accommodated ten soldiers. (Steven Zaloga)

HITLER'S FORTRESSES

WN73 KERNWERK IJMUIDEN, NORTH SEA CANAL, THE NETHERLANDS

DEFENCE OF THE PERIPHERY – THE ATLANTIC WALL

The Festung ports on the North Sea were typically based around a Kernwerk (core position) which covered the main port entrance – in this case, the North Sea Canal entrance into Amsterdam. The IJmuiden Kernwerk was built on Forteiland, a Dutch fortified island with the Kustfort built in 1880–87 and armed with German 24cm guns; it was modernized in the 1920s with several more modern small bunkers. The island was substantially rebuilt in the summer of 1943 while manned by 3./MAA. 201. The Dutch Kustfort was reinforced by adding three large M170 casemates for World War I 150mm naval guns with associated personnel bunkers, plus a fire control post. These bunkers were defended by a host of smaller bunkers containing anti-tank guns and machine guns, and two more artillery batteries were added, armed with war-booty Soviet 122mm A-19 field guns. The seaward beach was covered with dragon's teeth to prevent the landing of tanks or vehicles. This Kernwerk was part of an interlocking defence system with extensive artillery on both shoulders of the canal. Seezielbatterie Heerenduin, located on the IJmuiden coast south of the canal, had four 17cm SKL/40 naval guns in M272 casemates, while Seezielbatterie Wijk-am-See on the north had a battery of 15cm Tsts.K C/36 guns in Bauform 671 casemates. This Festung was also supported by a heavy concentration of naval Flak batteries for air defence along with fortified radar stations.

1. Bauform 636 SK fire-control post
2–4. M170 gun casemates for 15cm SKL/40 gun with adjacent Bauform 656 15-man personnel bunker
5. Bauform 671 SK gun casemate for British 3.7in gun
6–7. Bauform 611 gun casemate for Soviet 122mm A-19 gun
8–13. Bauform 631 anti-tank gun bunker
14–15. Bauform 633 mortar pit
16–19. Bauform 644 machine-gun casemate
20. Local design decontamination building
21. Bauform 635 Double group (20-man) personnel bunker
22. Water reservoir
23–24. Depth charge launcher
25. Storage bunker
26. Bauform 668 six-man bunker used as canteen

(Adam Hook © Osprey Publishing)

coastal batteries at the major harbours and major chokepoints leading into the Baltic, based primarily on old war-booty artillery taken from the Danish arsenal.

The autumn of 1940 saw the first major construction effort with a scheme to deploy two heavy coastal batteries in Denmark: one at Hanstholm opposite Norway to control the Skaggerak, and a pair on Bornholm in the Baltic to cover the Kattegat. In the event, the invasion of the Soviet Union in 1941 curtailed the Bornholm plans, but the Hanstholm project continued along with a corresponding battery on the Norwegian side of the Skaggerak, Batterie Vara. The Royal Navy raids on the Norwegian coast in early 1941 forced the Wehrmacht to recognize the weak protection on the Danish coast, and in late April 1940 the Army decided to deploy ten coastal artillery batteries to Denmark while the Navy expanded its coverage, especially the approaches to the Sound and the Small and Great Belts. As in Norway, most of the attention through 1944 was in providing defence for major ports, though in Denmark this effort extended to covering the various chokepoints into the Baltic. Since Denmark was often overflown by Allied bombers on their way to German ports, Denmark had a very substantial Luftwaffe fortification and construction effort with numerous radar and Flak sites.

By the summer of 1943, with the Atlantic Wall programme in full bloom in France and the Low Countries, the Wehrmacht began to examine a possible threat of an Allied amphibious landing in western Denmark aimed at reaching northern Germany. The most likely landing areas were considered to be northern Jutland or the Esbjerg area. One of the immediate outcomes of this assessment was to substantially augment the coastal batteries on Fano Island off Esbjerg as well as gun batteries to defend the port itself; 12 more Army artillery batteries were also allotted to Denmark. Four areas were declared Defence Zones (Verteidigungsbereiche): Esbjerg, Hansted, Frederikshavn and Aalborg. The various infantry and artillery positions were consolidated into strongpoint groups for greater unity of command and a total of 20 of these groups were organized, seven of which were airbases rather than coastal defence sectors.

In spite of the Normandy invasion in June 1944, the Wehrmacht continued to be concerned over threats to Denmark, based on the mistaken intelligence assessment that the Allies were withholding forces for possible operations against Denmark or Norway. The Kriegsmarine was convinced that the greatest threat was against the Kattegat on the eastern Jutland coast, the presumption being that Allied actions to control this area would block U-boats constructed in the Baltic ports from reaching their new operating bases in Norway. As a result, a programme to add 29 naval batteries was begun. In contrast, Hitler and the Army were more concerned about the threat posed to the western coast of Jutland as a potential shortcut into northern Germany. This resulted in the construction of three inland blocking positions, codenamed the Brunhild, Gudrun and Kriehild lines, consisting of anti-tank ditches and field fortifications rather than elaborate concrete fortifications. By late 1944, the situation was even more unsettled due to the advance of the Red Army from the east as well as Soviet naval operations in the Baltic. In consequence, AOK Dänemark was overruled, and priority for defensive construction shifted to the Kattegat coastline, as recommended by the Navy.

The Kriegsmarine planned to deploy 20 more batteries in early 1945, but the collapse of the German war economy prevented this; in April 1945 there were substantial shifts of coastal gun batteries from Denmark to the Eastern front. Likewise, there was considerable turmoil in the Army coastal artillery batteries as AOK Dänemark realized that the more likely threat to Denmark was not an Allied amphibious invasion, but an Allied advance into Denmark from the south via Germany. A number of the Army coastal batteries were moved to the southern portion of Denmark to set up a new defence line. In total, 22 Army and 46 Navy coastal artillery batteries were deployed in Denmark during the war, though the number was in flux through most of 1944–45. The Navy also deployed 16 Flak batteries for the defence of major ports.

Of the four countries surveyed in this section, only the Netherlands endured significant combat along its stretch of the Atlantic Wall, during the 85-day battle for the Scheldt estuary from September to November 1944. This campaign was a tortuous experience for Allied forces. The British commando assault at Westkapelle, for example, was thrown against heavy coastal batteries which were in turn protected by networks of pillboxes, strongpoints and minefields. Twenty of the 27 landing craft were subsequently sunk in the approach, with 300 casualties. Yet it was the Canadian First Army that suffered the most – nearly 13,000 casualties sustained by the time the Scheldt was brought under control.

By contrast, Belgium's short coast was liberated by the Canadian Army during the lightning advance of September 1944. Norway experienced some limited fighting in October 1944 when the Red Army stormed the arctic Finnmark region, chasing the Wehrmacht out of Finland. However, this did not involve extensive combat along the Atlantic Wall. Denmark experienced no significant combat on its portion of the Atlantic Wall.

EVALUATING THE ATLANTIC WALL

The commander of German forces in the west in 1944, Rundstedt was scathing in his later assessment: 'The Atlantic Wall was an enormous bluff, less for the enemy than for the German people. Hitler never saw the Atlantic Wall, not even one part of it! He was

HITLER'S FORTRESSES

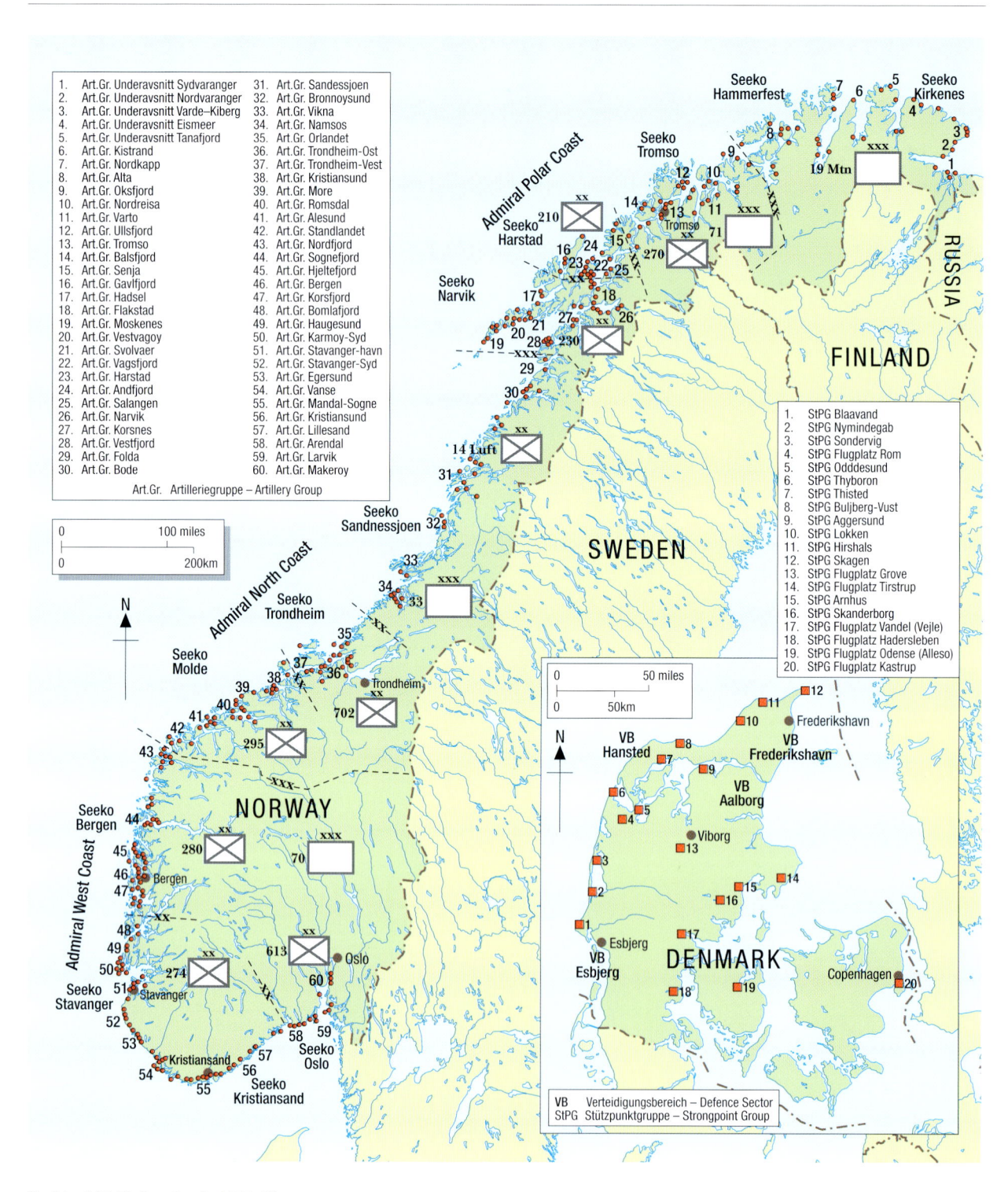

#	Art.Gr.	#	Art.Gr.
1.	Art.Gr. Underavsnitt Sydvaranger	31.	Art.Gr. Sandessjoen
2.	Art.Gr. Underavsnitt Nordvaranger	32.	Art.Gr. Bronnoysund
3.	Art.Gr. Underavsnitt Varde–Kiberg	33.	Art.Gr. Vikna
4.	Art.Gr. Underavsnitt Eismeer	34.	Art.Gr. Namsos
5.	Art.Gr. Underavsnitt Tanafjord	35.	Art.Gr. Orlandet
6.	Art.Gr. Kistrand	36.	Art.Gr. Trondheim-Ost
7.	Art.Gr. Nordkapp	37.	Art.Gr. Trondheim-Vest
8.	Art.Gr. Alta	38.	Art.Gr. Kristiansund
9.	Art.Gr. Oksfjord	39.	Art.Gr. More
10.	Art.Gr. Nordreisa	40.	Art.Gr. Romsdal
11.	Art.Gr. Varto	41.	Art.Gr. Alesund
12.	Art.Gr. Ullsfjord	42.	Art.Gr. Standlandet
13.	Art.Gr. Tromso	43.	Art.Gr. Nordfjord
14.	Art.Gr. Balsfjord	44.	Art.Gr. Sognefjord
15.	Art.Gr. Senja	45.	Art.Gr. Hjeltefjord
16.	Art.Gr. Gavlfjord	46.	Art.Gr. Bergen
17.	Art.Gr. Hadsel	47.	Art.Gr. Korsfjord
18.	Art.Gr. Flakstad	48.	Art.Gr. Bomlafjord
19.	Art.Gr. Moskenes	49.	Art.Gr. Haugesund
20.	Art.Gr. Vestvagoy	50.	Art.Gr. Karmoy-Syd
21.	Art.Gr. Svolvaer	51.	Art.Gr. Stavanger-havn
22.	Art.Gr. Vagsfjord	52.	Art.Gr. Stavanger-Syd
23.	Art.Gr. Harstad	53.	Art.Gr. Egersund
24.	Art.Gr. Andfjord	54.	Art.Gr. Vanse
25.	Art.Gr. Salangen	55.	Art.Gr. Mandal-Sogne
26.	Art.Gr. Narvik	56.	Art.Gr. Kristiansund
27.	Art.Gr. Korsnes	57.	Art.Gr. Lillesand
28.	Art.Gr. Vestfjord	58.	Art.Gr. Arendal
29.	Art.Gr. Folda	59.	Art.Gr. Larvik
30.	Art.Gr. Bode	60.	Art.Gr. Makeroy

Art.Gr. Artilleriegruppe – Artillery Group

1. StPG Blaavand
2. StPG Nymindegab
3. StPG Sondervig
4. StPG Flugplatz Rom
5. StPG Odddesund
6. StPG Thyboron
7. StPG Thisted
8. StPG Buljberg-Vust
9. StPG Aggersund
10. StPG Lokken
11. StPG Hirshals
12. StPG Skagen
13. StPG Flugplatz Grove
14. StPG Flugplatz Tirstrup
15. StPG Arnhus
16. StPG Skanderborg
17. StPG Flugplatz Vandel (Vejle)
18. StPG Flugplatz Hadersleben
19. StPG Flugplatz Odense (Alleso)
20. StPG Flugplatz Kastrup

VB Verteidigungsbereich – Defence Sector
StPG Stützpunktgruppe – Strongpoint Group

The Atlantic Wall in Scandinavia, 1944–45.

DEFENCE OF THE PERIPHERY – THE ATLANTIC WALL

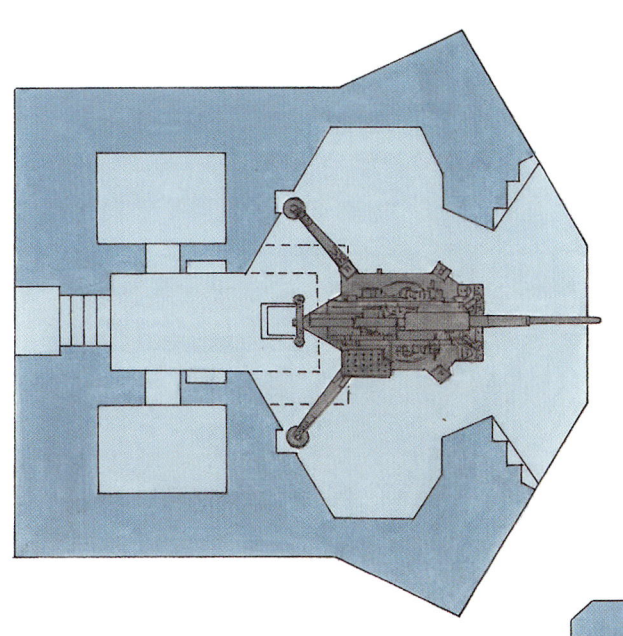

Batterie Westkapelle, 6./MAA. 202, Westkapelle, Walcheren, The Netherlands. This battery, better known by its British map designation as W15, was one of the two batteries of Kapitän Robert Opalka's MAA. 202 which fiercely resisted the British landings on Walcheren on 1 November 1944. This battery consisted of four Bauform 671 SK gun casemates armed with four British 3.7in anti-aircraft guns captured at Dunkirk. (Adam Hook © Osprey Publishing)

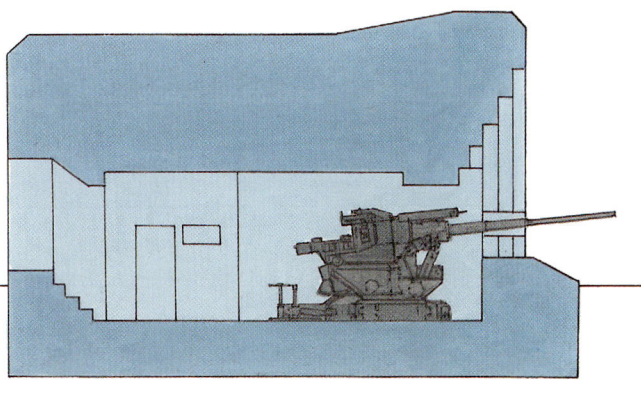

HITLER'S FORTRESSES

satisfied if OT reported that so many tonnes of steel and so many cubic metres of concrete had been used.' The Atlantic Wall failed to deter or seriously challenge the Allied amphibious invasion of France, and indeed, the coastal defences in Normandy were in most cases overcome in a few hours' fighting. The task of defending so long a coastline was impossible, especially given the limitations of Germany's wartime economy. The Atlantic Wall in France consumed some 17,000,000m^3 of concrete compared to about 12,000,000m^3 for the Maginot Line, and even then it never came near to the density needed to stop a determined attack. The programme was symptomatic of Nazi Germany's inability to provide rational and efficient direction to its defence economy due to Hitler's amateur enthusiasms. Throughout the war the Wehrmacht was usually short of tanks, ammunition and other war essentials, due in no small measure to the flagrant squandering of resources on dubious schemes such as this one.

An argument can be made that the heavy fortifications along the Pas-de-Calais forced the Allies to stage their attack further away from the German frontier in Normandy, but this hardly explains the extravagant wastage of concrete and steel at so many other sites along the French coast where there was no plausible threat of Allied invasion. Furthermore, it is debatable whether the Allied selection of Normandy was prompted primarily by the Atlantic Wall defences around Calais rather than the formidable concentration of German divisions, including much of the Panzer force,

The battlecruiser *Gneisenau*'s C turret was emplaced near Trondheim in MKB 1/507 near Orlandet in 1943; this image shows the battery shortly after its completion but before camouflage nets were attached. This battery remained in Norwegian service after the war and is currently preserved as a museum. (NARA)

in this area. Indeed, it can also be argued that Normandy was a more fortuitous location for confronting the Wehrmacht in France since it extended the German logistical lines, making them more vulnerable to the ravages of Allied airpower. Given Hitler's penchant for 'stand to the death' orders, the Atlantic Wall proved to be a trap for the nearly 200,000 German troops who were ordered to defend the isolated Festung ports.

The Atlantic Wall was more firmly rooted in Hitler's romantic fervour for architectural grandeur than in German military doctrine. Coastal fortification has fallen out of favour since then, and the Atlantic Wall is likely to remain the last major example of this long European tradition.

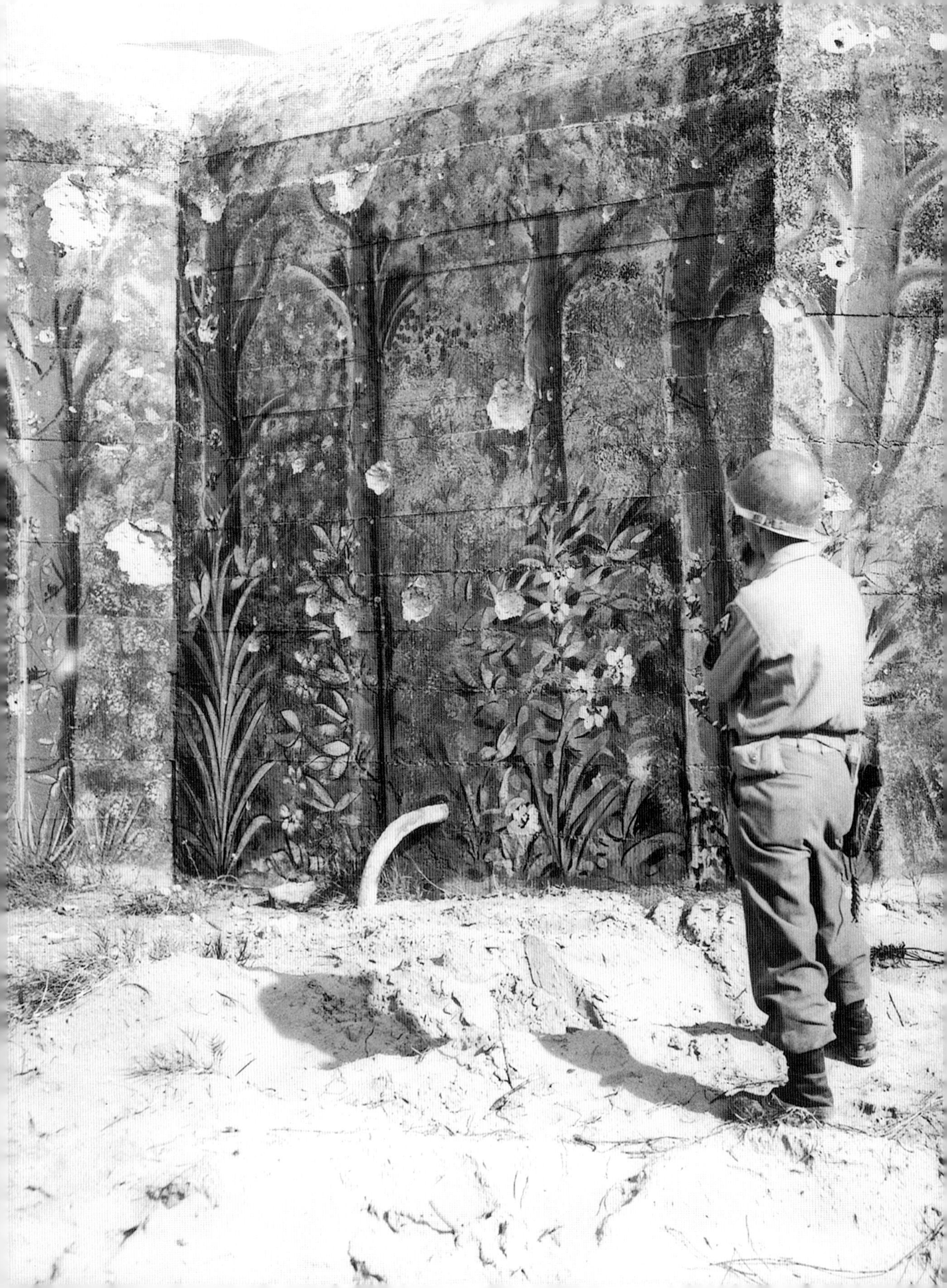

MOUNTAIN BARRIERS — GERMAN DEFENSIVE LINES IN ITALY

LEFT: A close-up of an artillery casemate. An American soldier admires the unusual camouflage scheme, which shows more than a little artistic flare. Superficial damage would suggest that the position was involved in some localized fighting or was strafed by Allied aircraft. (NARA)

Two Allied soldiers consider the all-round observation afforded by the concrete machine-gun nest in the Hitler Line. Metal hooks set in the roof were used to secure the camouflage net. The timbered entranceway is visible in the foreground leading to the communication trench. (Imperial War Museum, NA 15853)

In August 1943, the President of the United States, the British Prime Minister and the Combined Chiefs-of-Staff met at Casablanca to formulate future Allied strategy. The decisions they took at this meeting related to the whole conduct of the war against the Axis in Europe, but were particularly relevant to the strategy in the Mediterranean. The main aims were to eliminate Italy as a belligerent and to maintain the pressure on German forces to create the conditions for Operation *Overlord* and the eventual landings in southern France.

By this time Mussolini had been overthrown and, soon afterwards, an armistice was signed with Italy, which only left the final aim of maintaining pressure on German forces. Different people interpreted this in different ways. Certainly Churchill believed that Italy offered an inviting avenue of attack against what he saw as the 'soft underbelly' of the Third Reich. And following the Allied landings on the Italian mainland he hoped

MOUNTAIN BARRIERS – GERMAN DEFENSIVE LINES IN ITALY

The view through the aperture of a German pillbox located near San Giuliano. It shows how the position dominated the twisting section of road in front. (NARA)

that Field Marshal Harold Alexander's Fifteenth Army Group would make a rapid advance up the peninsula. However, geography, history and a resourceful enemy meant that the chances of realizing the Prime Minister's aspirations were slim.

For someone like Churchill with such a sharp military mind it should have been apparent that the topography of Italy favoured defence. 'The mountains are rugged and the Apennines make a continuous barrier between the eastern and western sides of the country. Many rivers, some fast flowing between precipitous banks, lie across the path of forces advancing from the south.' To make matters worse the weather in Italy is often inclement. The summers are very hot, especially in the south, the winters are cold and the spring and autumn are often wet, which gives an attacking army only a short window for operations.

After the loss of Sicily, the German forces had originally anticipated falling back to the Apennines, but Kesselring, the commander of Heeresgruppe C, convinced Hitler of the merit of a stand further south. This would keep the Allies further from Germany; would stop them creating air bases in Italy capable of attacking industrial targets in southern Germany or, more importantly, the Ploesti oil fields in Romania; and would also ensure that the symbolically important city of Rome would not be captured. German forces were rushed south and, having failed to repulse the Allied invasion, they fought a dogged rearguard action. This provided time for engineers, construction

HITLER'S FORTRESSES

German defensive lines in Sicily and Italy, 1943–45.

workers and labourers to build a series of defensive lines that took advantage of the country's many rivers and mountains. These were established from the ankle of the boot to its very top and were so numerous that the Germans used almost every letter in the military phonetic alphabet. Indeed in some respects the naming of the various lines seems to have been more taxing for the Germans than it was to construct them. They included letters of the alphabet; names of both sexes from Albert to Viktor and Barbara to Paula; almost all the colours of the rainbow; historical figures from Caesar to Genghis Khan; and, less adventurously, local place names. One line was even named after the Führer himself (although this was soon changed so as to avoid the Allies gaining a major propaganda coup).

In the end more than 40 defensive lines were established, but a lack of manpower and raw materials meant that the defences were too few in number, they lacked depth and were often poorly constructed. Yet in spite of this the fortifications did serve to delay the Allies. From the initial landings in September 1943 they took the best part of two years to reach the Alps; this was no soft underbelly but was in fact a 'tough old gut'.

DESIGN AND DEVELOPMENT

By the beginning of 1943 the face of the war had changed dramatically for Germany and the other Axis powers. On every front and in every field of combat the Wehrmacht was now on the defensive. In the oceans the U-boats had turned from hunter to hunted, in the air the Luftwaffe had to contend with Allied bombing raids on Germany and on land the Army had been defeated at Stalingrad and was on the retreat in North Africa.

Yet in spite of this reversal of fortune, Hitler was determined not to yield any territory to the Allies. This desire, bordering on an obsession, manifested itself in his insistence that 'the southern periphery of Europe, whose bastions were the Balkans and the larger Italian islands, must be held'. However, this resolve was complicated by uncertainty over what the Allies' strategy would be in the Mediterranean. Hitler was of the opinion that Sardinia was the most obvious target for an invasion, while others in the OKW believed they would attack Sicily. These divisions were exacerbated by Operation *Mincemeat*, a clever deception plan conceived by the Allies to convince the German military that the next attack would be directed towards the Balkans. To make matters worse, Hitler, in theory at least, was still part of an Axis with Fascist Italy and Mussolini was keen to continue the fight alongside his more powerful ally.

In spite of all this uncertainty one thing was clear. The threat of invasion could not be ignored and steps would need to be taken to protect the exposed coastline. However, with the time and materials available it was understood that there would have to be priorities and precedence was given to Sardinia. This decision meant that it was not until March 1943 that the Italians made a concerted effort to reinforce the coastal defences of Sicily. In this task they were aided by German engineers who arrived in the spring of the year and who had themselves been involved in the construction of the Atlantic Wall. Their Italian counterparts, some of whom had been on a fact-finding mission to a number of German coastal positions in France, were keen to create their own version of this great bulwark, but shortages made this difficult and efforts to improve and extend the existing fortifications were disappointing. The three naval bases on Sicily (Augusta, Palermo and Syracuse) were well fortified and were fitted with large-calibre guns, but the situation was very different around potential landing sites. The defences were thinly dispersed and those that existed often lacked weapons and camouflage. There was little in the way of barbed wire, mines or beach obstacles and aerial reconnaissance of one of the British landing beaches prior to the invasion showed a party of bathers.

The Apennines were an extremely strong natural feature, but the Germans still constructed a series of defences along the range and especially through the many passes. This concrete machine-gun shelter was built to cover the road along the Serchio Valley near Barga. (Imperial War Museum, NA21203)

The lack of beach defences was in part the result of a lack of time and materials, but was also partly the result of Italian strategy. The Italian Commando Supreme was of the view that the Allies would attack on a broad front and as such there was limited value in expending a great amount of effort on beach defences. Indeed, General Roatta, the commander of Italian forces on the Island, planned to construct a belt of fortifications and obstacles 19–24km inland – out of the range of Allied ships. These defences were designed to contain any Allied landing until the direction of the main thrust became evident and then the mobile reserve would be employed to decisively defeat them. The German military, by contrast, believed that the only way to defeat an invasion was to hit the enemy when they were most vulnerable and that was when they were coming ashore. In the end the arguments proved academic. The incomplete beach defences did little to stem the Allied landings and the belt of fortifications to the rear seems to have progressed little further than a line on a map.

Having secured their beachheads, the Allies pressed inland. With no prospect of repelling the enemy invasion the Italo-German force had little choice but to make a fighting retreat and now pinned their faith on a series of defensive 'lines' that it was hoped would stall the enemy advance sufficiently long to enable an orderly evacuation of the island. The term 'line' is somewhat misleading as these were not continuous belts of fortifications but rather were often simply naturally strong defensive positions that were strengthened with mines and fieldworks or demolitions.

The first of these 'lines' was the Hauptkampflinie (main defence line), which ran from San Stefano on the northern coast to Nicosia and then south-east to a point just south of Catania and essentially formed the base of a triangle with Messina at the apex. Behind this was the Etna Line (or Old Hube Line), which, as its name suggests, was constructed around the dormant volcano and ran from a point north of Acireale in front of Aderno and Troina to the coast at San Fratello. The troops manning defensive positions along the line would resist until they were in danger of being overrun or encircled before withdrawing along pre-arranged routes to the next position. There were four of these each with shorter bases that required fewer troops to defend; the surplus troops were to be evacuated to the mainland. The first of these was the 'New Hube Line', but there was seemingly no agreed set of names for the remainder and nor is it clear who fixed the lines.

The series of defensive lines enabled the German forces on Sicily successfully to evacuate the island across the Straits of Messina to the relative safety of mainland Italy. But the success of the operation could not disguise the fact that the Axis forces had been defeated, and soon after Italy surrendered. No longer able to rely on their ally, the German forces now anticipated pulling back to a defensive line running roughly from Pisa to Rimini. However, haggling over the Italian peace terms delayed the Allied occupation of Italy and gave Hitler the chance to reconsider his strategy. There was already some debate about where the outer boundary of the Third Reich should be and the Allies' prevarication offered a golden opportunity to set it at the furthest extent possible. Hitler was convinced and rushed 16 divisions south.

These units prepared to repel any invasion force and when the Americans landed at Salerno in September 1943 they were almost driven back into the sea. This success convinced Hitler that there was merit in fighting for Italy and Kesselring, the commander of German forces in Italy, planned to construct a series of delaying positions south of Rome. This strategy had much to commend it, and was not simply based on Hitler's psychological resistance to giving up territory. First, the Italian Peninsula was much narrower at this point and would need fewer divisions to defend it and, second, it would prevent the Allies capturing the symbolically important city of Rome, along with its airfields.

An Italian concrete pillbox constructed near San Giuliano. The position has a number of apertures that gave it good all-round observation. Rocks have been stacked in front to provide added protection and for camouflage. (NARA)

Before explaining these lines in detail it is worthwhile providing a little background information. Firstly, as in Sicily, the term 'line' is something of a misnomer. A line could be a rallying position, a delaying position or a position for protracted defence. Each of these in turn would be fortified according to its role. The rallying position might simply have been a naturally strong defensive position like a river or a mountain range. A delaying position might have some additional fieldworks, while a position for protracted defence might have had some 'permanent' defences and be built in some depth. Secondly, there is some confusion about the names of the various lines, which is not helped by the fact that certain names were used twice, and by the Germans' propensity to change them. To confuse the situation still further, the Allies and Germans often used different names for the same positions.

Initially the defensive lines were identified using the German military phonetic alphabet, for example, the A, A1 and B lines, but later they were given proper names, although often still having the same first letter. The first of these lines was the Viktor Line (A and A1 Lines), which followed the rivers Volturno, Calore and Biferno to Termoli on the Adriatic. Running parallel to this, some 16km to the rear, was the

Barbara Line. Both of these lines took advantage of natural features with only light fieldworks constructed, and were simply designed to slow the Allied advance to allow time for the completion of defences further north.

Further to the rear again was the Bernhardt Line (also known as the Rheinhardt or Reinhard Line), which broadly followed the rivers Sangro and Garigliano from Fossacesia to Minturno. This had initially been referred to as the B Line and still followed part of the original line. To begin with it was also only considered as a holding line with light fieldworks, but the decision by Hitler to stand and fight in Italy meant that further work was undertaken and it was reclassified as a permanent position. However, the defences were not uniform and the Eighth Army breached the weaker eastern end of

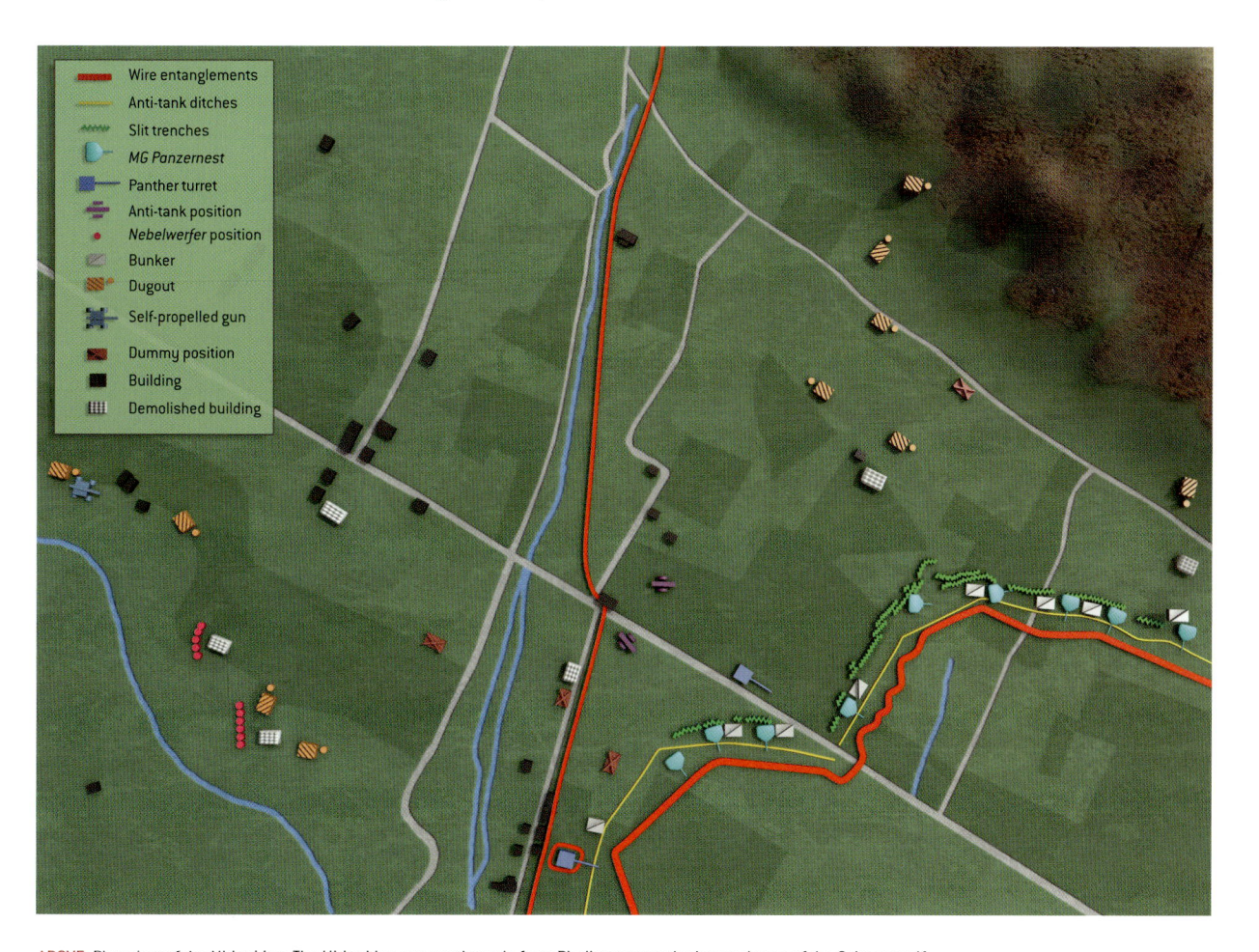

ABOVE: Plan view of the Hitler Line. The Hitler Line ran southwards from Piedimonte on the lower slopes of the Cairo massif to Aquino and Pontecorvo, and from there via Fondi and Terracina to the sea. The most heavily defended section of the line covered the Liri Valley and part of this is portrayed here, specifically the defences covering the strategically important Highway 6, showing how it would have looked prior to the battle in May 1944. (Chris Taylor © Osprey Publishing)

HITLER'S FORTRESSES

the line at the end of 1943 and a further position – the Foro Line – was established running along the River Foro. By contrast the western end of the Bernhardt Line was particularly strong, especially across the mouth of the Liri Valley where a switch position known as the Gustav Line was constructed.

The defences of the Gustav Line stretched from Monte Cairo in the north along the high ground to Monte Cassino, then along the east bank of the River Rapido before following the eastern face of the Aurunci mountains. The most strongly fortified section of the line was around the town of Cassino. The River Rapido, with its steep banks and swiftly flowing current, was in itself a formidable obstacle, but on the eastern bank it had been reinforced by a thick and continuous network of wire and minefields, while on the German side carefully sited weapons' positions and deep shelters to protect the defenders against air and artillery bombardment had been constructed. Additionally, the whole of the fortified zone was covered by mortar and artillery fire, which could be brought to bear with great accuracy from observation posts on the mountains that

An excellent view of one of the supporting Pak 40 anti-tank guns that protected the flanks of the Panther turrets. The Panther turret in the rear was destroyed by tanks of the 51st Royal Tank Regiment during the battle for the Hitler Line, May 1944. (Canadian National Archives, PA 114912)

228

overlooked the valley from north and south. Armour was kept to the rear for counter-attacking or used as static strongpoints.

In December 1943, the German troops began to build a reserve position known variously as the Führerriegel (Hitler Line), known later in German communications as the Sengerriegel, 13km to the rear of the Gustav Line. This line ran from Piedimonte, on the lower slopes of the Cairo Massif, to Aquino and then Pontecorvo, and from there via Fondi and Terracina to the sea. Again the most heavily defended section of the line covered the Liri Valley, essentially from Piedimonte to Pontecorvo.

Unlike the Gustav Line, the Hitler Line was not a naturally strong defensive position, and instead relied on an elaborate system of defences constructed by the OT. The defensive belt was between 500 and 1,000m deep. Its main strength lay in its anti-tank defences, which consisted of an anti-tank ditch and extensive minefields covered by anti-tank guns. These included emplaced Panther turrets supported by two or three towed PaK 38 or PaK 40 guns. Approximately 25 self-propelled guns gave depth to the position and also provided a counter-attack capability. All told there were some 62 anti-tank guns covering the 5km front. In support of these anti-tank defences the infantry were provided with deep bunkers built of steel and concrete, each with room for 20 men, which gave them shelter against artillery fire and which were connected with one or two covered emplacements, each mounting a machine gun. Additionally, a large number of semi-mobile armoured pillboxes or 'crabs' were installed behind the anti-tank ditch and barbed-wire entanglements. The whole line was covered by approximately 150 artillery pieces together with a considerable number of Nebelwerfer and mortars.

To prevent these elaborate defences being outflanked a series of defences at the western end of the Hitler Line were planned, running from Sant' Oliva through Esperia and then to Formia on the coast. This was known as the Dora Line. However, Kesselring and his senior commanders had largely neglected these defences because they considered the Aurunci and Ausonia mountains to be all but impenetrable. As a result the extension consisted of little more than minefields and a few simple earthworks dug to block the important roads and tracks. Covering the approaches to the Dora Line, and designed to bar the Ausonia Valley, was the Orange Line, which ran from the River Liri to Monte Civita, but it was similarly neglected.

Behind the Hitler Line, and the last major defensive position before Rome, was the Caesar Line. The main portion of the line ran from the coast just north of the Anzio bridgehead via the Alban Hills to Valmontone with the main fortifications concentrated on the coastal strip, Highway 6 and a number of other minor roads that led to Rome. The defences were cleverly sited to take advantage of the natural defensive features, but resources – materials, men and time – were scarce and they were far from complete when the Allies attacked.

HITLER'S FORTRESSES

German defensive lines in central Italy, 1943–45.

Not surprisingly the Caesar Line did little more than delay the Allied advance and on 5 June the Americans entered Rome. There was now only one major prepared defensive position before the Alps and that was the Gothic Line. Preparation of this position had begun when Italy surrendered and had continued intermittently thereafter, but it was not until June 1944 that work began in earnest.

The lack of progress prompted Hitler to change the name of the position from the Gothic Line to the Green Line. The original title was considered too pretentious and gave the impression that a strong fortified position existed, which was not the case. If the line was to be of 'fortress standard', as Hitler hoped, more time would be needed to complete the defences and that meant that Kesselring's forces would have to continue to fight further south. This would not only buy valuable time to finish the work but would also deny the Allies new air bases and limit the room they had to launch an amphibious operation from Italy, perhaps against the Balkans.

To realize these aims a further series of lines was established. The first of these was the Dora Line, which was a rallying position north of the Eternal City that ran to the eastern end of the Caesar Line. Behind this was 'Line E', which was a delaying position designed to slow the Allies before they reached the main line of defence – the Albert Line. This snaked from Ancona on the Adriatic to Perugia and then on to Lake Trasimeno before following the River Ombrone to the coast.

Behind the Albert Line were further delaying positions on the west coast, notably the Anton and Lilo lines that protected Leghorn and Siena respectively. And behind these lines, designed to protect Florence and the Arno crossings, were the Olga and Lydia lines, these running from Montopoli in the west to Figline on Highway 69. These positions, together with the Georg Line, a further intermediate withdrawal line that covered Volterra and Arezzo, would allow the German forces to fall back in good order to the next, and last, defensive line before the Green Line, the Heinrich Line. This started at Pisa on the west coast and ran along the north bank of the Arno and followed the line of the Apennines until it reached the coast at Senigallia.

Immediately in front of the Green Line were two further defensive positions that formed the outer bulwarks of the main line. The Vorfeld Line was a deep outpost zone that started at Fano on the Adriatic and followed the Metauro to its source in the Apennines and then on to a point just east of Florence where it effectively merged with the Heinrich position; behind this was a further intermediate position called the Red Line.

The 'Green Line' in actual fact consisted of two separate positions. Green I ran from Pesaro in the east to La Spezia in the west and Green II ran parallel to the first some 16km to the rear, but only as far as the Futa Pass where the two merged. At the rear edge of the Green Line was the Rimini Line. As its name suggests it was anchored on the

HITLER'S FORTRESSES

In order to safely store their ammunition for the weapons employed along the Gothic Line the Germans blasted a number of caves in the mountains. This cave was located near Castiglione Dei Pepoli. It was 5m deep and strengthened with timber props. It was used to house mortar rounds, as shown, and 17cm artillery shells. (Imperial War Museum, NA 19204)

Adriatic at Rimini and followed the River Ausa to the principality of San Marino. The value of these lines had long been recognized because they offered the last chance of a defensive action on a comparatively short front while at the same time taking advantage of the Apennine mountains, which at this point stretched from the Ligurian Sea almost to the Adriatic. If there was time to properly fortify and man these positions it was hoped that an attack on them would so weaken the enemy in a battle of attrition that further enemy operations would be much reduced or have to be cancelled completely. Moreover, it was important that the Apennine position was held because behind it lay the Plains of Lombardy. This flat expanse was perfect for large-scale operations and was rich in agriculture. An Allied breakthrough here would mean that extra food supplies would need to be provided for German forces in Italy and would also mean the loss of the industrial output from the Milan–Turin industrial basin.

MOUNTAIN BARRIERS – GERMAN DEFENSIVE LINES IN ITALY

The ramifications were unthinkable but eminently possible and even before the completion of the Apennine position a final defensive position had been identified – the Voralpenstellung (Forward Alpine Defences) – and in front of this a series of rallying and delaying lines were instituted. These intermediate positions were established along the line of the numerous fast-flowing rivers that ran from the Apennines, across the path of the Allies' advance, to the Adriatic. On the River Savio was the Erika Line and behind that on the Ronco was the Gudrun position, which protected Forli and blocked the Via Emilia (Route 9), one of the main arterial roads. Next came the Augsberger Line, which ran along the rivers Montone and Lamone and protected Ravenna. After that was the Irmgard Line, which followed the Senio, the Laura Line running along the Santerno, the Paula Line along the Sillaro and the Anna Line, which hugged the Gaiana.

In October 1944 a further defensive line east of Bologna was established. The Genghis Khan Line, as it was known, ran from Lake Comacchio along the River Idice

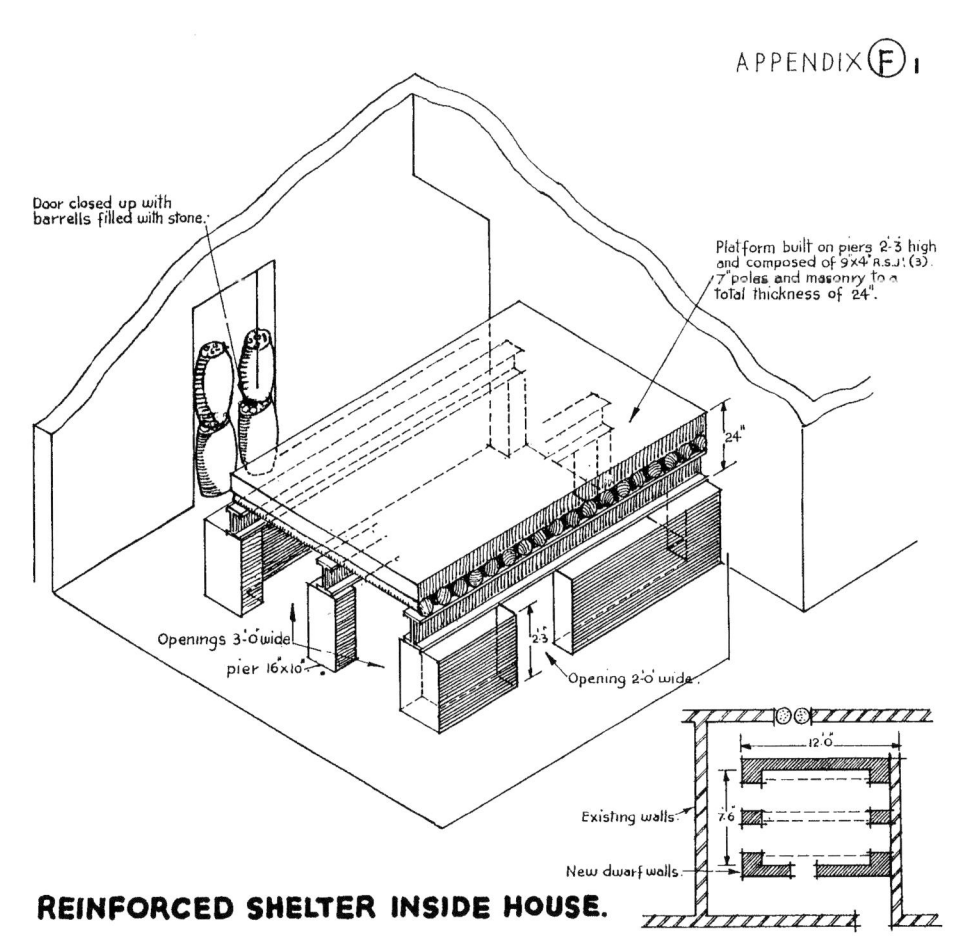

REINFORCED SHELTER INSIDE HOUSE.

An example of a reinforced shelter constructed inside a house in the Hitler Line. This example was constructed on piers which shouldered steel girders and logs. On top of this framework masonry and rubble were poured to a thickness of some 65cm. One of the entrances to the house was blocked with barrels filled with stones. (Public Record Office, WO291/1315)

233

to the foothills of the Apennines. This formed the forward line of a position that had already been prepared along the River Reno and which was sometimes referred to as the Reno Line.

The last line of defence before the Voralpenstellung was what the Allies referred to as the Venetian or Adige Line and what the Germans called the Red Line. This ran along the River Adige to the southern tip of Lake Garda.

The Voralpenstellung (also known as the Blue Line) was begun in July 1944 and included in its arsenal coastal artillery taken from the Ligurian Coast. The line ran from the border of Switzerland, across the Julian Alps to Monfalcone and was tied in with a series of defensive lines that ran along the rivers Brenta, Piave, Tagliamento and Isonzo that were to block the so-called Ljubljana Gap. The defences on the last two rivers were much more advanced and there were plans to emplace Panther tank turrets here in much the same way that they had been in the Hitler lines.

Technically speaking the National Redoubt, or Alpenfestung (Alpine Fortress), lay outside of Italy, but it warrants a brief mention for completeness. The Gauleiter for the Austrian province had floated the idea of a last redoubt in the Tyrolean Alps. Some work on the defences did begin but shortages of men and material, which had bedevilled previous attempts to build defensive lines in Italy, were now more acute and only a few fortifications on the Austro-Swiss border were completed.

Also worthy of mention are the fortifications constructed by the Italians and inherited by the Germans. Before World War I, defences had been constructed on the Ligurian Coast to meet the possible threat from France, but when Italy joined the Triple Entente this threat disappeared and in World War I these defences were largely abandoned and the weapons transferred to the front with Austria-Hungary. After the war the coastal defences were steadily improved with the building of a series of medium artillery batteries. These were subjected to a number of attacks by French and British naval forces in the early part of World War II and the weakness of the defences was highlighted, in particular the lack of any large-calibre artillery pieces. This shortcoming was rectified with the building of a number of large coastal batteries, but ironically these were not tested before the Italian surrender and the defences fell into the hands of the German forces. Some renovation and improvement work was undertaken by the OT, much of which was completed in a burst of activity in the spring of 1944 when there was a very real possibility of an Allied landing. This principally consisted of work to build obstacles and casemates to enfilade the beaches and also efforts to strengthen open positions against air attack. As it transpired the Allies landed in southern France and the defences of the rather grandly named Ligurian Wall were abandoned and the garrisons were relocated to France or to the Green Line. Ultimately, the only action the defences saw was against local partisans and in April 1945 the troops that remained surrendered to the Americans.

The other major defensive position inherited from the Italians was the Vallo Alpino. Ironically much of this had been constructed to deter an attack by Germany and as such most of the defences were of little use against an enemy attacking from the south. However, this was not true of the Ingrid Line, which ran along the Italian border with the former Yugoslavia. The defences here were strengthened by the OT with the addition of standard shelters and fieldworks against a possible Allied invasion of the Balkans, or, as became increasingly likely, a possible Soviet attack.

THE LINES OF DEFENCE

At an operational level each of the lines, and certainly those designed for protracted defence, were constructed in depth. At the leading edge were minefields, barbed wire and anti-tank ditches. Behind these defences were machine-gun and anti-tank positions that covered the line throughout its length. Further to the rear artillery, rockets and mortars were registered on the expected routes of advance. The idea was to separate the infantry and the armour and to isolate the attackers from their own forces, so making them vulnerable to counter-attack by reserves held in the rear, sheltered against the preliminary air and artillery bombardment, and earmarked for the purpose.

American soldiers inspect a section of the anti-tank ditch of the Gothic Line. The technique for revetting the sides is clearly evident with uprights held in place by wire securing the brushwood behind. (NARA)

HITLER'S FORTRESSES

GUSTAV LINE

Defensive lines had already been used in Sicily and in the early part of the campaign on the mainland. However, these lines tended not to be continuous and they certainly were not constructed in depth. The first real example was the Gustav Line. Here the River Rapido provided a difficult natural obstacle for any attacker to negotiate and this had been strengthened with the addition of mines and barbed wire. Behind these machine guns had been sited to provide interlocking fields of fire, especially around the most likely avenues of approach. Frequently these were housed in armoured pillboxes, which were known to the German forces as MG-Panzernester and to the Allies as 'crabs'. These firing positions were often linked to troop shelters at the rear. These were either prefabricated steel shelters or constructed from concrete with some large enough to contain sleeping accommodation for 20 or 30 men. Further to the rear mortars, Nebelwerfer and artillery were located to provide indirect fire support.

An Italian Cannone de 75/46 pressed into service by the Germans. This position was captured by the Allies north of Cervia and covered dragon's teeth on the coast below. The embrasure has been strengthened with the addition of sandbags. Ammunition ready for use is stacked to the side. (Imperial War Museum, NA20021)

MOUNTAIN BARRIERS – GERMAN DEFENSIVE LINES IN ITALY

An army observation post for a coastal battery (Type 637) positioned on the west coast. This example was only just completed when US forces captured it. The wooden shuttering is still in place on one side and is also evident in the foreground. (NARA)

In the town of Cassino itself and on the surrounding slopes a very different approach had to be adopted. Here the closely packed buildings meant that a traditional defensive position was not possible. Moreover, the heavy fighting and later Allied bombing had flattened many of the buildings. Far from being a handicap for the paratroopers assigned to this section of the line, this was a positive boon because, as the German troops knew from bitter experience at Stalingrad, rubble makes a better defensive position than undamaged buildings. Wherever possible shelters were constructed on the ground floor or in the cellars of buildings. These shelters were walled and roofed with heavy logs or girders and covered with a thick layer of rubble, which made them impervious to direct hits even from large-calibre artillery shells. Tanks and self-propelled guns were also positioned inside the shells of buildings as improvised strongpoints and proved extremely effective.

HITLER LINE

To the rear of the Gustav Line was the Hitler Line. This was not a naturally strong defensive position and as such German engineers went to great lengths to construct a continuous line of defences in some depth. With little time to complete the work a simple anti-tank ditch was blasted along the length of the line. In front of this was a thick band of barbed wire sown with mines. Behind these passive defences were machine-gun positions and, for the first time, Panther turrets mounted on steel shelters were used. These were positioned in a single defensive line in such a way that they were able to cover the line throughout its length. They were deployed in a series of spearheads. At the tip of each spear there was a Panther turret and echeloned back on either side were two or three towed 7.5cm or 5cm anti-tank guns. The turrets were located so that they commanded the approaches to the line with particularly long fields of fire to their front where trees had been cut down to approximately 45cm from the ground. They had more restricted fields of fire to the flank and particularly the rear, and towed anti-tank guns covered these weak spots. These were generally employed in pairs approximately 150–200m behind or to the flank of the turrets and were often hidden behind houses, in sunken roads or in thick cover. Some 25 self-propelled guns were also positioned along this same line with some held further to the rear to give depth to the defences, or to provide the punch for any counter-attack.

CAESAR LINE

The Caesar Line was to be constructed in much the same way as the Gustav and Hitler Lines, but because resources had been diverted south, work on the line was far from finished by the end of May. The defences protecting Rome were largely complete though with thick bands of barbed wire and mines laid to block the most favourable routes of approach. Covering these defences were machine-gun and anti-tank positions; mortars, Nebelwerfer and artillery provided indirect fire support. However, as General Eberhard von Mackensen, the commander of 14. Armee, was quick to point out, 'the Caesar Line was suitable for no more than a delaying action'.

GOTHIC LINE

The Gothic Line, or Green Line as it was later known, was the last major defensive line before the Alps. The Italian Army had identified the potential of a line running roughly from Pisa to Rimini and the merits of such a position were not lost on the OKW. Work on the defences had begun in late 1943, but had been suspended to concentrate resources on the Gustav and Hitler lines. Only in the summer of 1944 did work resume.

MOUNTAIN BARRIERS – GERMAN DEFENSIVE LINES IN ITALY

A rare photograph of one of the dug-in Panther tanks used by the Germans in the Gothic Line. Polish forces captured this example. The driver's and machine-gunner's hatches of the Ausf. A are clearly visible in the foreground. It is also possible to see the tank's original Zimmerit anti-magnetic-mine paste covering. (Polish Institute and Sikorski Museum)

The position was immensely strong, incorporating as it did the mass of the Apennines and a number of rivers that had their source in the mountains and flowed to the Adriatic. There were weak points, the principal one being the coastal plain around Pesaro, and this is where the bulk of the defences were concentrated. This was the responsibility of General Heinrich von Vietinghoff's 10. Armee and in this section of the line alone it was planned to lay more than 200,000 mines (although by the end of August 1944 less than half had been completed – 73,000 Tellerminen and 23,000 Schrapnellminen). A continuous anti-tank ditch almost 10km long had been dug and almost 120,000m of barbed wire had been used. Covering the line were almost 2,500 machine-gun positions, including MG-Panzernester and PzKpfw I and II turrets adapted for static employment. Panther turrets were also used, with particular concentrations in the section of the line that ran along the River Foglia from Pesaro on the east coast to Montécchio. By the end of August four of these positions had been completed in this section of the line with a further 18 under construction. In addition, seven disabled Panther tanks had been dug in with another one being installed. There were also almost 500 positions for anti-tank guns and Nebelwerfer and some 2,500 dugouts of various types, including OT steel shelters.

There had been little time to build the defences in any great depth and indeed Green II was little more than a reconnoitred line on German staff maps, although its natural features were strong. Panther turrets were installed to the rear, but this seems to have been the only attempt to provide depth to the position. As for possible outflanking manoeuvres, on the Adriatic Coast, which Kesselring regarded as the most vulnerable of the two, dragon's teeth were constructed on the beaches, laced with barbed wire and mines, to counter another Allied landing. Large concrete bunkers were also constructed to house coastal artillery.

The western section of the Gothic Line was dominated by the Apennine mountains and as such offered fewer opportunities for an Allied breakthrough. The weakest point was along Route 65 through the Futa Pass and it is here that General Joachim Lemelsen, the new commander of 14. Armee, concentrated his defences. The outpost zone consisted of minefields, an anti-tank ditch and barbed-wire entanglements. Behind these were fire trenches that covered the line throughout its length. Further to the rear were concrete pillboxes, troop shelters and the much-feared emplaced Panther turrets. One was installed close to the village of Santa Lucia, guarding the long anti-tank ditch dug a few kilometres south of the pass, and another on the pass itself. Similar defences were also constructed on Highway 6620 to the west, the Prato–Bologna road, and to protect Il Giogo Pass to the east, although both lacked Panther turrets. A Panther turret was installed at the Poretta Pass to protect Route 64 above Pistoia.

VORALPENSTELLUNG

The last of the major defensive lines was the Voralpenstellung, which was constructed in north-eastern Italy to block the so-called 'Ljubljana Gap'. According to German files this position was to be heavily fortified, with plans to install 30 tank turrets mounting machine guns, 37 Panther tank turrets, 100 Italian M42 tank turrets fitted with a German 3.7cm Kwk and 100 P40 turrets fitted with a German 7.5cm Kwk. It was also envisaged that a significant number of tank guns fitted to improvised mounts would be installed. However, it is unclear how many of these defences were completed. Certainly a number of the Panther turrets were being installed by January 1945, but others were destroyed or delayed in transit.

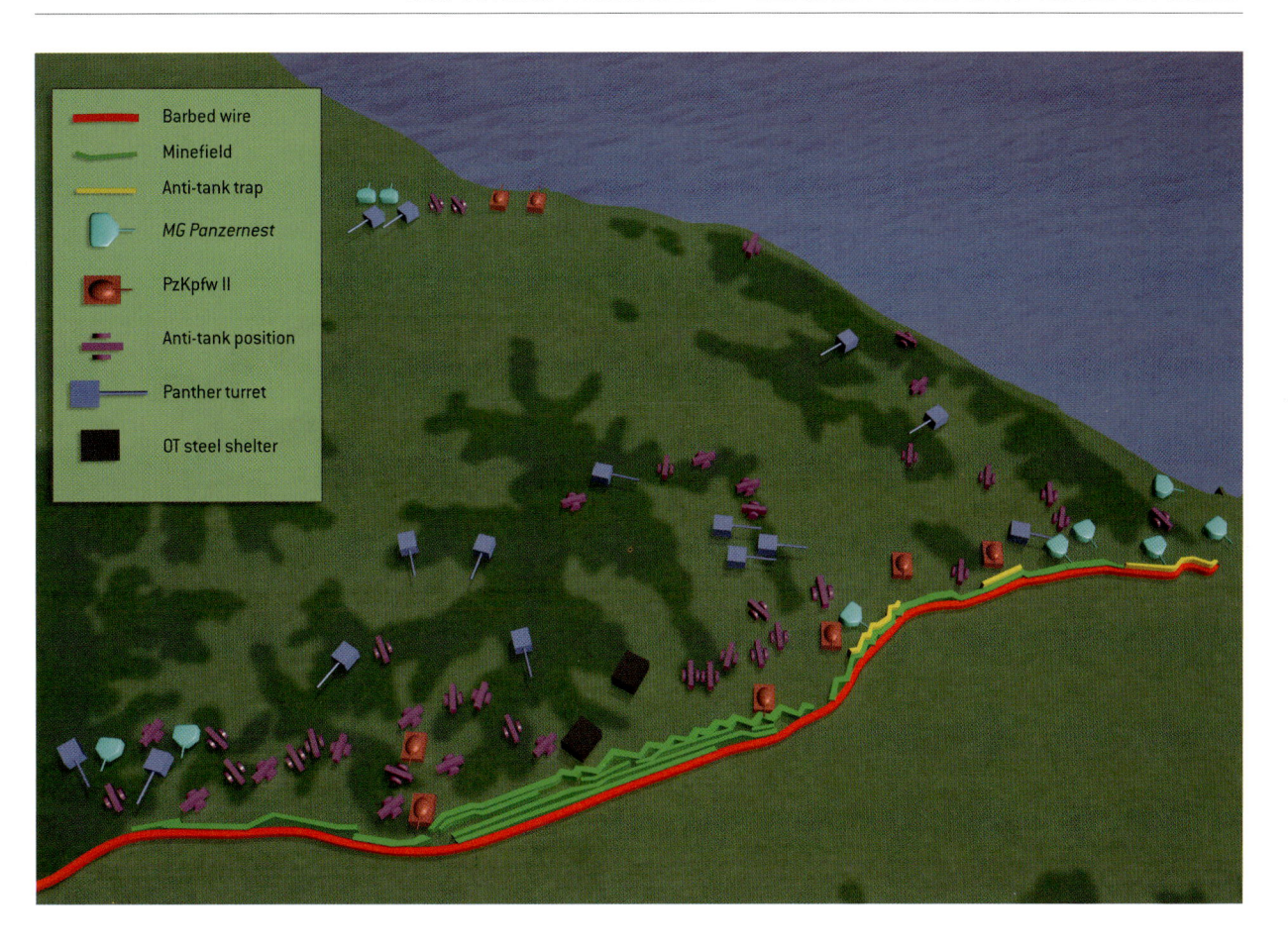

MOUNTAIN BARRIERS – GERMAN DEFENSIVE LINES IN ITALY

ABOVE: Plan view of a section of the Gothic Line. This plate depicts a small section of the Gothic Line that ran from Pesaro on the coast inland to Tomba di Pesaro and to the rear to Cattolica. The defences are depicted as they were planned in the autumn of 1944 and demonstrate the German concept of defence in depth. (Chris Taylor © Osprey Publishing)

ACHILLES' HEEL

For all the effort that went into the construction of the various defensive lines in Italy, they failed to stop the Allied advance. This judgement might seem harsh, because they certainly helped to delay the progress of 15th Army Group. However, it must be remembered that Alexander's forces were never significantly larger than those fielded by Kesselring and he certainly did not enjoy the 3:1 advantage that was considered necessary for a successful attack on such prepared positions. And yet in spite of this fact the Allies were still able to breach the defences. True, Alexander could field more armour and artillery, but these advantages were of less significance in a mountainous country like Italy. The same cannot be said of air power and this highlights one of the major shortcomings of such defences. They are by their very nature static and therefore

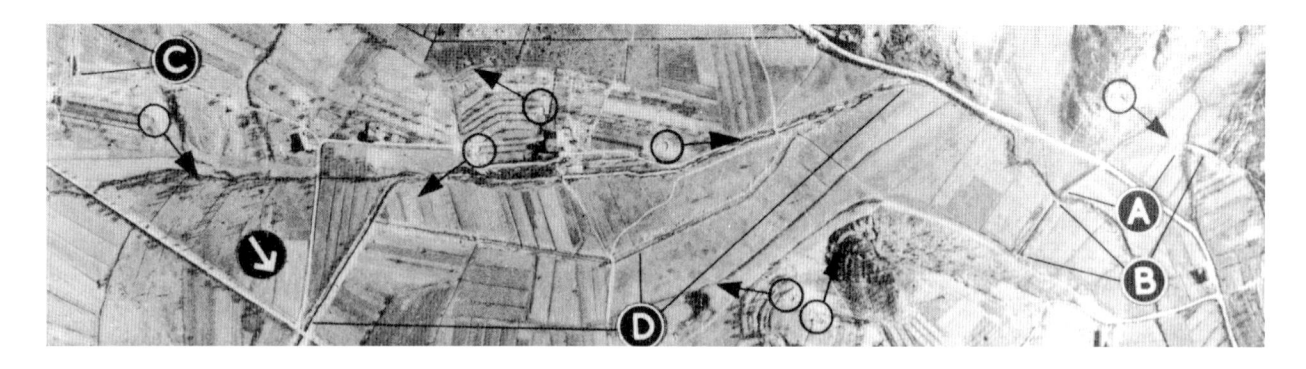

An aerial view of a section of the Voralpenstellung east of Gorizia. The arrows indicate anti-tank gun emplacements. 'A' shows a belt of dragon's teeth. 'B', 'C' and 'D' are anti-tank ditches. (TM30-246 Tactical Interpretation of Air Photos 1954, Figure 208)

vulnerable to attack from the air. Allied tactical and strategic bombing raids meant that work on the defences was constantly interrupted by direct interdiction or by delays in the supply of materials. This, together with sabotage and a less than committed workforce, meant that many of the defences were not complete or were sub-standard. Moreover, unfettered air observation meant that Allied ground forces always had good intelligence on enemy defences, despite the fact that much of the work was undertaken at night and camouflaged during the day.

The poor state of the defences also undoubtedly lowered the troops' morale. Goebbels' Propaganda Ministry made much of the strength of the defences, but its highly coloured description of the defences often did not match the reality. Indeed Engineer General Bessell, when taking over responsibility for the Gothic Line at the end of June, noted that,

> The line was without depth, lacked emplacements for heavy weapons, and was little more than a chain of light machine-gun posts. Fields of fire had not been cleared, anti-tank obstacles were rudimentary and the 'main line' ran across forward slopes.

And even where the defences had been completed there were often insufficient troops and weapons to employ in the positions. As Machiavelli famously stated, 'fortresses without good armies are incompetent for defence'. Furthermore, the rigid defences in many respects reduced the scope for the soldier on the ground to use his own initiative that had been such an important part of the German Army's early success.

At a strategic level the major problem with such defensive lines on the Italian Peninsula was that they could be outflanked by amphibious assault. In January 1944 VI (US) Corps landed at Anzio almost unopposed and had the chance of outflanking the Winter Line and capturing Rome. Overcautious commanders on the ground saw this opportunity squandered, but the prospect of a further landing was never far from the mind of German generals. These fears did diminish following Operation *Overlord* in June 1944 and certainly after the landings in southern France in August 1944, because it was recognized that the number of landing craft available to the Allies was finite. However, there was still concern about a possible landing on the Adriatic Coast and as such it was never possible to have complete faith in any defensive line, no matter how strong, for fear of it being outflanked by a landing in the rear.

THE NATURE OF THE DEFENCES

Each of the defensive lines built by the German soldiers in Italy was unique, built as they were to take advantage of natural features specific to that area, but often they shared common characteristics. The outpost zone consisted of passive defences: barbed-wire entanglements, minefields and, where there was no river or similar feature, an anti-tank ditch. Covering the whole were machine-gun positions, often mounted in MG-Panzernester or tank turrets, and to provide anti-tank defence Panther turrets were installed. Exceptionally, a number of other defences were constructed. Dragon's teeth,

The coast near Ravenna was fortified with pillboxes and protected with wire and, as seen here, dragon's teeth and mines. The mines are probably Italian anti-tank mines in wooden cases and were lifted by sappers to enable an airfield to be constructed nearby. (Imperial War Museum, NA 20897)

A PANTHER TURRET ON THE HITLER LINE

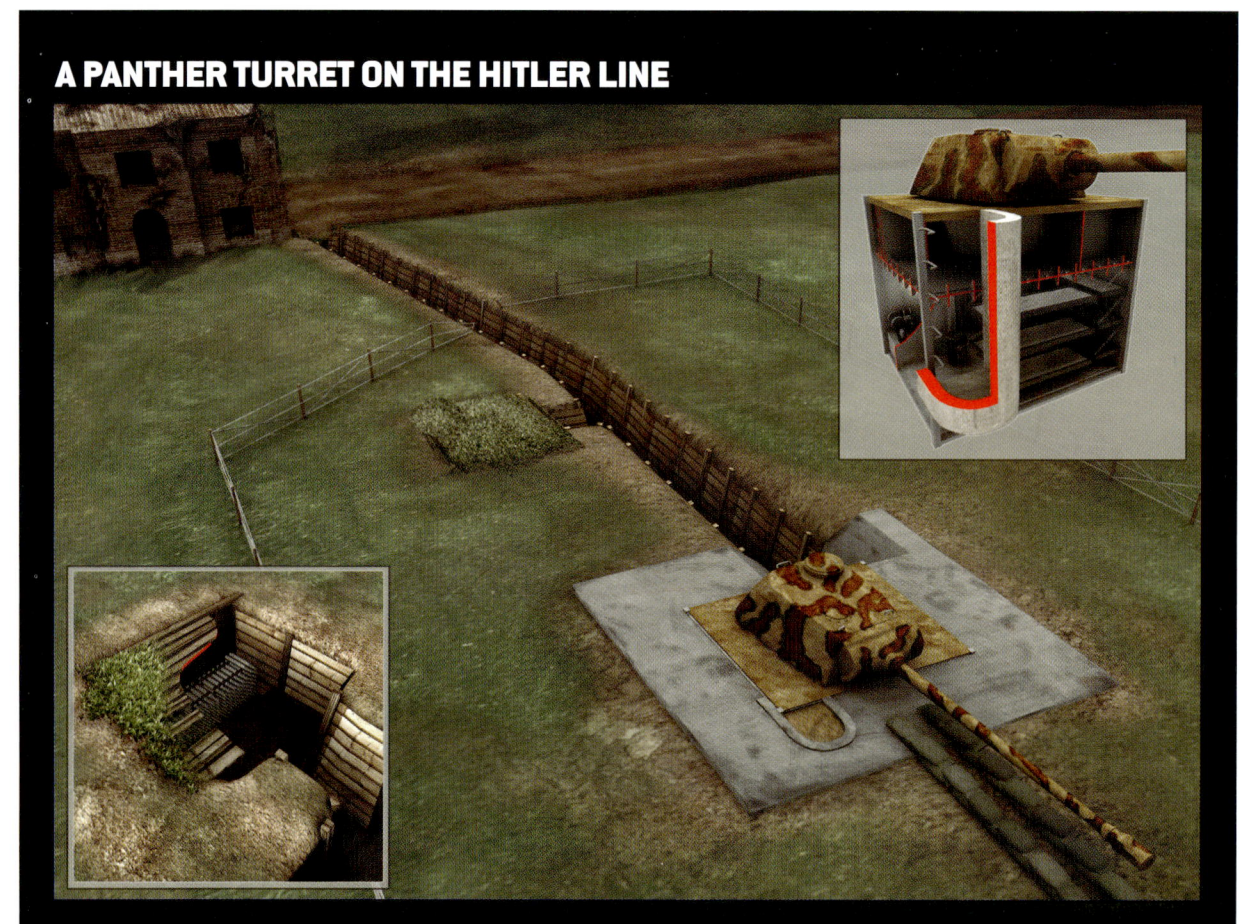

Along the length of the Hitler Line, Panther turrets mounted on specially designed shelters were installed. One of these turrets covered the strategically important Highway 6, which led from Monte Cassino to Rome. The turret, taken from a Panther Ausf. D tank, was positioned just behind the anti-tank ditch and wire and would have been heavily camouflaged but this has been omitted for clarity. At the front of the position was a shallow sandbag trench that was just deep enough for the gun to be depressed into so that it did not cast a telltale shadow for Allied aircraft to spot. The turret was mounted on an OT steel shelter that was buried in the ground and encased in concrete 1–1.5m thick. The shelter itself was constructed in two parts. The upper box incorporated the turret ball-race and housed the ammunition for the main armament. The lower structure was divided into three compartments. The largest of these was fitted with nine fold-down bunk beds and a stove for heat. In the right-hand rear corner of the compartment there was an escape hatch. The second compartment acted as home for a 2hp motor, together with a dynamo, a storage battery and a compressed air tank. The final compartment was fitted with a steel ladder that linked the upper and lower boxes and also incorporated the main access hatch. From here a revetted trench led away from the shelter. This was 60cm wide and 1.3m deep and ran to an abandoned building located on the Aquino road. Approximately two-thirds of the way along the trench was an ammunition shelter. This was 2.6m square and 1.3m deep and was covered with timber and spoil. This is shown separately in cutaway. All around the position was a barbed-wire fence. (Chris Taylor © Osprey Publishing)

which had first been used along the West Wall, were installed along the coast, and further inland large coastal guns were mounted in concrete casemates. Finally, in the last desperate days of the war there were plans to use tank guns mounted on swivel mounts as improvised anti-tank guns.

Two types of mine were employed: Tellerminen, which were used against vehicles, and anti-personnel mines. The mines tended to be laid in rectangular blocks to cover expected avenues of attack or, in the case of Tellerminen, they were often laid along roads and tracks. The weight of the vehicle would detonate the charge. The same principle applied to the Schützenmine 42, or 'Schu Mine', which was one of the most widely used anti-personnel mines. This consisted of a plywood box packed with 200g of TNT. Pressure on the lid would set off the charge. Because it was in a wooden box it was exceptionally difficult to detect. Captured Italian models were also employed and these were equally hard to find in Sicily because of the high iron content in the rock and lava. The Schrapnellmine 35 was slightly different. This was activated by direct

An Allied soldier inspects one of the flamethrowers that were used in the Gothic Line. The fuel tank of the Abwehrflammenwerfer 42 was buried in the ground so that only the nozzle was visible. They were often used in groups and when triggered would project a jet of flame for some 50m. (Imperial War Museum, NA 18338)

pressure on the head or by use of trip wires. A small charge would then propel the mine into the air where it would explode, scattering shrapnel over a wide area.

Often minefields were enclosed within a double-apron barbed-wire fence. This generally consisted of rows of concertina wire or wire stretched between screw pickets. Behind this, stretched just above the ground, was a broad band of trip wire.

In the absence of a river or similar anti-tank obstacle it was necessary to construct a man-made alternative. In the Hitler and Gothic lines anti-tank traps or Panzerabwehrgraben were dug. These varied in length and sophistication. In the Hitler Line this was little more than a consecutive series of craters that had been blown electronically with demolition charges at about 5m intervals. Accordingly, the width of the ditch varied from 7m to 11m and the depth from 2m to 4m. Only in a few places had any additional spadework been done. In a number of instances the explosive charges had not detonated and as a result there were irregular gaps in the ditch. A more elaborate affair was constructed at the eastern end of the Gothic Line running inland from the coast. It was dug to a depth of 2.5m, which with the spoil meant that the overall depth

Two Allied servicemen inspect a captured MG-Panzernest. The steel door, which was hinged at the base, lies flat on the floor. The position is perfectly located to enfilade one of the beaches south of Rimini where the Germans anticipated an amphibious landing. Just visible in the distance are stakes and barbed-wire entanglements. (Imperial War Museum, NA 18995)

was 3m, and was 4.5m wide. It was revetted with logs and brushwood held in place with anchor wires secured to stakes that were buried to protect them against enemy artillery. For every kilometre dug some 6,200m³ of soil had to be removed.

Covering the outpost zone were a variety of weapons. One worthy of mention because of its uniqueness was the Abwehrflammenwerfer 42, which was dug in at ground level in forward posts of the Gothic Line. This weapon was based on a Soviet design first encountered by the German soldiers in the Stalin Line. The 22.7-litre fuel tank was buried in the ground so that only the nozzle was visible. They were often used in groups spaced 10–25m apart and were ignited by a fuse or a trip wire. This would trigger a 50m jet of flame that lasted 5–10 seconds.

More normally the passive defences were covered by various machine-gun positions, including the MG-Panzernest. This was developed in the second half of the war and proved invaluable when the German Army was on the retreat. Weighing just less than 3,200kg it could be transported and installed relatively easily and provided valuable protection for the two-man crew against enemy small-arms fire and shrapnel.

The nest was constructed from two steel prefabricated sections that were welded together. The top half contained the aperture for the gun, air vents and the rear entrance hatch, which was hinged at the base. This section was most vulnerable to enemy fire and was cast accordingly with armour around the aperture 13cm thick and 5cm around the sides and the roof. The base of the unit, which was completely below ground, was about 12.5mm thick.

The frontal aperture was divided into two parts: the lower part accommodated the gun barrel and the upper part was for sighting. Two periscopes in the roof provided further observation. When not in use the aperture could be covered with a shield operated from within the shelter. The relatively small aperture meant that the machine gun had a limited field of fire of approximately 60 degrees. Because of this and because the nest could not be rotated they tended to be used for flanking fire with other positions providing mutual support.

A simple foot-operated ventilation system was provided that used holes at the side of the turret. These also acted as the mounting for an axle. With the nest upside down wheels could be fitted on either side. A limber was attached to the machine-gun embrasure and two further wheels were located in front. This was then hooked up to a tractor and the whole could then be towed.

Machine guns were also fitted in old tank turrets mounted on concrete bunkers. These were built to a standard design. Directly below the turret was the fighting compartment. This was fitted with wooden duckboards, which not only improved the crew's footing but also served as a repository for spent machine-gun cases. Any water that entered the fighting compartment would also collect here before being channelled through a drain to the lower level, where the floor was angled at 2 degrees to direct water out of the shelter to the soakaway at the entrance. Access to the fighting compartment was via a flight of steps from the anteroom inside the entrance, which in turn was linked to a revetted trench at the side. This room also housed the hand-operated ventilation system.

Turrets were taken from a number of obsolete German tanks. These included a number of modified PzKpfw I turrets. The original mantlet was removed and replaced with a 20mm-thick plate with openings for the machine gun and the sight. The two vision slits in the turret side were dispensed with and were covered by 20mm steel plates which were welded over the openings as ventilation ports. This meant they were much better suited for their new role. A number of PzKpfw II turrets were also used and a similar number of Czech PzKpfw 38(t)s were also made available for use in the Gothic Line.

There were also plans to use large numbers of Italian tank turrets that had fallen into German hands following their occupation of the country. These turrets were to be mounted on specially designed concrete bunkers (although a wooden design was also later developed). There were plans to install 100 P40 turrets and 100 M42 turrets in the Voralpenstellung, but it is unclear as to whether this work was completed. A number of other Italian tanks were simply dug in and used as improvised strongpoints. P40 tanks

One of the numerous MG-Panzernester, or 'crabs', used in the Hitler Line. This example was captured before it could be buried in the ground. Still attached at the front is the limber and a shattered wheel. The whole structure would have been towed upside down. (Imperial War Museum, NA 15778)

MOUNTAIN BARRIERS – GERMAN DEFENSIVE LINES IN ITALY

ABOVE: A cutaway view of a PzKpfw II turret. In addition to the heavier Panther turrets, a number of PzKpfw II turrets were installed along the Gothic Line. The view shows the steps leading from the trench down into the shelter and then the steps leading up into the fighting compartment. This was fitted with wooden duckboards, which served as a makeshift repository for the spent shell cases. (Chris Taylor © Osprey Publishing)

were used in this way in the Gustav Line and at Anzio when work to replace its unreliable diesel engine proved problematical; a number of L3 tankettes were used in a similar fashion.

In addition to the tank turrets, ten specially designed armoured revolving hoods (F Pz DT 4007) were installed capable of mounting either an MG34 or an MG42. These were constructed from steel plate, but were sufficiently light to be man portable. They could be mounted either on a prepared concrete or wooden shelter or, if necessary, simply on firm ground.

These, and the other tank turrets, were primarily for use against infantry, but a large number of Panther tank turrets were also used as improvised fixed fortifications. They retained their powerful 75mm gun and were often the main anti-tank weapon in the defensive line. The turrets were either taken from production models (Ausf. D and A) or specially designed for the role. The Ostwallturm (or Ostbefestigung) as it was known, differed from the standard turret in a number of ways. The cupola was removed and was replaced by a simplified hatch with a rotating periscope, and the roof armour was also increased in thickness because of the greater threat to the turret from artillery fire. The turrets were mounted on either concrete bunkers or, more often, on steel shelters. The OT had developed a series of prefabricated steel shelters and one of these was adapted to mount a Panther turret. It was constructed in two parts from electrically welded steel plates. The upper box essentially formed the fighting compartment. It held the ammunition for the main weapon and incorporated the turret ball-race onto which the turret was mounted. The lower box was divided into three compartments. The largest formed the living accommodation and was fitted with fold-down bunk beds and a stove. A further room acted either as a general store or as home to various pieces of equipment that provided power for the turret and shelter. Finally, there was a small anteroom fitted with a steel ladder that linked the upper and lower boxes and was also where the main entrance was located. A revetted trench, covered near the entrance, led away from the shelter and linked it to the main trench system at the rear.

A Panther turret and steel shelter ready for installation. In the foreground are the rails on which the lower box, which formed the crew's living quarters, was moved into place. The two sections have been covered in hay in an effort to camouflage them. (Imperial War Museum, NA 18343)

A large number of the original steel shelters developed by the OT were also installed in the various lines to provide protection for troops against enemy artillery and air attack. Other shelters were constructed from timber with soil and rocks heaped on top for added strength. These different shelters were often linked to fighting positions mounting a variety of weapons including machine guns, mortars, Nebelwerfer, artillery pieces and anti-tank guns.

Later in the war, there were plans to install tank guns in open pits as improvised anti-tank positions. The powerful 8.8cm guns taken from Jagdpanther tanks were to be fitted to pivot mounts and 5cm 39/1 L60 guns taken from PzKpfw IIIs were to be mounted on makeshift carriages. At the other extreme the German forces built a number of permanent positions. Around the Futa Pass, for example, a number of concrete bunkers to mount anti-tank guns were constructed. On the Adriatic coast near Rimini large coastal emplacements, not dissimilar to those found in the Atlantic Wall, were built. These mounted 15cm guns that had originally been designed for use on ships. Dragon's teeth were also used extensively around the coast in attempt to deter a further Allied amphibious assault. These were essentially reinforced concrete pyramids poured in rows and designed either to stop an enemy tank completely or to expose the thinner armour of the underside of the tank to the defenders' anti-tank guns.

OPERATIONAL HISTORY

SICILY

On 10 July 1943, the Allies landed on Sicily in what was the largest amphibious assault in Europe up to that point. This was a multinational force under the command of Field Marshal Alexander. Montgomery's Eighth Army landed on the east coast and experienced little opposition and, as hoped, the naval base of Syracuse was captured on the first day. Patton's Seventh US Army landed in the south-west of the island where the beaches were more heavily fortified and where resistance was stiffer. Nevertheless, by 12 July the beachhead had been secured and the German and Italian forces were on the defensive.

The Eighth Army made the main thrust of the Allied attack with the Americans securing the flank. But Alexander's strategy meant that the chance of splitting the island and isolating part of the enemy's forces in the west was lost. The Axis forces, under the command of General Hans Hube, fell back to the first of their defensive lines, the Etna Line. This held firm against a four-pronged attack by Montgomery and allowed 15. Panzergrenadier-Division to the west to fall back in good order and to dig in around Troina in the knowledge that its line of retreat was secure. Hube's forces were now

HITLER'S FORTRESSES

ensconced in a line that ran from Acireale to San Fratello. The British continued to press from the south while the Americans pushed east. The 1st (US) Infantry Division fought a fierce five-day battle to dislodge German troops from Troina and further north German positions along the San Fratello proved to be a bloody challenge for the 3rd Division. However, pressure from the Americans and the British eventually forced the German forces to withdraw and plans for a total evacuation were prepared. A series of defensive lines were established further back, each shorter than the last and requiring fewer troops to defend so allowing the rest to be evacuated. The Axis forces surrendered on 17 August, but by that point 40,000 German and 62,000 Italian troops with much of their equipment had been safely transported to the mainland.

GUSTAV LINE

A little over a fortnight later the Allies landed on the Italian mainland and, after an initial scare at Salerno, consolidated their hold and advanced north to the so-called Winter Line. The Allies hoped to bounce this position before the enemy had time to settle in. To the north of Monte Cassino the French Expeditionary Corps (FEC) attacked towards Atina. They successfully negotiated the perils of the River Rapido and closed on the outworks of the Gustav Line proper, but with the troops tired and cold

A US soldier examines the internal workings of a captured MG-Panzernest. It has been covered in rocks for added protection and camouflage. Just visible in the right foreground is a German mess tin. (NARA)

A destroyed army observation post for a coastal battery (Type 637) that was located on the west coast. In the front section a rangefinder would have been fitted to pinpoint enemy targets for batteries located further to the rear. (NARA)

from their exertions in the depths of a bitter Italian winter and meeting stiff German resistance the attack was suspended.

General Mark Clark, who now commanded American forces in Italy, had argued that attacks be launched on both flanks of the Gustav Line to increase the chances of a breakthrough and on 20 January II (US) Corps began what was hoped would be the decisive thrust across the Rapido and up the Liri Valley. General Fred Walker's 36th (US) Infantry Division was ordered to lead the attack. Covered by an artillery barrage the Texans advanced to the river with their assault boats and made their way across, but were met with a hail of machine-gun fire. The defenders, men of 15. Panzergrenadier-Division, had sheltered in deep dugouts during the barrage and now emerged to man their weapons in pre-prepared positions, which had been carefully sited to create a belt of interlocking fire.

Having reached the far bank there the Americans enjoyed no respite. Mines and barbed wire blocked their advance and, trapped in their tiny bridgehead with no easy route to retreat, they were subjected to intense mortar, artillery and Nebelwerfer fire that had been pre-registered on both banks. Eventually it was realized that the position was untenable. A few men managed to extricate themselves, but the rest were either killed or captured.

Still reeling from the bloody reverse crossing the Rapido, Clark tried to regain the initiative by launching another attack north of Cassino on the night of 24/25 January. General Charles Ryder's 34th (US) Infantry Division, supported by the FEC, was to cross the Rapido and, having secured a bridgehead, capture Monte Cassino. The defences in this section of the line were particularly strong and made any advance extremely difficult. The regimental commander of 133rd Infantry Regiment wrote, 'MG nests in steel and concrete bunkers had to be stormed. Progress was measured by yards and by buildings. Each building had been converted into an enemy strongpoint… Casualties were heavy.' Not surprisingly the Americans struggled to make any headway, and with no armoured support the attack faltered. A better crossing point was identified and a renewed attack proved more fruitful with tanks able to support the infantry. The signs looked promising and Clark signalled Alexander that Monte Cassino would fall soon, while von Senger und Etterlin, the commander of XIV Panzer Corps, suggested to Kesselring that German forces retire to the Caesar Line.

Victory seemed to be in sight and one more thrust was ordered on 11 February. But this proved to be ill conceived. The Americans had suffered terrible casualties and morale was low. Ryder's division was simply not capable of delivering the coup de

A section of German trench that was hewn out of solid rock. The trench formed part of the Gothic Line defences and dominated a hairpin bend in the Apennines. US forces captured it in 1944. (NARA)

An MG-Panzernest that formed part of the Gustav Line defences is removed from where it had been buried. An M32 tank recovery vehicle, more used to towing tanks, is used to transport the nest. (NARA)

grace. The first battle of Monte Cassino had ended and the Gustav Line had held firm.

The Americans were relieved by elements of 4th Indian Division, who were now tasked with capturing Monastery Hill. Meanwhile 2nd New Zealand Division was ordered to capture Cassino railway station. On 15 February, the operation was launched but both attacks were unsuccessful. However, the second battle for Monte Cassino is most noteworthy for the decision to bomb the abbey atop the hill which the Allies believed was occupied by the German forces. It later transpired that this was not the case, but the German troops were not slow to seize the opportunity and integrate the ruins into their defences.

A massive aerial and artillery bombardment similarly preceded the Third Battle for Monte Cassino, which it was hoped would smash the enemy defences and allow the Indians and New Zealanders to achieve their respective goals. On the morning of 15 March, the bombardment began. The results looked impressive and indeed the defenders in the town and on the surrounding hills suffered terrible losses, but enough survived in deep dugouts and caves hewn into the solid rock to man basement

ABOVE: Nebelwerfer position. The Nebelwerfer 42 was often employed in specially prepared positions, as depicted here. This was one of six such emplacements in this section of the Hitler Line and was located 1,000m behind the frontline. The emplacement consisted of a shelter 6 x 3.3 x 2.2m partly cut into the ridge at the rear and partly built up. Behind the shelter was a 2 x 1.3 x 0.5m concrete block, which was embedded so as to project just 15cm above a hardcore floor. Ammunition was stored in niches set into the side of the position. These were stacked in specially designed transport cages. (Chris Taylor © Osprey Publishing)

strongpoints and other positions. At the same time the bombardment served to flatten most of the buildings still standing, making navigation difficult and ensuring that it was all but impossible for the armour to support the infantry. Where the tanks did get forward the German soldiers easily picked them off using hand-held anti-tank weapons or mines. The New Zealand infantry did manage to reach Highway 6 and eventually some tanks wormed their way forward and engaged enemy strongpoints. One of these was centred on the Continental Hotel, which dominated the highway. A tank had been built into the entrance hall and it was key in preventing the New Zealanders from pushing armour down the road to Rome. By 23 March both sides were exhausted and the New Zealanders' attack was called off. Meanwhile, the Indians had captured Castle Hill and Hangman's Hill, but their hold was not sufficiently strong to act as a springboard for an attack on the monastery and they simply dug in to consolidate their gains. Eighth Army now reorganized and prepared for a new attack in the spring in what it was hoped would be the final breakthrough.

The Allies had tried to breach the Gustav Line on three occasions and although success had been tantalizingly close on a number of occasions the German forces held firm. This was partly because of the natural strength of the position with its fast-flowing rivers and mountains that dominated the main routes of advance. In part it was due to poor Allied leadership. The decision to bomb the Monastery gave the defenders an ideal defensive battleground and made combined operations almost impossible for attacking units. Crucially, the great opportunity of outflanking the position with the amphibious assault at Anzio was squandered by overly conservative commanders on the ground whose inaction was summed up by Churchill when he told the Chiefs-of-Staff, 'We hoped to land a wild cat that would tear out the bowels of the Boche. Instead we have stranded a vast whale with its tail flopping about in the water!' But the defences undoubtedly played a part in blunting the Allied attacks. The defences provided valuable protection against the Allied air and artillery bombardment and the strongpoints, carefully sited so that they could bring devastating fire to bear on the enemy, proved to be exceptionally difficult to neutralize. Eventually the Gustav Line was breached and the Eighth Army advanced along the Liri Valley, but it was now faced with the prospect of defeating the Hitler Line.

One of the 15cm naval guns in its concrete emplacement. Four of these positions were constructed in the vicinity of Rimini to protect against a potential amphibious assault. The New Zealanders captured them during their drive along the coast in September 1944. (Imperial War Museum, NA 18992)

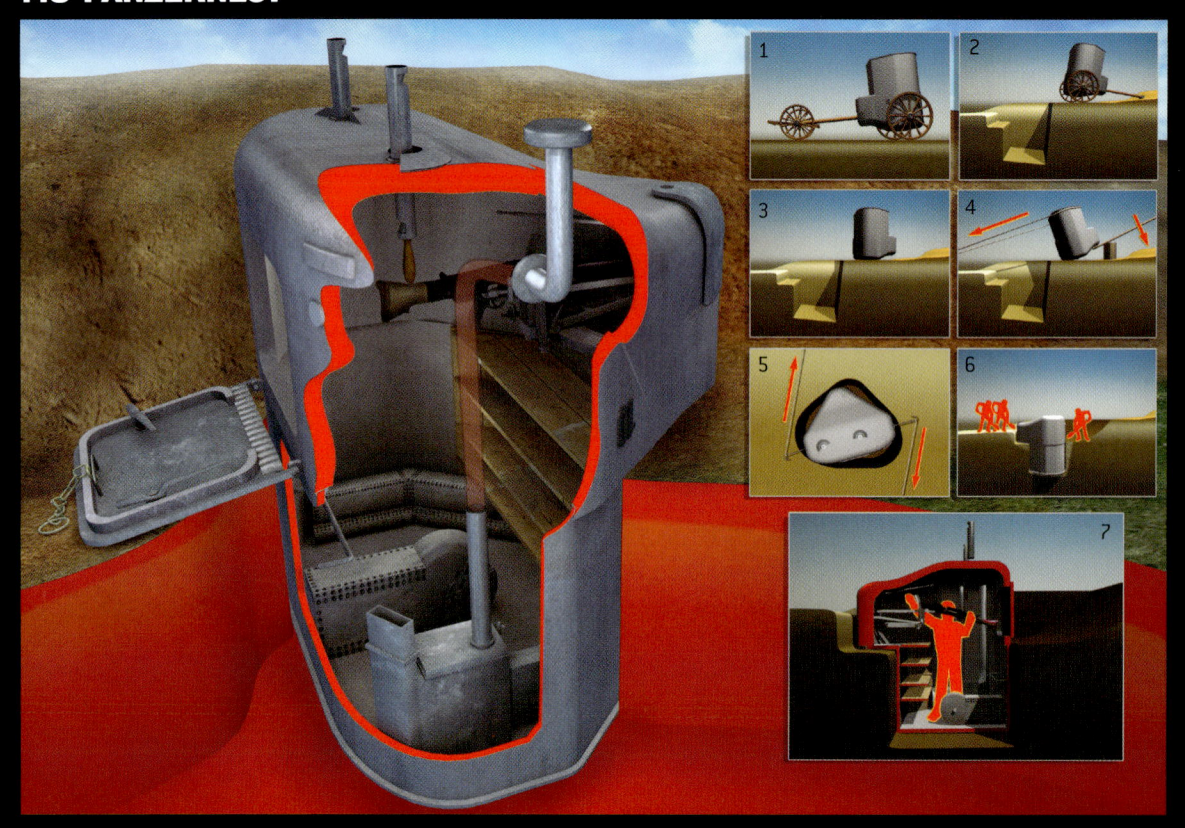

MG-PANZERNEST

The MG-Panzernest was developed in the second half of the war and was used extensively in Italy. The thick upper armour provided valuable protection for the two-man crew and the nest was easily transported with the opening at the front doubling as the housing for the towing limber and the holes for the ventilation acting as the mounting for an axle, which was then fitted with two wheels. The position was designed to mount a machine gun that could fire through a small aperture at the front. This limited the weapon's traverse and meant it only had a 60-degree field of fire. When the position was not in use the opening could be covered with a shield. The crew gained access to the position via a hatch at the rear and two periscopes in the roof provided them with observation. When they were firing the machine gun, fumes were extracted by a simple foot-operated ventilation system. The MG-Panzernest was installed in a simple seven-stage process.

1. Firstly, the Panzernest had to be transported to the site. To do this, the nest was turned upside down and was fitted with a limber, axle and wheels.
2. Once the nest arrived at the site the front limber was removed and a hole dug.
3. The nest was now manoeuvred into place. Earth under the turret was dug away so that the wheels could be removed.
4. A rope was now secured to the base of the nest and a lever inserted under the nose. Eight of the crew would pull on the rope and three other men would use the lever to tip the nest into the hole.
5. If the nest was not pointing in the right direction, crowbars could be inserted in the axle holes and ropes attached so that the team could pull the nest round.
6. Once installed spoil would be heaped around the sides.
7. Finally, the equipment was fitted.

(Chris Taylor © Osprey Publishing)

HITLER LINE

At first light on 19 May a probing attack was launched against the Hitler Line. Two battalions of infantry supported by tanks of 17th/21st Lancers and the Ontario Regiment of Canada advanced towards Aquino. Screened by early morning mist the composite force made good progress, but the fog cleared and an emplaced Panther turret quickly destroyed three US tanks. The tanks of the Ontario Regiment engaged the enemy, but it was an uneven struggle and under the cover of darkness those tanks that could withdraw did so. All of the tanks in the two leading squadrons suffered at least one direct hit and in total the Ontarios lost 13 tanks.

Another probing attack was put in against the defences around Pontecorvo on 22 May by 48th Highlanders of Canada and a squadron of tanks from 142nd Royal Armoured Corps (RAC; the Suffolks). The result was much the same with three of the Suffolks' tanks knocked out by an emplaced Panther turret. All efforts were now concentrated on the main attack planned for the following day, which was to be made by 1st Canadian Infantry Division supported by 25th Tank Brigade.

A view from one of the many concrete emplacements constructed around the Futa Pass that were captured by 91st (US) Infantry Division. This anti-tank emplacement had a clear field of fire across the tank trap in the middle distance and the road further on. (Imperial War Museum, NA 18929)

The main thrust was to be delivered by two battalions of 2nd Canadian Infantry Brigade – the Seaforth Highlanders on the left supported by two squadrons of tanks of the North Irish Horse and the Princess Patricia's Canadian Light Infantry on the right supported by a single squadron. At the same time the 48th Highlanders were to maintain the pressure on the enemy around Pontecorvo and, on their right, 3rd Infantry Brigade, supported by the 51st Royal Tank Regiment (RTR), was to launch a feint to keep the enemy guessing as to the Allies' true intentions.

Somewhat unexpectedly these secondary operations enjoyed a certain amount of success with the tanks of the 142nd RAC destroying an emplaced Panther turret protecting Pontecorvo and 51st RTR advancing to the Aquino–Pontecorvo road – the first objective of the main thrust – and in so doing also put a Panther turret out of action. However, the main attack of 2nd Infantry Brigade was not going as well.

The Patricias reached the enemy wire, but their supporting tanks were stopped by an undetected minefield and as they struggled to find a way through four of their number were picked off by enemy anti-tank guns and the remainder fell back to find another way forward. Unaware of their compatriots' difficulties the Loyal Edmontons, supported by a squadron of 51st RTR, followed the Patricias in accordance with the second phase of the attack. The tanks, however, were similarly balked by mines and a number fell victim to the Panther turrets and their supporting anti-tank guns.

To their left the Seaforth Highlanders and the North Irish Horse made better progress, but when only 100m from their first objective the tanks came under heavy anti-tank fire, which accounted for five of their number including the squadron leader. The remainder beat a hasty retreat and, together with tanks from C squadron that had been held in reserve, advanced on a new axis. This force accounted for another Panther turret, but lost seven tanks in the process.

In spite of the losses the unremitting pressure along the southern portion of the line had forced the enemy to retreat. The attack against Aquino was now resumed to exploit the enemy's disarray. Men of the Lancashire Fusiliers supported by two troops of tanks of 14th Canadian Armoured Regiment advanced on the town, but soon four of the six tanks had been destroyed and the others retired. Despite being outflanked it was clear that the enemy still held the defences in strength and it was not until the following day that the enemy finally withdrew, having first demolished the two Panther turrets defending the town.

In total 25th Tank Brigade lost 44 tanks (although some were later recovered): the heaviest tank losses inflicted on the Eighth Army in the Italian campaign. An intelligence report written after the battle noted, 'In front of each position there was a graveyard of Churchills and some Shermans… This is, at present, the price of reducing a Panther turret and it would seem to be an excellent investment for Hitler.'

CAESAR LINE

At the same time as General Oliver Leese's Eighth Army launched its attack to breach the Hitler Line, Alexander ordered Clark's Fifth US Army to break out of the Anzio bridgehead. General Lucian Truscott, the commander of VI (US) Corps at Anzio, planned to attack towards Cisterna and then advance to Valmontone with a view to cutting Highway 6, one of Vietinghoff's (AOK 10) main lines of retreat. This plan was endorsed by Alexander and initially VI (US) Corps made good progress towards its objective. However, on 25 May Clark changed the focus of the attack away from

A flight of steps constructed from logs held in place by wooden pegs. They led to a German position in the Gothic Line. Camouflage nets, that would have prevented Allied planes spotting the position, hang limply at the side. (NARA)

Valmontone towards Rome. This change of tack undoubtedly had a number of military advantages, but it was also fraught with danger because it would involve attacking the strongest section of the Caesar Line, which was held by General Alfred Schlemm's very strong and highly motivated I Fallschirmjäger Korps (I Parachute Corps), which was more than capable of defeating any such attack.

Only 3rd (US) Infantry Division continued its advance towards Valmontone. The Old Ironsides, 1st (US) Armored Division, which had been guarding its left flank, was now ordered to head north as were 34th and 45th (US) Infantry Divisions, which were tasked with capturing Lanuvio and Campoleone respectively. The new operation was launched on 26 May, but almost immediately the attack of 1st (US) Armored Division was stopped dead by mines and well-placed anti-tank guns manned by 4. Fallschirmjäger-Division. The advance of 34th (US) Infantry Division was similarly halted on 27 May and slightly later 45th (US) Infantry Division experienced the same fate. The assault on the Caesar Line was resumed on 29 May with an attack by 1st (US) Armored Division slightly further to the west, but this was also unsuccessful. As soon as the tanks approached the defences they were engaged by anti-tank guns and infantry armed with Panzerfaust hand-held anti-tank weapons. By dusk 37 American tanks had been knocked out, most of them destroyed. A further attempt to breach the line was launched the following day, this time with infantry in the lead, but the result was the same.

General Walker's 36th (US) Infantry Division had replaced 1st (US) Armored Division in the line after it had initially been withdrawn and it was envisaged that the infantrymen would launch another set-piece attack against the main defences of the Caesar Line. But General Walker, whose men had suffered heavy casualties by adopting such tactics at Salerno and, more recently, crossing the Rapido, was not keen and considered a number of alternatives. One that presented itself was to attack through the Alban Hills rather than going round. The OKW had largely ignored the hills, in part because they lay on the corps boundary, and in part because they were considered unsuitable for an enemy attack. A patrol ordered to reconnoitre enemy dispositions on Monte Artemisio found that it had not been fortified and nor was it occupied. But equally there were no obvious routes to the top save for a narrow farm track. However, engineers were convinced that the track could be widened to take military vehicles and so the decision was taken to attack on 30 May. Two infantry regiments made their way to the top of the mountain under the cover of darkness. They caught the small garrison completely by surprise and captured it without a shot being fired. Engineers soon set to work improving the track and men of Walker's division dug in on the heights. Through a mixture of complacency and élan the 36th (US) Infantry Division had captured the 1,000m peak. In so doing the Caesar Line had been turned and, on 5 June, Mark Clark was in Rome.

GOTHIC LINE

Clark's decision to attack the strongest portion of the Caesar Line not only allowed the German units to extricate themselves from a possible encirclement, but also meant that he unnecessarily weakened his divisions, which made it difficult for them to pursue the enemy north of Rome. This, together with the panoply of lines and defensive positions that the German forces had established between Rome and the Gothic Line, slowed the Allied advance. The Eternal City fell on 5 June but it was not until the end of August that the Allies were in a position to launch an attack against the last bastion before the Alps.

Although it was clear that the Allies would soon launch a new offensive, when it started on the night of 25/26 August it came as a complete surprise to Kesselring and Vietinghoff, the commander of 10. Armee. They had been considering the possible withdrawal to the Po, Operation *Herbstnebel* (Autumn Fog), while the movement of divisions in and out of the line distracted their immediate subordinates. At the same time, divisional commanders were preoccupied with the phased withdrawal of troops

An Allied soldier descends steps from a German machine-gun position that formed part of the Gothic Line. To the right is a shelter dug into the side of the slope with the walls strengthened with timber and brushwood. (Imperial War Museum, NA 18334)

This field position near Monghidoro formed part of the Gothic Line and was captured by US forces before it could be completed. The trench leading to the dugout is visible at the rear as are the ammunition niches. The pedestal in the middle might have mounted a small anti-tank or anti-aircraft gun. (Imperial War Museum, NA 19207)

from their forward positions into the Green Line proper; the tardy withdrawal in part driven by Hitler's insistence that no ground should be given up to the enemy. The result was that many of the troops had no time to familiarize themselves with the defences they were supposed to be manning. Not that all the positions were complete; a large number of Panther turrets had still to be installed in the ground and signs were still in place detailing safe lanes through the minefields.

With the German forces taken by surprise, Eighth Army, in the first phase of the battle, smashed through the defences of Green I with unexpected ease. Their advance was also facilitated by the devastating effect of bombing and strafing by the Desert Air Force. When 26. Panzer-Division was committed to the battle on 28 August, it found that air raids and shelling had smashed many of the positions it was to use.

The air and artillery bombardment also served to unnerve the enemy. When 2nd Canadian Infantry Brigade and their supporting tanks from 21st Tank Brigade launched their attack on Monteluro on 1 September, they found extensive defensive systems simply abandoned. Elsewhere, the enemy was more stubborn and was only

MOUNTAIN BARRIERS – GERMAN DEFENSIVE LINES IN ITALY

dislodged by small unit actions and individual bravery. In fighting on the previous day 46th Division captured Montegridolfo, Mondaino and Pt 374, the highest point along the ridge half way between the two villages.

Once through Green I, the Allies should have been faced with the equally daunting prospect of breaching the defences of Green II, but a lack of time and materials meant that no work had been completed. Nevertheless, it was naturally strong and manned by fresh divisions. Moreover, because no work had been completed the Allies were unaware of its existence and assumed that the German troops would fall back to their next prepared position – the Rimini Line. They were wrong. The German soldiers fought a vigorous rearguard action that provided valuable time for further work to be completed along the River Ausa.

In the middle of September the Germans began to man the Rimini Line in preparation for the next Allied assault, which began soon thereafter. The defences were again softened up by air attacks, but bombing could not always neutralize the enemy defences. On 15 September 1944, 3rd Greek Mountain Brigade supported by tanks of 18th New Zealand Armoured Regiment attacked Miramare airfield, near Rimini, which was protected by two emplaced Panther turrets. One of the turrets sited to cover Route 16 (the coast road) had been destroyed by its crew following an earlier engagement with the New Zealanders, but the other remained intact.

An Italian armoured pillbox, possible a Navy observation post, captured by the Americans at Anzio in 1944. The structure was constructed from steel plate and was accessed by a door at the rear. The apertures, which provided all-round observation, could be closed if necessary. (NARA)

HITLER'S FORTRESSES

On 17 September, the Seaforths of Canada supported by a squadron of 145th Regiment RAC put in an attack on San Martino. The attack started well, but soon six of the supporting tanks were knocked out. These it was believed were the victims of the second Panther turret located at the northern end of the airfield. This was engaged by artillery and ground attack aircraft, but neither succeeded in silencing the turret. The only alternative was a direct attack by the tanks of 18th NZ Armoured Regiment. But so complete was the turret's command of the terrain that it was decided that the best way of silencing the menace was an attack by a single tank. Covered by smoke the tank, commanded by Lieutenant Collins, advanced to within range of the turret and

ABOVE: An 8.8cm anti-tank gun pit. The plate depicts one of these pits in the Gothic Line in late August 1944. The 8.8cm Pak 43 has been dismounted from its limber and sits on its cruciform platform ready for action. The gun pit was dug to a depth of 60cm so that it provided the crew and the weapon with some protection but at the same time allowed the gun to be fully traversed. (Chris Taylor © Osprey Publishing)

with its fourth shot knocked it out before escaping under another smoke screen. For his bravery in the battle for Rimini airfield Collins was awarded the Military Cross.

In a little under a month, Eighth Army had broken through the three main lines in the Apennines and Leese could rightly claim that his men had smashed the Gothic Line defences. Eighth Army now stood on the Plains of Lombardy, but waiting for it was a further series of defensive lines and the autumn rains had come early, which extinguished any lingering hopes of a swift exploitation.

On Fifth US Army's front, General Mark Clark planned to make his main thrust through the Apennines towards Bologna. The most direct route, and the weakest point topographically, was along Route 65 through the Futa Pass. However, the German leaders had also recognized the significance of this pass and it had been heavily fortified. Moreover, intelligence intercepts suggested that Hitler had ordered Kesselring to concentrate his troops at this strategically important point. In light of this Clark considered his options. The Il Giogio Pass, some 10km east, was a less promising avenue of attack, but it was neither as heavily fortified nor as heavily defended (only one regiment of 4. Fallschirmjäger-Division guarded Il Giogio – there were two at the Futa Pass), and it also lay on the boundary between the German 10. Armee and 14. Armee, and as such was one of the weaker points on the enemy front. A breakthrough here would outflank the defences of the Futa Pass and open up the possibility of exploitation towards Bologna or Imola.

On 12 September, Clark launched his attack. The 91st (US) Infantry Division attacked Il Giogio with 85th (US) Infantry in reserve, while the 34th (US) Infantry Division launched a feint against the Futa Pass. Although undoubtedly less challenging than the Futa Pass, the capture of Il Giogio was nevertheless a daunting prospect. It was dominated by the Monticelli Ridge on the left and Monte Altuzzo on the right. These features had been fortified with the addition of concrete shelters or positions blasted into the rock that were almost impossible to identify. The main avenues of advance had also been covered with mines and barbed wire.

As the men of 91st (US) Infantry Division made their way up the slopes of the Monticelli Ridge they were engaged by the enemy firing from pillboxes and bunkers. Where possible these were met by anti-tank guns, tanks and tank destroyers, while positions out of range or too strong were targeted by heavy-calibre 8in guns and 240mm howitzers. But in the final reckoning it was down to the infantry to storm the enemy positions using small arms and grenades and, after a sanguinary struggle, the men of 363rd Infantry Regiment managed to secure part of the ridge by 15 September. With the defenders unable to call up reinforcements from the two regiments guarding the Futa Pass, who were themselves under pressure from the holding attack by 34th (US) Infantry Division, the Monticelli Ridge was captured on 18 September. Initially it was believed that 91st (US) Infantry Division would be able to capture this feature and Monte Altuzzo, but the stiff resistance meant that 85th (US) Infantry Division had to be ordered forward to attack the second feature. After further fierce engagements with the tenacious paratroopers the mountain was taken on the same day. The Americans paid a high price for this small section of the Gothic Line – 2,731 casualties – but the important breakthrough had been achieved. The OKW was acutely aware of this fact and Lemelsen ordered 4. Fallschirmjäger-Division to abandon the Green Line. The formidable defences of the Futa Pass had been outflanked and captured without a fight.

AFTERMATH

In the summer of 1943 the possibility that much if not all of the Italian mainland would escape serious damage seemed bright. Italian forces were continuing to fight in Sicily, but they had little stomach to continue to wage war on the mainland. Mussolini had gone and negotiations for an Italian surrender were under way. However, the negotiations stalled and Hitler, who had previously considered holding a line from Pisa to Rimini, sent his troops further south. It was now clear that the German forces would fight for every inch of ground with the primary aim of keeping the Allies as far away from the heart of the Third Reich as possible, and they would spare little or no regard for the country they were fighting over.

Roads and bridges were demolished to delay the Allies and houses and trees were cleared to provide better fields of fire. But for all that Rome and the other major cultural centres escaped with little or no damage and there were examples where culture triumphed over operational need. In Florence, for example, the German troops destroyed all the bridges over the Arno but following agreement with the Allies, who promised not to use it for military purposes, the Ponte Vecchio was saved.

But equally there were a number of aberrations, the most significant being the Allied bombing of the Benedictine Monastery at Cassino, which it was believed (erroneously as it turned out) was being used by the German forces as an observation post. While it is easy to criticize this action with benefit of hindsight, the attack was ordered with the intention of smashing the Gustav Line and easing the path of the ground forces. Some of the defences were destroyed and more were accounted for in subsequent raids. Others were silenced by artillery fire and by direct fire from tanks.

Indeed during the campaign as a whole many of the defences met a similar fate. Others still were demolished by the crew before they retreated or were simply abandoned. Frequently it was possible for the Allies to ignore them and continue to press the retreating German forces but some simply had to be demolished or, like a number of Panther turrets in the Green Line, lifted and removed to scrap heaps so that engineers could improve old roads, or build new ones. This was vital to the success of the Allies, whose lines of communication grew longer the further up the peninsula they advanced. Wherever possible the captured defences were studied by intelligence officers. For much of the campaign Italy was the only front on which the British and Americans were actively fighting and as such this information gave them a valuable insight into German tactics and innovations. It was in Italy that the Allies first came across the German tactic of elastic defence in depth. In terms of equipment the first MG-Panzernest was encountered here as were dug-in tank turrets used as improvised fixed fortifications. These were later to be found protecting the Normandy beaches and in the West Wall, where emplaced Panther turrets made an unwelcome reappearance. Detailed reports on these weapons were written and dispatched to the UK and America where they were analysed and the useful information disseminated to frontline units, which proved invaluable in the eventual Allied victory.

An American soldier inspects the shattered remains of one of the small artillery bunkers (Type 671) installed on the coast near Pisa. These casemates were extensively used along the Atlantic Wall. It would have mounted a 10.5cm gun. (NARA)

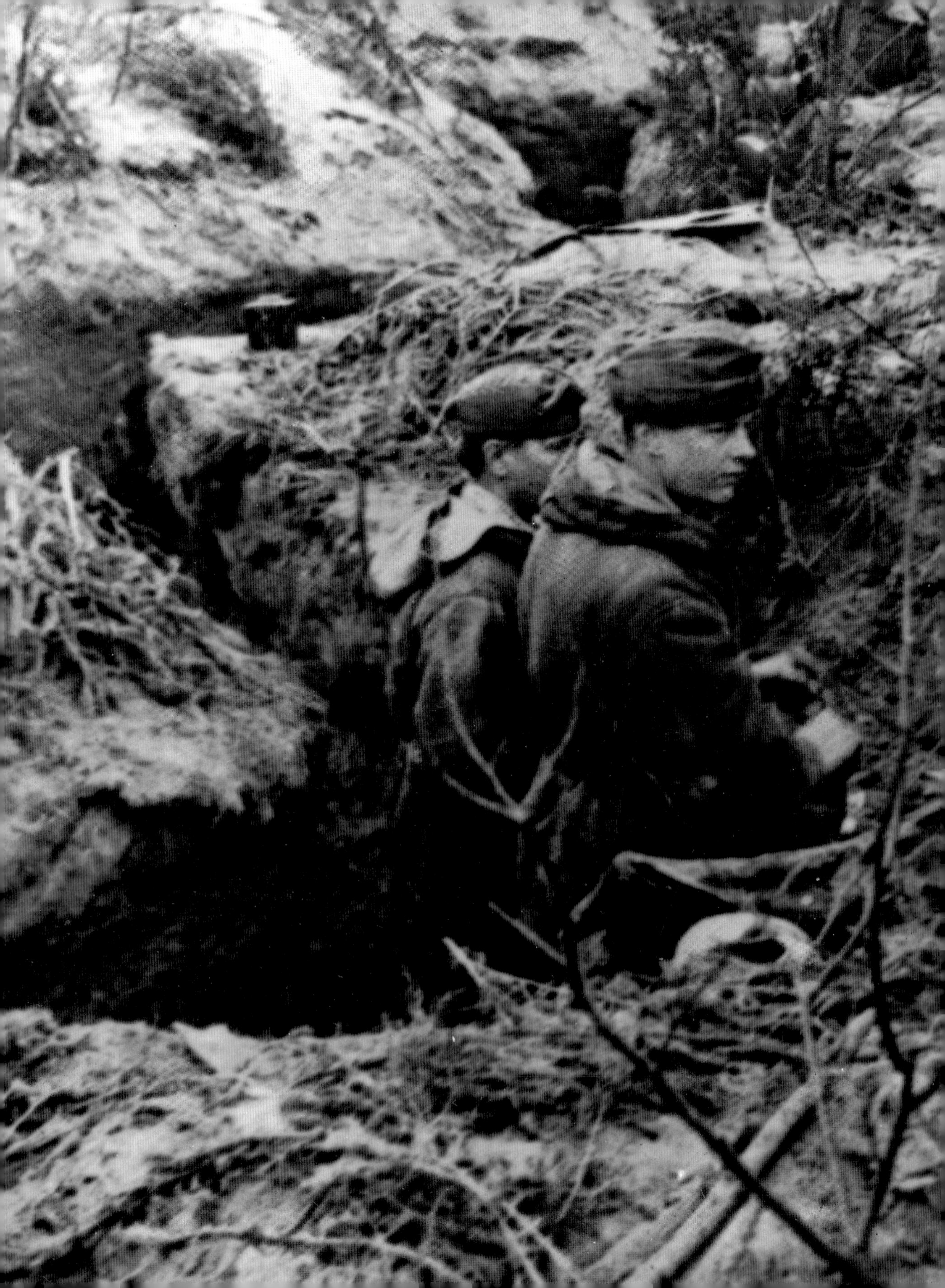

ETCHED IN THE EARTH – FIELD FORTIFICATIONS

LEFT: German Army troops man a defensive trench network at an unknown location, and wait for the inevitable enemy attack. Note the zig-zig configuration of the trench – this prevented enemies from delivering enfilading fire along a long, straight trench, and it also helped minimize casualties from artillery strikes. (Cody)

While the German Army is perhaps best known for elaborate, massive concrete and steel fortifications, such as the West Wall and Atlantic Wall, the fortifications that a German soldier was most familiar with were the ones he dug himself. Whether built on the sprawling steppes of Russia, in the deserts of North Africa, in the mountains of Italy, in European hills and forests, or among the rubble of countless battered cities, these were the fortifications that truly defined the boundaries of the Third Reich.

Building on the previous chapter's study of the Italian defensive lines, the focus of this chapter is the field fortifications constructed by combat troops defending the frontline. The core focus will be temporary and semi-permanent crew-served weapon positions and individual and small-unit fighting positions, built with local materials and occasionally construction matériel. Little engineer support was provided: pioneer troops may have provided advice, but the infantry mostly built these positions and obstacles. However, Pionier (pioneer) and Baupionier (construction) units and OT civilian labourers did sometimes prepare defences behind the front for units to fall back to.

While wartime intelligence studies and reports provide detailed information on German field defences, only limited post-war study has been undertaken. This is largely due to their temporary nature, and the fact that little survives of them today. The Wehrmacht used the same basic doctrine and manuals for positioning and construction purposes as did the Waffen-SS. With the exception of local improvisation, a factor common to all armies in the field, all branches of the German armed forces employed these field fortifications and obstacles.

Field fortifications were necessary during offensive movements too. Here infantrymen dig in for the night on a Russian steppe to provide protection to 7.5cm StuG III Ausf. F assault guns. These would be shallow slit trenches more suited to the role of a soldier's bed than a fighting position. (Gordon Rottman)

PLANNING THE DEFENCES

Regardless of the unique aspects of any given front, at all unit levels (defined by the German Army as regimental level and below) common principles for the establishment and conduct of defence were employed down to the squad. Space, distances, density of forces and support would vary, though, as would construction materials, types of fortifications, obstacles and how they were deployed and manned.

High ground was always desirable for defensive positions for its observation advantages, extended fields of fire and the fact that it is harder to fight uphill. In the desert even an elevation of a couple of metres would be an advantage. Natural terrain obstacles were integrated into the defence as much as possible. The routes and directions of possible enemy attacks were determined and infantry and supporting weapons were designated to cover these approaches. The goal was to destroy or disrupt the attackers by concentrating all available weapons before the enemy reached the main battle position. Effective employment of the different weapons organic to an infantry regiment was an art in itself, as each had capabilities and limitations: the weapons comprised light and heavy machine guns, anti-armour rifles, mortars, infantry guns, anti-armour guns and supporting artillery to include anti-aircraft guns employed in a ground role.

A commander preparing a defence (and an attack) needed to identify the main effort point or Schwerpunkt. In attack, this was the point at which he would concentrate effort and firepower to break through the enemy defences. In defence, it was the point (assessed by the defending commander) where the enemy would attempt to break through: he would concentrate his offensive forces and supporting weapons there. The defence would be established in depth, but not just using the four zones: each zone in itself would be organized in depth with the weapons providing mutual cover for each other. The employment of obstacles and minefields was critical, as it was fully understood that anti-armour weapons alone could not halt attacking tanks. Tank-hunting detachments with anti-armour rifles and hand mines were organized. In 1943 Panzerfaust and Panzerschreck shoulder-fired anti-armour rocket launchers began to replace these.

This Kampfgraben (squad battle trench) and Annäherungsgraben (approach trench) depicts the different positions incorporated into it: Schützenloch für 2 Schützen (rifle position for two riflemen), Stichgraben (slit trench), Schützennischen (fire steps), MG-Feuerstellung (machine-gun firing position), Unterstand (squad bunker), Schützenausstieg (exit ladder or steps), Unterschlupf (dugout). Note that the arrow points in the direction of the enemy. (Gordon Rottman)

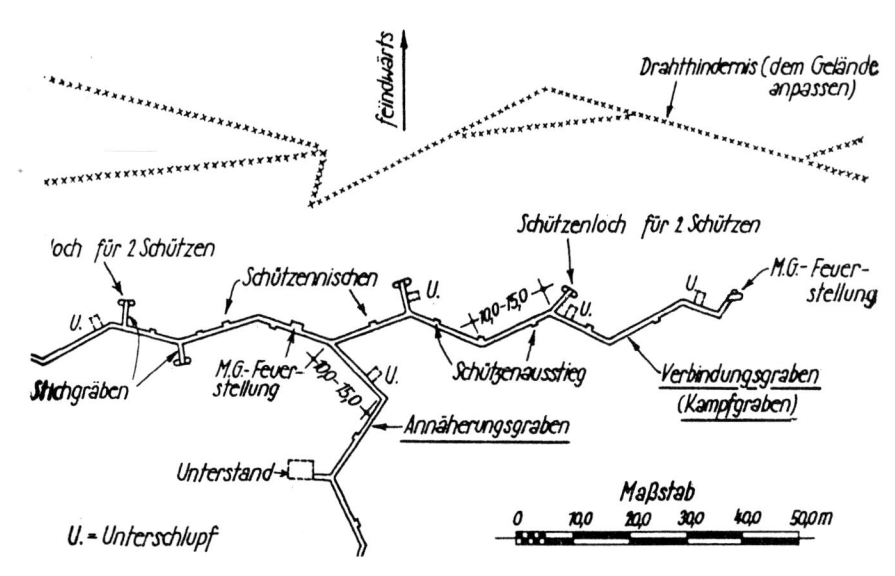

HITLER'S FORTRESSES

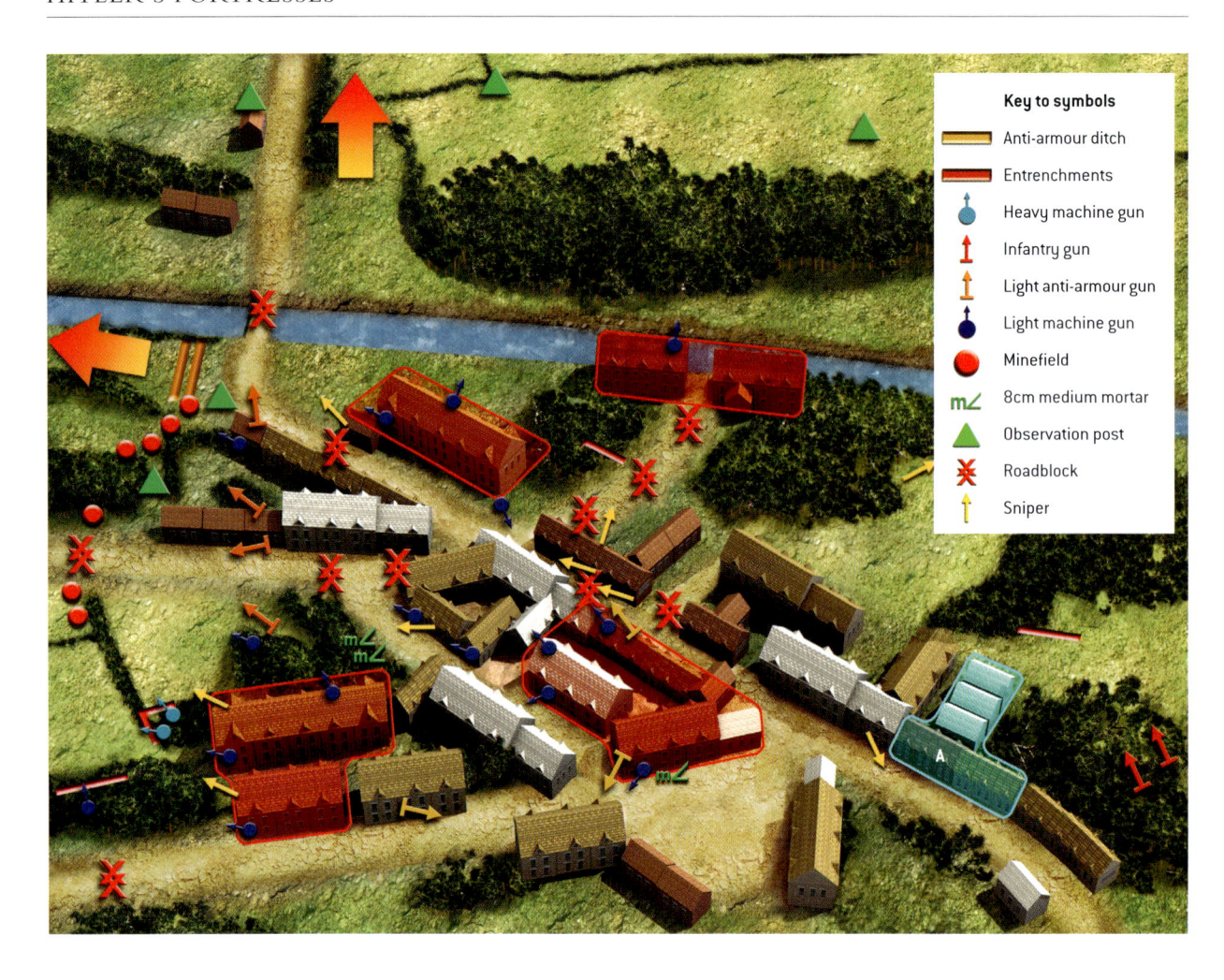

ABOVE: Defence of a village, north-west Europe. Villages were extremely irregular in pattern and layout, making the organization of the defence, the selection of strongpoints, the positioning of crew-served weapons and the placement of obstacles as difficult for the defender to determine as for the attacker to predict. The reserve platoon is located at A. Strongpoints are shown enclosed within red lines. (Ian Palmer © Osprey Publishing)

As the war progressed, anti-armour guns were increasingly employed in the main battle positions as well as in forward and outpost positions. Armoured fighting vehicles (AFVs – tanks and assault guns) tended to be held as mobile reserves to counter-attack breakthroughs. There were many instances, though, where AFVs were employed as mobile pillboxes. As Germany lost ever more AFVs and infantry units were reduced in strength, the availability of mobile reserves dwindled. Rather than large units conducting major counter-attacks, they became increasingly localized and smaller, greatly reducing the German ability to regain lost ground.

ETCHED IN THE EARTH – FIELD FORTIFICATIONS

ABOVE: 2cm Flak gun position. Although emplaced in positions optimised for ground fire, they could still engage ground attack aircraft. This well-developed position consists of four components: the gun position (1, Feuerstellung für 2cm Flak), gun shelter (2, Untersellraum), half-squad living quarters bunker (3, Halbgruppenunterstand) and an armour protection trench (4). The inset (A) shows the position in plan view. (Ian Palmer © Osprey Publishing)

Because of the extensive defensive frontages often required, 'strongpoint' defence was adopted on many fronts. There were no continuous frontlines, and the gaps between mutually supporting strongpoints were extensive, to be covered by outposts, patrols and observation, backed up by long-range fire. This reduced the numbers of troops necessary to defend an area, but not necessarily the number of weapons. Strongpoints had to be well armed with the full range of weapons, and significant mobile reserves were a necessity. Still, the basic German doctrine of four defensive zones was retained to provide depth to the defence.

Camouflage efforts and all-round local security were continuous during the development of defensive positions. Camouflage served to prevent the enemy from detecting positions from the ground and the air, and reconnaissance forward of the defensive zones was essential to warn of the enemy's approach and his activities. The German soldiers developed a dependable capability for determining when and where the enemy might attack by closely watching for signs of offensive action.

A wide variety of anti-personnel and anti-armour obstacles were employed in defensive systems. Maximum use was made of local and impounded materials. While it was difficult to conceal obstacles, the German soldiers would emplace barbed-wire barriers along natural contour lines, on low ground, on reverse slopes (Hinterhang), along the edge of fields and within vegetation. Terrain was important: swamps, marshes, forests, rivers, streams, gullies, ravines, broken and extremely rocky ground, all halted or slowed tanks. The Germans fully understood that to be effective an obstacle had to be covered by both observation and fire.

Manuals provided standardized designs for field fortifications, but there were many variations and exceptions in the field. This divergence was caused by assorted factors: the need to blend the fortification into the terrain, thus modifying its size, shape and profile; locally standardized designs induced by material shortages; types of material available; terrain conditions; weather; time constraints; preferences and concepts of local commanders; and the ingenuity and imagination of the officers and NCOs supervising construction. A common basic design can be seen in many examples, however.

DEPTH AND FRONTAGE

Infantry unit frontages could vary greatly. A major factor affecting the width of a division's sector was its internal organization. Standard German infantry divisions had three infantry/grenadier regiments with three battalions each. (On 15 October 1942 all regiments and smaller units designated Infanterie were redesignated Grenadier for 'morale' purposes.) This structure allowed for the standard 'two up and one back' formation: that is, two sub-units of any given unit were deployed in the main battle line with one behind them in reserve. From late 1943, due to manpower shortages, most infantry divisions were reorganized with only two battalions per regiment, and the Aufklärungs-Abteilung (Reconnaissance Battalion) was converted to a Füsilier-Bataillon as a mobile reserve. (The Germans employed two terms for 'battalion': *Bataillon* was used by infantry and pioneer battalions, and *Abteilung* or 'subdivision' was used by armour, artillery, smoke, cavalry and other branches.) This required regiments to place both battalions in the line without a reserve, although a company might be retained as

A Panzergrenadier-Division 'Grossdeutschland' command post. The Germans relied heavily on telephones when defending. The equipment includes two Feldfernsprecher 33 field telephones and a Feldklappenschrank 20-line field switchboard. (Gordon Rottman)

a regimental reserve. However, this also meant that one of the battalions was without a reserve. Often all three regiments had to be in the line with only the fusilier battalion as the divisional reserve.

In 1942 combat-depleted divisions consolidated the remnants of their reconnaissance and anti-armour battalions into a single unit to serve as a mobile reserve (Panzerjäger und Aufklärungs-Abteilung). The separate battalions were later reconstituted. It was common for the only effective mobile reserve to be found at corps or army level. Gebirgs (mountain) and Jäger (light infantry) divisions had only two regiments with three battalions, because they were expected to fight on rough terrain with narrow frontages. The 700-series occupation divisions raised in 1941 also had only two regiments and a single artillery battalion. Both of these divisional structures, three two-battalion regiments and two three-battalion regiments, greatly reduced a division's ability to defend in depth and field a viable reserve.

The depth of each of the positions depended much on the terrain and likely avenues of enemy approach: there was no specified depth. Depth would be achieved not only by positioning the two sub-units forward and the reserve sub-unit to the rear for each unit, but possibly by deploying elements of each sub-unit within the position providing mutual support and protecting the flanks. Various crew-served weapons attached from higher formations added to the width and depth of positions as well.

THE MAIN DEFENCE LINE

The Hauptkampflinie, analogous to the US 'main line of resistance', was determined by the commander using map reconnaissance. Subordinate unit commanders then reconnoitred the ground and moved their units into position. Commanders were cautioned not to spend too much time on reconnaissance so as not to delay construction of defences. They designated their sub-unit's area, primary sectors of fire, locations of support weapons, obstacles, minefields, command posts, aid stations, ammunition and supply points and so on. The higher commander might specify the locations and sectors of fire of crew-served weapons allocated from higher formations in order to ensure their integration into the overall defence plan. Artillery, infantry gun and mortar fire-support plans were developed. Reserve positions were established and counter-attack plans made.

THE ADVANCED POSITION

The Vorgeschobene Stellung (advanced position) was established 4,500–6,500m forward of the main defence line. It would be manned by reconnaissance troops, detachments from reserve units, and anti-armour and machine-gun sub-units. Artillery forward observers would be located there, and the approaches forward of the position were within range of medium artillery (15cm): these could be employed to break up any attack. The forces were widely scattered and in shallow depth. Small troop elements covered the roads, trails and railways approaching the position, plus crossroads, river crossings and key terrain such as high ground. They warned of enemy attack, prevented patrols from penetrating into the main defences, attempted to force the enemy to deploy early and called for fire on the enemy. The troops manning the advanced position would withdraw using concealed routes before they became too committed. The advanced position was not employed if the front was stabilized: that is, if enemy forces were in established positions or in close proximity to the German line.

COMBAT OUTPOSTS

The Gefechtsvorposten (combat outposts) were 2,000–4,500m forward of the main battle line. While similar in concept to the US combat outpost line, they were often better manned. This sector had much the same mission as the advanced position, but might be more heavily armed and manned in stronger positions. It could mislead the enemy as to the location of the main battle line: dummy positions might be constructed for this purpose. Obstacles and minefields were placed on avenues of approach and covered by fire. The combat outposts were within light artillery (10.5cm) range and forward observers from the howitzer batteries were located in these positions. Villages, tree lines and clumps, and hills covering the avenues of approach were developed as strongpoints. The German Army fully realized that enemy infantry would more than likely advance through woods and other terrain offering concealment rather than in the open, and so such areas were covered by Spähtruppen (reconnaissance patrols), Vorposten (outposts), Feldwachen (lookouts), Beobachtungstellen (observation posts), Horchstellen (listening posts) and fire positions. The same types of units manning the advanced position, especially if it was not employed, and also manned the combat outpost position – platoons and companies from the reserve regiment held the strongpoints here. They could also execute small-scale, limited-objective attacks to delay any enemy advance. The outposts were abandoned on order or when in danger of being overrun. Concealed withdrawal routes were selected so as not to interfere with covering artillery fire. Artillery and mortar fire was often registered on the forward positions to delay the enemy and cover the withdrawal. Artillery was usually emplaced approximately one-third of its maximum effective range behind the main battle line.

An MG34 machine gun in the embrasure of an Eastern Front bunker. The firing port is made from boards and snow-filled wicker ammunition containers. (Gordon Rottman)

THE MAIN BATTLEFIELD

The Hauptkampffeld (main battlefield) concentrated the bulk of the infantry and their supporting weapons on dominating terrain features or terrain that blocked or covered avenues of advance. Prior to 1942, the main battle position comprised mutually supporting platoon positions. Each company deployed two platoons forward and one in reserve. The reserve company of each battalion was similarly deployed to provide depth to the position. Light machine guns were deployed forward with riflemen, while heavy machine guns could be placed well forward, often slightly to the rear, covering gaps between units, possible enemy attack positions, and the flanks. Anti-armour rifles and light mortars (5cm) were located within the platoon positions to allow the gunners direct observation of targets. Heavy mortars (8cm) were placed on reverse slopes, as were infantry guns. Anti-armour guns were usually to the rear of forward positions and covering avenues of armour advance. Some anti-armour guns were emplaced in forward positions, though. Mines were laid and obstacles constructed to the extent allowed by limits of time and matériel. These could be continuous belts laid in depth in well-developed positions.

A division with three three-battalion regiments would normally have two regiments in the main battle position with a total of four battalions forward. This meant that eight of the division's 27 rifle companies were in the division's main battle line, each with two platoons forward. To all intents and purposes, the reserve platoons were in the battle line, as they were within sight of the forward platoons and supported them with direct fire. This meant that 24 of the division's 81 platoons were on the 6,000–10,000m frontline. The combat outpost position was manned by the forward regiments' reserve battalion and the advanced position, if established, was manned by detachments from the reserve regiment, reconnaissance and anti-tank troops.

THE STRONGPOINT CONCEPT, DECEMBER 1941

In December 1941, the German leadership adopted a new defensive concept to deal with the desperate situation on the Eastern Front. The initial plan for the winter of 1941/42 was to drive the Red Army towards the Ural mountains, seize the main population and industrial centres and withdraw two-thirds of the German forces, leaving the rest to establish a line of strongpoints to defend the Third Reich's new frontier. The strongpoint defence was an economy-of-force effort to employ the smallest possible number of troops to cover the widest possible front. German losses had been tremendous and replacements could not be trained fast enough. Understrength units could not man the required wide fronts in the traditional manner – a near-continuous linear defence. On 16 December Hitler issued his 'no retreat' order, putting a halt to local withdrawals then underway as units sought more easily defendable terrain in which to sit out the winter. The official term for a strongpoint was Stützpunkt, but Hitler preferred Igelstellung ('hedgehog position'): Stützpunkt generally remained in use in official publications, however.

The 'no retreat' order denied commanders a proven, effective counter-measure to massed Soviet attacks. Regardless of the order, it was still carried out in some instances. When a Soviet attack was imminent the forward troops were pulled back prior to the artillery barrages striking the strongpoints. Depending on the terrain, a withdrawal of 800–2,000m back to second-line positions was all that was required. The barrages fell on empty positions and obstacles, as Russian infantrymen rushed forward supported by tanks. The German soldiers would then open fire with artillery, mortars and machine guns from long range and wait for the assault's momentum to slow, and for formations to become disorganized and disorientated and then to either withdraw or stumble piecemeal into the prepared defences. The forward positions could usually be reoccupied following German counter-attacks.

Heeresgruppe Mitte had successfully employed the elastic defence in August and September, but by December German units were so severely under strength that such a defence could not be established other than as a thin screen. Sufficient troops were simply not available to man the multiple-zone, in-depth defence over such broad

Three Fallschirmjäger (paratroopers) fire an 8cm Gr.W.34 mortar from a standard mortar firing position. (Gordon Rottman)

fronts, and the necessary mobile reserves did not exist. Panzer divisions fielded only a dozen tanks and the remaining crews were serving as infantrymen. Rear service units were stripped to provide infantry replacements. Infantry battalions were at less than company strength, and companies had 25–70 men. The infantry strength of entire corps was less than 2,000 troops with a 250-man battalion deemed well manned. Many units possessed only a quarter of their heavy weapons. Rather than the doctrinal 6–10km sectors, the hollow divisions were assigned 30–60km fronts against the unexpected Soviet counter-offensive. All three regiments had to be placed in the main battle line, often with all nine battalions as well, allowing no regimental reserves other than the battalions' reserve companies, which were also manning deeper strongpoints. The Germans called it 'putting everything in the shop window'. Scattered squads and platoons would be held in reserve by battalions and companies to conduct immediate, local counter-attacks. An under-strength reconnaissance battalion served as the division's only mobile reserve, although if possible divisions retained one infantry battalion in reserve. To make matters worse, the strained German logistics system was on the verge of collapse.

Under-strength companies might organize into two platoons with three 6–10-man squads, each with a machine gun and positioned in a cluster of 3–5 two-man firing positions. Additional machine guns were often provided from service units as a substitute for riflemen. Remaining 5cm mortars were concentrated 50m to the rear under company control. Anti-armour guns were held in the rear to deal with tank breakthroughs. In some instances anti-armour guns were placed in strongpoints, making few available to block breakthroughs in the rear.

Strongpoints were established around villages to control roads and provide shelter from the brutal weather until fighting positions and bunkers could be built. Other strongpoints were built on the little available high ground. Weapons were positioned to engage the enemy at maximum range, provide mutual support to adjacent strongpoints, and cover the gaps between strongpoints.

The little remaining artillery was positioned further forward than normal (increasing the danger of its being overrun) to cover the different strongpoints. Many divisions fielded only an under-strength artillery battalion, rather than four, causing the few batteries to be widely dispersed to cover all the strongpoints. This prevented artillery fire from being concentrated en masse on main attacks, as not all batteries could range the wide division front. Mortars were distributed among strongpoints rather than being concentrated behind the forward units, meaning they were unable to range all the strongpoints. They could usually cover adjacent strongpoints though. Light air-defence units positioned their 2cm Flak guns in strongpoints, which proved ideal for breaking up mass infantry attacks.

The strongpoint defence remained into mid-1943/1944 in some areas. After that the German forces were in steady retreat. Defences consisted of hastily established lines in scattered sectors without continuous frontlines, little depth, and few if any reserves. As relentless Allied assaults hammered at the German units on all fronts, time and resources rarely allowed anything close to a doctrinal defence to be established. Pioneer units often built defensive positions and obstacles to await withdrawing infantry. Defences were built on rivers to provide major obstacles; villages and towns were turned into strongpoints and cities into Festungen. Some of these, however, were well defended with multiple rings of strongpoints protected by anti-armour ditches and minefields. In-depth defences were prepared on the roads leading into the fortress city. Switch positions were constructed between the fortified lines to protect against breakthroughs.

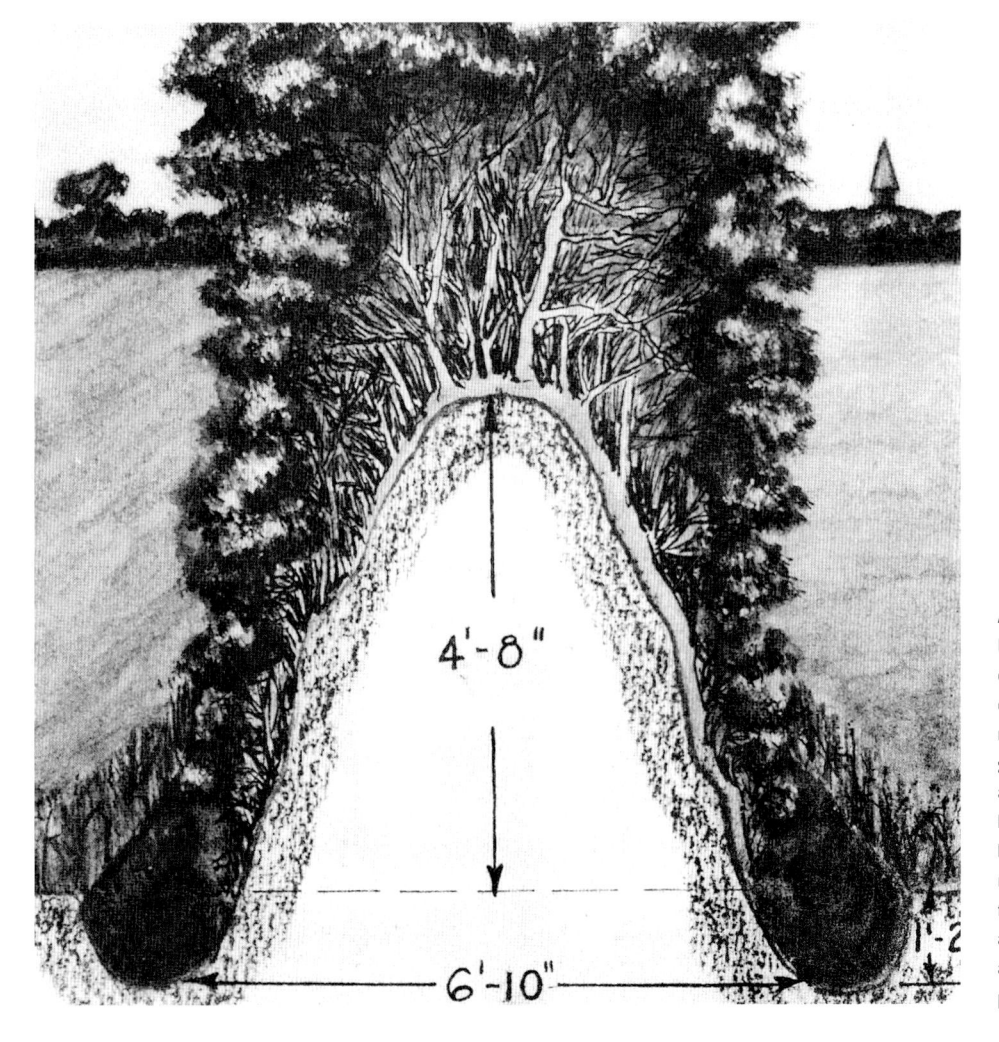

A cross-section of a typical Normandy hedgerow (the precise dimensions would vary). The core of the hedgerows comprised rocks gathered by previous generations and piled in lines along the edges of fields. Thick hedges then grew over these berms. The dense roots and rock core made the hedgerows formidable anti-armour and anti-personnel obstacles. They also provided ideal fighting positions. (Gordon Rottman)

HITLER'S FORTRESSES

HEDGEROW DEFENCES, NORMANDY 1944

In Normandy the Germans forces encountered a compartmented maze of cultivated fields, orchards and pastures atop the Collines de Normandie plateau 10–15km inland (the Bocage country). These fields were separated by earth and rock berms 0.5–1.5m thick and up to 1.5m high. They were topped with dense hedges and small trees from 1m to 5m in height. Ditch-lined roads and wagon tracks, often sunken, ran throughout the area bounded on both sides by hedgerows with small, gated openings into the fields. The enclosed fields could be relatively small, up to a few hundred metres to a side. They could be square, rectangular or triangular and were laid out in irregular patterns.

The German troops dug weapon positions and riflemen holes, often with an attached dugout, into the hedgerows as well as dugouts and positions for command posts, telephone exchanges, ammunition points, medical stations and others.

An M4 Sherman tank passes through a vertical log armour barrier inside a German village. The logs were buried as deep as 2m, and angled logs were sometimes set on the enemy's side to deflect any tank aiming to ram the German barriers. They required large quantities of demolition charges to breach them, as has been accomplished here. (Gordon Rottman)

Well camouflaged, they were difficult to detect from the ground or air. Observation between fields was impossible and an attacking force had no idea what was behind the next or adjacent hedgerows. The only way to approach a hedgerow was by crossing the open fields. The German soldiers would dig positions along the far side of the hedgerow and those on the flanks in the defended sectors. There were no continuous straight lines, resulting in more of a chequerboard pattern. Allied tactics evolved with alternating fields attacked with tank support while mortars and artillery suppressed the intervening fields' hedgerows. Hedgerow-cutter ploughs were fabricated for attachment to tanks, allowing them to burst through the berms. The compartmented nature of the hedgerows allowed the German troops to break contact easily, however, and withdraw to the next hedgerow.

MATERIALS AND CONSTRUCTION METHODS

The German troops made extensive use of local materials to build fortifications and obstacles. Concrete was always prized for any fortification. Its value was realized after the Allies began bombing the Atlantic Wall defences in 1943: field positions and trenches were destroyed while reinforced concrete positions were virtually unscathed. However, concrete and reinforcing bar were rarely available in the field, as these were being diverted to the construction of other major defensive works. Other available construction materials were insufficient, and were diverted to priority installations. The available local materials were dependent on the area of operations, with some offering abundant supplies (as in north-west Europe, Italy and parts of the USSR) and others (such as North Africa and the steppes of Russia) barren.

Timber was abundant in Europe and parts of Russia. Many of the plans for field fortifications, shelters and obstacles provided in German manuals called for the extensive use of logs; 20–25cm-diameter logs or 16 × 16cm cured timbers were recommended for overhead cover, horizontal support beams (stringers) and vertical support posts. Dimensioned wooden planks were used sparingly for revetting, flooring, doors, shutters, duckboards, ammunition niches, ladders and steps. Pioneer and construction units operated portable sawmills to cut lumber. Bunks, tables, benches and other furniture were also made from this and from discarded ammunition boxes. Nails, especially the large type required for timber construction, were often scarce.

The exterior of timber fortifications was banked with earth or buried below ground level. However, large-calibre penetrating projectiles could create deadly wood splinters. To reduce the risk of this, branches and saplings were woven horizontally like wicker

OPPOSITE: Hedgerow defences, Normandy, 1944. The faint lines represent the hedgerows and the double broken lines are sunken roads. This c.300m × 800m company area was self-contained and could fend off attacks from any direction. Note that the buildings were undefended, as they attracted artillery fire. If the perimeter were penetrated, troops would move to the flanking hedgerows to engage the attackers. There were several clusters of positions located in adjacent hedgerows on all sides of this area. (Ian Palmer © Osprey Publishing)

through 10cm vertical stakes or bundled brushwood fascines to create supporting revetments. The vertical stakes could be reinforced by securing anchor wires near the top and fastening them to shorter driven stakes a metre or so from the trench's edge.

Like all other armies, the German Army shipped munitions, rations and other matériel in robust wooden boxes and crates of all sizes. Wicker basket containers were also used, especially for artillery ammunition and propellant charges. These were often filled with earth and stacked like bricks to form interior walls of fortifications and for parapet revetting. They were braced by logs or timber or bound together by wire to prevent their collapse when the fortification was struck by artillery. Boxes were also disassembled and the boards used to construct firing ports, doors, shelves and the like. Nails removed from these boxes became a valuable commodity. German munitions (including grenades, mines and mortar rounds) were often transported in comparatively expensive metal containers (Muntionsbehälter). While they were supposed to be returned to the factories for reuse, they were sometimes filled with earth and used for shoring up parapets. Steel fuel and oil drums were available, although they too were supposed to be returned. British three-gallon petrol tins were much used in North Africa, being filled with earth and used to revet parapets.

Purpose-made cloth sandbags were scarce at the front as most production remained in Germany and in other rear areas. They were usually burlap tan, brown or grey. Other cloth shipping bags were used instead. Two layers of sandbags were sufficient to stop small-arms fire and provide protection from mortars.

Fortifications with firing ports, which needed to be above ground level, were kept as low as possible. Banked earth was piled high on the sides and angled at a fairly steep slope to absorb armour-piercing projectiles and the blast and fragmentation of high explosives. Layers of logs were sometimes laid just below the surface of the side banking as a burster layer. The above-ground portion of covered fortifications tended to be uniform rather than irregular.

Rocks were used for fortifications wherever they could be found, but were especially common in North Africa and Italy, where fortifications were often constructed entirely of these. Rocks and logs were laid in layers beneath the piled-earth overhead covering to act as shell-burster material. Rocks were also used as in-fill between double log walls to detonate projectiles or deform armour-piercing rounds. One particular hazard to the occupants was from fragments caused by bullet and shell strikes. Trenches and positions were sometimes revetted with rock walls, but unless stakes and horizontal bracing or wire mesh were used to anchor this, a near miss artillery round could make it collapse. Materials such as corrugated sheet metal, lumber, timbers, roofing tiles and shingles, doors, masonry, structural steel, pipes, railroad rails, concrete and steel railroad ties were frequently salvaged from local structures, and applied to defensive positions.

ETCHED IN THE EARTH – FIELD FORTIFICATIONS

Legend:
- Machine gun/antitank gun
- Mortar
- Bazooka
- Dugout
- Rifle pit
- Roadblock

La Mare

Command Post

HITLER'S FORTRESSES

A square 3.7cm Flak 36 gun emplacement made of concrete, with much of the formation planking left in place. Some effort was made to camouflage-paint the emplacement's sides. Ammunition and gun equipment niches were built into the interior sides. The gun's wheeled carriage was removed and the jack-stands set on earth-filled ammunition boxes. A second emplacement can just be seen in the background, to the left of the US soldier. Such weapons were usually employed in threes. (Gordon Rottman)

On the Eastern Front, ice and frozen snow proved to be ideal for fortifications and shelters. The duration and average depth of snowfall varied depending on the region. In the north it began in December, accumulated 100cm or more, and remained into June. In the south it began in January and remained until April with only 10–40cm falling. Temperatures remained 20–40°F below zero through the winter. Ice blocks and packed snow were surprisingly bulletproof, and simple to work. They required no revetting, but bale of hay or straw were sometimes used to support trenches and walls and to provide additional insulation.

THE PRINCIPLES OF CONSTRUCTION

Detailed and elaborate plans for the construction of field fortifications, shelters and obstacles were provided, and many of the principles on which they were based had been developed in World War I. Even though time and resources did not always allow these ideal positions to be built, they served as guides and their influence can be seen in the design of those actually constructed. A great deal of local initiative was used.

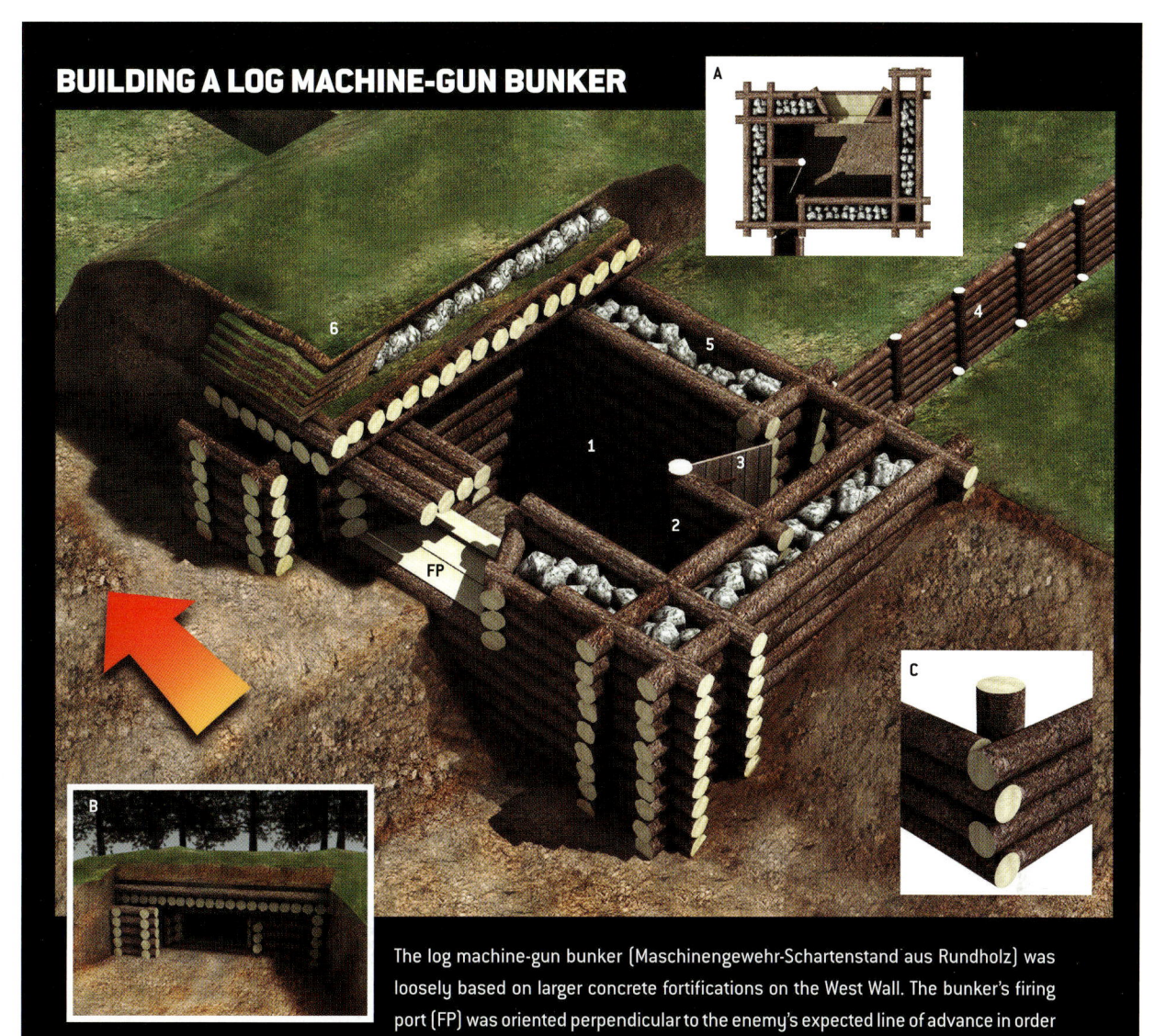

ETCHED IN THE EARTH – FIELD FORTIFICATIONS

BUILDING A LOG MACHINE-GUN BUNKER

The log machine-gun bunker (Maschinengewehr-Schartenstand aus Rundholz) was loosely based on larger concrete fortifications on the West Wall. The bunker's firing port (FP) was oriented perpendicular to the enemy's expected line of advance in order to engage him from the flank. This allowed positions to have a thicker than normal wall on the enemy side, and to inflict a surprise attack from an unexpected direction: it also made it much easier to conceal the bunker. The interior included a battle room (Kampfraum, 1) for the light machine gun (a tripod-mounted heavy machine gun could be installed); an adjacent ammunition room (Munitionsraum, 2); and an entry alcove (Vorraum, 3). A communications trench (4) connected it to other positions. The double-log walls were filled with rock or packed earth (5). The roof was made of multiple layers of logs, clay, rocks and earth (6). The sides and roof were covered over with sods of turf and care was taken to ensure that it blended into the terrain. The large red arrow on the main illustration indicates the direction towards the enemy (feindwärts): bunkers of this type were also built with the firing port oriented forward. Image A shows the bunker in plan view; image B shows the bunker with its full earthen covering in place, without cutaway details; and image C depicts an alternative method used to mate the corners of log walls. (Ian Palmer © Osprey Publishing)

289

For the most part defensive positions were dug as deep as possible and kept low to the ground in order to present a low profile, both for concealment and to offer less of a target. Positions not requiring firing ports were usually flush with the ground. This was not always possible because of a high water table, swampy ground or shallow bedrock. In such instances the position had to be completely above ground level. In addition, the roof had to protect the position from heavy artillery: its thickness might also mean that the position's profile was not always as low as desired. In some instances the firing port had to be well above the ground in order to cover its field of fire effectively, especially if firing downhill, which could also raise the position's profile. Positions dug into the sides of hills, ridges, gorges and the like were usually built flush with the surface if possible, making them difficult to detect when camouflaged.

Most covered positions and shelters were built from logs, usually laid horizontally and with the ends notched for assembly, or spiked together. Horizontally constructed log walls were supported by vertical pilings with the ends often held together by steel staples. Wire was sometimes used to bind logs together. The upper ends of vertical load-bearing support posts were sometimes bound by wire to prevent the end from splintering from high-explosive impacts. Interior walls were built of logs, planks, woven branches and saplings, rock, sandbags or hay bales to prevent collapse when hit by artillery or bombs.

Overhead cover comprised a layer of large-diameter logs with a second layer laid perpendicular to them on top. Manuals called for no more than two or three layers, but in practice up to half a dozen layers could be used to ensure protection from heavy artillery. Waterproof roofing felt, if available, was laid atop the roofing logs before they were covered with earth. A 5cm layer of clay was sometimes laid over the logs providing marginal waterproofing. If above ground, sods or peat blocks were stacked brick-like to shore up the angled sides. The whole fortification was covered over with sods removed from the site before digging began. If needed, additional sods were brought for the rear. This was supposed to be removed from areas beneath trees and brush so that it was undetectable from the air. While the manuals provided precise dimensions for fortifications, they often did not specify the thickness of overhead cover. This depended on how deep the position could be dug: the deeper it was, the thicker the overhead cover. Examples of specified overhead thickness are 160cm for a below-ground squad bunker and 130cm for an above-ground machine-gun bunker. The spacing of vertical support posts and stringer logs varied from approximately 1m to 1.5m.

Light mortars (US 60mm, UK 2in, USSR 50mm) did not possess the ability to penetrate most bunkers. Medium mortars (US 81mm, UK 3in, USSR 82mm) were more effective, but heavy mortars (US/UK 4.2in, USSR 120mm) were best suited, especially since they sometimes had delay fuses. Light artillery (75mm, 105mm, 25pdr) had limited effect, whereas medium artillery, like the 155mm, could destroy a well-prepared bunker.

Firing ports or embrasures (Schießscharten) were kept small to make them more difficult to detect and hit. A 60° field of fire (Wirkungsbereich) was recommended, but the angle could be narrower or wider. The ports were made of smaller-diameter logs, planks or sandbags. There was usually only one firing port; seldom did additional ports exist to cover alternate sectors. These were usually placed very low to the ground, if not flush with it.

Open-topped fighting positions, such as rifleman's holes, trenches and holes for machine guns, mortars, infantry guns and anti-tank guns, were kept as small as possible. Small positions, just large enough to accommodate the weapon and crew and allow them to function effectively, required less construction time and camouflage, were more difficult to detect, especially from the air, and made a smaller target. Manuals called for trenches to be 60–80cm wide at the top and 40cm wide at the bottom, providing

Panzergrenadiers from the 'Grossdeutschland' Division in a two-man rifle position. They have erected a parapet to their front, and have provided it with a loophole. 'Egg 39' and 'Stick 29' hand grenades lie ready on the edge of the hole.
(Gordon Rottman)

slightly sloped sides. In practice they tended to be narrower if the soil was stable enough to support it, with the sides almost vertical. They were either without an earth parapet or had a very low parapet for concealment. Parapets were used if the hardness of the soil, a lack of time, or a high water table did not allow the positions to be dug sufficiently deep. It also required significant time and effort to remove the spoil, conceal it, and return the ground around the position to a natural state.

The idea of removing soil and keeping the position level with the ground was learned from the Italians in North Africa. On flat, barren desert floors natural features and vegetation were non-existent and concealment was achieved by blending the positions into the ground. For machine-gun positions the Italians developed an underground shell-proof shelter and magazine with a small circular chamber. Its ceiling tapered to a neck, serving as the machine-gun position. The tobruk pit provided a small, circular, difficult to detect opening with 360° fire for the machine gun. Separate entrances were provided or they were connected to central bunkers by tunnels. The German Army developed similar positions for the 5cm mortar and the Panzerstellung.

Entrances to positions were normally in the rear, but in some instances they might be on the side of a position depending on the protection and concealment afforded by surrounding terrain. Entrances were often protected to prevent direct fire, blast

A light machine-gun position with a large firing platform and a niche for the ammunition bearer. The parapet is low in order to reduce the profile of the position. This practice was first adopted in the featureless landscape of North Africa and was later used in other open areas. (Gordon Rottman)

ETCHED IN THE EARTH – FIELD FORTIFICATIONS

DEFENSIVE POSITIONS

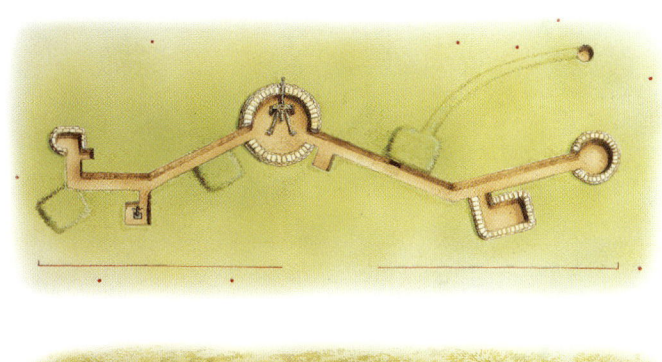

Top: 'Tobruk turret' (Ringstand). This standard machine gun position was used in many German defensive schemes in the second half of the war. Only the uppermost ring of the buried concrete pillbox showed above the surface. This firing position was provided with two fixed concrete steps up the side, and a removable wooden platform below. Ammunition was stored in the 1.9m-high compartment at the bottom of the steps, inside a subterranean entrance. The walls and most of the roof were 38cm thick, the floor 18cm thick.

Middle: Reinforced squad position. An outer defence of barbed wire and anti-tank mines would typically ring the position about 50m out from the trenches. Dug off the zigzag trenches are bunkers with overhead protection, sandbagged MG positions, and an advanced listening or sniping post at the end of a tunnel from an underground bunker. Apart from the squad's own weapons, an anti-tank gun is emplaced centrally and a mortar at left, attached from the unit support elements. The red dots are randomly scattered anti-personnel mines. The position is designed to be defensible against attack from almost any direction, the weapons being turned as required.

Bottom: 8cm mortar pit. This is the regulation 'winged' pit which was dug whenever time allowed, with a central weapon pit and separate ammunition and crew shelters at the ends of short trenches. The earth spoil has not been gathered into a parapet, but scattered – concealment takes priority. (Peter Dennis © Osprey Publishing)

fragmentation, grenades and demolitions from entering. This protection might be in the form of a blast barrier inside the position, or a similar barrier or wall on the outside. A trench with at least one right-angle turn usually formed the entry passage. Many positions, though, had only a straight, unprotected entry way. This often proved to be the strongest defensive point: if the attackers gained the position's rear, they would usually come under fire from adjacent positions. Larger positions often had a vestibule or entry hallway separated from the main compartment by a log wall. Such helped protect occupants from grenades and demolition charges as well as from external blast overpressure and chemical agents. It also served as a changing area for wet clothes and helped keep out cold draughts as troops entered and exited for guard duty and patrols.

Frontline open positions for crew-served weapons were provided with Panzerdeckungslöcher (armour protective trenches). These were narrow, deep slit trenches on either side of the position – 'wings' that provided cover for the crew if overrun by tanks. Often they would be dug with an angled turn, in the form of a wide 'V'. For protection from the crushing action of a tank, the trench had to provide 75cm of clearance above the crouching occupants. They were also used if the position came under artillery or mortar fire, or air attack, as well as for firing positions for close-in defence. Ideally these would be covered if time and resources permitted.

Munitionslöcher (ammunition niches) were dug into the sides of trenches and other positions, and usually a wooden box was inserted there. Anti-armour gun, infantry gun, and artillery positions had ammunition niches dug into the ground at an angle and lined with a box with a lid. These were located a minimum of 10m to the rear of the position.

TYPES OF DEFENSIVE POSITION

INFANTRY POSITIONS

The basic rifleman's position (Schützenloch – literally 'firing hole') was a two-man slit trench, analogous to a foxhole; it was also nicknamed a *Wolfgrabhügel* (wolf's barrow). While a one-man hole was used when necessary, the two-man was preferred. It offered soldiers moral support and allowed one to rest with the other on watch. Also, if a one-man position was knocked out, a wide gap was created in the defensive line, whereas in a two-man hole if one was lost the other could still conduct the defence. The one-man rifleman's position, nicknamed *Russenloch* (Russian hole), was a simple 70cm-wide, 60cm-deep hole – deep enough to allow a man to kneel in. Soil was piled in a crescent to the front to reduce the amount of digging required. As with other positions the soil was meant to be removed, but often time constraints meant the parapet remained. In the absence of a parapet, the rifle was propped on a small mound of earth or a Y-shaped fork driven into the ground. The 'Russian hole' could be deepened to allow a standing position and could later be widened for two men. Initially, Schützenloch für 2 Gewehrschützen (two-man positions) were specified as a short straight trench, 80cm × 1.8m. A slightly curved trench was also approved and this became standard in 1944. This version had two firing steps with a deeper centre section, allowing the riflemen to sit on the firing steps with their legs in the centre hole during shelling and offering protection from overrunning tanks. Panzerdeckungslöcher (armour protection trenches) used the same concept and they too were suitable as rifle positions. They could be V-, W- or U-shaped, or a shallow crescent. The firing steps were recommended to be 1.4m deep and the deeper central portion 1.8–2m. All of these positions were recommended to be 60–80cm wide at the top and 40cm at the bottom. The recommended distance between positions was 10m, but this varied depending on the unit's assigned frontage, the terrain and vegetation.

Anti-armour rifles were placed in two-man positions. No special positions were provided for Panzerfäuste; they could be fired from any open position with a few considerations. This rocket launcher was normally fired held under the arm, but it could be fired from the shoulder from a dug-in position. In the latter case the rear of the breech end had to be clear of any obstructions because of the 30m back-blast, meaning no rear parapet; nor could the breech-end be angled down too far. They could not be fired from within buildings unless from a very large room, such as a warehouse, with open doors and windows to relieve blast overpressure. The same restrictions applied to the 8.8cm Panzerschreck, but it had a greater back-blast. They were often employed in threes with two positioned forward and one to the rear, the distances dependent on terrain. This allowed the

A squad trench in the final days of the war, in East Prussia. Firing steps have been cut into the trench's sides. In the upper centre is the entrance to a squad bunker. (Gordon Rottman)

HITLER'S FORTRESSES

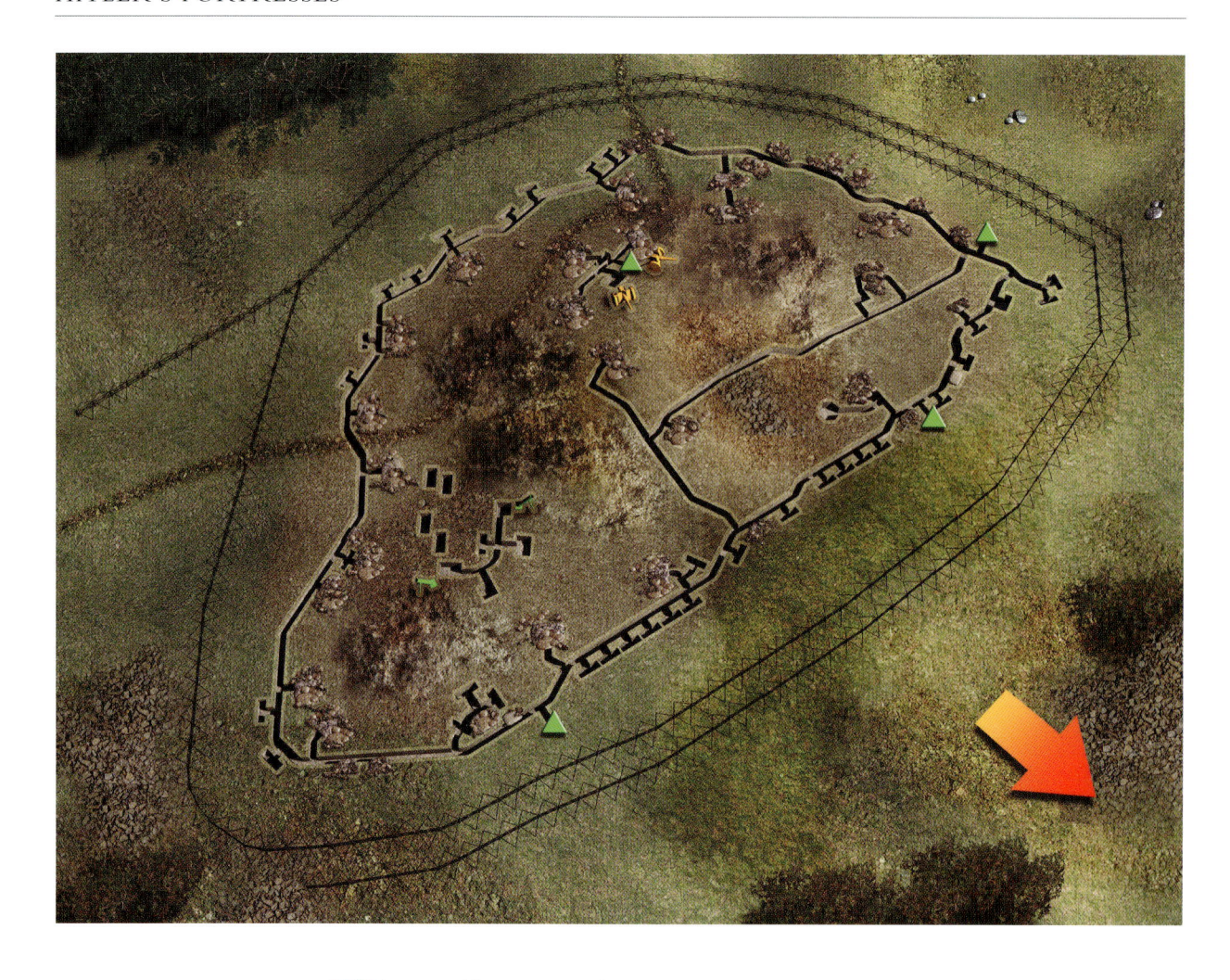

ABOVE: A company hilltop strongpoint. Stützpunkt Zuckerhutl was typical of the company strongpoints in the far north of Finland in 1944. It was surrounded by two parallel double-apron barbed-wire fences with anti-personnel mines. A firing trench revetted with rock and mortar ran around the entire perimeter with communications trenches connected to support positions in the centre. The large red arrow indicates the direction towards the enemy. (Ian Palmer © Osprey Publishing)

launchers to engage enemy tanks approaching from any direction plus provided an in-depth defence: at least two of the launchers could engage a tank. A 2m-long, V-shaped slit trench without parapet was used, with the two ends of the 'V' oriented away from the enemy. The gunner would occupy the arm of the 'V' that offered the best engagement of the target tank, and the assistant would load and take shelter from the back-blast in the other arm.

The squad's Schützenloch für leichtes Maschinengewehr (two-man light machine-gun position), or Maschinengewehrloch oder Nest (literally 'machine-gun hole or nest'), was a slightly curved, 1.4–1.6m trench with two short armour protection trenches angled to the rear. On the forward side was a 20cm-deep U-shaped platform for the bipod-mounted gun. The position could be placed anywhere within the squad line that provided it with the best field of fire. Alternative positions were meant to be up to 50m from the primary position, but were often closer. The three-man Schützenloch für schweres Maschinengewehr (heavy machine-gun position) was similar to the light one, but with armour protection trenches extending from the ends. The platform was still 20cm deep, requiring the long tripod legs to be dug in to lower the weapon's profile. The difference in design between the light and heavy positions was a weakness, as it allowed aerial photographic interpreters to differentiate between the types. A common design would have prevented this.

Expedient efforts and materials were used to construct positions. As the Soviets swept into East Prussia in late 1944, the German forces employed civilians to construct defensive positions and obstacles behind the field army, so that it could fall back on them. Two sections of 1.5m-diameter, 2m-long concrete culvert pipe were used to build tobruk machine-gun positions. A pit was dug and one section laid horizontally on the bottom with one end shored with sandbags or planks, creating the troop shelter. The second pipe was set vertically, with a U-shaped section cut out of one side of the bottom end to mate with the horizontal pipe. The top end of the vertical pipe was flush with the ground. It was quick to build and easily camouflaged.

Squad (Gruppenunterstand) and half-squad bunkers (Halbgruppenunterstand) were built in many forms, from simple single rooms to large, complex, multi-room bunkers. (Gordon Rottman)

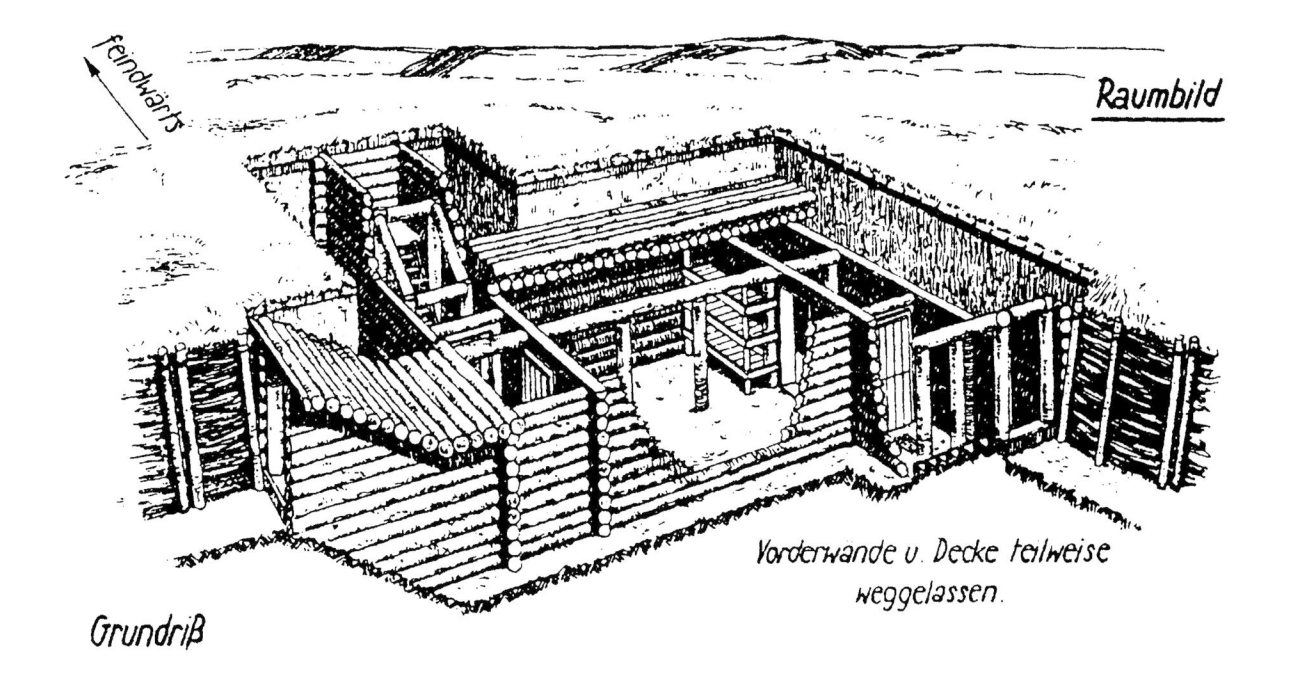

If a position was occupied for long enough, the rifle and machine-gun positions might be connected by trenches. Trench systems were widely used in the desert as they allowed concealed movement between firing positions in terrain otherwise devoid of cover. They were also used extensively within strongpoints. Trenches followed the terrain's contours in contrast to the geometric patterns laid out in World War I-style that ignored the terrain. Trench systems were not necessarily continuous. Some sections may have been covered with branches and saplings and perhaps a light covering of earth or snow. Trench patterns were zig-zag with each section 10–15m in length: in this way, artillery or mortar rounds striking the trench would only inflict casualties in the section struck. The angled trench sections also prevented any enemy troops that gained the trench from firing down its full length. Kriechgraben (crawl trenches) were 60–80cm wide at the top (as specified for all trenches), 60cm deep and 60cm wide at the bottom. Verbindungsgraben (connecting trenches) or Annäherungsgraben (approach trenches) were 1.8–2m deep and 40cm wide at the bottom. Kampfgraben (battle trenches) were the same, but with Schützennischen (firing steps) and ammunition niches cut into the sides. Some firing steps might be cut into the trench's rear side for all-round defence. Connecting trenches too might have firing steps, and adjoining armour protection trenches were recommended every 40–50m. Two-man rifle and machine-gun positions were usually dug 2–3m forward of the battle trench and connected by Stichgraben (slit trenches). These were located at the points of trench angles and along the straight sections. Unterschlupfe (dugout shelters) protecting one to six men were situated in the trench's forward side at intervals, and nicknamed *Wohnbunker* (dwelling bunkers). These provided protection from sudden artillery and air attacks and tank overruns. They were built as small as possible and in a variety of manners. As the position developed, squad and half-squad bunkers were built off connecting trenches for both protection from artillery and as living quarters. In muddy and wet conditions, plank duckboards might be placed in the trench's bottom over a central drainage gutter.

CREW-SERVED WEAPONS POSITIONS

The Schützenloch für leichten Granatwerfer (5cm mortar position) was a simple slit trench similar to a two-man rifle position, with a 70cm x 1m x 70cm step in the front for the mortar. Shallow rectangular pits were also dug as hasty positions with a U-shaped parapet open in the front. The pit for the 8cm heavy mortar (Nest für schweren Granatenwerfer) was a 1.6m-deep circular pit, 1.8m in diameter at the bottom. The top would be slightly larger, the degree of side slope depending on the stability of the soil. A $1m^3$ shelf was cut in the back for ammunition. On either side were armour protection trenches.

In 1943 the '8cm heavy mortar pit' was redesignated the Feuerstellung für mittleren Granatwerfer (firing position for medium mortar), as the new 12cm had been adopted as a heavy mortar. The latter's Feuerstellung für schweren Granatenwerfer was simply an enlarged version of its 8cm counterpart, 2m deep and 2m in diameter. Since mortars were highly mobile and relatively small, they were often simply emplaced behind any available cover such as in gullies and ditches, or behind mounds, walls or rubble.

'Nests' for anti-armour and infantry guns too were redesignated 'firing positions' in 1943. Anti-armour gun positions were circular or oval, about 4m across (though this varied), and shallow (40cm for 3.7cm anti-armour guns, and slightly deeper for the 5cm and 7.5cm). Slots were sometimes dug for the wheels to lower the profile of these anti-armour guns. Infantry-gun positions were similar, but deeper (3m in diameter, 50cm deep for the 7.5cm; 6m in diameter, 1.3m deep for the 15cm). Ramps dug in the position's rear allowed the gun to be emplaced and withdrawn. A low

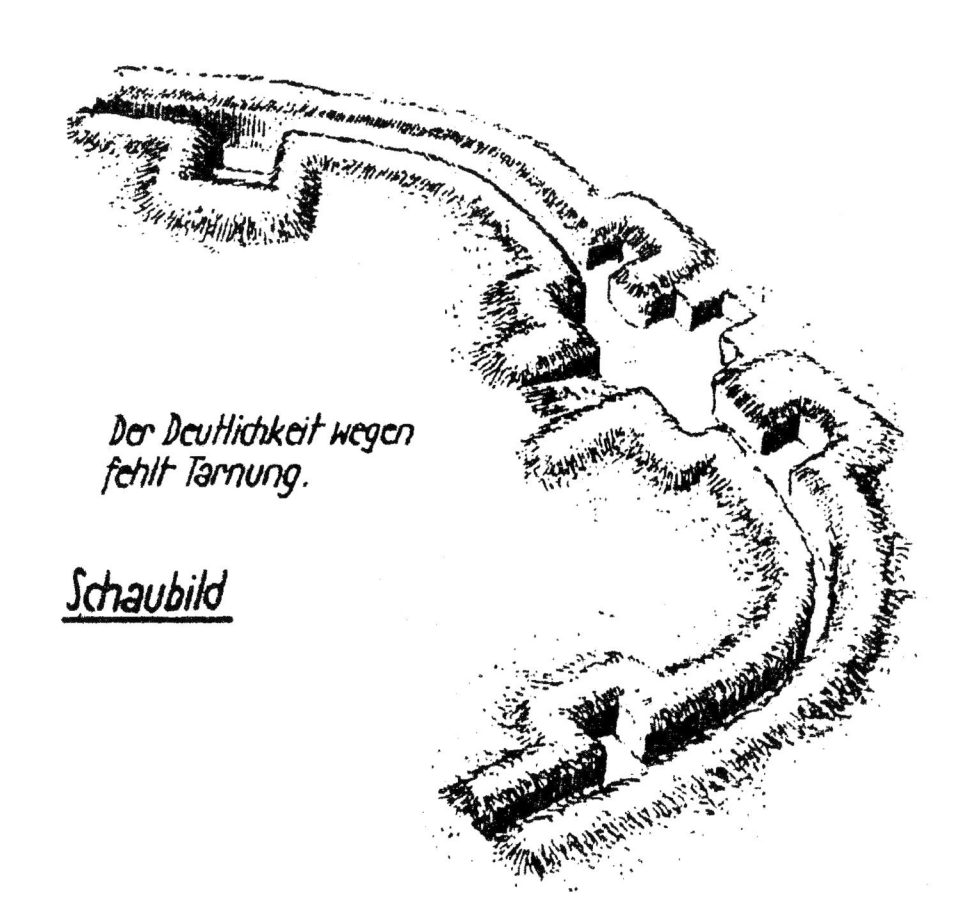

A firing position for the 15cm rocket projector (Feuerstellung für 15cm Nebelwerfer) required substantial protection for the crew and ammunition from the launcher's considerable back-blast. The launcher would be in the central position, and there are ammunition niches on either side. The crew shelters are in the curved trench wings. (Gordon Rottman)

HITLER'S FORTRESSES

RIFLE PLATOON DEFENSIVE POSITION

An early-war rifle platoon (Zug) defensive position is depicted here with all three squads (Gruppen, labelled A, B and C) deployed on line. 19 two-man rifle positions (1) are used. It was intended that the squad light machine guns (2) be positioned to cover the entire platoon front without gaps, but this was not always possible. Alternative machine-gun positions may have been prepared to cover gaps as well as the flanks and the gaps between adjacent platoons. Time permitting, some scattered rifle and one or two light machine-gun positions may have been dug in the rear and oriented in that direction (3). On this type of terrain the positions were typically at 10m intervals, less in densely wooded terrain. In some exceptional circumstances one squad may have been deployed to the rear, oriented forward, to provide depth to the position. If the platoon had four squads one would normally be deployed in the rear. The platoon's 5cm light mortar (4) is positioned to the rear, but in a place where it could observe its target area, as it had no observers. A 3.7cm anti-armour gun (5) and two heavy machine-gun squads (6) have been attached to the platoon along with an anti-armour rifle troop (7). The forward perimeter and flanks are protected by a double-apron barbed wire fence (a 'Flanders fence', 8) some 30–50m from the positions, keeping the troops beyond hand-grenade range. Sods of earth for camouflaging the positions have been removed in the rear from beneath trees and brush (9). The Zugführer's (10) and Zug-Truppführer's (11) positions are also indicated. An observation or listening post (12) is located to the front of the platoon, beyond the wire fence. The large red arrow indicates the direction towards the enemy. (Ian Palmer © Osprey Publishing)

ETCHED IN THE EARTH – FIELD FORTIFICATIONS

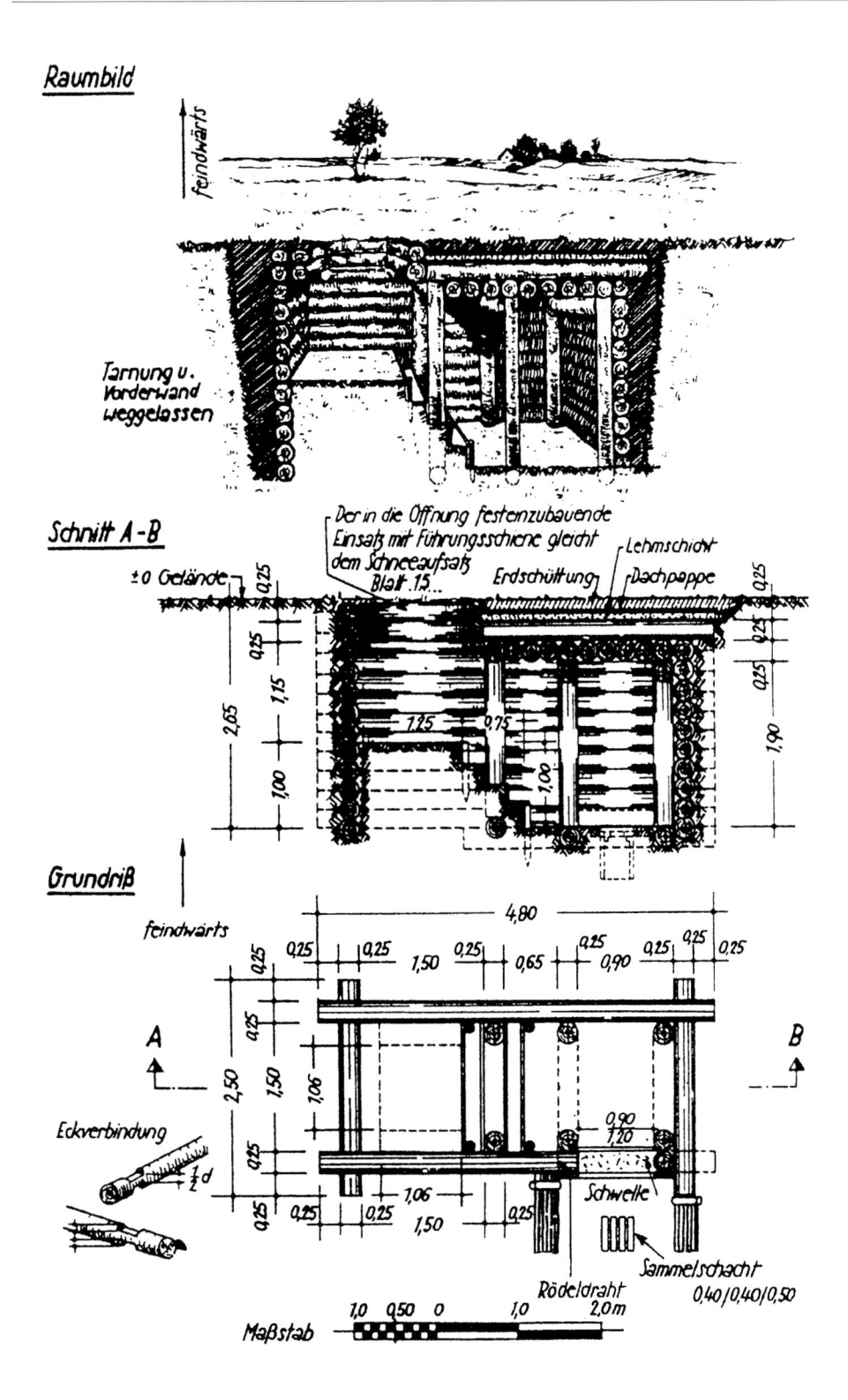

A tobruk light machine-gun position built from logs rather than the usual concrete (Maschinengewehr-Ringstand aus Rundholz). The overhead cover was always flush with the ground, making the position difficult to detect. Note the inset illustration at the bottom left, showing the method of notching logs. (Gordon Rottman)

An incomplete tank turret emplacement (Ringstand für Panzerkampfwagen Turm), here using a 7.5cm Panther PzKpfw. V turret. The turret was mounted on a steel frame and could be hand-traversed. The frame's sides would be strengthened with timbers or logs and banked with earth. Beneath the frame is the crew's log-built shelter. While under construction, the position was camouflaged from aerial detection by branches, which have been pulled away to allow it to be photographed. (Gordon Rottman)

parapet was placed some 2m behind the ramp's upper end to protect the position's rear opening. If armour protection trenches were not dug on either side of the position, shallow slit trenches were dug inside the position immediately adjacent to the gun and in some instances beneath the gun between the wheels. In fully developed positions a downward angled ramp was sometimes dug, and the gun could be rolled down this to place it below ground level. The lower end of the ramp was sometimes provided with overhead cover.

Infantry guns, being smaller and lighter than artillery pieces, were often emplaced in hastily built positions, like mortars. Anti-armour guns by necessity had to be in well-concealed positions to survive and inflict losses on enemy tanks. They also had to be able to relocate to other positions quickly once detected by the enemy. For this reason, while a gun's initial position may have been a fully prepared one, subsequent positions were often only partly prepared or simply a hastily selected site providing concealment and the necessary field of fire.

During the war 2cm Flak guns, single and quad, were increasingly employed in forward positions in the ground-fire role, especially on the Eastern Front. When deployed so, they were positioned on their own in the frontline. The firing position for 2cm Flak (Feuerstellung für 2cm Flak) was circular, 5.5m in diameter and 45cm deep, and was lined with ammunition niches and compartments for gun equipment. 2cm and 3.7cm guns were set on a slightly elevated triangular platform.

The 8.8cm Flak gun was employed as an ad hoc anti-armour gun on all fronts. While extremely accurate at long range and capable of knocking out any tank with high rates of fire, it had its limitations in this role. It was very large and had a high profile, making it difficult to conceal and requiring a great deal of effort to dig in. Its large size and the need for a heavy prime mover made it difficult and slow to withdraw and reposition. When used in the anti-armour role, the '88' was hidden among buildings, or in wooded areas, or defiladed in gullies and road cuts.

The 7.5cm and 15cm infantry gun positions comprised a circular pit with armour protection trenches on two sides. This one has a low berm behind the exit ramp and ammunition niches are located to either side and to the rear. (Gordon Rottman)

HITLER'S FORTRESSES

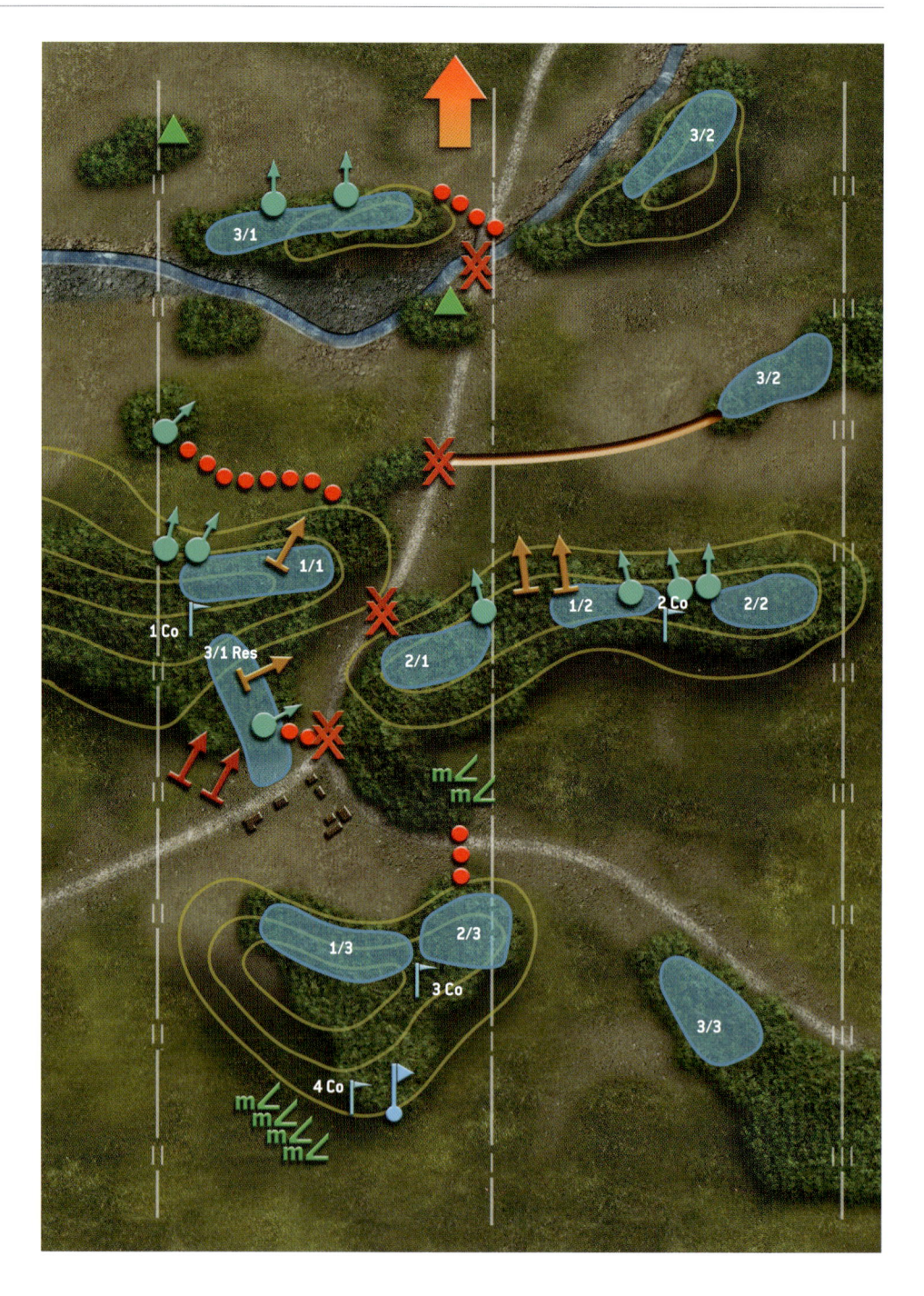

ABOVE: Infantry battalion defence sector. A full-strength infantry battalion normally deployed for defence with two companies forward on its 800–2,000m front. The positions of the heavy machine guns and mortars of the battalion machine-gun company (4th) are depicted along with the four 3.7cm anti-armour guns and two 7.5cm infantry guns attached from the regiment. (Ian Palmer © Osprey Publishing)

Divisional field artillery pieces were provided with circular or roughly triangular firing positions called Geschützestellungen. These usually had substantial all-round parapets and were deeper than other more forward gun positions for protection from counter-battery fire. Ready ammunition niches might be dug into the forward side, armour protection trenches attached to the sides, a rear entry/exit ramp added and separate ammunition niches and crew shelters located to the rear. A simple artillery firing position was prepared by digging a shallow pit and piling the earth to the front. Any existing cover might be used for this purpose. Armour protection trenches or merely simple slit trenches were dug to either side of the gun to protect the crew from ground, artillery and air attack. As air attack became common, these slit trenches were placed further from the gun position. Several ammunition niches were dug to the rear. A battery's four gun positions were set 30–50m apart and could be placed in a straight or staggered line, a square or a diamond formation. The battery headquarters was to the rear of the positions. The horse and ammunition wagon parking was well to the rear of the battery position (up to 200m) in a concealed area to protect it from artillery. Camouflage was essential for the battery to survive, and so positions were often covered with camouflage nets. Each battery had two light machine guns for ground and air defence.

Slit trenches were dug in rear areas as Luftschutzräume (air raid shelters). These varied in form and dimension, but two typical examples were the straight trench (2m long, 40–60cm wide and 1.6m deep), and the three-leg zig-zag trench of which each leg had approximately the same dimensions as the straight trench. Trenches might be roofed over with earth-covered logs or bundled brushwood fascines. Interestingly, such shelters were dug in at distances as great as 40km behind the front.

SQUAD BUNKERS

A variety of different designs of squad and half-squad underground shelters or bunkers (Gruppen und Halbgruppenunterstände) were available for protection and living. These bunkers were built to the rear of the main defences, within strongpoints and near crew-served weapons positions. They were not fighting positions, being completely below ground and lacking firing ports. They were to provide more practical living quarters than small dugouts, trenches and holes. They also provided good protection from artillery and air attack, as well as the extremes of wind, rain, snow and cold. Wherever possible, they were built completely below ground level, with the top flush with the ground. If the water table or extremely hard or rocky ground prevented a buried bunker they were dug as deep as possible with double log walls (50cm between logs), filled with rock or packed soil, and the above-ground sides and roof banked with packed soil and covered with sod. Entry was gained through a trench (connected to a communications trench), down some stairs, and into a vestibule separated from the main room, although this last luxury was not always present. Wood floors were provided if sufficient dimensioned lumber was available. When it was not, straw was used, which had to be changed periodically. Individual or multi-person two- or three-level platform bunks were integrated. A table and benches were provided. Rifle racks might be mounted on a wall near the door. Sometimes a short emergency exit tunnel was provided.

If available a wood or oil stove was installed with a stovepipe. Small, canister-like, gasoline-burning heaters were used such as the motor vehicle heater and the smaller Juwel 33 heater. Little folding stoves, fuelled by hexamethylene tetamine tablets, were used to heat mess tins. Sand-filled cans soaked with petrol were used for heat during cold nights. Light was provided by kerosene lanterns, candles (with melted wax remoulded into new candles) and small ration cans fitted with a wick burning rifle oil known as a *Hindenburger Lampe*. Expended cartridge cases, 2cm or 3.7cm for example, had the mouth crimped to a narrow slit, filled with oil, and a wick inserted to make a crude lamp. Issue field pocket lamps were used sparingly, as batteries were scarce.

The elaborate bunkers pictured in manuals could not always be built in urgent situations. During December 1941, 6. Panzer-Division, with its former tank crews

On the Russian steppes, long snow-bank barriers formed defensive lines with firing positions. Dugouts too were set in the snow berms, which were revetted with snow-filled fuel drums and hay bales (as shown here). Canvas tarps sometimes covered the dugout entrances. (Gordon Rottman)

ETCHED IN THE EARTH – FIELD FORTIFICATIONS

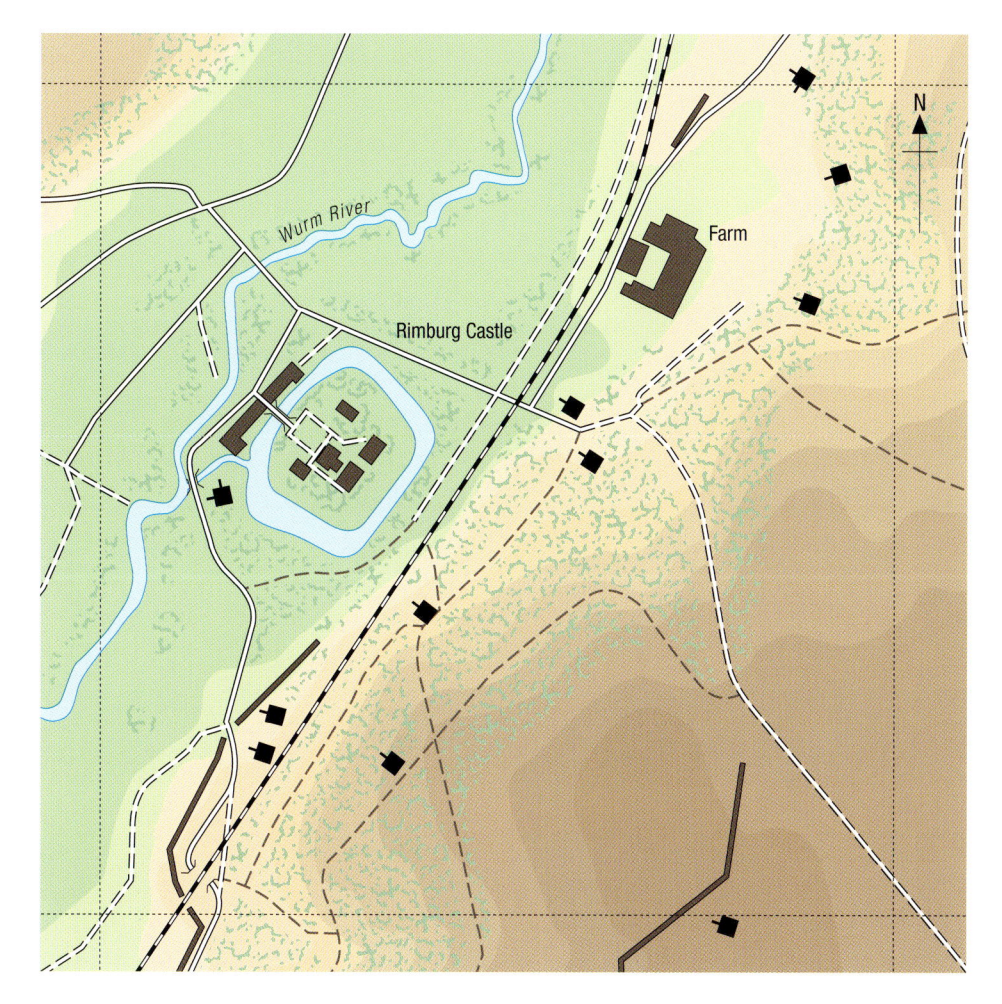

West Wall defences, Germany, October 1944. The 1,100m² area shown lies immediately to the south of Palenberg. The moated Rimburg Castle, to the centre left, was heavily defended, as was the large farm complex to the upper right of the castle. The River Wurm flows through the upper left area – itself an obstacle with its bridges blown. (Ian Palmer © Osprey Publishing)

fighting as infantry, was forced from a chain of villages within a forested area. Either it could withdraw to another line of villages and possibly be enveloped, or it could establish a hasty defensive line in a temperature of -49°F without adequate shelter, which would mean death from exposure. During the previous few days' engagements on open terrain, daily casualties from frostbite had risen drastically to 800 per day. The division would soon lose its ability to function.

The immediate construction of bunkers for both fighting and shelter was essential. The single corps and two divisional engineer battalions had only 40–60 men each and very little equipment. However, the division had recently received a large quantity of demolitions. The engineer battalion commanders were ordered to disregard the harsh weather conditions and blast multiple lines of craters in the solidly frozen ground along the specified battle line to shelter all combat units and reserves. The craters were sighted to provide mutual in-depth fire support. Each crater/bunker could hold three to five

OPPOSITE: The well-built, multi-storey, interconnected buildings of European urban areas provided robust defensive positions. When destroyed, the rubble created countless hiding places for defenders and obstacles to the attackers. (Gordon Rottman)

men. The engineers also mined approaches and built tank obstacles at three sites. The reserves and service troops packed down paths between the craters and to the rear, essentially snow communications trenches. They used readily available lumber and logs to cover the craters.

The blasting of the crater lines began the next morning. The enemy appeared to think that the blasting was artillery fire and did not advance. The blasting was completed by noon and by night the craters were finished by infantrymen with hand tools, covered with lumber, logs and snow, and occupied. Smoke soon rose from the bunkers, where the troops kept warm with open fires. Outposts were established forward of the bunkers, and abatis obstacles were laid in front of these, with anti-armour guns emplaced on higher ground covering the tank obstacles. The entire line was prepared within 12 hours of the first detonation. The engineers who prepared the positions suffered 40 per cent frostbite casualties, but the next day division frostbite casualties dropped from 800 to four. The line withstood all enemy attacks and was not abandoned until ten days later, in milder weather, when the adjacent units on both flanks were forced to withdraw after enemy tanks had penetrated their lines.

PRINCIPLES OF CAMOUFLAGE

German camouflage practices attempted to blend fortifications into the surrounding terrain and vegetation to prevent detection from both the ground and air. Efforts were made to hide positions outright as well, an example being the personnel bunkers which were completely buried below ground. Natural materials were used alongside camouflage nets, screens and pattern painting. German directives stated that cover and camouflage measures should not obstruct a weapon's field of fire.

Basic camouflage principles of frontline positions included positioning emplacements within vegetated areas and among rubble and broken terrain, avoiding a neat orderly appearance (although manuals depicted fortifications as tidy, in practice they were not), avoidance of silhouetting against the sky and contrasting backgrounds, removing spoil or concealing turned earth, concealing firing ports with tree branches or wreckage materials, building fortifications inside existing buildings, and the fabrication of screens from brushwood to mask movement along roads and tracks. The dispersal of fortifications, positions and facilities in irregular patterns was also common.

In barren, snow-covered and featureless desert areas it was cautioned that camouflaged positions should not be located near any existing features, otherwise this would allow an enemy observer to reference the position's location. Snow positions were not as easy to camouflage as may be assumed. Dug-up snow looks very different to undisrupted

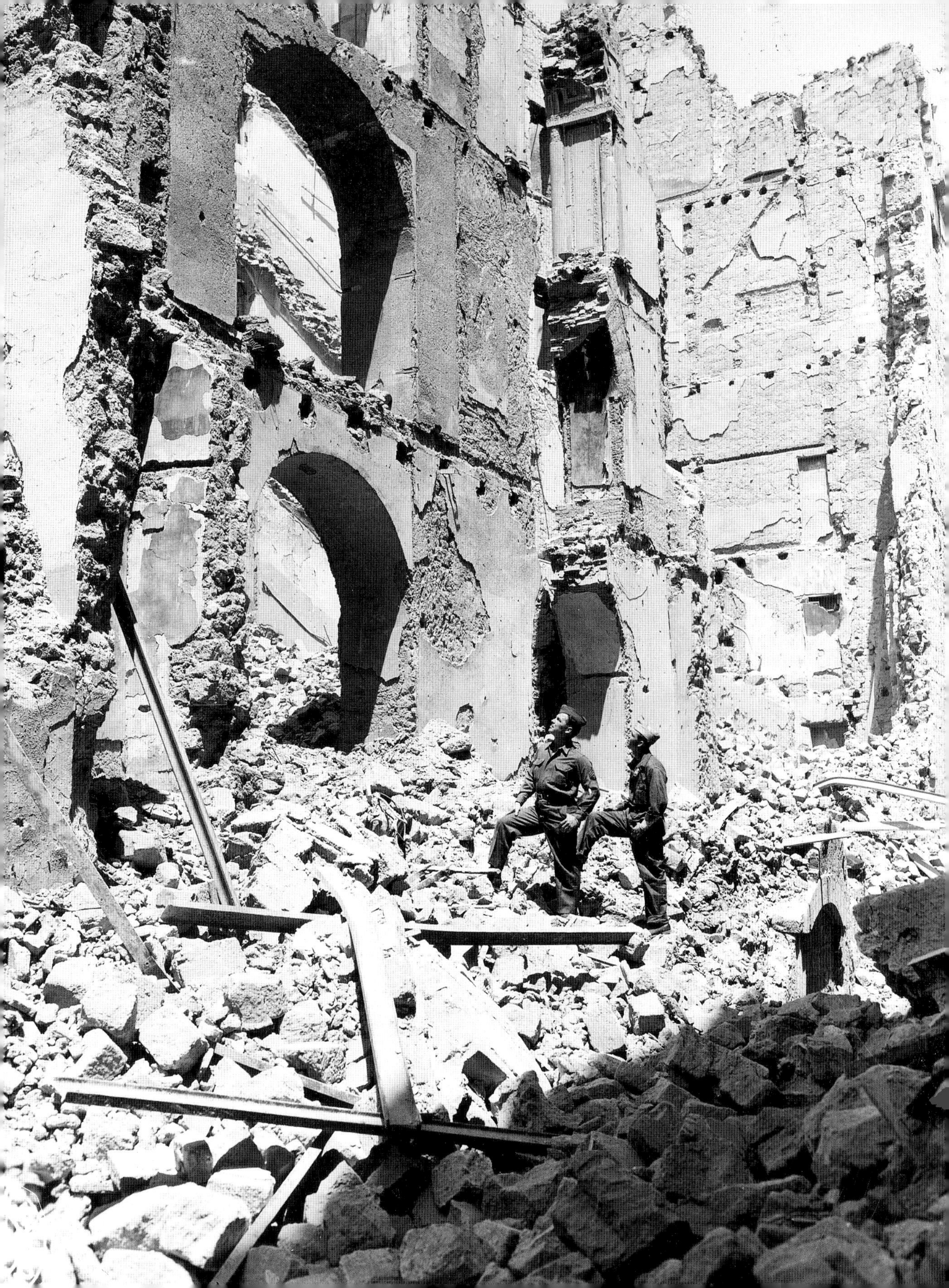

HITLER'S FORTRESSES

DESERT STRONGPOINT

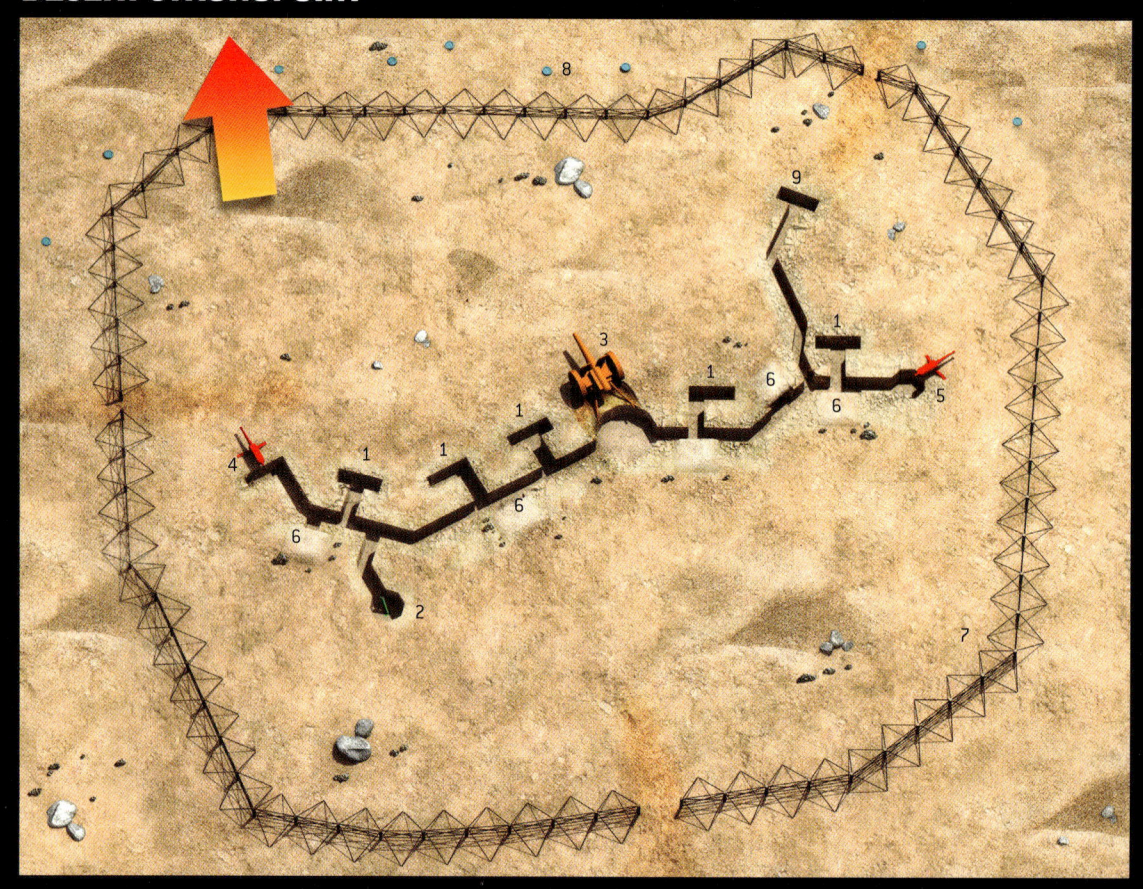

A squad strongpoint in the desert. Because of the need to defend wide frontages in the desert and the expansive fields of observation and fire, German units often built self-contained, widely scattered, reinforced squad strongpoints. An ideal example is shown here. The weapons positions and dugouts were to be at least 6m apart along the 40–60m zig-zag trench. One- and two-man rifle positions (1) were set 1–2m forward of the trench. Firing steps might be used, including on the trench's rear side. Not all such strongpoints had an 8cm mortar (2). A 2cm Flak gun may have been substituted for the 3.7cm or 5cm anti-armour gun (3, shown above scale for clarity). Some strongpoints may have had two machine guns, one at each end (4 and 5). Lacking a Flak gun, one of the machine guns (5) would be provided with an air-defence mount as well as an alternative position for ground fire. This combination of weapons provided the strongpoint with direct and indirect anti-personnel fire, direct anti-armour fire and air defence. Sufficient dugouts and small bunkers (6, hidden) were available for all personnel. Such a strongpoint might be manned by 16–24 troops. It would be sighted on any piece of high ground, even if only a couple of metres above the surrounding desert. Camouflage nets might have been used. The barbed-wire barrier (7), if present, was erected c.50m from the strongpoint. Anti-armour mines would be emplaced outside the barbed wire along with some anti-personnel mines (8). The listening post (9), accessed via a crawl trench, was manned at night to guard against infiltration. Flare pistols were used to signal other strongpoints and command posts that a strongpoint was under attack, with coloured flare combinations identifying the type of attack and direction. The large red arrow indicates the direction towards the enemy. (Ian Palmer © Osprey Publishing)

ETCHED IN THE EARTH – FIELD FORTIFICATIONS

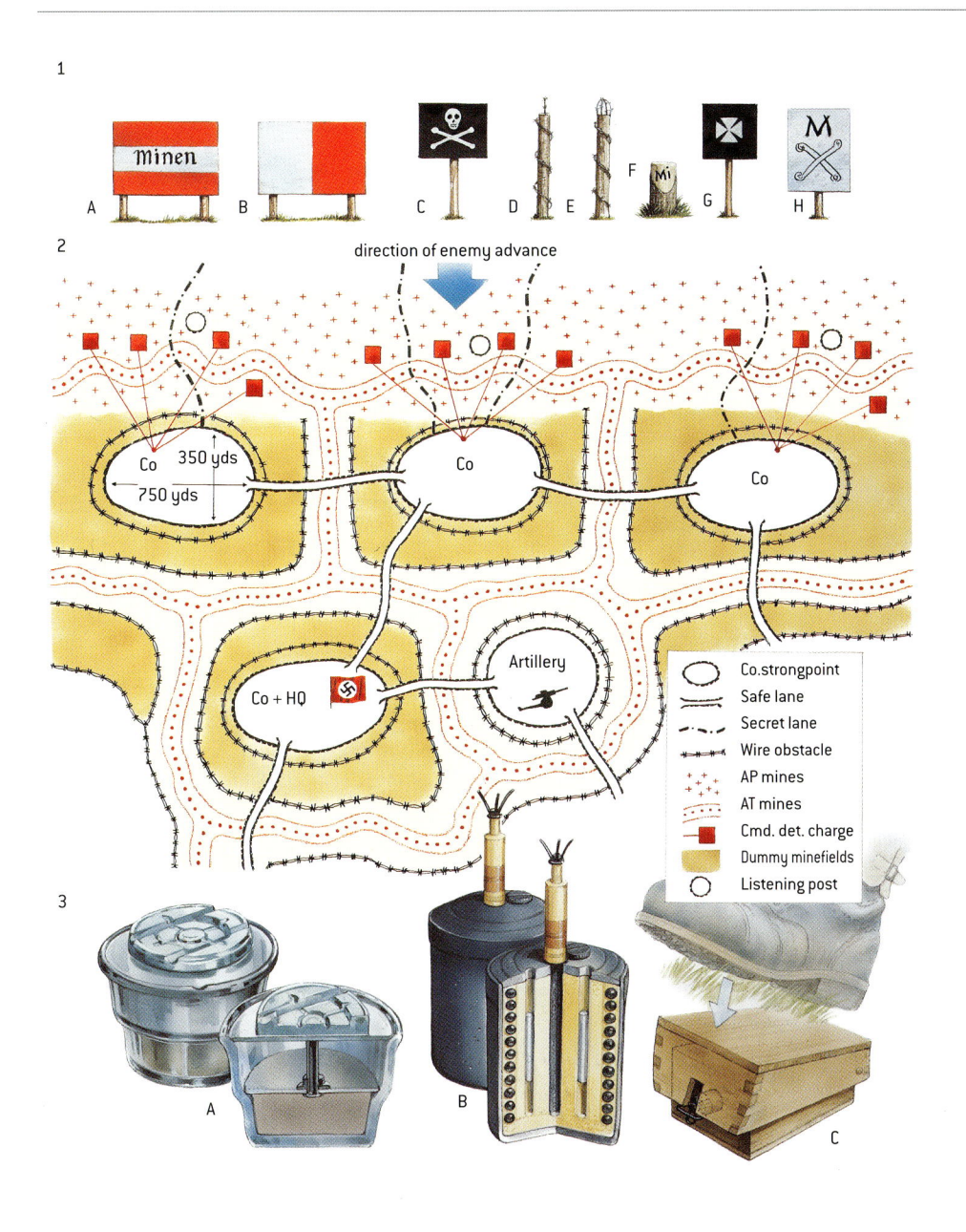

ABOVE: (1) Minefield signs – (A) Actual minefield; dummy minefields were sometimes marked with this sign but with 'Minen' in italic lettering. (B) Minefield gap sign – gap on the white side, mines on the red. (C), (G) & (H) Alternative painted signs for actual minefields. (D) & (E) 'Subtle' signs made with barbed wire and stakes; (D) = anti-personnel mines, (E) = anti-tank. (F) Hastily painted sign on shaved tree stump. Diagram (2) shows a reinforced company position, while in (3) we see three common German mine types: (A) Glas-Mine; (B) S-Mine; (C) Schu-Mine. (Peter Dennis © Osprey Publishing)

snow and even after additional snowfall it appears different. Vehicle and foot tracks point to positions. Machine guns cause black powder marks in front of firing ports making them easy to detect. Any movement, even by white-clad troops, is easily detectable against snow backgrounds. Smoke from heating and cooking fires also signals the locations of positions. White sheets were often used to conceal crew-served weapons, but were easily detected at close range.

The removal of soil from around positions and the lack of parapets were for concealment purposes. It is extremely difficult to detect such positions from ground level, especially if all signs of work have been removed or concealed. Soil parapets around positions are easily detectable from the air because of the turned soil's contrast with surrounding undisturbed soil and vegetation, which appears white or very light grey. Parapets also cast shadows, which are detectable from the air. The lack of parapets for concealment was especially effective in the desert and Russian steppes.

One determining factor might be the location of a position in relation to enemy ground-level observers. A parapet might be thrown up behind a position so that the occupants would not be silhouetted against the sky or contrasting terrain. When parapets were built they were sometimes camouflaged with sod removed from the position's site and beneath where the parapets would be thrown. The soil was spread outward from the position and the parapet kept low. Evergreen tree branches were also used to conceal parapets, but had to be replaced every couple of days: in the Russian winter they froze

Pre-war photograph showing the MG34 used in the sustained-fire role on its tripod mount, here angled close to the ground to allow the crew to fire prone. The No.1 is looking through the x3 power prismatic telescopic sight while the gun commander observes with binoculars. (Gordon Rottman)

and remained green for some time. If the ground was covered with fallen leaves these too were spread over parapets and other turned soil for camouflage. Positions were often placed on the reserve slopes of hills and ridges to conceal them from ground observation and direct fire. Camouflage nets were used to conceal the entrances to bunkers, erected over artillery positions, and sometimes laid on the ground to cover trenches and their parapets. In the latter case the nets were supported by taut wire staked in a zig-zag pattern over the trench, and it also supported camouflaging brush and branches.

Riflemen's positions were sometimes camouflaged with camouflage tent quarters (Zeltbahn rain capes), covers woven from vines and twigs, and sections cut from camouflage nets. Lift-up lids for riflemen's positions were made by constructing a criss-crossed stick frame and wiring on sections of sod trimmed to match the surrounding ground. These are known as 'spider holes'.

The use of dummy positions and facilities and mock-up vehicles was very common, especially in Africa. Since it was impossible to conceal activity in the desert, deception efforts were widespread. To be effective, dummy vehicles had to be moved nightly, at least partly camouflaged, and fake tracks had to be made. Dummy bunkers were constructed by simply piling, shaping and lightly camouflaging spoil removed from actual positions, which provided a means of disposing of excess soil. Knee-deep dummy trenches connected dummy positions and were filled with brush to make them appear deeper from the air. Sentries manned dummy positions and fires were burned to make them appear occupied.

AN ASSESSMENT OF GERMAN FIELD FORTIFICATIONS

German field fortifications were highly developed and were as effective as any others employed during the war. The specified designs of individual positions were well thought out, and were designed to protect against direct and indirect fire and from being overrun by tanks. They could accommodate troops and weapons, allowing them to take full advantage of their capabilities. However, individual positions, no matter how well designed, were ineffective unless fully integrated into a defensive system that coordinated the various elements of adjacent positions, obstacles, fire support, reserves and command and control. Avenues of approach and obstacles (including minefields) needed to be kept under constant observation to prevent surprise attacks. Camouflage and concealment from both ground and air observation were essential, including deception measures such as decoys and dummy positions. The overall layout and layering of the defences in depth was also essential to a successful defence. German troops were capable of achieving all of

HITLER'S FORTRESSES

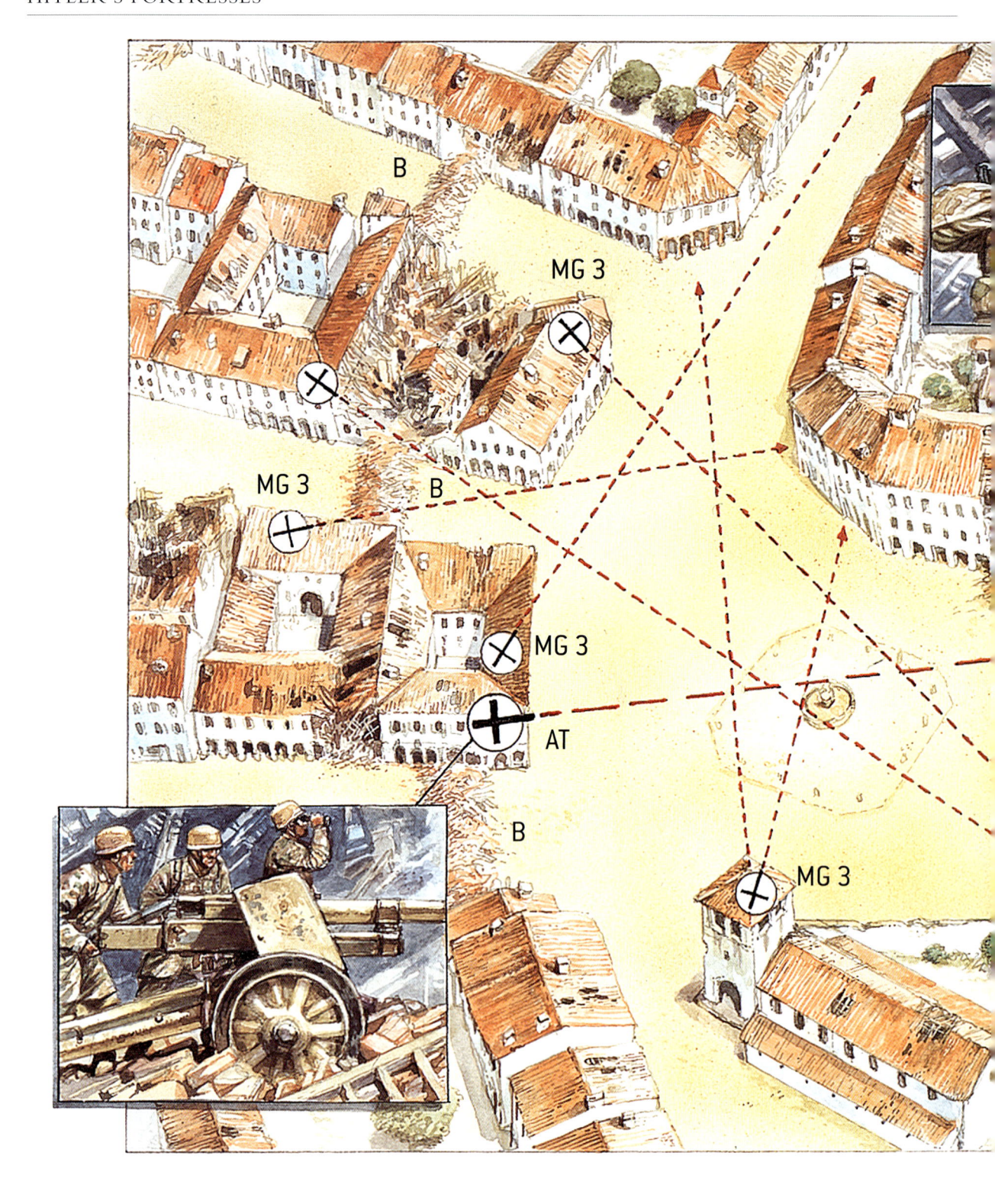

ETCHED IN THE EARTH – FIELD FORTIFICATIONS

German street fighting in defence, Ortona, 1943. (B) Barricades of rubble formed by blowing down houses on each side of streets; height varied from 1.2m to 1.8m. (AT) 7.5cm PaK 40 AT gun hidden to cover barricade. (MG1) Automatic weapon covering barricade from third floor of house in next street, with field of fire over demolished buildings between. (MG2) MG42 dug into actual barricade. (MG3) Automatic weapons – MG42s, FG42s and MP40s – in second and third floors of houses, to cover barricades, the whole square and all roads leading into it. (Peter Dennis © Osprey Publishing)

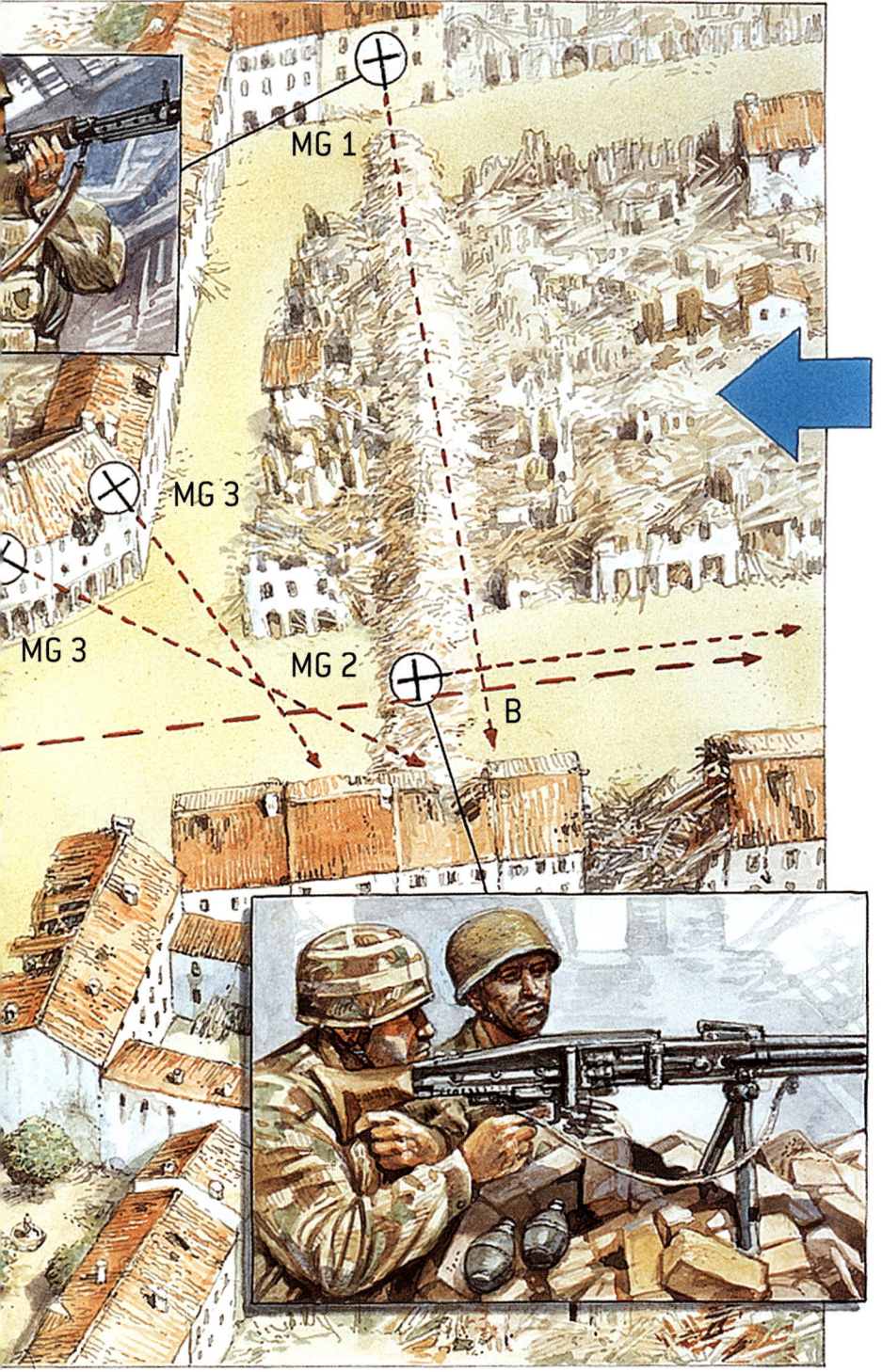

Direction of Canadian advance

this, and often did so (with time, resources, weather and the tactical and operational situations permitting).

In most instances the German soldiers, at all levels, adhered to the basic precepts of selecting, locating and building field fortifications. Generally these fortifications were well positioned, effectively covered their assigned sectors of observation and fire, provided mutual support to adjacent positions, made good use of their weapon's capabilities, were well camouflaged (especially at ground level) and fitted well within the terrain and avenues of approach to their positions. In particular, the obstacles employed made good use of natural features to create more effective barriers, but there were many instances when the German troops failed to maintain observation and fire on these areas – more a result of a specific tactical situation or a lack of resources as opposed to the neglecting of key principles. Camouflage was sometimes deficient, especially overhead, a factor usually due to insufficient time and resources, coupled with the inherent difficulties of hiding from airborne observation.

The German units demonstrated a great deal of flexibility, ingenuity and initiative in adapting their doctrinal defensive tactics and techniques to the varying terrain and weather conditions on different fronts. Field fortifications and obstacles were modified and new ones designed to exploit locally available materials (vital when considering how limited supplies were) as well as to attempt to counter new Allied assault tactics and heavier armour.

Regardless of the front on which the German forces defended, the most significant problem they faced was the lack of sufficient troops to provide adequate in-depth defence, and of armour and other motorized units for a mobile reserve allowing rapid and hard-hitting counter-attacks. No defence could resist a strong, well-coordinated, combined-arms attack supported by massive artillery and air resources. The defence line could be restored or partly restored if strong mobile reserves could conduct substantial counter-attacks, but the lack of air defence cover, or rather the air superiority of the Allies, prevented the timely commitment of mobile reserves even when they were available.

The Allies developed extremely effective offensive tactics to deal with German defences. Allied basic doctrine was repeatedly modified and perfected as new weapons became available and lessons were learned. No two units, even within the same division, used the same assault tactics.

German combat troops in particular realized the fallacy of fixed, permanent defences, such as on the West Wall: these were used to strengthen the field fortifications, and not vice versa. Ultimately, the German soldiers were rarely able to develop complete mobile or elastic defences as specified by doctrine. What the defences did do was buy time at a strategic level. It should be noted that it took the Soviets from February 1943 (after the fall of Stalingrad) until 30 April 1945 (the fall of Berlin) – some 27 months – to bring the Germans to the point of defeat.

Little remains today of these field fortifications. In most areas new construction, agriculture and government polices have covered over the mostly temporary sites. Many of the semi-permanent concrete fortifications have been demolished too. However, in some remote areas of Germany, France, the former USSR and other countries, traces of trench lines and shallow, overgrown depressions can be found, marking the vanished frontiers of the Third Reich.

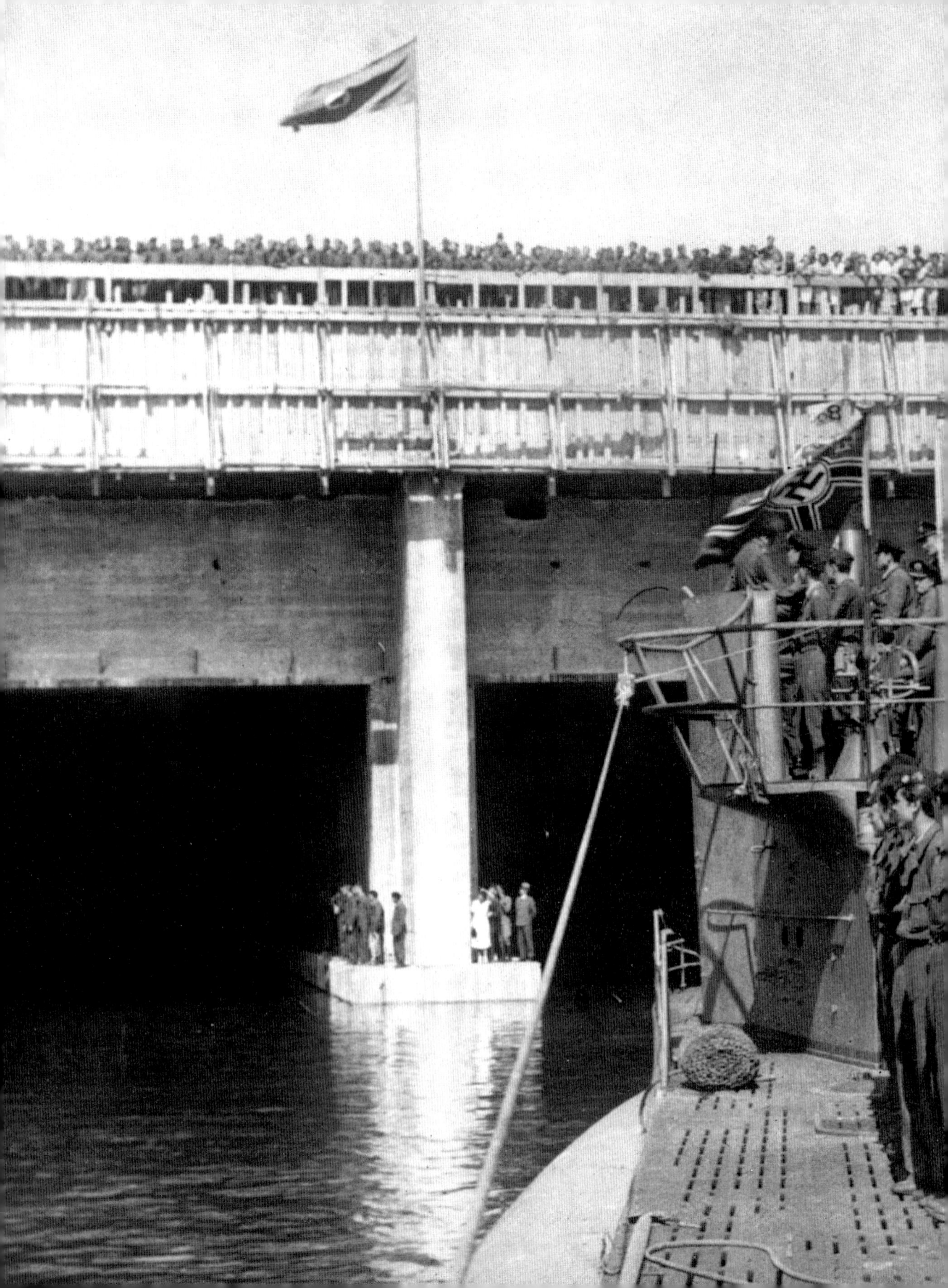

SPECIALIST FORTIFICATIONS – PROTECTING THE U-BOATS AND V-WEAPONS

LEFT: The first German submarine to enter the U-boat bunker at La Baule, St Nazaire in July 1941 is pictured here, in full ceremonial display. (Topfoto)

The formidable reach and punishing payloads of Allied air power had a profound effect on the physical structure of the Third Reich. To be seen, and to be exposed, was to invite explosive destruction, so Hitler's engineers and builders were compelled to create a range of defensive facilities for its sites of military and political importance. In this chapter, we will consider two particular forms of defensive works: U-boat shelters and V-weapon pens. Both demonstrated German ingenuity and resilience, particularly in the adaptation of ferro-concrete structures to different tactical and geographical requirements.

U-BOAT BASES

DESIGN AND DEVELOPMENT

The U-boat bunkers dotted along the coastline of occupied Europe were but one aspect of Germany's programme of defensive construction. Similar protective housing was planned to shelter S-Boote (E-Boats) and Räum-Boote (R-Boats) and to provide protected locks: damage to these could effectively seal off a port. In addition storage bunkers for munitions and matériel, general defensive pillboxes and artillery bunkers were planned. It should also be remembered that the work on the U-boat bunkers effectively competed for materials and manpower with the construction of the Atlantic Wall coastal defences.

As far as the German Navy was concerned, the responsibility for providing these defensive structures belonged to the Marinebauwesen (Naval Construction Department) under the command of Ministerialdirektor Eckhardt. The experience of building similar large-scale defensive structures on the German naval base at Helgoland was put to good use when the U-boat bases began to appear in the various captured French ports in 1941, and the general designs themselves closely followed the basic principles established during the construction of the Imperial German Navy U-boat base at Bruges.

As well as providing shelter for the U-boats themselves, the bunkers contained repair workshops, power generating plants (general power was drawn from the local electricity supply but diesel generator plants were provided to produce power in emergencies should the local supply be knocked out), pumping stations, storage facilities, offices, accommodation, ventilation units, heating units, telephone and communication rooms and first aid posts. Narrow-gauge rail tracks also ran into the bunkers themselves to allow heavy equipment to be brought inside and to the U-boats. For safety's sake, munitions such as torpedoes were generally stored away from the U-boat pens in their own well-protected bunkers and brought into the complex when needed, by means of the narrow-gauge tracks.

OPPOSITE: This interior view shows one of the highly important dry-dock-capable pens in which a Type IX is undergoing a major overhaul and repairs. The depth of the pen itself is clear to see. Note also the exterior doors in the background, and the gap between the top of these doors and the roof of the pen. Also note the powerful arc lights along the pen wall which allowed work to continue around the clock if necessary. (Gordon Williamson)

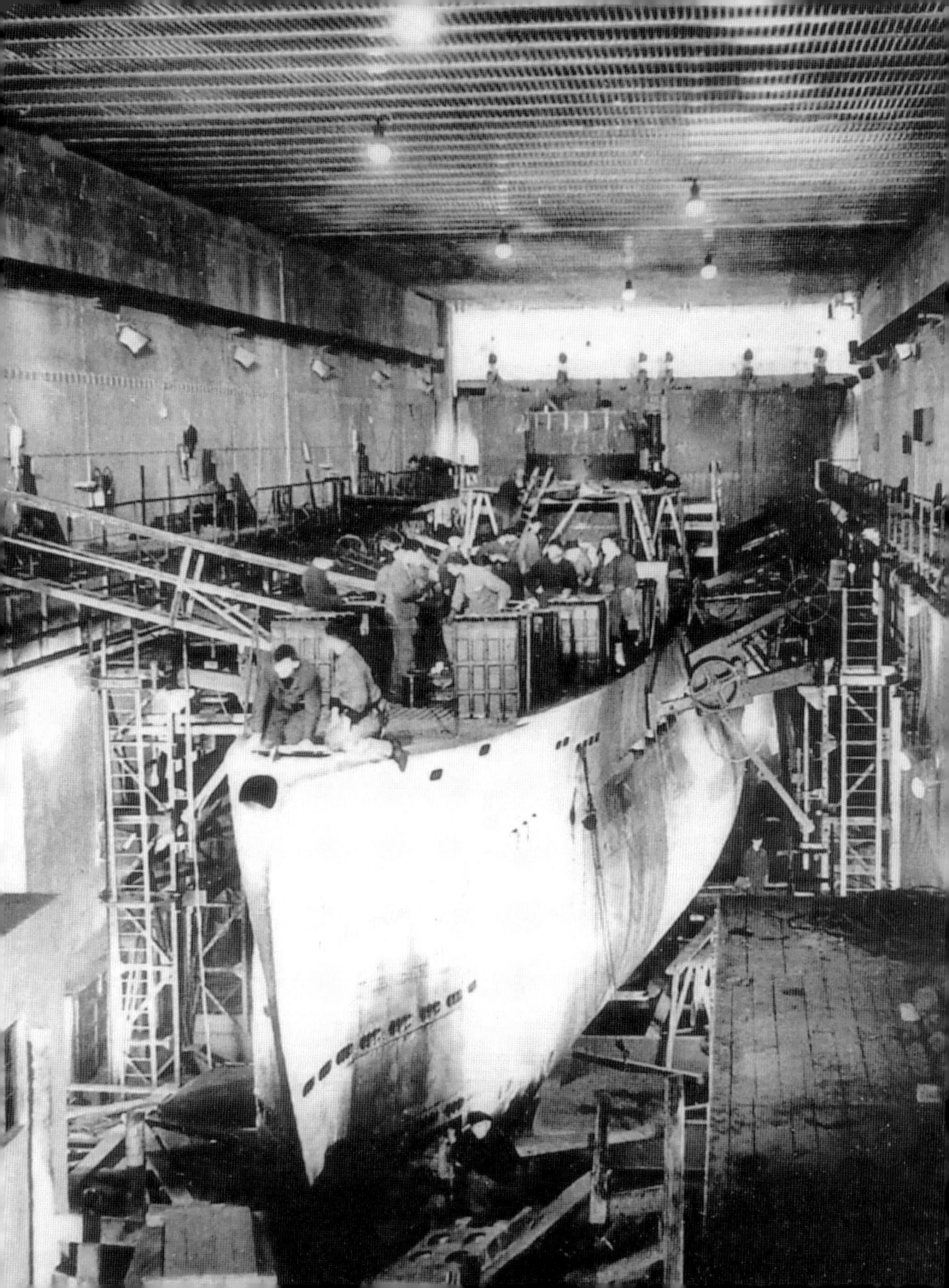

LONG-RANGE DEFENCES OF THE FRENCH BASES

Faced with the threat of intensive Allied bombing raids, the first significant bunker defensive measure which would come into play was the Luftwaffe's system of early-warning radar and spotter posts. At various sites along the French coast were establishments equipped with the Freya and Würzburg radar systems (1 and 2). These would detect formations of Allied bombers approaching the coast. Depending on the time of day, single-engined day fighters (such as the Fw 190, 3) or twin-engined Me 110 or Ju 88 night-fighters would be scrambled to intercept the enemy. Allied bombers could boast fairly powerful defensive weaponry, particularly when flying in close formation, but despite this many fell victim to the determined attacks of the Luftwaffe fighters. Those who survived such attacks would face a concentrated barrage of heavy anti-aircraft fire from large-calibre weapons (such as the 12.8cm Flak gun, 4) which protected important installations such as the ports in occupied France. In many cases poor visibility, bad weather or heavy cloud over the target prevented a number of planes from reaching their objective, as shown by events at Brest. At the end of the day, the single greatest factor in the successful defence of the bunker was its inherent, massive strength (5). (Ian Palmer © Osprey Publishing)

The pens themselves were constructed in two styles, 'wet' and 'dry'. Dry pens were those capable of being pumped out and effectively used as dry-dock facilities for submarines requiring repair and maintenance. The actual dimensions of the pens varied, but as a general rule the distance from the base of the pen to the level of the quay allowed for approximately 10m water depth, with a similar distance from quay level to ceiling. The height of the ceiling had to allow the overhead cranes to remove the periscopes fully from their housing for repair or replacement. The quayside was normally around 1.5m wide.

Each pen had at least one overhead crane running down its length. These had capacities ranging from 1 ton up to 30 tons, the U-boat being directed into whichever pen had a crane or cranes of the requisite capacity for the work required. Each pen was served by main pumps with a 3,000m³ capacity and smaller auxiliary drainage pumps with a 380m³ capacity. These pumps were located at pumping stations between each pen, usually with two of each of these pumps per station. This was by no means a universal arrangement, but it was by far the most typical set-up: some bases had all the pumping equipment located in the service areas in the main block behind the pens themselves. These powerful pumps took anything from three hours upwards to empty a pen completely and create a dry-dock facility.

Protection for the pen interiors was provided by massive armoured steel plates, some up to a metre thick. These could be in the form of steel shutters, which were lowered vertically from above the entrance to the pen, or conventional hinged doors. These armoured plates would in some cases extend down to the level of the quay (for dry pens) whilst others only provided cover for some two-thirds of the opening, leaving just under 2 metres of the entrance open. Some of the protective doors to the bunker complexes were hollow boxes made from thick plate, which were then filled with concrete.

The Bordeaux U-boat pens under construction. This aerial view shows the sheer size of the construction site. The basic layout is already clearly visible with the individual pen foundations completed and the separating walls between the pens being erected. To the rear of the pens can be seen the structures which would contain the various workshop areas. No site this large can be hidden from enemy aerial reconnaissance, yet the U-boat bunker complexes were all successfully completed without incurring significant damage from enemy attacks. (Gordon Williamson)

Given the Kriegsmarine's urgent need for protected repair facilities for their U-boats, the dry-dock-capable pens were generally the first to be constructed. It was common for the first pens to be put into use as soon as they were ready, whilst the remaining pens were still under construction.

With the greatest threat to these bunkers coming from enemy aircraft, it is no surprise that the most innovative development work was carried out on the design of the bunker roof. The result of this was the creation of roofs that were virtually impregnable.

PROTECTED LOCKS

As several of the U-boat bunkers were located in basins in the inner harbour of their port, access would normally be via a set of lock gates. Though the bunker complexes themselves were immensely strong, the unprotected locks were definite weak spots. If these were put out of action, boats would be unable to enter or leave their pens. In order to protect this Achilles heel, especially after the British attack on the lock at St Nazaire, it was decided to enclose these locks in their own protective bunkers: St Nazaire, La Pallice and Bordeaux were all to have these. Effectively, these looked like miniature U-boat bunkers. The locks at St Nazaire and La Pallice still stand to this day. The partially completed lock at Bordeaux was demolished after the war.

At St Nazaire the lock was built a few yards along from the lock which gave access to the inner harbour via the Normandie dry dock, which had been damaged when it was rammed during the St Nazaire commando raid by HMS *Campbeltown*. She was one of the old 'four-stacker' destroyers supplied by the USA under the lend-lease programme. After the destroyer was rammed into the lock gates, a huge cargo of explosives carried on board was detonated, destroying the gates.

The new protected lock was almost directly in front of pens 8 and 9 of the bunker complex. This lock, begun in August 1942, was some 155m long, 25m wide and 14m high. A roadway ran through the lock, entering via doors in its side, and crossed the lock waters by means of a bridge, which could be raised when a vessel passed through. The lock was capable of being pumped dry, and in addition to the intrinsic protection offered by the reinforced concrete roof and walls, had its own Flak defences on the roof, with four emplacements for 2cm Flak guns on a special platform on the western side. At La Pallice, the massive sheltered lock was 167m long, 26m wide and 14m high. It was not used until August 1944.

A number of fascinating new projects were planned, the most interesting of which was the proposal to turn the eastern portion of the Rove Tunnel at Marseilles (which opened out in the north-west part of the harbour at Port de la Lave) into a U-boat bunker, suitable for handling the smaller Type XXIII coastal boats. It was also

SPECIALIST FORTIFICATIONS – PROTECTING THE U-BOATS AND V-WEAPONS

planned to build bunkers at Rügen, at Gotenhafen and at Nikolajew in the Crimea, and to create additional bunker facilities at Kiel, Bremen and Hamburg.

Pens at the massive Keroman complex at Lorient under construction, watched over by an armed sentry. This was the biggest and most successful of all U-boat bunker sites, with much of it still being in use today. (Gordon Williamson)

BUILT TO RESIST

Each bunker complex was subtly different to its counterparts in its layout: however, there were a number of standard features. The example we will use here to tour the layout of a bunker site, namely the complex at Brest, will illustrate most of the common features found in all the operational sites.

When the German Army, in the form of 5. Panzer-Division, occupied the port of Brest in June 1940, it was to discover that the withdrawing British troops had destroyed most of the port facilities. The German troops began urgent repair works immediately and within two months the first of Admiral Karl Dönitz's U-boats, U-65 under the command of Kapitänleutnant Hans-Gerrit von Stockhausen, entered Brest for repairs. By the middle of the following month, the port of Brest was fully functional once more.

HITLER'S FORTRESSES

ABOVE: This illustration shows the construction of the massive Valentin factory bunker near Bremen, near to the village of Farge. The second largest bunker to be built, it covered just over 49,000m² of ground on the northern bank of the River Weser. Almost a quarter of a million tons of concrete were used in its construction, as well as 27,000 tons of steel. (Ian Palmer © Osprey Publishing)

Almost immediately, preparations began for the establishment of an operational U-boat base. Construction of protective concrete pens began in January 1941 and lasted for approximately nine months. The layout actually consisted of two bunkers in one. The first contained five wet pens, 115m long and 17m wide, each capable of accommodating up to three boats: the second contained eight dry repair pens 99m long and 11m wide, and a further two 114m long and 13m wide, each capable of accommodating just one boat. Overall, the bunker measured 333m in length and 192m in width, and its height was 17m.

SPECIALIST FORTIFICATIONS – PROTECTING THE U-BOATS AND V-WEAPONS

The first U-boats to arrive at Brest were from 1. Unterseebootsflotille 'Weddigen', transferring from Kiel in June 1941, followed four months later by 9. Unterseebootsflotille. The first recorded use of the U-boat pens was in September 1941, though the complex was not fully completed until the summer of 1942.

The harbour at Brest was bounded by a protective mole (a harbour wall), the bunker being tucked in the eastern corner of the harbour, with the mole emerging from the eastern side of the bunker. The forward part of the bunker, containing the individual pens, opened out into the harbour or basin. In the Brest complex, there were five pens lettered A to E, then a further ten pens numbered in sequence.

BELOW: Defending the base from low-flying aircraft. On the roof of the bunker are a number of concrete emplacements equipped with the four-barrel 2cm Flakvierling (1). In addition, the pilot would have to avoid the cables of barrage balloons anchored to vessels in the harbour near to the bunker (2), as well as extended masts fitted to such ships to provide further hazards for low-flying aircraft (3). An anti-torpedo net drawn across the harbour in front of the pens (4) would provide yet another obstacle to a successful strike. (Ian Palmer © Osprey Publishing)

Pens A and B were fractionally under 116m in length and 17m in width. Each could accommodate two U-boats side by side. The external wall was some 7m thick, and there was a 6.3m-wide quay separating the two pens, with a 1.3m-thick dividing wall between them running down its centre. Pen C was slightly shorter, at 114m, but wider at 17.5m. It too could accommodate two boats. A 7m-wide quay separated Pen C from Pen B, with a 2.7m-thick dividing wall running along its centre. Pens D and E were 96m in length, Pen D being 17.8m wide and Pen E 16.8m wide. Again, each could accommodate two boats. The internal dividing wall between Pens C and D was 2.5m thick, that between pens D and E 1.3m thick and that between Pen E and the first of the numbered pens 2m thick. The dividing walls between each pen had five openings in the case of the longer pens and four in the case of the shorter to allow for movement between the pens, spaced approximately every 13m.

Moving westwards there were eight numbered pens, all around 11m wide, with each being slightly longer than its predecessor at 96.1m, 96.5m, 96.8m, 97.1m, 97.5m, 98m, 98.5m and 99.1m respectively. The dividing walls between these pens alternated at between 2m and 1.3m thick. These were all dry-dock pens capable of handling only one boat each. Then followed an 11m-wide section running the entire length of the complex from front to back, containing various offices. Finally, at the east end of the complex were two larger dry-dock repair pens, both 12m wide: Pen 9 was just under and Pen 10 just over 114m in length. The fact that virtually no two pens were identical, each differing by a metre or so in length and width, was by no means unusual.

All pens were provided with overhead travelling cranes, which differed in their handling capacity. These cranes were located as follows: Pens A, C and D – 4-ton capacity; Pen B – 12-ton capacity; Pen 1 – 10-ton capacity; Pens 2, 3, 5 and 8 – 3-ton capacity; Pens 4, 6 and 7 – 2.5-ton capacity; Pen 9 – 5-ton capacity; and Pen 10 – 30-ton capacity.

Running parallel with the rear of pens 1 to 8 was a corridor separating the front part of the complex from the rear. The front faces of pens A to E were set much further

The completed U-boat bunker complex at Brest. The enormous size of the base is clear from this photograph. In the background is the École Navale (Naval Academy) which has been painted with a disruptive-pattern camouflage. (Gordon Williamson)

forward than the numbered pens, so that there was a space between the rear of these pens and the corridor. Immediately behind Pen A was a ship repair workshop, behind Pen B a mechanical workshop and behind Pen C a torpedo storage room. Behind Pen D was a torpedo workshop and behind Pen E lay the complex Orderly Room. On the northern side of the corridor were, moving from east to west, a weapons repair shop, mechanical workshop, ship repair workshop, diesel room, electrical repair workshop, three further mechanical workshops and three ship repair workshops, the pump room and the firefighters' room. Powerful electric lighting allowed skilled machinists to work to fine tolerances on lathes and milling machines in the workshops deep within the bunker's gloomy interior. The standard format of having the rear of the complex provide all forms of repair workshops was highly typical. The east end of the corridor ran through to the entrance: on the northern side of this was the main boiler house which provided heating for the complex, and to the south of the entrance opening was a pillbox with firing slits to protect the entrance.

Moving to the roof, above pens A, E and 4 were concrete Flak gun emplacements providing an element of protection against low-flying aircraft. These were relatively small-calibre weapons, rarely larger than 4cm calibre, and incapable of reaching the four-engined RAF and USAAF bombers which flew at very high altitude, but could put up enough fire to force smaller aircraft to abandon a bombing/torpedo run. Above Pen 10 was a small tower containing the radio and signals equipment for the bunker.

Although certain bunkers, such as that at Brest, stored some torpedoes within the bunker, in general the bulk of torpedo storage was remote from the bunker site for safety reasons, usually in equally strong though much smaller bunkers connected to the main complex by narrow-gauge railway tracks.

BUNKERS, BOMBS AND RAIDS – THE BASES AT WAR

HAMBURG

Elbe II

Plans for a new U-boat bunker at the Howaldtswerke yards on the River Elbe at Hamburg were approved in 1940, with construction commencing at the end of that year. Erected by the firm of Dyckerhoff & Widmann AG at the east end of the Vulkan basin, the bunker was completed in March 1941 and consisted of two pens. Each pen was 112m in length and 22.5m in width and could accommodate three boats moored side by side.

To the rear of the bunker at ground level were a storage area on the west side, and offices and electrical switch-gear on the eastern side. The entire upper floor of this rear area was fitted out with workbenches and various equipment such as drills, vertical and horizontal boring machines, and lathes. Landward access was via small, well-protected steel doors on each side of the bunker.

The Elbe II bunker was used primarily to provide cover for new Type XXI U-boats being fitted out, and for existing boats returning to the yard for refit or repair. Despite numerous Allied bombing raids, the boats in the interior of the bunker remained safe, though some damage to the roof of the structure was achieved. On the night of 8 March 1945 a force of over 300 RAF bombers attacked the Hamburg dock area, dropping almost 1,000 tonnes of bombs. This was only the start of a concentrated bombing campaign against the dock installations in Hamburg. At the end of March, the RAF returned with a force of over 450 bombers and dropped over 2,200 tonnes of bombs on the area, laying waste to the Howaldtswerke yards but doing little or no damage to the bunker. The massive hanging steel doors covering the entrance were blown off during an air raid on 8 April 1945, when once again over 400 bombers attacked the area.

Six submarines, U-2505, U-3004, U-2501 and U-3506 (all Type XXIs) plus U-684 and U-685 (Type VIICs), were sheltering in the Elbe II bunker when the war ended. The Type XXIs were all awaiting repair and the Type VIICs were not fully completed. All six boats were crammed into the westernmost pen.

Following the German agreement to surrender the city of Hamburg to British forces on 3 May, the crews of the Type XXIs made immediate preparations to scuttle their boats using explosive charges. U-3506, U-3004 and U-2505 were scuttled inside the pen; the others were moved out into the harbour waters before being sunk.

The exterior of the Elbe II bunker. The interior walls were blown out and the roof collapsed: its massive sloping slabs are clearly visible leaning against the top of the remaining wall. (Gordon Williamson)

Fink II

The Fink II bunker, the largest to be built on German soil, was also constructed at Hamburg. Erected at the Deutsche Werft yards at Hamburg Finkenwerder, the main contractors involved were Wayss & Freytag and Beton & Monierbau AG. Although plans were approved in 1940, work did not commence until March 1941.

The bunker was actually built on dry land at the Deutsche Werfte yards, then a large triangular area of ground between it and the inlet from the River Elbe was excavated and the resulting area flooded. The structure consisted initially of four pens, all at just over 111m in length. The first was 27.5m in width, and the three remaining pens each 22.5m in width. A fifth pen was approved in September 1942 with construction beginning in May 1943 and completion in April 1944. This fifth pen,

ABOVE: This illustration shows the interior of a U-boat bunker. An operational boat is undergoing repair and maintenance in one of the dry-dock-capable pens. These were generally intended to accommodate only one boat at a time, unlike the wet pens that could normally take at least two boats. The pen has been fully drained, but water would continue to leak in and so pumps were used to keep the pen as dry as possible. (Ian Palmer © Osprey Publishing)

The Elbe II bunker at Hamburg. Although consisting of only two pens, it was still a sizeable structure. On the roof of the bunker various office and workshop facilities were built. A Type VII U-Boat is moored beside the bunker. (Gordon Williamson)

like the first, was 27.5m in width. Overall dimensions of the bunker were 153m in width and 139m in length.

The fifth pen was built slightly higher than the original pens, so that its roof could be supported by the edge of the original fourth pen. To the rear of the first four pens was a work area stretching back a further 20m: this same area behind the final, fifth pen stretched back for 39.5m.

The bunker could accommodate up to 15 boats, with three side by side in each pen. Landward access was by a single door on the west side of the bunker and a double door on the east. To the rear, on the east side of the projecting fifth pen, was a further single entrance door.

As with Elbe II, the Fink II bunker was intended primarily to give shelter to U-boats constructed at the adjacent yards whilst fitting out or being repaired or refitted. Protection against low-level bombing was provided by three 3.7cm Flak positions on the bunker roof.

The bunker did not suffer any particularly serious bombing raids until April 1945 when it suffered two separate attacks. The first, on 4 April, was a daylight raid carried out by US bombers with special armour-piercing bombs, and caused little or no damage. The second, on 9 April, was carried out by 17 Lancaster bombers carrying the massive 5.5-tonne Tallboy bombs, as well as two of the Grand-slam 10-tonne bombs. Of the 17 bombs dropped, six hit the bunker. The roof of the bunker was actually penetrated, but it was the pressure wave from the explosion that caused the greatest damage. A number of Type XXIII boats inside received minor damage, whilst the floating dry dock containing two boats in the new fifth pen sank: the boats inside, U-677 and U-982, although submerged, remained relatively undamaged. The massive structure survived, however, and ended the war virtually intact.

HELGOLAND

Nordsee III

Helgoland was a long-established German naval base and a logical spot for the construction of a U-boat bunker. Plans were drawn up as early as 1939 and by 1940 work was well under way: construction was completed in June 1941. The principal contractor for excavation work was Grün & Bilfinger and for actual construction the Hamburg firm of Dyckerhoff & Widmann AG was selected.

The bunker was a fairly modest one, lying in the east basin of the harbour on Helgoland. It comprised only three pens, all of which were wet pens: each could accommodate three submarines. A floating dry dock was also provided which could be towed into one of the pens should dry repair facilities be required. The dry dock could accommodate only a single submarine.

The bunker was 156m in length and 94m in width, each pen being approximately 108m long and 22m wide, with a 6m-wide quay separating each pen. The roof was some 3m thick and the walls 2m thick. To the rear of the easternmost pen lay a workshop for periscopes and optical equipment as well as torpedo storage, whilst to the rear of the westernmost pen was a workshop area with welding facilities and also an oxygen tank storage area and a carpenters' workshop.

Of less importance to the U-boat war than many other bunker complexes, Nordsee III did not come in for much attention from Allied bombers until late in the war. There were no resident flotillas, and once the French and Norwegian bases fell into German hands, Nordsee III saw only 'passing trade' with boats calling in for repair or resupply. In fact, the U-boat bunkers were used just as often, if not more often, to shelter small surface craft such as E-Boats.

After the Allied landings in Normandy in June 1944, the Nordsee III bunker became a staging point for the Seehund-type midget submarines under Vizeadmiral Heye, on their way from Wilhelmshaven to the invasion front, and at one point even housed a number of so-called Sprengboote. These were small motor boats packet with explosives which were driven directly at their targets, the operator leaping overboard at the last possible moment and being picked up by a control boat.

Defences on the bunker itself were fairly light, comprising just two 3.7cm Flak guns and one 2cm Flak gun together with a 2m searchlight. From late-1944, however, both the USAAF and RAF began to mount raids against the Helgoland base. A total of six major raids were launched against the complex between 1941 and 1945, the RAF raid on 18 April 1945 involving over 960 bombers. A final raid on the following day saw just 36 bombers drop 22 Tallboy bombs. The U-boat bunker suffered no significant damage in any of these attacks and was still completely intact at the end of the war.

KIEL

Kilian

Sited on the east bank of Kiel harbour, the relatively small Kilian bunker was built during the winter of 1941/42 to provide protection for newly built U-boats before they were allocated to their operational flotillas, as well as for the repair of operational and training boats.

Two pens were provided, separated by an internal dividing wall, each 138m long and 23m wide, allowing two boats to be accommodated one behind the other with three side by side. The bunker could therefore accommodate a total of 12 boats at full capacity. On the north-west (front) corner of the bunker was a small concrete tower to accommodate a Flak gun position. Only a relatively small area of the bunker was allocated to workshop space, though this was spread over three floors (ground and two upper floors).

The overall length of the bunker was 176m, with walls just over 3m thick and a 4.8m-thick roof. Protection for the interior was provided by seven thick, hanging, overlapping steel plates forming a door, which reached down to water level. There was no special protection below water level.

The bunker was finally completed on 13 November 1943, having taken around one year to construct. U-1101, a Type VIIc, became the first U-boat to enter the bunker. The labour force consisted of well over a thousand men, working around the clock in two shifts, and comprising to a large degree forced labourers, camp inmates and prisoners of war. The death rate amongst the workers for whom no provision for shelter was made during bombing raids was extremely high.

The principal contractor for the construction of Kilian was the firm of Dyckerhoff & Widmann AG. Initially, the bunker escaped the attentions of the Allies, and general raids on Kiel harbour facilities saw Kilian remain unscathed. On 9 April 1945, however, a massive bombing raid, which sank the pocket battleship *Admiral Scheer*, saw the protective doors of the bunker blown off by a near miss. Inside the bunker at this time were two U-boats, U-170 (not a new boat, but being used as a test-bed) and U-4708. So great was the pressure wave from the bomb blast that the small Type XXIII U-4708 was lifted into the air and smashed against the side of the pen causing such damage that it sank almost immediately. The larger and more robust U-170 escaped destruction. The concrete structure of the bunker remained intact and survived the war. The last few U-boats resident within were scuttled or blown up at the end of the war.

Konrad

This bunker was in fact a conversion of an existing facility, namely the Dry Dock III of the Deutsche-Werke construction yard. Work commenced in April 1943, the intention being to provide shelter for boats undergoing minor repair or fitting-out work. During construction, the decision was made to change this to a production facility. Bombing raids slowed construction, which was not completed until October 1944. Work on this bunker was shared by a number of contractors including Wayss & Freytag AG, Habermann & Guckes AG, Holzverartbeitung GmbH and G. Tesch of Berlin.

The bunker was just over 162m in length, 35m in width and 13m in height. It was used to facilitate the construction of Seehund mini-submarines and also modular sections of the Type XXI. Subsequent bombing raids after the completion of the facility did little damage and the bunker survived the war intact.

BREMEN

Hornisse

Built on the north bank of the River Weser at Bremen, this complex was commissioned in early 1944. It was basically a sheltered construction complex which would be used (together with the much bigger Valentin bunker) to build the revolutionary Type XXI U-boat. The Type XXI's design integrated modular sections so that the construction work could be distributed to suitable sites throughout Germany, sometimes far inland, then transported to assembly points at various shipyards for completion, launch and fitting out. A Type XXI could be built in about 176 days, about half the time it took to put together a Type VII or Type IX. The bunker was to be erected on land belonging to the Deschimar firm in Bremen on which an assembly yard had already been established. The bunker would simply protect this facility with a reinforced concrete shell. The construction contract was awarded to the Hamburg firm of Wayss & Freytag.

In the eastern end of the bunker, which lay on a virtual east–west axis, an assembly line for the production of sectional modules was planned, whilst the centre section of the complex was to consist of two dry-dock pens for repair work. These pens would be connected to the westernmost section that consisted of two wet pens (but capable of being pumped out for dry-dock work) each capable of housing two Type XXIs. The pen areas were connected to each other, and to the exterior, by lock gates.

A heavy bombing raid by the USAAF on 30 March 1945 destroyed much of the construction, which was never completed.

Valentin

Plans were first made in 1943 for the erection of a protected assembly facility on the banks of the River Weser at Farge near Bremen. This was to be a custom-built facility for the assembly of the Type XXI U-boat (see above). One of the principal reasons why this excellent submarine could not be brought into service soon enough to influence the war at sea was the interruption to the building programme caused by Allied air raids – hence the decision to build this massive, reinforced concrete protected facility. The facility was a virtual assembly line: the partially assembled boats moved through various stages until, finally finished, they were lowered into a wet pen and sailed out into the River Weser from the bunker.

The Type XXI consisted of eight hull sections, numbered from stern to bow, plus the conning tower. Main assembly points for this submarine were at the Blohm & Voss yard at Hamburg, Schichau in Danzig and at Deschimar AG Weser in Bremen, with Blohm & Voss producing the greatest number. As soon as the Allies became aware that this revolutionary new boat was being assembled at Blohm & Voss, the yard came under persistent attack by Allied bombers and suffered serious damage. Valentin, had it reached completion, would have been a valuable asset.

Over 12,000 workers were employed in the construction of this gigantic bunker, of which around one third were foreign, and over 2,500 were either prisoner-of-war forced labourers or concentration camp inmates. It is estimated that at least 4,000 died during the construction work on this bunker. Work ceased on 7 April 1945, at which point the bunker was around 90 per cent complete.

Allied bombing raids in late March 1945 succeeded in penetrating the partially completed structure with Tallboy bombs, but little damage was caused to the interior. There were only two major air raids, one on 27 March 1945 by the USAAF and one on 30 March by the RAF. The latter saw 15 Tallboys dropped, of which six were direct hits.

SPECIALIST FORTIFICATIONS – PROTECTING THE U-BOATS AND V-WEAPONS

TYPE XXI U-BOAT CONSTRUCTION, VALENTIN, BREMEN

The 13-stage assembly process would have begun in the south-west corner of the complex (A), where stages 1 to 3 would see the keel being laid and the partially completed hull modules welded together. Moving on 30-ton trolleys, each unit would be shifted northwards right to the opposite end of the bunker, where it would then be traversed into the central section (B) and moved back along the bunker. Here, during stages 4 to 8, the welding work would be completed, machinery installed, the tanks tested and the conning tower added.

On reaching the far end of the bunker, the boat would undergo stages 9 and 10 where its batteries, periscopes and schnorkel tube would be fitted: the periscopes were lowered into place using a 5-ton overhead crane (C). The roof of the bunker was higher at this point to allow for the extreme length of the periscope. The boat then reversed direction again, and moved towards the bunker exit. Through stages 11 and 12 the final fitting out was done, the antennae installed. Then (stage 13) the boat moved sideways into the flooded end chamber and into water some 9m deep, where it was tested to ensure it was watertight and fuel and oil taken on. The completed boat would then be moved out into the River Weser. The seaward entrance/exit was protected by lock gates. The rear area (D), as in most bunkers, was given over to workshops, stores and similar units. (Ian Palmer © Osprey Publishing)

BERGEN

Bruno

Shortly after the invasion of Norway in 1940, the Kriegsmarine established naval bases at several ports, Bergen being one of the most important. In May 1942 work commenced on the construction of a U-boat bunker at the Norwegian port. The bunker was built on a rocky outcrop in a small bay to the west of the town.

The bunker was planned to consist of ten pens, three of which would be wet and six dry. The tenth would be used for fuel storage. In the event, just seven pens were constructed: one of these was used for fuel storage, and of the remaining six, three were wet and three dry. The roof was up to 6m thick in places and the walls up to 4m thick. A further mezzanine level was built above the main bunker to provide additional storage space. This also had the beneficial effect of enhancing the level of protection against air attack for the bunker interior. The overall size of the Bruno bunker was 130m by 143m.

Unusually for such construction projects outside Germany, responsibility was not in the hands of the OT. Instead a commercial construction firm, Wayss & Freytag AG, which had also worked on similar projects within Germany, was the main contractor. Each of the three wet pens, on the north side of the bunker, was 11m wide, and the dry pens 17m wide. Their entrances were protected by 3cm-thick steel doors formed by hanging, overlapping plates.

The western face of the Valentin bunker. On the left is the entrance through which component sub-assemblies could be brought by barge and through which the completed Type XXI would exit into the River Weser. Since the end of the war, the entrance has been blocked off and the embankment built up alongside this west face. Although the opening is closed off by a wire-mesh screen, it is still possible to see into the interior of the complex. (Gordon Williamson)

SPECIALIST FORTIFICATIONS – PROTECTING THE U-BOATS AND V-WEAPONS

The base was to be the home of 11. Unterseebootsflotille for most of the war and following the Allied invasion of Normandy took on an even greater strategic importance as the French bases were, one by one, closed down and abandoned. Work to enlarge and improve the bunker continued throughout the war. As the importance of the Bergen U-boat base grew, so did the Allied determination to destroy it. The first major bombing raid, comprising over 130 RAF bombers, took place on 4 October 1944. Although the RAF raid caused widespread destruction to the surrounding area and serious civilian casualties, its effect on the bunkers was minimal. Direct hits were achieved, but none succeeded in penetrating the thick, reinforced concrete shell.

The interior of the Bruno bunker in Bergen. The U-boats of the Kriegsmarine have been replaced by the submarines of the Royal Norwegian Navy. (Photo courtesy Hans Lauritzen)

HITLER'S FORTRESSES

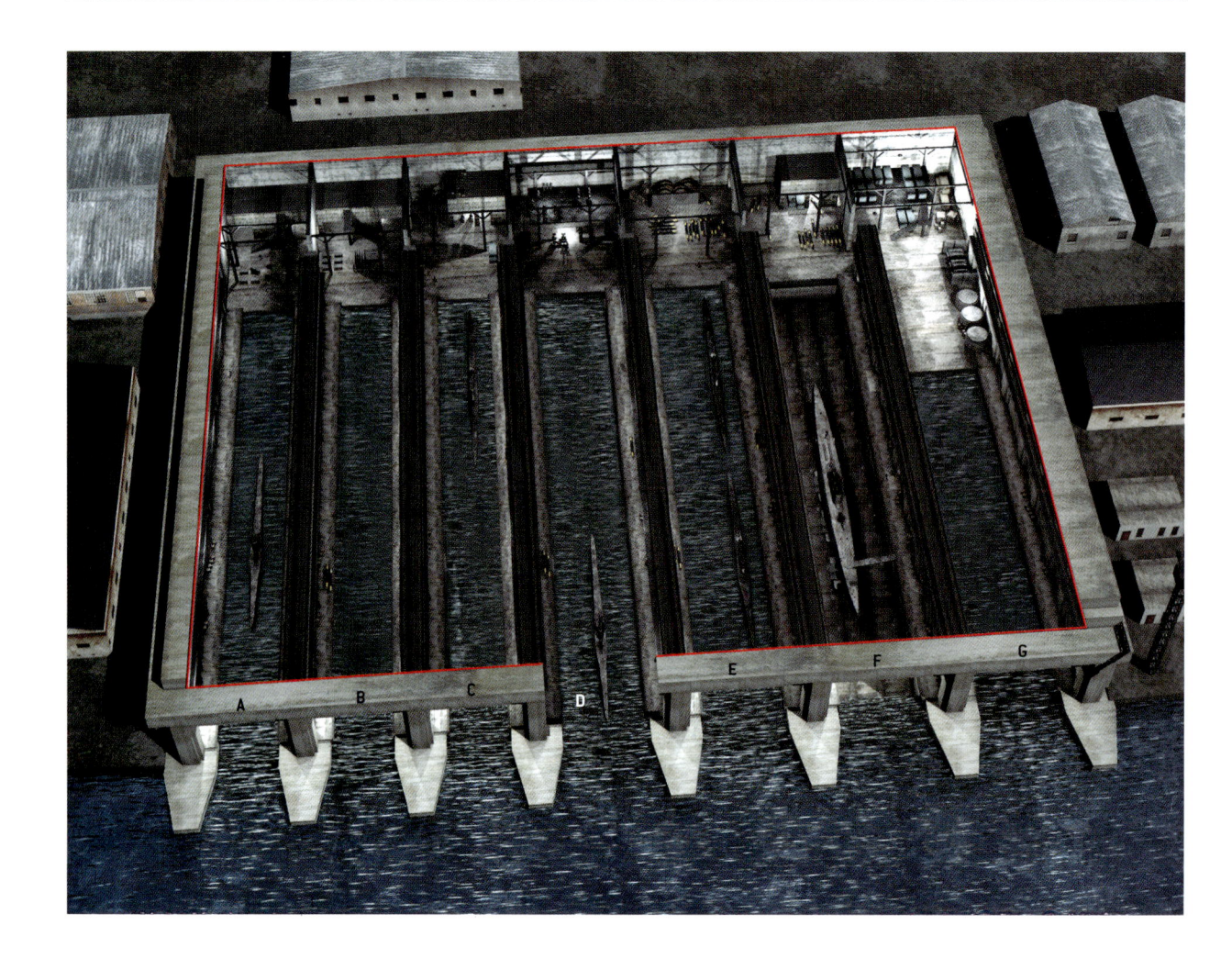

ABOVE: The Bruno bunker at Bergen was originally intended to comprise a total of ten pens but in the event only seven were constructed. Of these, six (A–F) were used to accommodate U-Boats, whilst the seventh (G) was used for fuel storage. The complex covered an area of around 18,600m^2 and was protected by a roof almost 4m thick. Although entrances to the three dry-dock pens (D, E and F) were protected by vertical, overlapping steel plates, the wet pens (A, B and C) were open to the harbour. (Ian Palmer © Osprey Publishing)

A further attack on 29 October saw almost 250 RAF aircraft involved, though fewer than 50 eventually found and bombed the target. Not one German casualty was inflicted though once again there was considerable loss of civilian life. No damage was suffered by the bunker interior, all of the blast effect being dissipated in the space between the outer and inner roof levels. A third and final raid on 12 January 1945 was launched by 32 RAF bombers carrying Tallboy bombs. The bunkers at Bergen survived the war intact.

TRONDHEIM

Dora I

The U-boat bunker at Trondheim was the first to be constructed in Norway. It was a relatively small structure, measuring some 153m in length and 111m in width, with just five pens. Of these, three were 15m in width, had dry-dock capabilities and could accommodate just one boat each; two were 21m-wide wet pens, and each of these could accommodate two boats. The main purpose of the bunker was to provide repair facilities for 13. Unterseebootsflotille. Air raid protection was provided by three 2cm Flak installations on the bunker roof.

As with most bunkers outside Germany, construction was overseen by the OT, and specifically by the OT-Einsatzgruppe Wiking. The principal contractor was the Munich firm of Sager & Wörner. Orders for construction of the bunker were issued at the start

The Dora I bunker in May 1945. Tied up alongside the quay are U-861 and U-995. (Gordon Williamson)

of 1941 and it took fully 27 months to complete the work. Several thousand workers were involved, including around 800 Soviet prisoners of war used as forced labour. Only one major air raid, on 24 July 1943, was suffered by the Dora I bunker: a subsequent raid launched on 22 November 1944, comprising over 170 RAF bombers, was abandoned due to poor visibility over the target area. Dora I survived the war intact.

Dora II

Almost as soon as work on Dora I had commenced, it was realized that a greater capacity would be required and planning began for a new bunker (Dora II) in the same harbour and just 140m away. Dora II was to have four additional pens, two 13.5m-wide wet and two 20m-wide dry, thus allowing for the accommodation of a further six boats.

Immediately behind the dry pens was the boiler room, and behind the wet pens a storage space. Running the full width of the bunker behind these would be all of the electrical gear for the bunker, and further to the rear were workshops for repairing the boats' battery cells and torpedo storage areas. Unfortunately, the demand for skilled workers by the huge bunkers being constructed in France meant that the small

The interior of the U-boat bunker at Trondheim. Note the corrugated metal shuttering on the ceiling. As shown here, most of the wet pens were capable of accommodating two boats. (Gordon Williamson)

workforce available for the second bunker at Trondheim made slow progress, and the structure was only 60 per cent complete when the war ended. A third bunker, Dora III, was also planned at Leangen, just to the east of Trondheim, but the project was cancelled before any serious construction work had been done.

BREST

Almost as soon as construction work on the pens began in January 1941, the site was subjected to Allied air raids. In the spring of 1943, work began on strengthening the roof of the bunker. Ultimately the roof had a thickness in excess of 6m, and a layer of concrete beams was laid across the roof some 3.8m above its surface (the Fangrost concept): these beams were around 1.5m high and spaced about the same distance apart.

Continued air raids caused very little damage to the bunkers and cost the Allies dearly in lost aircraft. Air defence for the bunker itself was provided by three 4cm Flak guns in concrete emplacements and controlled by their own radar equipment. Eventually, however, a series of Tallboy raids in early August 1944 was launched against the Brest U-boat bunkers. A total of nine direct hits were scored from 26 bombs dropped. Of these five actually penetrated the roof, but caused little or no damage to the interior and none whatsoever to the U-boats inside.

Throughout the war the U-boat bunker at Brest suffered more enemy air raids than any other base. Over 80 large-scale raids were launched between 1941 and 1945, and of these 11 were the so-called 'hundred-bomber raids' with up to 154 aircraft taking part. Around 50 aircraft were either shot down in these raids, or so badly damaged that they were destroyed on landing.

The rapid progress being made by Allied troops following the Normandy landings in June 1944 saw the U-boat bunker at Brest under serious threat. The last U-boat to depart from the bunker was U-256, under the command of Korvettenkapitän Heinrich Lehmann-Willenbrock, which left on 4 September. Lehmann-Willenbrock was the real-life commander of U-96, upon which the fictional film *Das Boot* was based.

US forces finally captured the port on 21 September 1944 after four weeks of extremely bitter fighting. The US Army suffered over 10,000 casualties in this battle by the end of which the port itself had been almost totally destroyed – except for the U-boat bunker, which remained intact.

LORIENT

The port of Lorient fell to the German Army on 21 June 1940, and just 16 days later the first U-boat (U-30 under Kapitänleutnant Fritz-Julius Lemp) docked at the port for

KEROMAN I, II AND III, LORIENT

The largest and most impressive of all complexes was the one at Lorient. This illustration shows the entire complex. At the former fishing-boat repair site (1) boats would be pulled up the ramp by winch onto the central turntable unit (2), which would then rotate to send the boat on its cradle towards one of the 'Dom' bunkers shown around the central turntable (3 and 4). At bottom right is the Keroman III bunker (A), a large unit with seven pens opening out into the River Le Ter. In the lower left of the illustration is the original Keroman I bunker (B): note the pen opening into the Le Ter (5). This entrance led to the ramp (6) that gave access to the upper-level Keroman II bunker (C), protected by a lock gate. The pen interior would be drained and the boat lowered by an overhead crane onto a special cradle on a wheeled trolley. It would then be winched up the 160m-long slope and onto the traversing unit (7) running between Keroman I and Keroman II. This unit was 48m long and 13m wide and ran along an eight-rail track. In addition to the entrance pen, Keroman I (B) had a total of five dry repair pens. Directly opposite, in Keroman II (C), there were a further seven repair pens. The traversing unit allowed the boat to be lined up with any of the repair pens and winched along a four-rail track into the appropriate pen. It would normally take around two hours for a boat to be taken out of the water, winched up the slope and received into one of the repair pens. The traverser units themselves were stored in a separate pen alongside Keroman II (8). An extension to Keroman II (Keroman IVb) and an extension to Keroman I (Keroman IVa) are shown under construction (9), though neither was ever completed: the resources were channelled into the construction of Keroman III instead. (Ian Palmer © Osprey Publishing)

SPECIALIST FORTIFICATIONS – PROTECTING THE U-BOATS AND V-WEAPONS

resupply. Lorient soon became one of the Kriegsmarine's most vital U-boat bases. The base eventually housed two flotillas, 2. Unterseebootsflotille 'Salzwedel' and 10. Unterseebootsflotille.

The first facility provided for U-boats was a winching system for pulling smaller vessels out of the water for inspection and repair. This was based around a smaller pre-existing facility for fishing boats on the Keroman peninsula, which was upgraded and enlarged. Here fishing boats were winched up a ramp onto a turntable, which could then direct them onto one of six sets of stocks. Due to both the limited capacity of the winching mechanisms and the size of the bunkers, these were used only for smaller U-boats.

The next major improvement was the building of the two so-called Dombunker or 'cathedral bunkers', also at Keroman: they acquired their name because of their high, arched roofs. These small bunkers were built at the fishing-boat repair facility, immediately to the east of the main complex, over the two southernmost positions. Built by the firm of Carl Brand of Düren, each bunker was 81m long, 16m wide and 25m high and had walls some 1.5m thick. U-boats could be winched on trolleys directly from the water and along into these dry bunkers. They were nowhere near as well protected as the main bunker complex: they were intended to provide U-boats undergoing repair and maintenance some measure of protection from shrapnel and the like. They were strong, but would not have been able to withstand a direct hit from a Tallboy as the main bunkers did on several occasions.

In April 1941, a more conventional-style U-boat bunker was also built further up the River Scorff, on the eastern bank across from the existing port dry-dock facilities. Known as the 'Scorff bunker' for obvious reasons, this structure consisted of two pens just over 100m long with workshop and repair facilities to the rear of the structure. The overall length of the bunker was 128m.

Surveyors meantime had been searching for a suitable location for the creation of a larger bunker complex. Once again the Keroman peninsula was chosen, and an area extending to around 20 hectares was taken over by the Kriegsmarine. Work on the first bunker, subsequently known as Keroman I, began in 1941 with over 15,000 workers being employed in construction.

A rather ingenious design was created for this particular complex. The bunker consisted of a well-protected, enclosed wet bunker with five pens. On the east side of the bunker was an enclosed berth, the floor of which was sloped. Sitting on this ramp was a 45m-long cradle into which the boat sailed. The water in this berth would then be pumped out, effectively lowering the boat into the cradle which sat on a wheeled trolley, with the aid of an overhead crane. The trolley was then winched up a 160m sloped slipway: at the top, the cradle was moved from the trolley onto a similarly

Another of Lorient's interesting structures was the turntable fitting at the top of the old fishing-boat repair ramp. This was strengthened and improved to handle small Type II coastal U-boats. Here a Type II, partially covered by tarpaulins, has been winched up out of the water and into one of the repair areas. However, these boats were dangerously exposed to enemy attack. (Gordon Williamson)

designed 48m-long traversing unit. This unit moved backwards and forwards along eight sets of rails, running between the two sets of five dry pens, allowing it to be brought perfectly in line with any of the individual pens. The trolley unit was then run off the traverser into the selected pen. The operation to move the submarine from Keroman I across exposed open space into the safe bunkers of Keroman II took between one and two hours from start to finish. The unique equipment was manufactured by the M.A.N. (Maschinenfabrik Augsburg-Nürnberg) firm, and this amazing system was so well built that it is still fully functional today.

The pens in Keroman I were 120m long, 85m wide and 18.5m in height, with 2.4m-thick walls and a roof over 3m thick. Each pen was provided with a travelling crane. Keroman I was completed in September 1941. At the same time, work was under way on a further bunker complex, known as Keroman II, directly in line with the existing complex at the top of the slope. This contained a further seven dry pens, each 138m long, 120m wide and 18.5m in height. Each pen in Keroman II was provided with two travelling cranes. An eighth pen was also built but this contained the equipment for the traversing unit.

A third bunker, Keroman III, was begun in October 1941 and completed in January 1943. This provided a further seven pens, all opening out directly into deep water and capable of being used for both wet and dry docking. The pens were 170m long, 135m wide and 20m in height and each was provided with a travelling crane. The concrete roof was over 7m thick. A further bunker complex, Keroman IV, was planned to provide facilities for the new Type XXI submarines, but due to Germany's wartime reversals, this project was not carried through.

In addition to the bunker complex proper, the entire Lorient base was liberally peppered with smaller bunkers, including a complex of six torpedo storage bunkers to the north-west of the Keroman complex, linked to the base by a narrow-gauge track. The Lorient base was also heavily defended by a huge range of anti-aircraft artillery ranging from light 2cm Flak guns, of which there were over 200, through medium 7.5cm and 8.8cm pieces, up to heavy 10.5cm and 12.8cm Flak guns.

The bunker complexes at Lorient were bombed on numerous occasions but no serious damage was ever inflicted. A total of 33 significant air raids on the bunkers were recorded, though only one of these, on 17 May 1943, involved over 100 aircraft. At least 60 enemy aircraft were either shot down or seriously damaged during these raids. Additional protection against low-level attack by enemy aircraft was provided by mooring two elderly ships directly in front of the bunkers: they had particularly tall masts and barrage balloons tethered to their superstructure. Despite the Allied advances through France, the German garrison at Lorient held out right until the end of the war. The last U-boat to leave, U-155, departed on 5 September 1944, with two other boats, the severely damaged U-123 and U-129, left behind. The port finally surrendered to US Army troops on 10 May 1945, two days after VE-Day.

HITLER'S FORTRESSES

This photo shows a Type IX U-boat being winched up in its special cradle onto dry land from the docking pen at Keroman I at Lorient. This pen was not a working area as such, and therefore had only a very narrow walkway along one side. (Gordon Williamson)

ST NAZAIRE

The port of St Nazaire fell to German forces in the summer of 1940. Work on constructing the U-boat bunkers began in March 1941 in the southern basin of the harbour. The first four of an eventual total of 14 pens were ready for use by July 1941 whilst work continued on the remainder of the structure. The first five pens were some 130m long and 18m high. Each was 14m wide with a dividing wall between each pen 1.25m to 1.5m thick. Separating Pen 1 from the north-side exterior was a 22m-wide storage space area, running the full length of the pen. Between pens 5 and 6 was a storage area running the length of the pen and some 8m wide. Pens 6 to 8 were identical to the first five. Then followed pens 9 to 12, shorter than the previous pens at just 124m in length, but wider at 20m and separated by dividing walls 1.25m thick. A further spaced area some 8m wide separated Pen 12 from pens 13 and 14 which once again were 20m wide.

To the rear of the bunker complex, immediately behind each pen, were a number of workshop areas, each the same width as the pen. On the north and south side walls of the complex, in line with the rear of the pens, was a 5m-wide entrance door leading to a corridor running the full width of the complex. Overall the bunker complex was 295m wide. Six of the pens were wet whilst the others were capable of being pumped out and used for dry-docking. Its first resident U-boat flotilla, 7. Unterseebootsflotille 'Wegener', arrived in June 1941. In February 1942, the Wegener flotilla was joined at St Nazaire by 6. Unterseebootsflotille 'Hundius'.

In mid-1943 the OT began work on reinforcing the bunker roof, adding almost 4m to its thickness. Originally, U-boats had to first enter the main (north) basin via the Normandie dock, and then pass through a smaller lock into the southern basin. The British commando attack in March 1942, when the explosive-laden destroyer HMS *Campbeltown* was rammed into the gate of the dock and detonated, highlighted the vulnerability of the system. Accordingly, a new lock was built directly opposite the entrance to the bunkers, giving direct access to open water and protected by a concrete bunker.

The bunkers proved themselves during numerous Allied air raids, with no loss or damage suffered by any U-boat inside – despite the almost total destruction of the town. In all, 30 major raids were recorded on the St Nazaire bunkers, three in particular being extremely heavy. On 28 February 1943, more than 430 RAF bombers pounded the port. This was followed on 22 March by another raid involving more than 350 aircraft, with another one on 28 March of over 320 aircraft. A total of 58 enemy aircraft are recorded as having been lost during these raids.

Following D-Day, the U-boats based at St Nazaire were withdrawn to Norway, the last of this batch (U-267) departing on 23 September 1944. The base, though,

HITLER'S FORTRESSES

The side wall of the St Nazaire bunker. The figure to the bottom right gives some idea of the sheer size of this amazing structure. Like most of the French bunkers, it is in surprisingly good condition. (Chris Boonzaier)

was rigorously defended, having been declared by Hitler to be a 'fortress'. Troops under the command of Generalleutnant Werner Junck resisted all Allied attempts to take the port until the very last day of the war. During this period however, numerous U-boats made the trip to St Nazaire carrying essential supplies: as late as February 1945, U-275 docked for repairs to its Schnorkel equipment. The very last boat to leave was U-255, which had been languishing at St Nazaire for some time awaiting repairs. Following the arrival in the autumn of 1944 of a seaplane carrying spare parts, repair work was carried out and U-255 eventually left St Nazaire on 8 May 1945, just in time to surrender to the Allies.

The last boat to put in to St Nazaire was U-510, which arrived at the end of a long voyage from the Far East on 23 April 1945. It was still there when the Allies finally took over the port, and was in such good order that it was taken into the French Navy where it served as the *Bouan*.

LA PALLICE

This base, often erroneously referred to as La Rochelle, fell to German forces in 1940, but did not become a major U-boat operational base until the autumn of 1941. Initially, it was used by the submarines of the Italian Navy, but in the spring of 1941 it was decided that a new U-boat base would be built on the eastern side of the main basin of this port. Construction of the bunker began in April 1941 and on 27 October of that year, following the completion of the first two pens, it became home to 3. Unterseebootsflotille Lohs. The first U-boats arrived within three weeks.

Around 490 OT personnel were involved in the construction of this bunker, overseeing 1,800 forced labourers. The bunker complex was to consist of ten pens. The first two to be completed were wet pens, 92.5m in length and 17m in width, allowing each to accommodate two boats. Pens 3 to 7 were dry-dock capable, also 92.5m in length but just 11m wide, each able to accommodating a single boat. Pens 8 and 9 were also dry-dock capable but slightly longer at 100m. Pen 10, also intended to function as a dry dock, was never fully completed. It was to be 17m wide and could accommodate two boats.

The quays separating each pen were between 4.25m and 5m wide with a dividing wall running down the centre of each. The exception to this was the space between pens 7 and 8, which consisted of a 15m-wide quay running all the way through the bunker complex and extending out into the basin as a 200m-long mole. This mole also carried twin railway lines.

Overall, the complex measured 195m by 165m and was 14m high. The roof thickness over pens 1 to 5 was in excess of 7m. Work was still ongoing to increase the existing

The Bordeaux bunker complex today, still in remarkably good condition. The remains of the painted numbers above each pen are still visible. (Gordon Williamson)

6.5m-thick roof over the remaining pens and to install bomb traps when the worsening war situation brought this to a halt. On the exterior, at the north-eastern corner of the rear of the bunker, was a 30m-wide and 50m-long concrete structure, some 25m high: this contained a generating station for the bunker. Against the southern side wall of the bunker by the side entrance door was an oil storage bunker.

The bunker suffered much less from the attentions of enemy bombers than some of its counterparts, only eight major raids being launched against it, none of which did any serious damage to the pens. Anti-aircraft defences on the bunker complex consisted of three concrete emplacements for 2cm light Flak guns. In addition to the U-boat bunker complex, numerous other subsidiary bunkers were constructed, including three large torpedo storage bunkers around a kilometre to the north-east of the U-boat bunker complex. A command bunker and a small bunker housing the electricity transformer were located to the west of these storage bunkers. Also, a large bunker-type construction was built over the lock that allowed entrance into the basin where the U-boat bunker complex was located.

As with the other French bases, its usefulness decreased after 6 June 1944 and its boats were dispersed to other bases, primarily in Norway. This base, too, was declared a 'fortress' and its garrison held out until 8 May 1945. A Type VIIC U-boat (U-766) was still in residence when the base finally surrendered, and was taken into the French Navy as the *Laubie*.

BORDEAUX

The port at Bordeaux became an operational Axis naval base in the autumn of 1940 when it became home to the Italian Navy's submarine flotilla Betasom, whose operational success was, it must be said, somewhat limited. Admiral Dönitz decided in mid-1941 to erect a protective U-boat bunker in the port's Number 2 basin, entered first through a lock from the River Gironde into the Number 1 basin, then through a further lock between the two.

The U-boat bunker comprised 11 pens. Pens 1 to 4 were wet pens 105m long and 20m wide, capable of accommodating two boats each. Pens 5 to 8 were also 105m long, but just 14m wide, designed to accommodate one boat each. Pens 9 to 11 were dry-dock capable, and were 95m long and 11m wide. Overall, the complex was 245m wide, 162m long, and 19m high, with roofing just under 6m thick. At the north-east corner of the structure was a 58m-wide and 73m-long concrete blockhouse containing the bunker boiler room and electrical equipment.

This base primarily served the larger Type IX boats used for long-distance cruises, as well as the Type XIV 'Milk Cows' and the Type XB minelayers. Bordeaux became the home base for 12. Unterseebootsflotille, which also took over the remaining Italian submarines after Italy's surrender. All but one of these Italian submarines sailed from Bordeaux to the Far East on transport missions, some eventually being taken over by the Imperial Japanese Navy – thus having served three different masters.

Earlier in the war, Bordeaux was also visited by Japanese submarines, which successfully made the long journey from Japan to occupied Europe. As with all the French bases, Bordeaux came under attack by Allied bombers. However, the port suffered only seven major air raids from 1940 through to mid-1944: two larger bombing raids in August 1944 saw the bunkers suffer little or no serious damage. The base was finally abandoned in late-August 1944 and was occupied by Free French Forces on the 26th of that month, the last few U-boats having put to sea just two days earlier.

V-WEAPON SITES

The A-4 missile programme – what would become the V-2 – was officially initiated in 1936. By the summer of 1942, the German Army sought Hitler's approval to begin preparing for the mass-production of the A-4, a major issue due to the enormous cost of the programme, which was also likely to have an impact upon German aircraft production, while engineers began discussions about possible launch configurations for the weapon. From a strictly technical standpoint, a fixed site was preferred for many reasons. To begin with, the A-4 missile was extremely complicated, requiring a substantial amount of test equipment to monitor the missile subsystems prior to launch. In addition, the A-4 used liquid oxygen (LOX) as the oxidizer for its fuel, and this chemical had to be maintained at super-cold temperatures using elaborate refrigeration and insulation techniques that were easier to undertake at a fixed site than at a mobile field site.

Although a fixed site would be more efficient, the missile would have to be launched from locations well within the range of Allied medium bombers, and so any fixed site was likely to be heavily bombed. Such a site could be fortified, but this would add to the expense of the programme. Two different bunker designs were prepared in 1942 including sketches and architectural models. The B.III-2a design envisioned erecting the missile inside the bunker and then towing the launch pad outside the bunker for launch; the B.III-2b design had two openings in the roof which would permit the missiles to be elevated from within the protective confines of the bunker and launched from the roof.

The alternative to fixed basing was mobile basing. This would require a mobile erector system to place the missile vertically on its launch pad, and it would require that

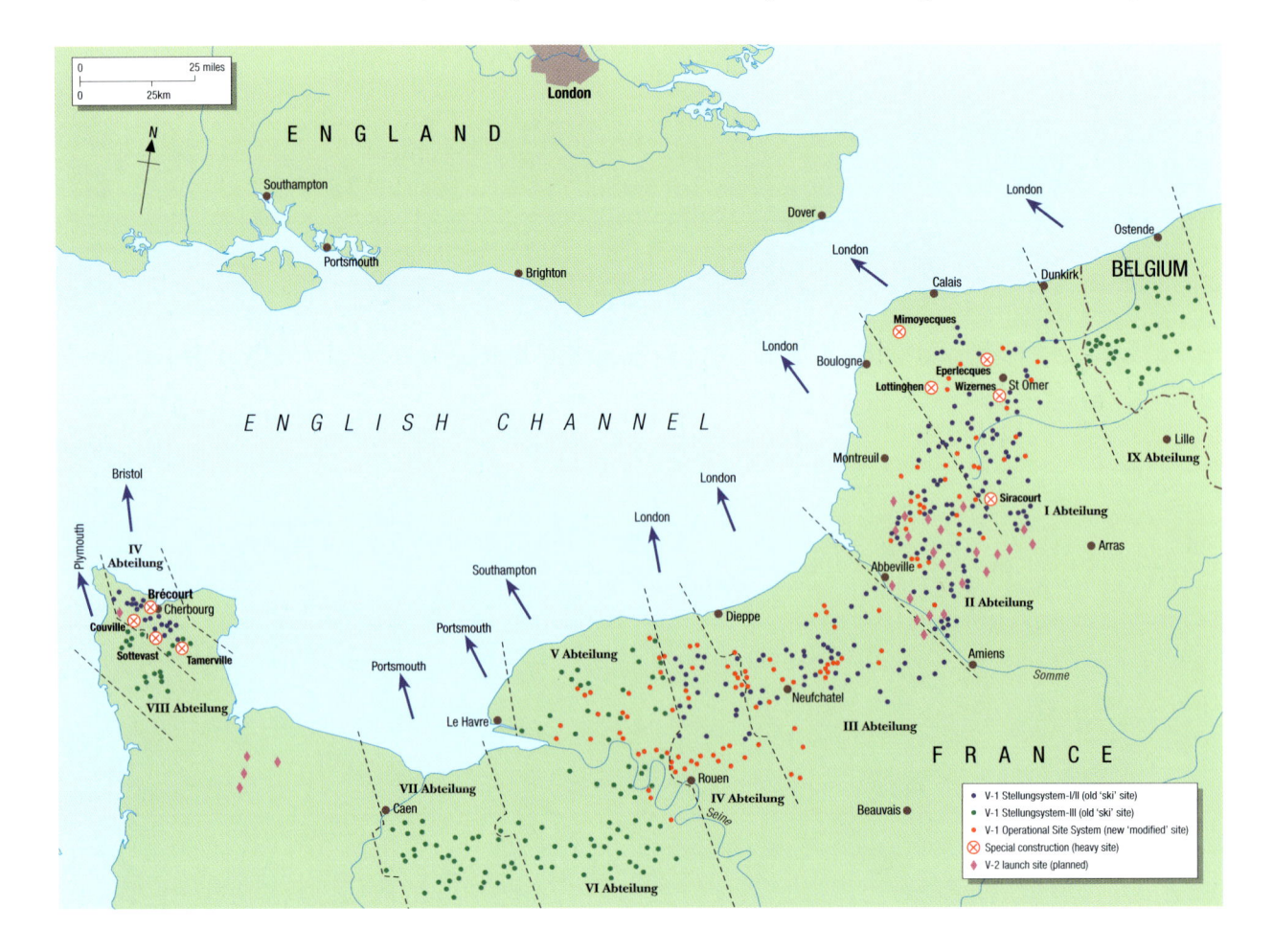

German V-Weapon sites in France 1944.

SPECIALIST FORTIFICATIONS – PROTECTING THE U-BOATS AND V-WEAPONS

all the elaborate testing and fuelling equipment be re-packaged to fit on either railway cars or trucks and trailers to accompany the launcher into the field. While this launch configuration would be less vulnerable to air attack than a fixed site, it would be far less efficient and the rate of fire considerably less.

The head of the A-4 programme, Oberst Walter Dornberger, laid out the various launch options in a study completed in March 1942. The study suggested that fixed sites could be created similar to the U-boat bunkers being built on the French Atlantic coast that would be impervious to aerial attack. However, Army artillery officers favoured a mobile basing system, as they were not convinced that any structure could withstand repeated air attacks and still remain functional. The issue wasn't simply the bunker itself, but the roads and railroad lines leading to the bunker, which would be needed to provide a supply of missiles and fuel. Although a final decision was put in abeyance until the A-4 missile proved viable, initial design work began on a mobile missile launcher in

The Wehrmacht remained torn between mobile and fixed basing for its new secret weapons. The artillery branch, which controlled the V-2 ballistic missile, favoured mobile basing using simple pad launchers like those seen here at Test Stand X at Peenemünde during training exercises for the experimental Batterie 444 in 1944. (MHI)

OPPOSITE: The enormous internal volume of the Kraftwerk Nordwest at Watten is evident from this photo inside one of its cavernous halls. The painting on the wall depicts a full-sized V-2 missile. (Steven J. Zaloga)

early 1942 including both road-mobile and rail-mobile options. Some more exotic launch options were considered, including a submersible launch barge that could be towed behind a U-boat. None of these progressed beyond paper designs.

The problem posed by the need for liquid oxygen for the A-4 led to the first construction effort connected with the V-weapons. In October 1942, a technical mission was sent to northern France and Belgium to inspect potential locations for the creation of two plants capable of producing 1,500 tons of liquid oxygen per month. The sites selected were Tilleur near Liège in Belgium, codenamed WL; and Stenay in the French Ardennes, codenamed WS.

THE KNW LAUNCH BUNKER

The first successful launch of an A-4 Feuerteufel (fire-devil) missile from the Peenemünde test site in October 1942 led to a discussion about the programme between Hitler and armaments minister Albert Speer on 22 November 1942. Hitler was shown models of the proposed launch bunkers as well as details of the proposed mobile launchers. He agreed to a production plan for the missile, but made clear his preference for the bunker launch sites in addition to the Army's preferred mobile launcher option. As a result, Speer met with Dornberger in Berlin on 22 December 1942, to lay out the programme in more detail. Speer instructed that the bunkers be designed to the special fortification standard (Sonderbaustärke) with a 5m-thick steel-reinforced concrete ceiling and 3.5m-thick walls. Each bunker would contain enough missiles for three days of launches, totalling 108 missiles, along with sufficient fuel and liquid oxygen. Each bunker would be manned by 250 troops. Construction of the first bunker somewhere in the Boulogne area would begin as soon as possible and would be followed at the end of June 1943 with a second bunker on the Cotentin Peninsula in France opposite southern England. The OT would undertake construction. Supervision of the missile construction programme was undertaken by director-general of the OT, Xaver Dorsch, due to the high priority afforded the programme by Hitler.

The survey of potential launch sites began in the final days of December 1942. The team concentrated on sites in the Artois region of France and finally settled on a site near the town of Watten, since the area was easily accessible by rail and canal, there was a good local electrical power-grid, and there were several forested sites that appeared suitable for construction while at the same time being remote enough to prevent the local French villagers from observing the work. The first bunker was given the cover-name KNW (Kraftwerk Nordwest: Northwest Electrical Works). Initial plans were completed on 12 February 1943, and it was decided to merge the planned Stenay

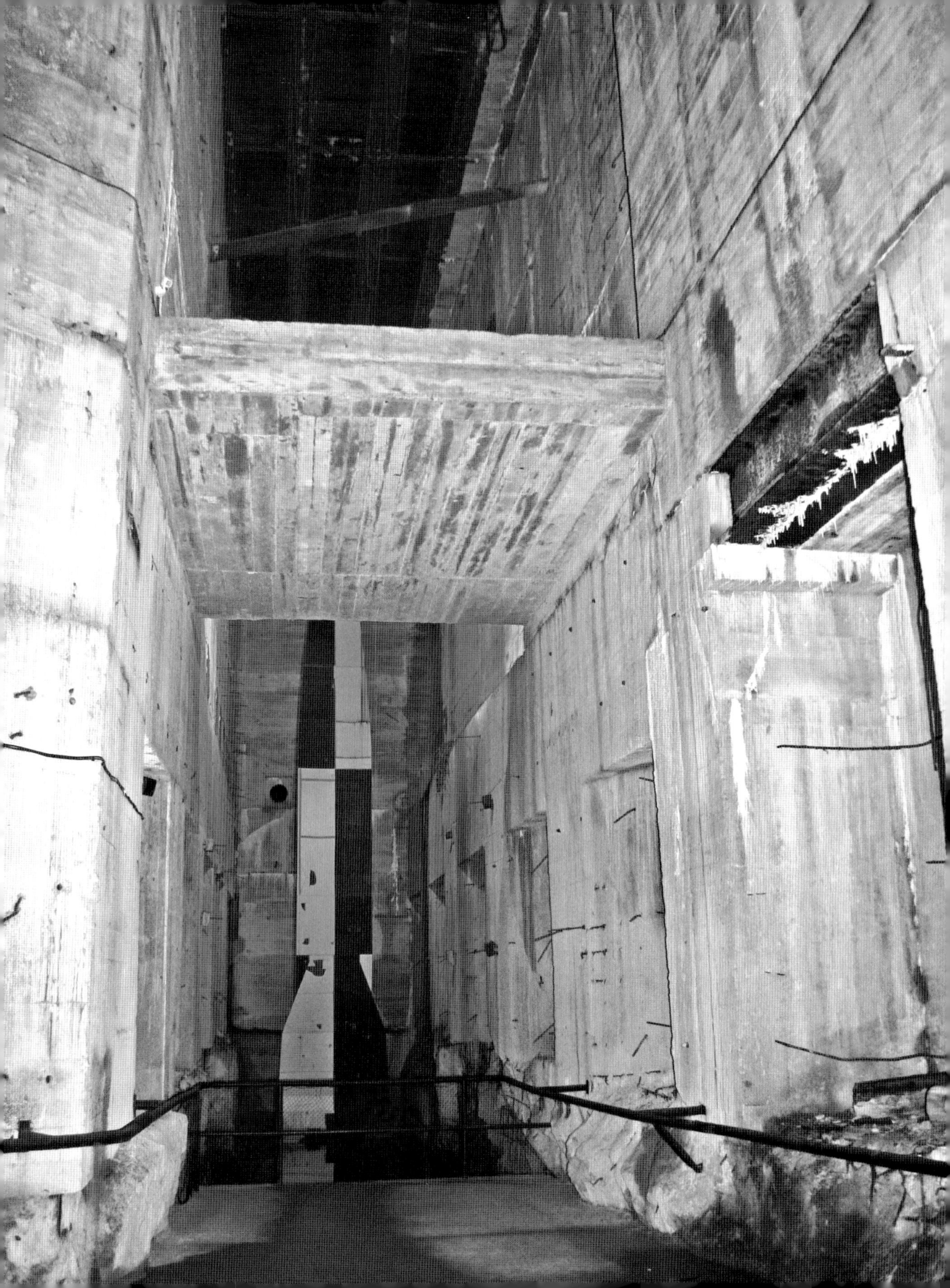

HITLER'S FORTRESSES

Oxygen Plant within the KNW Bunker. This meant enlarging the bunker considerably beyond that envisioned in the preliminary studies, requiring some 120,000m³ of concrete and about 360,000 tonnes of material during the four months of construction. Besides the bunker itself, the plan included a substantial upgrade to the neighbouring railroad lines to permit re-supply once the missile campaign began, and also included preliminary efforts to create supporting sites for stocking missiles and other necessary supplies. The nearby town of Wizernes was selected as the location for the main supply base, codenamed SNW (Schotterwerk Nordwest; Northwest Gravel Works). A limestone quarry in the town was selected since it would permit extensive tunnels to be dug for sheltering the missiles prior to delivery to the launch bunker. Hitler approved the plan on 29 March 1943, with the KNW Bunker scheduled to be ready for combat by 31 December 1943.

This illustration shows a typical V-2 launch site during the critical fuelling process including the:
1. Hanomag SS-100 tractor
2. Opel 3-ton KW Kfz. 385 B-Stoff (alcohol) Kessel-KW.3500 l. tanker
3. SdKfz 7 8-ton half-track armoured fire-control vehicle
4. fuel pump trailer
5. A-Stoff (liquid oxygen) Anhänger 6 insulated trailer
6. Meillerwagen transporter-erector
7. A-4 ballistic missile
8. B-Stoff (alcohol) Kessel-KW.3500 l. trailer
9. Opel Blitz Kessel-KW.2100 l. T-Stoff (hydrogen peroxide) tanker.
(Steven J. Zaloga)

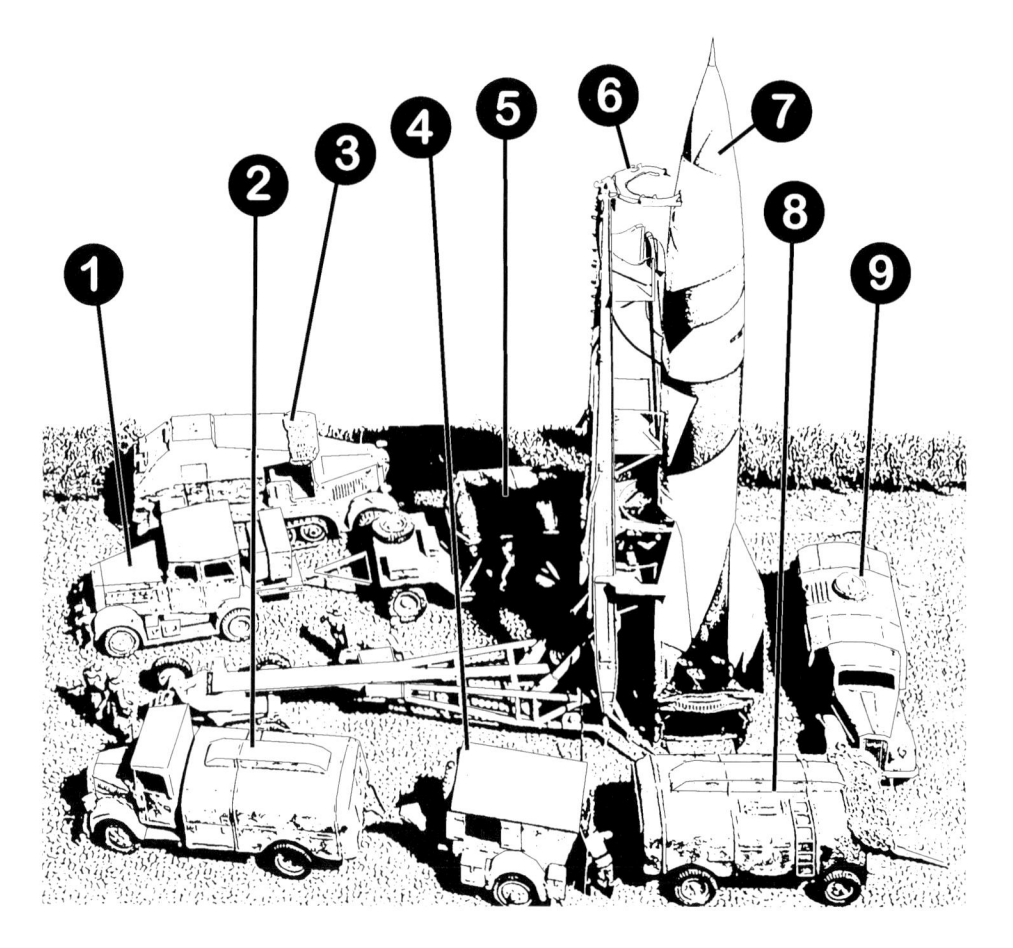

SPECIALIST FORTIFICATIONS – PROTECTING THE U-BOATS AND V-WEAPONS

ABOVE: Wasserwerk No. 2 (Ersatz B8), Brécourt, France. Brécourt was also called Wasserwerk No. 2, as it was planned to use this as the model for a new series of protected launch bunkers from the spring of 1944. Aside from adapting the tunnels, the main work at Brécourt focused on the creation of a pair of heavily protected launch areas, both of which would be fitted with a standard Walther catapult launcher. (Hugh Johnson/Chris Taylor © Osprey Publishing)

THE V-1 WATERWORKS

The FZG-76 (V-1) cruise missile was the last of the V-weapons to receive deployment approval. The launch system for the missile was determined by the engine choice, a simple pulse-jet engine. A Walther steam-catapult system was attractive since it provided more than enough power to get the missile airborne, and also was cheap to operate since it was reusable. On the negative side, it required the use of a very long 49m (160ft) launch rail, which was cumbersome to deploy. The awkward launch rail would prove to be the Achilles heel of the V-1 missile system.

The FZG-76 cruise missile used a Walther steam catapult to get up enough speed for its Argus pulse-jet engine to ignite. This is an early test version of the launch system at the main experimental range at Peenemünde in the autumn of 1943. (NARA)

As was the case with the Army, so too was there a strenuous debate within the Luftwaffe over fixed versus mobile basing. The Luftwaffe's Flak arm was assigned responsibility for the launch sites, and the Flak commander, General der Luftwaffe Walther von Axthelm, wanted the missiles deployed in a large number of small 'light' launch sites that could be easily camouflaged. However, the head of the Luftwaffe production programme, Generalfeldmarschall Erhard Milch, knew that Hitler favoured large launch bunkers, so he argued for this approach. A compromise was finally worked out during a meeting with the head of the Luftwaffe, Hermann Göring, on 18 June 1943, with a plan to create four heavy Wasserwerk (waterworks) launch bunkers along with 96 light installations.

The first of the heavy bunker sites were Wasserwerk Desvres located near Lottinghen and Wasserwerk St Pol located near Siracourt, both in the Artois region of north-eastern France. Another two would follow on the Cotentin Peninsula west of Normandy, Wasserwerk Valognes near Tamerville and Wasserwerk Cherbourg at Couville to the south-east of the port; the eventual goal was ten Wasserwerke. Even though this programme started several months later than the A-4 ballistic missile

SPECIALIST FORTIFICATIONS – PROTECTING THE U-BOATS AND V-WEAPONS

programme, the plan was to have the four Wasserwerke operational at the end of December 1943 to start the missile campaign against London, plus four additional bunkers by March 1944. However, work on the sites was badly delayed by other priorities as OT was stretched thin by its commitments to reinforcing the Atlantic Wall for the expected Allied invasion as well as a major rebuilding effort in Germany after the RAF's 'Battle of the Ruhr' bombing campaign in the autumn of 1943.

THE ALLIES INTERVENE

British intelligence had some significant breakthroughs in discovering the German secret weapons programmes in 1942, and bombing of the sites began in earnest in 1943. Both Peenemünde and the KNW Bunker received punishing blows, and the heavy

The RAF raid on Peenemünde forced the Wehrmacht to abandon plans to mass-produce the V-2 missile there. Instead, the main centre became the underground Mittelwerke tunnel complex in the Harz Mountains near Nordhausen. (NARA)

damage sustained by the KNW Bunker in August and September turned the German leadership's attention to mobile basing. The November 1943 plan therefore envisioned a total of four A-4 battalions along the French coast, each with three batteries. Two battalions would be stationed in Artois near the Pas-de-Calais with 26 launch bases and five guidance bunkers; one battalion with six launch bases and two guidance stations would be completed near Dieppe, and one battalion with nine launch bases and three guidance bunkers near Cherbourg. Two other large bunkers associated with the A-4 ballistic missile were also added, the Reservelager West (RLW; Reserve Store West) near Brix/Sottevast and the Ölkeller Cherbourg (Cherbourg Oil Cellar) near Brécourt. As late as November 1943, the precise role of these two facilities had not been finalized. Sottevast was a large protected bunker, comparable in size to the original Watten design, which could be used for housing one of the mobile missile regiments as well as serve as a store for about 300 missiles, fuel and other supplies. Brécourt included a series of protected tunnels for storing the missiles.

The first Allied air attacks forced changes in the construction plans for the Wasserwerke as well. Instead of creating a bunker in the traditional fashion, a new six-step process called Verbunkerung or Erdschalung would be undertaken to shield the bunker from air attack during construction: the side walls would be created first while protected by an earthen berm, the cavity between the walls filled, the roof poured over a temporary inner earthen core, and then the internal cavity excavated to form the main bunker chamber. Completion of the Wasserwerk 1 design permitted construction to begin in late September 1943. The bunker was essentially a 212m-long protected

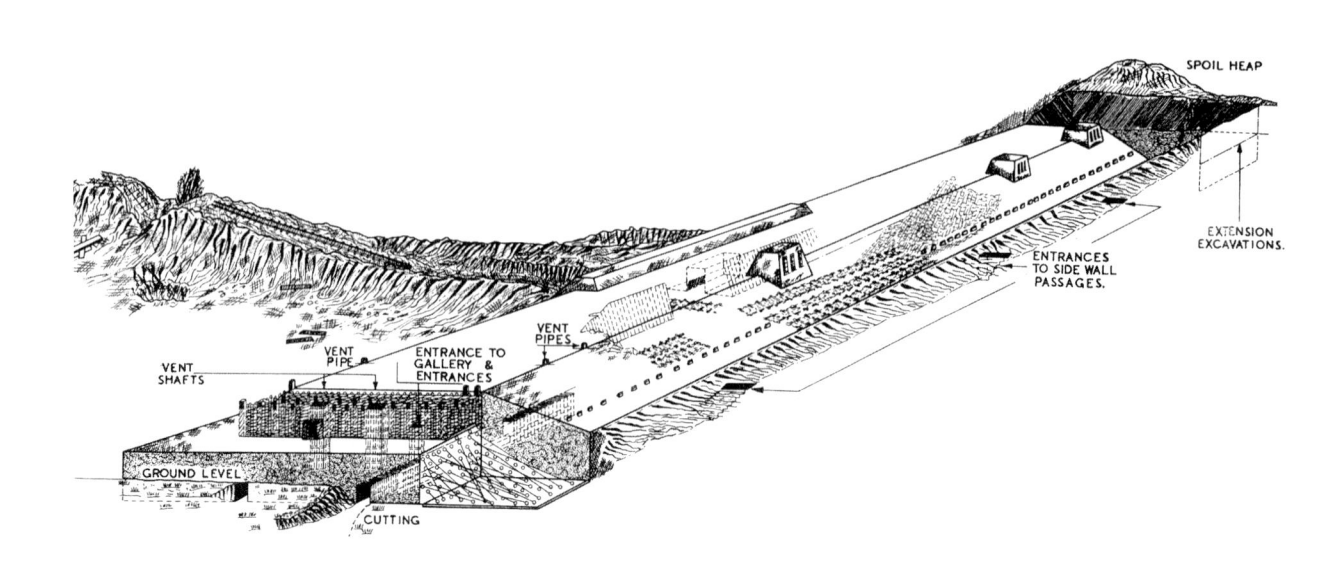

Wasserwerk St Pol near Siracourt was the only one of the first four waterworks to be nearly completed. This drawing from one of the wartime technical intelligence reports shows the state of the building in the summer of 1944. The precise launcher configuration has never been determined; Allied sketches show a single launch ramp as seen here but German accounts indicate that two launch rails were planned. (NARA)

SPECIALIST FORTIFICATIONS – PROTECTING THE U-BOATS AND V-WEAPONS

ABOVE: The chalk quarry outside Wizernes was first selected in 1943 as a supply base for A-4 missile operations on the Pas-de-Calais as it could be easily tunnelled. This facility was originally codenamed SNW (Schotterwerk Nordwest: Northwest Gravel Works). (Hugh Johnson/Chris Taylor © Osprey Publishing)

tunnel. Each Wasserwerk could contain up to 150 FZG-76 cruise missiles along with their associated fuel and support equipment, and this entire inventory could be expended in one or two days depending on the launcher configuration. Although the design was ready, the construction programme for the Wasserwerke came at an inopportune time and the deadline for starting the missile campaign in December 1943 was not met. OT was diverted to reconstruction efforts in Germany as a result of RAF attacks on the Ruhr. The Sonderbauten effort required about 1.83 million cubic metres of concrete, competing with other construction programmes such as the Atlantic Wall. To further undermine the programme, there were significant delays in the mass-production of the missiles after the RAF had bombed the Fieseler plant in Kassel on the night of 22/23 October 1943.

The last of the V-weapons sites to enter construction were the FZG-76 cruise missile 'light' launch sites. Although Generalfeldmarschall Erhard Milch, the head of Luftwaffe production, originally favoured the heavy waterworks, by September 1943 he had changed his mind. He became convinced that a large number of FZG-76 missile sites would inevitably divert the attention of the RAF away from Germany, relieving the pressure on the Luftwaffe, and making the bombers more vulnerable to fighter attack since precision daylight missions would be needed. He dubbed the Sonderbauten effort on the Pas-de-Calais 'the graveyard of the RAF'.

In mid-August 1943, Luftwaffe personnel began to visit locations in the Pas-de-Calais area, informing the local farmers that their property was being requisitioned. In many cases, the farmers were allowed to continue to work their farms, though they were kept away from some areas that were being used for construction. This was the first step in the creation of Stellungsystem-I, the 'light' launch sites for the FZG-76 missile. The plan was to deploy the newly formed Flak Regiment 155(W) in these sites. At the time, FR 155(W) was still training on test launchers at Peenemünde, and it was anticipated that it would have four launch battalions ready by the start of the missile campaign scheduled for December 1943. Each battalion had four launcher batteries with four launchers each, for a total of 64 launch sites under the regiment's control. These 64 launch sites formed Stellungsystem-I and they were located primarily in the Pas-de-Calais region of north-eastern France from Lille through Dieppe. Besides the 64 primary launch sites, steps were also underway to create Stellungsystem-II, with a further 32 sites that were intended to serve as reserve launch locations as well as supply bases, two per launch battery. The last portion to be started was Stellungsystem-III, located south-west of the Seine from Rouen to the Cotentin Peninsula in lower Normandy. Stellungsystem-III was located for attacks on British cities in southern England after London had been destroyed and would be manned by a second regiment, FR 255(W), which was organized in the late spring of 1944.

Construction of Stellungsystem-I began in the late summer and early autumn of 1943 under the direction of the Luftwaffe's Sonder Pionier-Stab Frisch (Special Engineer Staff Frisch) of 15. Armee (AOK 15) in the Pas-de-Calais area and Sonder Pionier-Stab Beger of AOK 7 in the Normandy area. These units supervised the construction work undertaken by OT, though most of the actual labour was subcontracted to French construction firms. Each site centred on a platform for a Walther catapult, protected on either side by a concrete blast wall. Each site included a standard assortment of support buildings, though the layout of the buildings varied from site to site. The layout was intended to facilitate a high missile launch rate. The Walther launch rail could be fired and reloaded in 20-minute intervals so it could launch 72 missiles per day at its maximum rate. This was not entirely realistic since each site had accommodation for only 21 missiles, so a more realistic rate of fire per site was about 20 per day.

Certain of the structures essential for the launch process were located near the launch rail, while other preparation buildings were arranged based on the layout of the terrain, for example placing the long storage building along hedgerows to provide natural camouflage. The missiles arrived at the site, usually by truck, in a partially assembled form on special dollies. The launch battery had to complete the final assembly of the missile, as well as fuel, fuse and arm the missile. Besides the missile-related facilities, most sites also had a few 2cm or 3.7cm Flak guns to protect the site from air attack.

While construction was underway at the launch sites, a parallel programme was in progress to create storage facilities for the missiles in the neighbouring areas. In some cases these were converted from tunnels or other existing structures. The first nine of these were planned for the Pas-de-Calais while the last four were located in Normandy.

As construction of Stellungsystem-I progressed in the autumn of 1943, it increasingly came to the attention of British intelligence, attracted by the distinctive visual profile of the sites from the air. By late November 1943, some 75 sites had been spotted in the Pas-de-Calais area, and seven near Cherbourg. In mid-November, a sub-committee of the JIC was created codenamed 'Crossbow' to coordinate the intelligence collection directed against the German missile programme. As a result, the German missile sites in general were often referred to as 'Crossbow sites', a term that will be used here for convenience.

The first Allied air attacks on the new Crossbow sites began on 5 December 1943, and were only the beginning of a long air campaign against the 'ski sites' (another Allied term for the V-1 launch facilities, so called after the visually distinctive missile storage buildings). Hitler's plan to start the missile campaign on London by the end of December 1943 proved impossible, and in January 1944, the first steps began to devise a new launch system. FR 155(W) had already begun to consider the needs of a minimal launch site without the distinctive buildings such as the 'ski' buildings that disclosed the site's location. The development of the new site system was entrusted to Oberst Schmalschläger. The Luftwaffe decided to continue construction and repairs on the now-battered Stellungsysteme using available French construction firms in order to distract Allied attention from the new sites.

In the spring of 1944, with the Crossbow campaign well underway, Oberst Schmalschläger's team had developed a new simplified site system. The firing sites were configured with an absolute minimum of permanent structures. Basic pilings for the launch ramp, a flat platform for the steam generator trolley, and a foundation for the non-magnetic guidance shed were made from concrete. The new sites were generally

HITLER'S FORTRESSES

The Walther catapult for the FZG-76 was eventually configured as a modular unit to make it easier to assemble in the field. This is a partial launcher preserved at the Eperlecques Museum near the Watten Bunker, which can be seen in the background. This launcher is missing the distinctive blast deflector found at the end of the catapult. (Steven J. Zaloga)

positioned near French farms where the existing buildings could be used for crew accommodation and storage. Certain of the specialized buildings such as the navigation correction building used prefabricated wooden sheds instead of concrete structures. The distinctive ski buildings were not used and missiles were either stored in available buildings or left under camouflage nets. When time permitted, some small structures were built, especially the steam generator preparation shed, workshops for preparing the missile, fuel storage sheds and the launch bunker near the catapult, and in some cases, prefabricated structures were used. It took a work party of 40 men only about two weeks to construct such a site.

None of these buildings were especially conspicuous, and the new sites proved to be almost invisible to air detection until the launch ramps began to be erected in June 1944. A network of local caves, tunnels and mines was taken over for use as improvised ordnance storage areas. In total, the 'Operational Site System' consisted of five launch sites (Feuerstellungen) for each launch battery plus a support site, for a total of 80 launch sites and 16 support sites, located from Calais westwards into lower Normandy. The original 'ski sites' were then called Stellungen alter Bauart (old-pattern sites) while the new simplified sites were called Einsatzstellungen (special sites).

The V-1 missile campaign began in earnest on 12 June 1944. The strikes against the ski sites had no effect in delaying the start of the campaign, and indeed the German Flak officers later argued that the initial December 1943–January 1944 attacks on the first ski sites had the positive consequence of forcing the Luftwaffe to design more survivable sites months before the actual missile campaign could begin. The Crossbow campaign did largely derail efforts to deploy the FZG-76 from the Wasserwerke. Yet the main delay in the start of the missile campaign was not the attacks on the launch sites, but rather the strategic bombing raids against the German aircraft industry, which delayed mass production of the FZG-76 until the spring of

V-1 Launch Site. The V-1 launch site centred on the Walther WR 2.3 Schlitzrohrschleuder catapult. The prerequisites for the site were modest – a concrete platform for attaching the catapult and supporting the gas generator trolley, and concrete pilings for the catapult support. (Hugh Johnson/Chris Taylor © Osprey Publishing)

The Allied success in pre-emptive bombing of the first set of Wasserwerke forced the Organization Todt to try less conspicuous approaches to heavy launch sites. The extensive tunnel network created originally for V-2 storage at Brécourt near Cherbourg was converted to a V-1 launch site with this massive set of blast walls erected at the end of one of the tunnels to accommodate a Walther catapult. In the event, the site was captured before any missiles could be fired. (NARA)

1944 instead of the autumn of 1943 as planned. As a result, FR 155(W) did not have an adequate inventory of missiles, launch ramps and other necessary equipment until late May 1944.

The smaller number of Sonderbauten sites were also attacked as they were identified, starting in October 1943. Even though the Wehrmacht was increasingly sceptical of the value of these bases, Organization Todt continued their construction as a matter of pride to prove that it could build in the face of bombing attacks. The proposed Wasserwerk sites fared very poorly under heavy bombing, in spite of the innovative construction techniques. To make up the shortfall of large launch bunkers, in March 1944, the Luftwaffe decided to reinvigorate construction of the proposed Army Ölkeller Cherbourg, a series of tunnels near Brécourt in the Cherbourg suburbs that had been intended for storing A-4 ballistic missiles. The A-4 was not yet ready for production; instead the tunnels would serve as the preparation and storage area for

SPECIALIST FORTIFICATIONS – PROTECTING THE U-BOATS AND V-WEAPONS

V-weapons launch sites, autumn–winter 1944.

the FZG-76 missiles, while two protected launch ramps were added to turn the facility into a gigantic protected launch site. This new configuration was called Wasserwerk No. 2, and the Brécourt site was variously codenamed the Minenlager (mine storage) or Ersatz B8, since it was intended to replace the ill-fated B8 Waterworks at nearby Couville. The Minenlager was expected to be able to contain 300 FZG-76 missiles, enough for about six days of launches. As expected, the Minenlager attracted far less attention than the more obvious early configurations and even though only 40 per cent of the concrete work was ready by mid-May 1944, the work progressed so well that most of the main construction was completed in the week after D-Day. In March 1944, a second FZG-76 site of this type was considered for the Roche de Tronquet tunnels near Nardouet. These tunnels were in use by the Kriegsmarine, but could be modified with four sheltered launchers emanating from the tunnels. It did not progress beyond the design stage.

The Allied amphibious invasion in Normandy on 6 June 1944 forced a premature start of the missile campaign against London. The attacks caused widespread damage and panic on the UK mainland, and Churchill was adamant that the highest priority must be afforded the efforts to stop the missiles, now officially dubbed the 'V-1' by Hitler. In spite of the diversion of large numbers of heavy bomber attacks against the V-1 sites in the final two weeks of June, there was no appreciable decline in German missile launches. In part, this was due to the problem of actually finding the new sites; of 8,310 sorties in late June, only 4,500 bombed actual launch sites. The summer Crossbow bombing campaign placed a new emphasis on the heavy sites, in spite of a lack of evidence that they were operational. Yet by July, a new weapon had entered the RAF arsenal that sounded the death knell of the heavy sites – the Tallboy heavy bomb. Air attacks with these weapons forced the Luftwaffe to disperse the storage areas, and as a result slowed the supply of missiles to the launchers. The FR 155(W) war diary indicates that the main bottleneck on the number of missiles launched was the interruptions in supply of missiles and equipment rather than the attacks on the launchers themselves. Other smaller depots and supply areas were bombed during the Crossbow campaign as they were identified, but the attacks had a much less dramatic effect on dampening down the missile launches.

The other effective attacks of the Crossbow campaign were those by the US Eighth Air Force against the V-1 production sites, notably the Volkswagen plant at Fallersleben with two raids in late June and another in early July. These raids, combined with attacks on the gyroscope plant near Weimar, helped to suppress the scale of V-1 production. The plan had been to raise production to 8,000 missiles by the end of the summer, but the air attacks capped the production at 3,419 in September after which production declined, even after the opening of a second production facility at Nordhausen.

SPECIALIST FORTIFICATIONS – PROTECTING THE U-BOATS AND V-WEAPONS

The new sites were almost invisible from the air until the Walther catapult was erected. This shows one of the launch sites of Abteilung IV on the Cotentin Peninsula abandoned after D-Day. The concrete launch pad and rails are camouflaged with hay. (NARA)

The intensifying Crossbow campaign during the summer of 1944 made it quite clear that mobility and concealment were far better defences for missile sites than fortification. The heavy sites never became operational due to their vulnerability to air attack. Even without the use of Tallboy bombs, the sites were useless since aerial bombardment could sever the rail and road connections vital to a steady supply of missiles and supplies. In contrast, the 'new' light launch sites proved durable to intense air attack due to the difficulty of locating and identifying them, and the relative ease of repair even when they were bombed. On the other hand, the light V-1 launch sites were not especially efficient as a weapon system as their lack of handling and storage facilities slowed the process of preparing the missiles for launch. The cumbersome Walther catapult took days to disassemble and more than a week to reassemble in another location, making the transfer of batteries from one location to another a difficult and time-consuming process.

The start of Operation *Cobra* by the First US Army on 24 July 1944 marked the beginning of the Allied breakout from Normandy. The last launch battalion withdrew from France on August 29, 1944, destroying their launchers before leaving the sites.

Plans to restart the missile campaign in Belgium faltered due to the rapid Allied advance, which overran the new V-1 launch sites in the first week of September 1944. Launch sites had already been scouted in the Eifel forests along the Belgian frontier,

V-2 LAUNCH SITE

The V-2 launch site was located in an area about 500m in length and this shows the textbook configuration. The prescribed deployment pattern was in a wooded area, or a road network edged with trees to help camouflage the launch site from aerial observation. The launch area itself was ideally a flat clearing about 50m wide with good access to roads. The firing platform (A) was located at the centre of this clearing with three key pieces of equipment nearby: the battery fire-control vehicle (B), electrical generator trailer (C) and an air compressor trailer (D). Each was positioned about 90m from the launch pad, as there was the constant danger that the missile engine turbopump would fail shortly after take-off, with the missile and its fuel crashing down on the pad and exploding. The fire-control vehicle, based on a Krauss-Maffei SdKfz 7 half-track, was deployed with a clear line of sight to the launch pad since the battery commander conducted the launch from this site. The generator and compressor trailers provided electrical power and hydraulic air pressure to the missile and launcher and the associated support equipment. Usually the Meillerwagen transporter-erector trailer and Magirus servicing ladder were parked near the launch pad as well (E). The fuel equipment was kept further away from the launch pad, usually 365m due to the dangers of the launch. The A-Stoff (liquid oxygen) detachment consisted of an Anhänger 6 insulated liquid oxygen trailer and its tractor, usually a Hanomag SS-100 (F). The T-Stoff (hydrogen peroxide) detachment usually consisted of a Opel Blitz Kessel-KW.2100 1 tanker truck towing a support trailer used to heat the hydrogen peroxide (G). The B-Stoff (alcohol) fuel detachment was the largest of these units, usually consisting of an Opel 3-ton KW Kfz. 385 Kessel-KW.3500 1. tanker (H); a Kessel-KW.3500 1. trailer along with its Hanomag SS-100 tractor (I), and a fuel pump trailer. These fuel vehicles would be driven to the launch pad only after a missile had been erected, and would depart as soon as the fuelling process was complete for security reasons. (Hugh Johnson/Chris Taylor © Osprey Publishing)

SPECIALIST FORTIFICATIONS – PROTECTING THE U-BOATS AND V-WEAPONS

and the border area had only scattered German villages that were less likely to be hit by wayward missiles. The new launch sites followed the pattern of the new sites in France with minimal construction, and an accent on the use of camouflage to prevent detection and attack. The first launches of Operation *Donnerschlag* (Thunderclap) began from Germany on 21 October 1944, mostly aimed at Antwerp.

The activation of launch sites in Germany remained contentious. By December, 20 sites had been completed along the Rhine and eight launchers erected, but continued high rates of crashes led to a reluctance to launch from sites near German cites.

Although the dome of the Wizernes missile base remained largely intact, near misses by Tallboy bombs so undermined the construction that the site was abandoned in the summer of 1944. The small square bunker to the left covered a vent shaft for the missile complex. (Steven J. Zaloga)

HITLER'S FORTRESSES

With the Watten Bunker no longer viable as a missile launch base, the tunnel complex in the chalk quarries at Wizernes was expanded to include a massive missile complex under a special reinforced concrete dome. Two tunnels would have exited the complex to permit V-2 missiles to be launched from the open plaza below the dome that were sealed by Allied bombing. The tunnel entrance to today's museum as seen here is based on the Ida railroad tunnel. (Steven J. Zaloga)

Instead, the regiment decided to establish new sites in the Netherlands since according to the regimental diary, 'in Holland there is no need to worry about the civilian population in respect to premature crashes'. Two battalions deployed to new sites in the Netherlands around Deventer, beginning their campaign against Antwerp on 16 December, with other batteries installed around Rotterdam in the New Year.

The V-1 launches continued from various locations into the spring of 1945. Meanwhile, the new A-4 missile debuted in the autumn of 1944 after long delays, renamed by Hitler as the V-2. Three missile launch battalions had been formed in late 1943, Artillerie Abteilungen 485, 836 and 962 (Mot.). In the spring of 1944, SS-Werfer Battalion 500 began converting from their conventional artillery rocket launchers to the A-4 as part of Himmler's efforts to place the SS in control of the new secret weapons.

SPECIALIST FORTIFICATIONS – PROTECTING THE U-BOATS AND V-WEAPONS

The original scheme was to deploy these in Normandy and the Pas-de-Calais at heavy sites such as Wizernes and Sottevast, as well as from mobile launch sites. A-4 missile production began at the damaged Peenemünde plant in late 1943, but a new production facility, codenamed Mittelwerke, was created in the Harz mountains near Nordhausen by tunnelling under a mountain. Production began in the tunnels there in January 1944 using slave labour from the notorious Dora camp nearby. However, the A-4 was plagued with technical problems, disintegrating in the final stages of flight, and these problems were not resolved until the summer of 1944. In spite of the obvious failure of the heavy sites, there were plans to create three more fortified bunkers for the V-2 in the western area of Germany, but these plans never came to fruition due to the resistance of the Army, which saw the V-1 experience in the summer of 1944 as confirmation of the tactical benefits of mobile versus fortified launchers. As a result, all V-2 operations in 1944–45 were based on the mobile launcher configuration.

Both the U-boat bunker and the V-weapon sites had exposed the strengths and the weaknesses of fortified positions in an age of aerial warfare. While some of the most resilient sites did prove to be resistant to many conventional bombing efforts, eventually the sheer disruption and devastation of the raids critically hampered functionality. Furthermore, weapons such as the thunderous Tallboy meant that even the most titanic of fortifications could eventually be breeched. As demonstrated by the V-weapon site experience, not being seen in the first place was the best form of defence.

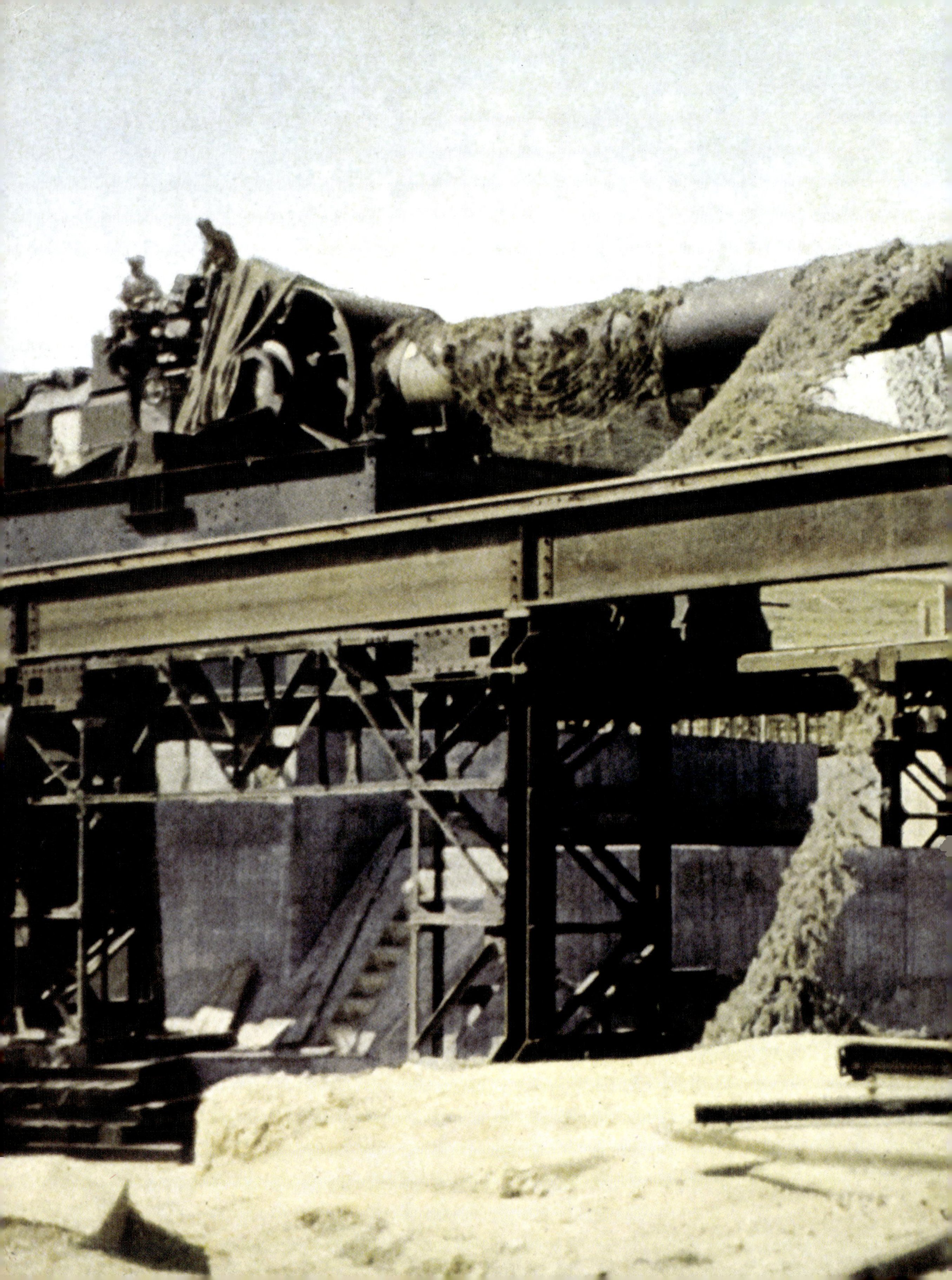

CONCLUSION

LEFT: Camouflaged artillery on the Atlantic Wall, one of the most infamous of Hitler's defences. (Topfoto)

Fortifications, by their very durability in design, are one of the lasting legacies of war. The fortifications of Hitler's Third Reich are no exception, and can be found in locations ranging from the tourist traps of the French coastline, through to hidden corners of dark forests in Poland. To this day, these structures draw interest from the military minded, and sometimes from those with a more ideological perspective.

Generating understandable fascination are the remnants of Hitler's headquarters. A large proportion of the Führerhauptquartiere were destroyed either by retreating German forces during the war, or by the Allies after the cessation of hostilities. In spite of this, and with a little research to put the place in context, there is still much to be had from a visit to these places. The sites themselves are scattered across Germany and what had been occupied Europe.

Belgium, somewhat surprisingly, has gone to great lengths to preserve Hitler's headquarters at Brûly-de-Pesche. The village itself has been preserved much as it was when Hitler used it as a headquarters in 1940, and it is still relatively easy to compare photographs taken at the time with modern views. Almost uniquely, Hitler's bunker is still in situ and undamaged and two new wooden chalets – not dissimilar to the originals – have been erected and house a museum devoted to the Führerhauptquartier and also a wider study of the war.

Unlike its near neighbour, France has not embraced the fact that Hitler established a series of Führerhauptquartiere on its territory. Part of the reason for this is that Wolfsschlucht II near Margival, the largest and best-preserved example, was used by NATO after the war and later as a training site for French commandos with access restricted. Although now disused, the site is still fenced off and impromptu visits are actively discouraged. However, the site is opened to the public at certain times of the year.

Understandably, perhaps, little remains of the various Führerhauptquartiere in Germany. The bunkers of FHQ Adlerhorst were demolished after the war and the area redeveloped with the concrete bunkers sometimes used as the foundation for new buildings. Schloß Ziegenberg remains, and, although badly damaged in the war, it has been restored. Führerhauptquartier Felsennest was also demolished and the area around it has seen significant changes, but, despite the fact that it is not advertised, the determined historian can still find vestiges of the bunkers outside the village of Rodert. Slightly farther south it is also possible to find remains of the bunkers at FHQ Tannenberg. Despite the fact that it was witness to one of the most momentous events of the 20th century, the Führerbunker in Berlin was demolished and the remains buried, and today nothing is left to visit except a map of the bunkers.

Poland remains home to three of Hitler's wartime Führerhauptquartiere. The most famous of these, FHQ Wolfsschanze, is located in the north of the country near Ketrzyn

CONCLUSION

One of the three concrete pillboxes built around the tunnel at Stepina to protect the facility. Each pillbox was fitted with three apertures for machine guns. Access was through a single entrance sealed with a steel door, though, if necessary, an emergency exit was provided. (Neil Short)

and is a popular tourist attraction. The facility was completely destroyed by the retreating Germans in January 1945, but the remains can still be visited. Some of the original buildings have been restored and are now used as a hotel and restaurant for visitors to the site. Nearby, the remains of the OKH headquarters 'Mauerwald' are much better preserved and are well worth a visit.

Farther to the south, near Lodz, is Anlage Mitte (Tomaszów Mazowiecki) where an artificial tunnel was constructed for the Führer's train. It was never used by Hitler, but is still intact and can be viewed by the public. A similar facility was built at Stepina and is where Hitler met Mussolini in August 1941. Today the tunnel is used as a museum with a collection of Soviet and German militaria on show. The disused rail tunnel at Strzyzów, which was adapted for Hitler's use, is also open to the public. Führerhauptquartier Riese is in south-west Poland and is a massive complex. Parts of it are open to the public like the Osówka Complex, near Głuszyca, but many of the tunnels are dangerous and should not be visited without specialist equipment and local guides.

These sites, and those remaining of the West Wall, Atlantic Wall and other fortifications, are immensely evocative. Some, such as the easily accessible sections of the Atlantic Wall around Normandy and the Pas-de-Calais, still convey brute strength and force. Casual tourists should not, however, go wandering into bunkers unprepared. Many large bunkers had sub-basements for storage, and over the years wooden floors have rotted, making them a natural trap for the unwary. Also, some of the bunkers are on private property and tourists are not necessarily welcome without permission. As always, do your research first before making a visit.

What attracts many people to view these fortifications is not just their technical or tactical significance, but also the mood that they evoke. When we enter a bunker or fortification, there is a sense of descent into history, and the ghosts of the past seem somehow vividly present in the damp walls and dark corridors. The fortifications also provoke the unsettling sense of being both places of protection, yet also potential graves. Such unsettling landmarks of the Third Reich will remain with us for decades, if not centuries, to come.

GLOSSARY

Alpenfestung	Alpine Fortress
Annäherungsgraben	approach trenches
Armee	army
Armeeoberkommando AOK	Army High Command
Heeres-Küsten-Artillerie-Abteilung/ -Regiment HKAA/HKAR	army coastal artillery regiments
Atlantikwall	Atlantic Wall
Baupionier	construction
Befehlswagen	command car
Behelfskreuzlafette	improvised cruciform mount
Beobachtungstellen	observation posts
Blitzkrieg	lightning war
Brückenkopf	bridgehead
Deutsches Heer German Army Ersatzheer	Replacement Army
Fallschirmjäger	paratrooper
Feldheer	field army
Festungs-Artillerie-Abteilung	fortress artillery unit
Festung	fortress
Festungsdienstelle Düren	Düren Fortification Sector
Fliegerabwehrkanone	Flak (anti-aircraft)
Führer Begleit Bataillon	Führer Escort Battalion
Führerhauptquartier FHQ	Führer Headquarters
Führerriegel	Hitler Line
Führersonderzuglit	'Führer Special Train'
Gefechtsvorposten	combat outposts
Hauptkampffeld	main battlefield

Hauptkampflinie	main defence line
Heeresgruppe	Army Group
Heimatheer	Homeland Army
Höckerhindernis	'dragon's teeth' (anti-tank obstacle)
Horchstellen	listening posts
Kampfgraben	battle trenches
Kesselbettungen	kettle positions
Kriechgraben	crawl trenches
Kriegsmarine	German Navy
Küstenverteidigungs-Abschnitt KVA	coast defence sector
Lebensraum	living space
leichte Marine-Artillerie-Abteilung	leMAA: light naval artillery regiment
Luftverteidigungszone	Air Defence Zone West
Luftwaffe	German Air Force
Marine-Artillerie-Abteilung MAA	naval artillery battalion
Marine-Befelshaber Kanalküste	Channel Coast Naval Command
Marine-Gruppekommando West	Naval Group Command West
Maschinengewehrloch oder Nest	literally 'machine-gun hole or nest'
MG-Panzernest	armoured steel pillbox
Munitionslöcher	ammunition niches
Nachrichtenbunker	communication centre
Oberkommando der Wehrmacht OKW	Armed Forces High Command
Oberkommando des Heeres OKH	Army High Command
Operationsgebiet	operational zone
Organisation Todt	OT; Todt Organization
Pantherkanone	Panther gun
Panzerabwehrgraben	anti-tank traps
Panzerabwehrkanone	PaK; anti-tank gun
Panzergraben	anti-tank ditches
Panzersperren	tank barriers
Reichsarbeitsdienst RAD	Reich Labour Service

Reichsbahn	German Railways
Reichssicherheitsdienst RSD	Reich Security Service
Reichsverteidigungskomissare RVK	Reich Defence Commissars
Schwerpunkt	main emphasis
Sonderzüge	special trains
Spähtrupp	reconnaissance patrol
Sperrkreis	Security Zone
Stützpunkt	StP; strongpoint
Unterseebootsflotille	U-boat flotilla
Verbindungsgraben	connecting trenches
Verteidigungsbereich	defence zone
Vogesen-Stellung	Main Vosges Line
Volkssturm	People's Army
Voralpenstellung	Forward Alpine Defences
Vorgeschobene Stellung	advanced position
Vorposten	outposts
Wehrgruppen	defence groups
Wehrkreise	military districts
Wehrmachtführungsstab Wfst	Armed Forces Operations Staff
West-Stellung	West Position
Widerstandnest WN	resistance points

FURTHER READING

Astor, G., *The Bloody Forest. Battle for the Huertgen: September 1944–January 1945* (Presidio Press, 2000)

Baur, H., *Hitler At My Side* (Eichler Publishing Corporation, 1986)

Beevor, A., *Berlin: the Downfall, 1945* (Viking, 2002)

Below, N. von, *At Hitler's Side: The Memoirs of Hitler's Luftwaffe Adjutant 1937–45* (Greenhill Books, 2004)

Bernage, Georges, *Gold-Juno-Sword* (Heimdal, 2003)

Bernage, Georges, *Omaha Beach* (Heimdal, 2002)

Blocksdorf, Helmut, *Hitler's Secret Commandos: Operations of the K-Verband* (Pen & Sword, 2008)

Breuer, William, *Hitler's Fortress Cherbourg: The Conquest of a Bastion* (Stein & Day, 1984)

Burnal, Paul, *Batterie Lothringen: Archive Book No. 10* (Channel Islands Occupation Society, 2002)

Cohen, Frederick, *The Jews in the Channel Islands during the German Occupation 1940–1945* (Jersey Heritage Trust, 2000)

Cruickshank, Charles, *The German Occupation of the Channel Islands: The Official History of the Occupation Years* (Guernsey Press Co., 1975)

D'Este, C., *Bitter Victory: The Battle for Sicily July–August 1943* (Collins, 1988)

Darlow, Steve, *Sledgehammers for Tintacks: Bomber Command Combats the V-1 Menace 1943–44* (Grub Street, 2002)

Davenport, Trevor, *Festung Alderney* (Barnes Publishing Ltd, 2003)

Delaforce, Patrick, *Smashing the Atlantic Wall: The Destruction of Hitler's Coastal Fortresses* (Cassell, 2001)

Dungan, T.D., *V-2: A Combat History of the First Ballistic Missile* (Westholme, 2005)

Fest, J., *Inside Hitler's Bunker – The Last Days of the Third Reich* (Pan Books, 2005)

Fisher, E., *Cassino to the Alps* (Center for Military History, 1977)

Forty, George, *Fortress Europe: Hitler's Atlantic Wall* (Ian Allen, 2002)

Garland A. & H. McGaw Smyth, *Sicily and the Surrender of Italy* (Center of Military History, 1986)

Gavey, Ernie, *A Guide to German Fortifications on Guernsey* (Guernsey Armouries, Revised Edition 2001)

Ginns, Michael, *Jersey's German Bunkers: Archive Book No. 9* (Channel Islands Occupation Society, 1999)

FURTHER READING

Gückelhorn, Wolfgang, & Paul Detlev, *V1-Eifelschreck* (Helios, 2004)

Henshall, P., *Hitler's V-Weapons Sites* (Sutton, 2002)

Hewitt, R.L. *Work Horse of the Western Front: The Story of the 30th Infantry Division* (The Battery Press, 1980)

Hinsley, F.H., *British Intelligence in the Second World War, Its Influence on Strategy and Operations*, 4 volumes (HMSO, 1979–90)

Hoffmann, P., *Hitler's Personal Security: Protecting the Führer, 1921–1945* (Da Capo Press, 2000)

Hogg, Ian V., *German Artillery of World War Two* (Greenhill Books, 1997)

Hölsken, D., *V-Missiles of the Third Reich* (Monogram, 1994)

Jentz, Thomas & Hilary Doyle, *Panther Turrets* (Panzer Tracts, 2005)

Jentz, Thomas & Hilary Doyle, *Panzer Turrets on Concrete and Wood Stands* (Panzer Tracts, 2004)

Johnson, A.L., *Hitler's Military Headquarters: Organization, Structures, Security and Personnel* (R. James Bender Publishing, 1999)

Junge, T., *Until the Final Hour: Hitler's Last Secretary* (Phoenix, 2004)

Kaufmann, J.E. & H.W. Kaufmann, *Fortress Third Reich: German Fortifications and Defense Systems in World War II* (Da Capo Press, 2003)

Kaufmann, J.E. & R.M. Jurga, *Fortress Europe: European Fortifications in World War II* (Combined Publishing, 1999)

Kennedy, G., *Vengeance Weapon 2* (Smithsonian, 1983; Shiffer reprint, 2006)

Kieser, Egbert, *Hitler on the Doorstep: Operation Sea Lion*, trans. Helmut Bögler (Arms & Armour Press, 1997)

Lehmann, A.D., *In Hitler's Bunker: A Boy Soldier's Eyewitness Account of the Führer's Last Days* (Mainstream Publishing, 2004)

Lehrer, S., *The Reich Chancellery and Führerbunker Complex* (McFarland & Company, Inc., 2006)

Lepage, Jean-Denis, *The Westwall: Siegfried Line 1938–1945* (Nafziger, 2002)

MacDonald, C.B., *United States Army in World War II. The European Theater of Operations: The Siegfried Line Campaign* (Center of Military History, 1984)

O'Donnell, J.P., *The Bunker* (Da Capo Press, 2001)

Oldham, P., *The Hindenburg Line* (Leo Cooper, 2000)

Pantcheff, T.X.H., *Alderney Fortress Island: The Germans in Alderney, 1940–1945* (Phillimore and Co., 1987)

Partridge, Trevor & John Wallbridge, *Mirus: The Making of a Battery* (The Ampersand Press, 1983)

Prefer, N., *Patton's Ghost Corps Cracking the Siegfried Line* (Presidio Press, Novato, 1998)

Renn, Walter, *Hitler's West Wall: Strategy in Concrete and Steel 1938–45* (UMI, 1970)

Rudi, Rolf & Peter Saal, *Fortress Europe* (Airlife, 1988)

Ruge, Friedrich, *Rommel in Normandy* (Presido, 1979)

Saunders, Anthony, *Hitler's Atlantic Wall* (Sutton, 2001)

Sauvary, J. C., *Diary of the German Occupation of Guernsey 1940–1945* (Self Publishing Association, 1990)

Schmeelke, Karl-Heinz & Michael Schmeelke, *Guns on the Atlantic Wall* (Schiffer, 1998)

Schmeelke, Karl-Heinz & Michael Schmeelke, *Fortress Europe: the Atlantic Wall Guns* (Schiffer, 1993)

Schroeder, C., *He Was My Chief: The Memoirs of Adolf Hitler's Secretary* (Frontline Books, 2009)

Seidler, F.W. & D. Ziegert, *Hitler's Secret Headquarters* (Greenhill Books, 2004)

Shachtman, T., *The Phony War 1939–1940* (Harper & Row, 1982)

Short, Neil, *Tank Turret Fortifications* (Crowood, 2006)

Short, Neil, *Hitler's Siegfried Line* (Sutton, 2002)

Shulman, M., *Defeat in the West* (Secker and Warburg, 1986)

Speer, A., *Inside the Third Reich* (Weidenfeld and Nicolson, 1970)

Taylor, B., *Hitler's Headquarters: From Beer Hall to Bunker, 1920–1945* (Potomac Books, Inc., 2007)

Taylor, T., *Munich The Price of Peace* (Hodder and Stoughton, 1979)

Thompson, Peter, *V3: The Pump Gun* (ISO Publications, 1999)

Trevor-Roper, H., *The Last Days of Hitler* (Pan Books, 2002)

Verbeek, J. R., *V2-Vergeltung: From The Hague and its Environs* (V2 Platform Foundation, 2005)

Warlimont, W., *Inside Hitler's Headquarters 1939–45* (Presidio Press, 1997)

Whaley, B., *Covert German Rearmament, 1919–1939: Deception and Misperception* (University Publications of America Inc., 1984)

Whitaker, W.D. and S. *Rhineland: The Battle to End the War* (Leo Cooper, 1989)

Whiting, C., *The Battle for the German Frontier* (The Windrush Press, 2000)

Whiting, C., *West Wall: The Battle for Hitler's Siegfried Line* (Spellmount, 1999)

Williamson, D.G., *The British in Germany, 1918–1930: The Reluctant Occupiers* (Berg, 1991)

Wilt, Alan, *The Atlantic Wall* (Enigma, 2004)

Wray, Timothy A., *Standing Fast: German Defensive Doctrine on the Russian Front During World War II: Pre-war to March 1943*. Research Survey No. 5 (Combat Studies Institute, 1986)

Young, Richard A., *The Flying Bomb* (Ian Allen, 1978)

Ziegler, Philip, *Mountbatten* (Collins, 1985)

INDEX

References to maps and illustrations are in **bold**

A

A-4 missile programme *see* V-Weapon sites
Aachen **82**, **89**, 94, 117–118, 122
Aachen-Saar Programm 73, **84**
Adlerhorst, FHQ 17–18, **20,** 22–24, **24**, **37**, **48**, 64–65, 378
advanced position 9, 278
air defence zone (West) **72**, 73, **80**, 84
air raid shelters **56**, 305
Alderney **191**, 195, 197
Alexander, Field Marshal Harold 241, 251
Allies
  6th Army Group 127
  Ardennes offensive 64–65
  and the Atlantic Wall 138–139, 175–185, 198–199, 212
  in Italy 164–165, 220–225, 231, 241–243, 251–269
  and the Rhine 119–131
  and U-Boat bunkers 330, 333–336, 339–340, 342, 343, 347, 349, 351, 352, 353
  and V-Weapon sites 361–363, 365, 368, 370–371
  and the West Wall/West-Stellung 93–95, 98–100, 107, 119–131
Alsace, defence of 126–131
amphibious assaults 164–165, 242–243
Anlage Mitte, FHQ 18–19, 25, **37**, **48**, 379
Anlage Mitte II & III, FHQ 25
Anlage Süd, FHQ 19, **20**, **26**, **26**, **37**, **48**, **54**, 57
anti-tank defences
  Atlantic Wall 166, 168
  Channel Islands 193
  ditches 110, 235, 238, 229, 239, 240, 246–247
  dragon's teeth 68–69, 76, 78, 82, 85–86, 100, 243, 243, 245, 251
  field fortifications 273, 276
  hedgehogs 166, 192, 193
  Hitler's priority 109, 111
  improvised 166
  in Italy 229, 235, 238, 239, 240, 243, 246–247
  mines 85, 166, 168, 229, 243, 245–246
  natural terrain 243, 276
  timber 95, 130, 192
  West-Stellung 78, 103, 109, 110, 130
  West Wall 68–69, 78, 82, 85–86, 95, 109, 111, 130
  see also anti-tank guns
anti-tank guns
  3.7cm PaK 35/36; 83
  4.7cm PaK 36(t) 85, 189
  5cm KwK 115, 167
  5cm PaK 38; 176, 229, 238
  7.5cm PaK 40; 111, 115, 228, 229, 238
  8.8cm PaK 85, 112–113, 162–163, 172, 266
  mountings 114–115
  West-Stellung 111–119
anti-tank positions **93**, **266**, 299, 302, 303, **304**
Apennines **224**, 232–233, 240, **254**, 267
Aquino 260
Ardennes offensive 64–65, 98–99
artillery **98**
  2cm Flak guns 275, 303
  3.7cm Flak guns 215, 288
  5cm Flak guns 175
  8.35cm Flak guns 85
  8.8cm Flak guns 80, 303
  10.5cm guns 188
  10.5cm K331(f) guns 172
  10.5cm SK C/32 203
  10.5cm naval guns 204
  10.5cm SKC/32U submarine guns 194
  15cm C/36 destroyer guns 180, 188
  15cm naval guns 257
  15cm SKC/28 naval guns 205, 208
  15cm Tbts.K.L/45 guns 169
  15.5cm K420(f) guns 171–172
  17cm K(E) 201
  17cm SKL/40 naval guns 202
  24cm naval guns 83–84
  28cm K5E railway guns 144
  28cm Kurze Bruno 196

30.5cm naval guns 83–84
30.5cm SKL/50 guns 182
240mm SKL/50 guns 169
Adolfkanonen 208
camouflage 376–377
Cannone de 75/46; 236
Cockerill 120mm mle. field gun 190
Flakwerfer 44 Föhngerät 101
Jagdpanther guns 115
Krupp 28cm SKL/40 MO6; 142
Krupp 203mm K(E) 138
Nebelwerfer 42; 256
Pantherkanonen 115
Rheinmetall 150mm C/36 destroyer guns 158–159
Rheinmetall 15cm SKC/28; 160
Rheinmetall-Borsig R300 rockets 195
Saint-Chamond 155mm K220(f) 141
Saint-Chamond 155mm K420(f) 161
shortage of 115–116
Skoda 210mm K39/40 guns 183
artillery gun pit **112–113**
artillery positions 302–305
assaulting techniques, US Army **129**
Atlantic Wall
    Allies attack 138–139, 175–185, 198–199, 212
    Army coastal artillery 139–143, 152–157, 170–173, 208
    Army infantry strongpoints 173–175, 174, 201
    Army v Navy 141, 148–157
    in Belgium 198, 200–201
    Channel Islands 186–197
    construction of 138–145, 148, 166, 205
    defence principles 157–168
    in Denmark 199, 209, 212–213, 214
    evaluation of 138–140, 178, 179, 183, 213, 216–217
    in France 139–185, 200, 216–217
    and Hitler, Adolf 157, 213, 216–217
    infantry strongpoints 173–175, 174, 201
    maps 140, 198, 214
    naval coastal artillery 139, 141, 148–154, 168–170, 200–204, 208–213
    in Netherlands 197–198, 198, 200, 201–204, 210–211, 213, 215
    northern section 197–213
    in Norway 144–145, 197, 199, 200, 204–209, 214, 216
    origins of 139–145
    post-war 380
    and Rommel, Erwin 161, 164–165

B

B.III-2a & 2b bunkers 354
B-Gerüst C/39 turrets **150–151**
B-Werke bunkers 84, 91, **96–97**, 134–135
Balkans campaign 55–56
Bärenhöhle, FHQ 20, 26–27, **37**, **48**
Bauform bunkers/casemates **188**, **194**, **205**, **209**, **210–211**, **215**, **269**
Baur, Hans 34
beaches, defences on **156**, 165, 166, **167**, 168, **192**, 193, 224
Belfort Gap 127
Belgium
    Ardennes Offensive 64–65
    Atlantic Wall 198, 200–201
    V-1 missiles 371
    see also Wolfsschlucht I, FHQ
Below, Nicolas von **30**, **49**
Bergen
    Fjell Batterie 206–207
    U-Boat bunkers 338–340, 339, 340
Berlin
    Hitler's bunker 20, 21, 23, 28–29, 29, 50–51, 65, 66, 66–67
    Soviet invasion of 66–67
Bernhardt Line 227–228
Black Forest 128, 131
    Tannenberg, FHQ 20, 32, 37, 48, 53, 378
Blue Line 234
Bordeaux, U-Boat bunkers **323**, **352**, 353
Boulogne 181–183
Brauchitsch, Walther von **16**
Brécourt **359**, 362, 368, **368**, 370
Bremen, U-Boat bunkers **10**, **326**, 335–336, **337**, 338
Brest
    Atlantic Wall 179
    U-Boat bunkers 325–329, 328, 343
    bridge defences **91**, **101**, 121, 122, 126, 127
Britain
    and the Atlantic Wall 138–145, 175, 179
    Channel Islands 145, 186–197
    V-1 missile campaign 365, 370
    see also Allies; British armed forces
British armed forces
    Eighth Army 251–252, 257, 264, 267
    I Corps 179–180
    51st Royal Tank Reg 260
    142nd Royal Armoured Corps 259, 260

INDEX

RAF 166, 330, 334, 339–340, 370
  see also Allies
Brûly-de-Pesche 18, 38–39, **40–41**, **45**, 52, **63**, 378
  see also Wolfsschlucht I, FHQ
Brunhilde, FHQ 22, 27
Bruno, U-Boat bunker 338–340, **339**, **340**

C

C-Type bunkers 134
Caesar Line 229, 231, 238, 261–262
Calais 183, 185
camouflage
  artillery 376–377
  bunkers 114, 132, 164, 187, 233
  casemates 149, 218–219
  Hitler's bunkers 30, 32, 35
  MG-Panzernest 252
  Panther turrets 250
  pillboxes 226
  principles of 308, 312–313
  V-weapons launch sites 371
  West Wall 74
Canadian forces
  1st Inf Div 259
  2nd Inf Brigade 260, 264
  3rd Inf Div 181–182, 185
  14th Canadian Armoured Reg 260
  25th Tank Brigade 259, 260
  48th Highlanders 259, 260
  Ontario Regiment 259
  Seaforth Highlanders 260, 266
  see also Allies
Cassino 228, 237, 254–255, 268
  cathedral bunkers 140, **144**, 345
caves **232**
Chancellery see Führerbunker (Berlin)
Channel Islands 145, 186–197
Cherbourg
  Atlantic Wall 141, 177–178
  Ölkeller 362, 368, **368**, 370
Churchill, Winston 220–221, 257
Clark, Gen Mark 253–254, 261–263, 267
combat outpost zones 8, 9, 75, 240, 243, 247, 274, 278–279
concrete
  amounts used 48, 108, 138, 216, 363
  reinforced 76, 154
  thickness of 38, 155
crew-served weapons positions 298–305

Crisbeq battery **183**
Crossbow campaign 365, 367, 370–371
crust-cushion-hammer strategy 160–161
cupolas **78**, **79**, 82–83, **128**, 189, **203**

D

D-Day 61, 138–139, 176
defence concepts/systems 8–9, 74–85, **88**, 157–168, 273–284
defensive positions **293**
  crew-served weapons positions 298–305
  infantry battalion 304
  infantry positions 294–298
  rifle platoon 300
  squad position 305–308
Denmark 199, 209, 212–213, **214**
desert strongpoints 310
Dombunkers 140, **144**, 345
doors, bunkers **15**, 86–87, 89
Doppelgruppenunterstände 190
Dora I U-Boat bunker 341–342, **341**
Dora II U-Boat bunker 342–343
Dora Line 229, 231
dragon's teeth **68–69**, **76**, **78**, **82**, 85–86, **100**, 243, **243**, 245, 251
dummy positions **227**, 313
Dunkirk 53, 185

E

East Wall 131–135
Edelweiss, Stützpunkt **203**
Eifel defences 121–123
Elbe II U-Boat bunker 329–330, **330**, **332**
emergency exits, bunkers 89–90
Erft-Stellung 118, 122
Etna Line 225, 251

F

Felsennest, FHQ 18
  building of 37, 48
  demolition of 28
  design of 25, 27, 30
  Hitler at 20, 30, 52
  life in 48
  post-war 53, 378

Festung-Panzer-Drehturm **134**
Festungs-Pionier Korps designs, bunkers 157
field fortifications
    camouflage 308, 312–313
    construction materials 270–271, 284–288
    construction methods 285–294
    defensive positions 294–308
    defence principles 273–283
    evaluation of 313, 316–317
    today 317
field telephones **277**
Fink II U-Boat bunker 331–333
Finland **296**
fire-control bunkers/posts 153, 169, **180**, **199**, **202**, **205**
firing positions 294–305, **310**
firing steps 295, **295**, 298
Fjell, Batterie **206–207**
flame-throwers 84, 193, **245**, 247
France
    Atlantic Wall 139–185, 200, 216–217
    D-Day 61, 138–139, 176
    hedgerows, use of 270–271, 283, 284–285, 287
    Operation *Gelb* 52–53
    surrender of 52–53
    U-Boat bunkers 318–319, 323, 325, 325–329, 328, 343–353, 344, 346, 350, 352
    V-Weapon sites 356–358, 362
    and the West Wall 70–71
    see also Allies; Wolfsschlucht II, FHQ; Wolfsschlucht III, FHQ
French armed forces
    1ère Armée 127, 130–131
    2e Corps d'Armée 131
    French Expeditionary Corps 252–253, 254
Friedrich August, Batterie 182
FT-17 tank turret **171**
Führerbunker (Berlin) 23, **66**
    daily life in 50–51
    design of 28–29, 29
    Hitler at 20, 66–67
    post-war 21, 65
Führerhauptquartiere (Führer headquarters)
    accommodation 23–44
    construction of 19, 37, 48
    daily life in 46–51, 49
    finding locations for 14, 17–23
    map of 14
    occupation of 20
    operational history 51–67
    origins of 14–17
    post-war 378–379
    sites 23–44
    Führerriegel *see* Hitler Line
Führersonderzug 'Amerika' **16**
    accommodation for 26, 35, 39
    design of 43–44
    use of 15–17, 20, 51, 52, 54, 55–56
Futa Pass 240, **259**, 267–268
FZG-76 *see* V-Weapon sites, V-1s

G

gas locks, bunkers 87, 89
gas-tight sheet metal doors 87, 89
Gefechtsvorposten (combat outposts) 8, 9, 278–279
German armed forces
    1.Armee (AOK 1) 124, 126, 152–153, 200
    4.Fallschirmjäger-Div 262, 267, 268
    5.Panzer-Armee 64–65
    6.Panzer-Division 306–308
    6.SS-Panzer-Armee 64–65
    7.Armee (AOK 7) 64–65, 152–153, 200
    10.Armee (AOK 10) 239, 263
    14.Armee (AOK 14) 240
    15.Armee (AOK 15) 152–153, 200, 201, 204
    15.Panzergrenadier-Division 251, 253
    19.Armee (AOK 19) 127, 130, 131
    709.Inf Div 173–174
    coastal artillery regiments/units 148–149, 170–173, 198
    Flak Regiment 155 (W) 364, 370
    fortification companies 118, 119
    Heeresgruppe B 120, 121–123
    Heeresgruppe G 120, 123–124, 125, 126–131
    Heeresgruppe H 119, 121
    HKAR. 1261; 170–171
    infantry unit structure 276–277
    MAA.240; 182
    MAA.242; 169
    MAA.244; 168–169
    MAA.266; 169
    manpower problems 105, 281–282
    Unterseebootsflotille 327, 339, 341, 345, 349, 351, 353
    see also Luftwaffe
Gerstfeldhöhe tunnel system **92**
Gneisenau, use of turrets **206–207**, 216

INDEX

Görlitz Forest 35
Gothic Line 231, **232**, **235**, 238–240, **241**, 242, **245**, 246–247, **254**, **261**, **263**, 263–268, **264**
Green Line 231, 238–240
Green Line I 231, 264–265
Green Line II 231, 240, 265
Gruppenunterstände 190
Guernsey 186, **187**, 188–190, 193, 196–197
Gustav Line 228–229, 236–237, 252–257, 268

H

H612 casemates 174
H633 bunkers **181**
H667 casemates **167**, 176
H677 casemates **162–163**, **172**, 174
H679 casemates **161**, 171–172
H683 casemates **183**
Hagen/Siegfried, FHQ 31, **37**, 48
half-squad bunkers **275**, **297**
Hamburg, U-Boat bunkers 329–333, **330**, **332**
Hauptkampffeld 280
Hauptkampflinie 225, 278
heating, bunkers 91, 306
hedgerows **270–271**, **283**, 284–285, **287**
Helgoland, U-Boat bunkers 333–334
Heerenduin, Seezielbatterie **199**, **202**
hilltop strongpoint **296**
Himmler, Heinrich 103
Hindenburg Line 75, **77**
Hindenburg Stands 154
Hitler, Adolf **12–13**, **30**, **61**
    Ardennes offensive 64–65
    assassination attempts on 50, 60, 62
    and the Atlantic Wall 157, 213, 216–217
    and the Balkans 55–56
    and Berlin 66–67
    daily routine 46–48
    and France 52–53
    headquarters 12–13, 14–67
    health of 48, 50
    inner circle 44–47, 49
    and Italy 221, 223, 225
    no retreat order 280–281
    radio broadcast 61
    and Soviet Union 57–60, 61, 63
    suicide of 46, 66, 67
    his train 15–17, 16, 20, 26, 35, 39, 43–44, 51, 52, 54, 55–56
    and V-Weapons 356
    and the West-Stellung 104–105
    and the West Wall 71–72, 78, 80
Hitler Line **220**, **227**, 229, **233**, 238, **244**, **256**, 259–260
Hochrhein-Stellung 128, 130
Höckerhindernis *see* dragon's teeth
Hook of Holland 202–203
Hornisse U-Boat bunker 335–336
Hube, Gen Hans 251–252

I

ice, for fortifications 288
Ijmuiden **199**, 203–204, **210–211**
Il Giogio Pass 267
Indian forces, 4th Indian Div 255, 257
infantry positions 294–298, 299, 302, **303**, **304**
infantry-section trench **125**
infantry unit structure 276–277
Italy
    Allied strategy 220–221, 223–225, 231, 257, 268–269
    Allies attack 164–165, 241–243, 251–269
    defensive lines 218–269
    defensive shortcomings 241–243
    early defences 234–235
    German strategy 221–225, 227–231, 241–243, 268–269
    Germany defends 251–269
    and Hitler, Adolf 221, 223, 225
    identification of Lines 222–223, 226–227
    manpower problems 242
    maps of defence lines 222, 230

J

Jersey **155**, 195, 196–197

K

Kammhuber Line **191**
Katzenkopf bunker **96–97**, 99–100
Keitel, Wilhelm **12–13**, **16**
Keroman I U-Boat bunker **325**, **344**, 345–347, **348**
Keroman II & III U-Boat bunker **344**, 347

K

Kesselring, Albert 221, 225, 229
Kiel, U-Boat bunker 334–335
Kilian U-Boat bunker 334–335
Kitzinger-Stellung 71
Kleinau 87
KNW (Kraftwerk Nordwest) bunker 356–358, **357**, 361–362
Konrad, U-Boat bunker 335
Kyll-Stellung 122, **130**

L

La Pallice U-Boat bunker 324, 351–352
Le Havre **164**, 179–181
Lembach 95
Les Dunes de Varreville 174
lighting, bunkers 32–33, 90–91, 306
Ligurian Wall 234
Limesprogramm 73–74, **81**, 83–84
Lindemann, Batterie **146–147**, 185
linear defensive system 75, 157
Liri valley **227**, 229
living conditions, bunkers 46–51, 90–91, **96–97**, **209**, 306
locks
  gas 87, 89
  U-Boat bunkers 324–325
logs, use in fortifications **284**, 285–286, **289**, 290, **301**
Longues-sur-Mer gun battery 180
Lorient U-Boat bunker 325, 343–348, **344**, **346**
Lossberg, Oberst Fritz von 75
Luftverteidigungszone (West) **72**, 73, **80**, 84
Luftwaffe
  command bunker 191
  radar posts 322
  and V-Weapons 360, 364, 368, 370

M

M272 casemates **160**, 169, **180**, **202**
machine-gun positions 224, **263**, 289, 296–298, **300**, **301**, **304**, **310**
machine guns **314–315**
  MG08s 82, 83, 111
  MG34s 82–83, 111, 189, 279, 312
  MG42s 111, 125, 191
Maginot Line 27, 52, 123–124, 126
main battle position 280

Margival **42**, **47**
memorials 19
MG-Panzerneste 119, **124**, **128**, 236, **246**, 247, **248**, **252**, **255**, **258**
MG-Schartenstand 89
Minenlager 370
mines **156**, 168, **192**, 193, 239, **243**, 245–246, **311**
Mirus, Batterie **187**
Mittelwerke tunnel complex **361**, 375
Mont de Coupole **143**
Mont Lambert 182
Monte Artemisio 262
Monte Cassino 254–257
Montgomery, Field Marshal Bernard 185, 251
Monticelli Ridge 267–268
mortar pits **293**, 298–299
mortar positions **293**, 298–299, **300**, **304**
mortars
  5cm 84
  8cm Gr.W.34; 281
  bunker penetration 290–291
  M19s 96, 181, 189
Moselle Gate 123
museums **17**, **92**, **188**, **194**, **216**, **366**, **374**, 378–379

N

naval artillery towers **155**
naval casemates 154–155
naval guns *see* artillery
Neckar-Enz line 70, **72**, 128, 131
Netherlands
  Atlantic Wall 197–198, 198, 200, 201–204, 210–211, 213, 215
  V-Weapon launch sites 374
  West-Stellung 103, 105, 108, 115
New Zealand forces 255–257, 265–266
Nordsee III U-Boat bunker 333–334
Normandy
  fortifications 152, 170, 176, 177, 178, 179–181, 180, 216
  use of hedges 270–271, 283, 284–285, 287
North Sea, Atlantic Wall **198**
Norway
  Atlantic Wall 144–145, 197, 199, 200, 204–209, 214, 216
  Britain attacks 144
  torpedo batteries 208–209
  U-Boat bunkers 338–343, **339**, **340**, **341**, **342**

INDEX

O

OB 600 gun platforms **178**
observation points **65**, **143**, **164**, **237**, **253**, **265**
Oder-Warthe Bend (OWB) 133–135
Oldenburg, MKB **148**, 169
Olga, FHQ 21, 31
Ölkeller Cherbourg 362, 368, **368**, 370
open-topped positions 82, **142**, 175, **178**, **190**, 291–292, **291**, **292**, 294
Operation *Astonia* 179–181
Operation *Bagration* 61, 63
Operation *Barbarossa* 57–58
Operation *Blau* 58–59
Operation *Blockbuster* 121
Operation *Citadel* 59–60
Operation *Frühlingssturm* 55–56
Operation *Gelb* 52–53
Operation *Nordwind* 124, 126
Operation *Seelöwe* 139–141
Operation *Undergo* 183, 185
Operation *Weiss* 51–52
Operation *Wellhit* 181–183
Orscholz Switch Line 95, 98
Ostwallturme **102**, 117, 250
outpost zones 8, 9, 75, 240, 243, 247, 274, 278–279

P

Panther-Stellung **108**, 115, 121
Panther turrets **83**, 85, **102**, **116**, 117–119, **118**, **228**, 238–240, **244**, 249–250, **250**, 260, 265–267, **302**
Panther-Wotan Line 135
Patton, Gen George 95
Peenemünde test site **355**, 356, **360**, 361
pillboxes **77**, 86, **86**, 90, **129**, **221**, **226**, **265**, **379**
see also MG-Panzerneste
Poland 14–16, 378–379
Pontecorvo 259, 260
post-war sites **17**, **53**, 378–380
PzKpfw turrets 119, **134**, 239, 248, **249**, **302**

R

R600 casemates **182**
R621 bunkers **184**
radar **191**, **322**
RAF 166, 330, 334, 339–340, 370
railway tunnels **15**, **17**, 18, 25, 26, **26**, 39, 43
Rapido, River 228, 236, 253, 254
Regelbau 10 bunkers **81**
Regelbau 687 bunkers 117, **118**
Regelbau 703 bunkers **108**
Reichswald **109**, 121
Rhein-Stellung 131
Rheinhardt Line 227–228
Rhine, River
    Allies attack 119–131
    arms 111–119
    defence system 101–111
    lower defences 121–126
    upper defences 126–131
Riese, FHQ 22, 31–32, **37**, **48**, 379–380
rifle platoon defensive position **125**, **300**
rifleman's position **273**, **291**, 294–295, 298, **300**, **310**, 313
Rimini Line 231–232, 265–267
Ringstand *see* tobruks
roadblocks **130**
rockets, firing positions **299**
rocks, for fortifications 286
Rodert 27
Rommel, Erwin 161, 164–165
Ruhr-Stellung **112–113**, 118, 122, **134**
Rundstedt, Gerd von 213
Russian hole 294–295

S

Saar, River **91**
Saarland, defence of 123–124, 126
Saltzwedel, Batterie **190**, **194**
San Martino 266
Scharnhorst-Stellung **109**
Scheldt Estuary 204, 213
Schiessgerüst C/39 turrets **146–147**
Schloß Ziegenberg 17, 22–23, 23–24, 378
Schotterwerk Nordwest (SNW) 358, **363**, **373**, **374**
Schveningen-Nord, Seezielbatterie **205**
Schwerpunkt (main effort point) 273
Sechsschartentürme 189
Seeckt, Generaloberst Hans von 9
Sengerriegel *see* Hitler Line
ships, turrets from 154, **206–207**, 208, **216**
Sicily **222**, 223–225, 251–252
Siegfried Line *see* West Wall

Siegfried Line misnomer 102
Siegfried Line (World War I) **70**
Siegfried Switch Line 95, 98
SK design casemates **148**
snow
    camouflage 308, 312
    for fortifications 288, 306
Sonderbauten sites 363, 364, 368
Soviet Union
    border defences 135
    German tactics 280–282
    Hitler's view of 18–21
    invade Berlin 66–67
    invasion of by Germany 57–60
    on the offensive 59–60, 61, 63, 66–67, 280–282
Speer, Albert 17–18, 38, 356
squad bunkers **120**, **297**, 305–308
squad position **293**
squad strongpoint **310**
squad trenches **273**, **295**
St Nazaire U-Boat base **318–319**, 324, 349–352, **350**
Stauffenberg, Claus Schenk von **60**, 62
steel shelters 250–251
Steinfeld **114**, **120**, **132**, **133**
Stellungsystem-I 364–365
Stellungsystem-II & III 364
Stepina **15**, **17**, **57**, 379, **379**
strongpoint defence concept **174**, 275, 280–283, **296**, **310**

T

Tallboy bombs 336, 343, 345, 370, 371
tank turrets **170**, **171**, 174, 175, **177**, **239**, 240, 247–249, **302**
tanks **82**, **95**, 182, 183, **239**, **255**, 260, **284**
    see also anti-tank defences; Panzer turrets; tank turrets
Tannenberg, FHQ **20**, 32, **37**, **48**, 53, 378
timber, for fortifications 34, 116, 285–286, **289**, 290, **301**
tobruks 85, 157, **170**, **171**, 175, **177**, 189, 292, **293**, **297**, **301**
Todt, Batterie **150–151**, 169
toilets, bunkers 90
torpedo batteries 149, 208–209
train, Hitler's *see* Führersonderzug 'Amerika'
trenches **133**
    approach 273

armour protective 294, 302, 305
dimensions 291–292, 298
infantry-section 125
in Italy 254, 264
machine-gunners position 296–298
rifleman's position 294–296
rock 254
slit 272, 273, 294–296, 298, 302, 305
squad 273, 295
types of 298
Trier-Flankenstellung 123, 126
Trondheim, U-Boat bunkers 341–343, **341**, **342**
Truppenführung (Troop Command) 9
tunnel systems 27, **92**, **94**, 196–197, **361**, 375
turntable **346**
Type 102V shelters **57**

U

U-Boat bunkers
    Allies attack 330, 333–334, 335, 336, 339–340, 342, 343, 347, 349, 351, 352, 353
    Bergen 338–340, 339, 340
    Bordeaux 323, 352, 353
    Bremen 10, 326, 335–336, 337, 338
    Brest 325–329, 328, 343
    construction of 325–329, 331, 334, 335, 336, 342–343
    defences on 324, 327, 329, 334, 347
    France 318–319, 323, 325, 325–329, 328, 343–353, 344, 346, 350, 352
    Germany 10, 326, 329–337, 330, 332, 337, 338
    Hamburg 329–333, 330, 332
    Helgoland 333–334
    Kiel 334–335
    La Pallice 351–352
    layout of 320–334, 337, 338, 340, 341–343, 344, 345–347, 349, 351–352, 353
    locks 324–325
    Lorient 325, 343–348, 344, 346
    Norway 338–343, 339, 340, 341, 342
    operational history 329–353
    St Nazaire 318–319, 324, 349–352, 350
    Trondheim 341–343, 341, 342
U-Boats **321**, **332**, **341**, **348**
    construction of 336, 337
    Type XXI 335, 336, 337
    see also U-Boat bunkers
United States armed forces

INDEX

First Army 122–123, 177–178, 371
Third Army 126, 179
Fifth Army 261, 267
Seventh Army 126, 127, 130, 131, 251
Ninth Army 121
II Corps 253–254
1st Armored Div 262
1st Inf Div 252
10th Armored 'Tiger' Division 95, 98
28th Inf Div 94–95
30th Inf Div 94
34th Inf Div 254, 262, 267
36th Inf Div 253, 262
45th Inf Div 262
76th Inf Div 99
83rd Division 179
90th Inf Div 98
91st Inf Div 267–268
95th Inf Div 98
Air Force 370
assaulting techniques 129
and the Atlantic Wall 177–178, 179
in Italy 251–257
and the Rhine 120–124, 126, 127
and the West Wall 82, 94–95, 98–100
see also Allies
Unterstand 230/10 bunkers **120**
urban defences 237, **309**, **314–315**

V

V-Weapon sites
Allies attack 361–363, 365, 368, 370–371
background to 353–356
Crossbow campaign 365, 367, 370–371
deployment of 367–368, 370, 371, 373–374
fixed or mobile launch sites 354–356, 360, 362, 375
KNW bunker 356–358, 357, 361–362
launch sites 356–375
light launch sites 364–365, 371
maps 354, 369
Ölkeller Cherbourg 362, 368, 368, 370
simplified site system 364–367, 371, 371, 373
V-1s 354, 359–367, 368, 369, 370–371, 374–375
V-2s 353–356, 355, 358, 358, 361, 369, 372, 374–375

Walther catapult 359, 360, 364–365, 366, 367, 371
Wasserwerke bunkers 359, 359–361, 362–363, 370
Valentin U-Boat bunker **10**, **326**, 336, **338**
Vasouy, MKB 169
Vazon Bay 186, 188–190, 193
Verbunkerung 362
Vf600 gun emplacements 175, **178**
village defences **274**
Voralpenstellung (Blue Line) 233, 234, 240, **242**
Vorgeschobene Stellung 278
Vosges Mountains **6**, 117, 126–127

W

Waldwiese, FHQ 32, **37**, **48**
Walker, Gen Fred 253, 262
Walther catapult 359, **360**, 364–365, **366**, **367**, 371
Warlimont, Gen W. 49, 63
Wasserburg, FHQ 20–21, 32–33, **37**, **48**
Wasserwerk bunkers **359**, 360–361, **362**, 362–363, 368, 370
water supplies, bunkers 27, 33, 34, 50, 91, **96–97**
Wehrwolf, FHQ
building of 20, 37, 48
daily life in 49–50
demolition of 60
design of 33–35, 33
Hitler at 20, 58, 59
post-war 19, 64
West-Stellung
Allies attack 107, 121–124, 126–131
anti-tank defences 78, 103, 109, 110, 130
armaments 105–106, 108, 111–119, 128, 132, 134
construction of 103–107, 108–109
definition of 101–102
design of 107–111
map 104
and the Rhine 119–131
Rhine Panzer-Stellung 117–119
Rhine-Stellung 131
success of 103, 105–106
and tactics 105
and the West Wall 102–103
see also West Wall

395

West Wall
   abandonment of 93
   aim of 71
   Allies attack 93–95, 98–100, 107, 119–131
   anti-tank defences 68–69, 78, 82, 85–86, 95, 109, 111, 130
   armaments 81–92, 96–97, 98–100
   construction of 68–69, 70–74, 73, 74, 76, 76, 78, 80, 106–107
   defects 76, 80, 81–82
   defence principles 74–85, 88
   demolition of 87
   and Hitler, Adolf 71–72, 78, 80, 123, 126
   maintenance of 81
   manpower problems 99, 126
   maps 72, 104
   parts for the Atlantic Wall 79, 83, 111
   post war 87
   pre-war 78
   rejuvenation of 101
   and the Rhine 101–131
   strengthening of 83, 85
   tunnel systems 92, 94
   and the West-Stellung 101–103
   see also West-Stellung
Westkapelle, Batterie 213, **215**
Wetterau-Main-Tauber line **72**
Wizernes missile base 358, **363**, **373**, **374**
WN10, Strongpoint **174**

Wolfsschanze, FHQ 18, 22
   assassination attempt in 60, 62
   building of 37, 48
   design of 34, 35–38, 36, 50
   Hitler at 12–13, 20, 57, 58–59, 63
   life in 12–13, 46–48, 49, 50
   post-war 378–379
   radio broadcast from 61
Wolfsschlucht I, FHQ
   building of 18, 37, 45
   design of 38–39, 56
   Hitler at 20, 52–53
   life in 48–49
   post-war 63, 378
Wolfsschlucht II, FHQ
   building of 18, 37, 48
   design of 39, 39, 41–42, 42, 46, 47, 55, 58
   Flak batteries 44
   Hitler at 20, 61
   post-war 22
Wolfsschlucht III, FHQ 21, **37**, 43, **43**, **48**
World War I; 8, 9, **70**, 74–75

Z

Ziegenberg, Schloß 17, 22–23, 23–24, 378